EU Competition Law

EU Competition Law

CASES, TEXTS AND CONTEXT

Eleanor M. Fox
Walter J. Derenberg Professor of Trade Regulation, New York University School of Law, USA

Damien Gerard
Director, Global Competition Law Center (GCLC); Visiting Professor, College of Europe and Université catholique de Louvain, Belgium

Edward Elgar
PUBLISHING

Cheltenham, UK • Northampton, MA, USA

© Eleanor M. Fox and Damien Gerard 2017

All rights reserved. No part of this publication may be reproduced, stored in a retrieval system or transmitted in any form or by any means, electronic, mechanical or photocopying, recording, or otherwise without the prior permission of the publisher.

Published by
Edward Elgar Publishing Limited
The Lypiatts
15 Lansdown Road
Cheltenham
Glos GL50 2JA
UK

Edward Elgar Publishing, Inc.
William Pratt House
9 Dewey Court
Northampton
Massachusetts 01060
USA

A catalogue record for this book
is available from the British Library

Library of Congress Control Number: 2017939824

ISBN 978 1 78643 083 0 (cased)
ISBN 978 1 78643 085 4 (paperback)
ISBN 978 1 78643 084 7 (eBook)

Printed and bound by CPI Group (UK) Ltd, Croydon, CR0 4YY

Contents in brief

Preface	xii
Table of cases	xvi
Introduction	xxv
Abuses of dominance: the Intel *judgement of the Court of Justice*	xxix
Abuses of dominance: the Google *decision (search)*	xxxiii
1 The Treaty, objectives and the Single Market	1
2 Cartels	33
3 Horizontal restraints	69
4 Vertical restraints	123
5 Abuses of dominance	159
6 Merger control	234
7 The State and competition	274
Afterword	334
Index	335

Full contents

Preface	xii
Table of cases	xvi
Introduction	xxv
Abuses of dominance: the Intel *judgement of the Court of Justice*	xxix
Abuses of dominance: the Google *decision (search)*	xxxiii

1 The Treaty, objectives and the Single Market — 1
   A. The objectives of EU competition policy — 1
   B. Institutions and procedures — 8
      1. From Regulation 17/62 to Regulation 1/2003 — 9
      2. The innovations brought about by Regulation 1/2003 — 10
         Note on the effects-based approach — 12
      3. The private enforcement of EU competition law — 15
   C. Introduction to Articles 101 and 102 TFEU — 16
      Note on the notion of undertaking — 18
   D. Market integration and the blockage of imports — 20
      1. Overview — 20
      2. Parallel imports — 21
         a. *Consten and Grundig v. Commission* (Cases 56–58/64) — 21
         b. Development of the rule against market partitioning — 27
   Conclusion — 31

2 Cartels — 33
   A. Cartels and the economics of competition — 35
   B. Proof of cartels — 40
      1. The *Quinine* case — 41
         ACF Chemiefarma v. Commission
         (Case 41/69) (*'Quinine'*) — 41
      2. The *Dyestuffs* case — 45
         Imperial Chemical Industries Ltd v. Commission
         (Cases 48, 49, 51–57/69) (*'Dyestuffs'*) — 46
      3. The *Sugar Cartel* case — 47
      4. The *Wood Pulp* case — 49
         Ahlström Osakeyhtiö v. Commission (Cases C-89, 104,
         114, 116–117, 125–129/85) (*'Wood Pulp'*) — 49

	C.	World cartels and offshore cartels: jurisdiction, comity, and cooperation	54
		1. Effects, sovereignty, and restraint	54
		Ahlström Osakeyhtiö v. Commission (Cases C-89, 104, 114, 116–117, 125–129/85) (*'Wood Pulp'*)	55
		2. Cooperation, and seeds of a global regime	61
	D.	May cartels be justified? Crisis cartels	62
		Competition Authority of Ireland v. Beef Industry Development Society Ltd (Case C-209/07) (*'BIDS'*)	62

3 Horizontal restraints — 69

	A.	Agreements among competitors: general	69
		Note on the notion of '(block) exemption'	70
	B.	The reach of Article 101(1)	71
		1. 'By object' restrictions	72
		Groupement des Cartes Bancaires (CB) v. Commission (Case C-67/13 P)	73
		2. 'By effect' restrictions	77
		Note on market definition	78
		Mastercard v. Commission (Case C-382/12 P)	82
		Note on agreements of minor importance ('de minimis')	88
	C.	Article 101(3): Effects of the agreement on competition, efficiency, innovation	91
		1. Introduction and guidelines	91
		2. Loose agreements	93
		a. Agreements to exchange information	93
		Note on *John Deere Ltd v. Commission*	94
		Note on *Wirtschaftsvereinigung Stahl*	96
		Asnef-Equifax v. Asociación De Usuarios De Servicios Bancarios (Case C-238/05)	97
		b. Standard setting	100
		3. Tighter agreements	101
		European Night Services Ltd v. Commission (Cases T-374–375, 384 and 388/94)	101
		4. Relationship to innovation and competitiveness	106
	D.	Article 101(1) and (3): public policy and non-competition goals	108
		1. Labour	108
		Albany International BV and Textile Industry Pension Funds (Case C-67/96)	108
		2. The liberal professions	112
		Wouters et Cie (Case C-309/99)	113

		3.	The environment and competitiveness	116
			CECED	118
	E.	Block exemptions		120
		1.	Research and development	120
		2.	Specialization	121

4 Vertical restraints 123

	A.	Vertical restraints and their effects	123
		Note on the effect of modernisation	124
	B.	Is there an agreement within Article 101(1)?	125
	C.	Parallel imports and exports, and dual pricing	126
		Consten and Grundig v. Commission (Case 56/64)	126
		Note on *Distillers Company Ltd v. Commission*	127
		GlaxoSmithKline Services Unlimited v. Commission (Case T-168/01) (Spanish price ceiling)	128
		Sot. Lelos KAI SIA EE v. GlaxoSmithKline AEVE (Joined Cases C-468 to 478/06)	132
	D.	Resale price maintenance: Europe, and a view from the US	135
		Leegin Creative Leather Products, Inc. v. PSKS, Inc.	136
	E.	Single branding (exclusive purchasing), tying and related foreclosures	144
		Stergios Delimitis v. Henninger Bräu AG (Case C-234/89)	144
		Schöller Lebensmittel v. Commission (Case T-9/93)	147
		Pierre Fabre Dermo-Cosmétique v. Président de l'Autorité de la Concurrence (Case C-439/09)	152
	F.	Block exemptions: history and reform	156

5 Abuses of dominance 159

	A.	Dominance			161
		Note on collective dominance			163
	B.	Abusive conduct			164
		1.	Excessive and discriminatory prices and unfair terms		165
			British Leyland Plc v. Commission (Case 226/84)		165
			United Brands Co. v. Commission (Case 27/76)		167
		2.	Exclusionary conduct		171
			a.	Refusal to deal	172
				(i) Essential facility and duty to give access	172
				(ii) Other duties to deal that may or may not involve an essential facility	174

>
> *Istituto Chemioterapico Italiano Spa v. Commission*
> (Joined Cases 6 and 7/73) ('Commercial
> Solvents')   174
> *Verizon Communications Inc. v. Law Offices
> of Curtis V. Trinko*   177
>   (iii)   The special relevance of intellectual property   180
> *Radio Telefis Eireann v. Commission* (Joined
> Cases C-241 and C-242/91 P) (*'Magill'*)   181
> *IMS Health GmbH & Co.* (Case C-418/01)   184
>   (iv)   Interoperability   186
> *Microsoft Corp. v. Commission* (Case T-201/04)   186
>   b.   Exclusive dealing and loyalty rebates   193
> *Hoffmann-La Roche & Co. AG v. Commission*
> (Case 85/76)   194
> Note on British Airways Plc v. Commission   197
> *Tomra Systems ASA v. Commission* (Case C-549/10 P)   199
> Note on Intel Corp. v. Commission   201
> *Post Danmark A/S v. Konkurrencerådet*
> (Case C-23/14) (*'Post Danmark II'*)   204
>   c.   Tying and bundling   207
> *Microsoft Corp. v. Commission* (Case T-201/04)   209
>   d.   Price predation and price discrimination (continued)   211
> *AKZO Chemie BV v. Commission* (Case C-62/86)   212
> *Brooke Group Ltd v. Brown & Williamson
> Tobacco Corp.*   215
> Note on France Telecom SA v.
> Commission ('Wanadoo')   218
> *Post Danmark A/S v. Konkurrencerådet*
> (Case C-209/10) (*'Post Danmark I'*)   220
>   e.   Margin squeeze   223
> Note on Pacific Bell Telephone Co. v. linkLine
> Communications, Inc.   223
> *Deutsche Telekom AG v. Commission*
> (Case C-280/08 P)   224
> *Konkurrensverket v. TeliaSonera Sverige*
> (Case C-52/09)   228
>   f.   Abusive leveraging   232

6 Merger control   234
  A.   The Merger Regulation   235
    1.   Coverage and procedures   235
    2.   The substantive standard   237

	B.	The economics of merger analysis	239
		1. Competition-lessening effects	239
		2. Positive effects	241
		3. Competitiveness	241
		4. Markets, concentration, barriers, and efficiencies	242
	C.	Substantive law under the Merger Regulation	244
		1. Mergers of competitors that create or increase dominance	244
		a. Note on Aerospatiale-Alenia/De Havilland	245
		b. Note on Boeing/McDonnell Douglas	246
		c. Contemporary mergers to monopoly	250
		d. The failing firm defence	253
		France v. Commission (Joined Cases C-68/94 and C-30/95) ('Kali + Salz')	253
		2. Mergers that create unilateral or non-coordinated effects	255
		3. Mergers of competitors that facilitate coordinated behaviour (collective dominance)	257
		Gencor Ltd v. Commission (Case T-102/96)	258
		Airtours v. Commission (Case T-342/99)	261
		4. Mergers other than mergers of competitors: vertical and conglomerate effects	265
		Tetra Laval BV v. Commission (Case C-12/03 P) ('*Tetra/Sidel*')	266
	D.	The international dimension	269
		Note on *Gencor Ltd v. Commission*	270
7	**The State and competition**		**274**
	A.	State ownership, and a note on liberalization	276
		Merci Convenzionali Porto di Genova v. Siderurgica Gabrielli SpA (Case C-179/90)	279
	B.	State monopolies of a commercial character: application of Articles 34 and 37 TFEU	282
		Franzen (Case C-189/95) (*Swedish alcohol monopoly*)	284
	C.	Exclusive privileges: Article 106 TFEU	290
		Hofner v. Macrotron GmbH (Case C-41/90)	290
		Commission v. DEI (Case C-553/12 P) (*Greek lignite*)	293
		Albany International BV and Textile Industry Pension Funds (Case C-67/96)	296
	D.	State measures that restrict competition or facilitate private restrictions	299
		1. State responsibility	299
		Consorzio Industrie Fiammiferi (Case C-198/01) ('*Italian matches*')	301

			Cipolla v. Fazari and Macrino v. Meloni (Joined Cases C-94 and C-202/04)	303
		2.	Private responsibility	306
			Commission and France v. Ladbroke Racing Ltd (Joined Cases C-359 and C-379/95 P)	306
			Commission v. Italy (Case C-35/96) ('CNSD')	308
	E.	State aid		311
		1.	Notion of State aid	312
			a. State aid criteria and ex-ante review	312
			b. Compatible aid	313
			c. The market economy operator test	314
			d. Public service compensation	315
			e. State v. private resources	315
			f. Selectivity	316
		2.	State aid policy	319
			Note on tax rulings and Apple	329

Afterword	334
Index	335

Preface

[T]he function of EU competition rules is to prevent competition from being distorted to the detriment of the public interest, individual undertakings and consumers, thereby ensuring the well-being of the European Union.[1]

From the outset, the development of a competition policy was considered an inherent part of the establishment of the EU single market and, as a result, of the whole European integration enterprise. The 1956 Messina Report, which provided the foundations for the subsequent adoption of the Treaties of Rome, identified monopoly power as a threat to the fundamental objectives pursued by the opening of domestic markets, inasmuch as open markets were to contribute to a 'more rational allocation of resources' and 'a general increase in welfare' in post-World War II Europe. Specifically, the original concerns spelled out in the Messina Report related to: (i) cartels allocating markets between 'undertakings' (which is the term used to designate businesses in EU competition parlance) that would lead to partitioning effects contrary to the integration project; (ii) agreements limiting output or hampering innovation that would hinder productivity improvements; and (iii) monopolization practices that would pre-empt the welfare gains expected from market integration. Hence, the overarching goal of market integration has since the very beginning encompassed the setting up of 'a system ensuring that competition is not distorted' (former Article 3(g) EC Treaty, now Protocol 27).

The historical connection between competition policy and the establishment of the EU internal market has naturally influenced and continues to affect the enforcement of the EU rules on competition, as now contained in Chapter 1 of Title VII of the Treaty on the Functioning of the European Union ('TFEU'). The prohibition of absolute territorial restrictions in contractual arrangements, the protection of passive cross-border sales in distribution agreements, the particular sensitivity of discriminatory pricing practices, and the control of State subsidies, all illustrate that filiation. Since the beginning, however, market integration and competition policy were

---

1 Case C-52/09, *TeliaSonera* [2011] ECR I-527, ECLI:EU:C:2011:83.

conceived as complementary forces aimed at achieving an optimal allocation of resources, i.e., allocative efficiency, without entailing the submission of one to the other. This is not to say that tensions cannot, or have not arisen, between both endeavours. Still, since the origins of the Union, competition policy was meant to stand on its own as the recognized engine of a well performing market economy. Today, the TFEU continues to promote 'the principle of an open market economy with free competition, favouring an efficient allocation of resources' (Article 120 TFEU).

In effect, the protection of the dynamic process of rivalry between firms aimed at ensuring that the market economy reaches a level of allocation of resources close to an optimal efficiency situation, lies at the core of EU competition policy. It is a robust competitive process that best enables consumers to benefit from lower prices and wider choices of products and services, and that best preserves the incentives of enterprises to perform and innovate. As a result, EU competition policy is naturally tinged with concerns for the protection of the various elements that contribute to shaping competitive market environments. Yet again, competition is viewed as a dynamic process, and competitive markets are not static frameworks. Market players come and go as a result of competitive interactions and industry concentration, including the acquisition of a certain level of market power, is an acceptable outcome of competition geared towards efficiency. On balance, however, the EU rules on competition are designed in such a way that the protection of competition prevails in the final analysis over alleged benefits arising from the exercise of market power, jointly or unilaterally.

The focus of EU competition law on the protection of the process of competition goes a long way in explaining the outcome of many hard cases brought by the European Commission, as its main original enforcer. In operational terms, it also has the consequence of requiring in each case a contextual assessment of all the circumstances and factors affecting competition in order to evaluate the (likely) effects of the practice(s) in question or the applicability of existing presumptions. Likewise, this process-based focus means that EU competition law enforcement can adjust its analytical framework to the distinctive features of particular industries and also to the evolution of the state of economic knowledge, as well as accommodate other public policy interests, within certain limits. In turn, the focus on the protection of the competitive process requires determinations as to the optimal or acceptable level of competition in particular cases, which are open to various influences, be they particular schools of thought or the views of sophisticated parties. This phenomenon is by no means peculiar to the EU, or to the enforcement of competition law, but the broad wording of the EU rules on competition and the diversity of legal and economic traditions prevailing across the Union make the enforcement of EU competition law particularly open to varying sources of inspirations.

Among these sources, the case law of the US courts in the field of antitrust, combined with the experience of US agencies and the rich scholarship of US academics, has been a constant point of reference for all stakeholders involved in the development of EU competition policy. The benchmarking of the EU experience against that of the US has highlighted over time the specificities of the EU enforcement framework and put a magnifying glass on their shortcomings. That process increased significantly as from the late 1980s with the introduction of EU merger control and the opening of a Brussels office by many US law firms attracted by the completion of the EU Single Market. Since then, a significant body of comparative literature has emerged and revealed differences across the institutional, procedural and substantive dimensions of competition law enforcement on both sides of the Atlantic, as well as the intrinsic interdependence between these three dimensions within each system. Combined with constraints arising from the enlargement of the Union, these iterative transatlantic interactions—including outright criticisms on the occasion of diverging outcomes in the assessment of particular cases—played a significant role in stimulating the comprehensive review of the EU competition law enforcement framework that took place over the turn of the century, as part of the so-called 'modernisation' initiative.

While covering all aspects of EU competition policy, this casebook offers various comparative references to the US enforcement context in order to stimulate critical discussions. In fact, it originates in an endeavour to introduce EU competition law to a US audience as part of a broader presentation of the development of EU law.[2] As such, that original endeavour reflected more than two decades of continuous study of the EU enforcement practice as part of an effort to promote transatlantic cooperation and convergence in the field of competition policy. The materials assembled over the years, reused with the generous permission of West Academic Publishing, have been carefully updated, completed and expanded in order to turn them into this stand alone volume reflecting the current state of EU competition law as profoundly modified by modernisation and the turn to a network enforcement model associating the European Commission, national competition authorities and EU and national courts.

---

2 See R. Goebel, E. Fox, G. Bermann, J. Atik, F. Emmert and D. Gerard (2015), *Cases and Materials on European Union Law*, 4th edn, St Paul, MN: West Academic Publishing.

Nowadays, EU competition law has grown to become a model for various other regimes across the world, notably because of its openness and ability to adjust to different legal and economic traditions. This remarkable evolution makes the study of the EU experience enforcing competition rules ever more important and indeed informative for (future) practitioners and policy makers beyond Europe. This casebook has therefore been designed to be accessible to a broad audience, including non-EU specialists. As such, it reflects the authors' shared conviction that competition law enforcement benefits from the continuous sharing of experiences and knowledge across forums while equally mirroring the complex social arrangements and tensions underlying each of them. Hence, this casebook is meant to become a collaborative tool by reflecting the outcome of classroom experiences and by adjusting to the requirements of practice in Europe and elsewhere. Users' feedback would therefore be very much appreciated in order to refine the scope and presentation of materials for future editions.

Eleanor M. Fox and Damien Gerard
31 January 2017

Table of cases

EU Cases

1&1 Telecom v. Commission, Case T-307/15 [2015], OJ C 270/35..257
ACF Chemiefarma v. Commission, Case C-41/69, [1970] ECR 661, EU:C:1970:71.................. 41–5
Aegean/Olympic II, Commission Decision of 23 April 2013 in Case COMP/M.6796..................254
Aerospatiale/Alenia/de Havilland, Commission Decision of 2 October 1991 in Case
    COMP/M.53, [1991] OJ L 341/42 245–6
Ahlström Osakeyhtiö v. Commission (Wood pulp) (jurisdiction), Joined Cases C-89, 104,
    114, 116–117, 125–129/85, [1988] ECR 5193, EU:C:1988:447 .... 54–60, 269, 271
Ahlström Osakeyhtiö v. Commission (Wood pulp) (proof of concert), Joined Cases C-89,
    104, 114, 116–117, 125–129/85, [1993] ECR I-1307, EU:C:1993:120 49–53
Airdata v. Commission, Case T-305/15, [2015] OJ C 270/34 257
Airtours v. Commission, Case T-342/99, [2002] ECR II-2585, EU:T:2002:146.........................261–4
AKZO Chemie BV v. Commission, Case C-62/86, [1991] ECR I-3359, EU:C:1991:286............163,
                                                                                                                                                                            212–15,
                                                                                                                                                                            218, 221
Albany International BV and Textile Industry Pension Funds, Case C-67/96, [1999] ECR
    I-5751, EU:C:1999:430...108–12, 296–9
Allianz Hungária Biztosító Zrt. and Others v Gazdasági Versenyhivatal, Case C-32/11,
    EU:C:2013:160...73
Alrosa Co. Ltd v Commission, Case C-441/07 P, [2010] ECR I-5949, EU:C:2010:377.................. 12
Alrosa Co. Ltd v Commission, Case T-170/06, [2007] ECR II-2601, EU:T:2007:220..................... 12
Altmark Trans GmbH and Regierungspräsidium Magdeburg v Nahverkehrsgesellschaft
    Altmark GmbH, and Oberbundesanwalt beim Bundesverwaltungsgericht, Case C-280/00,
    [2007] ECR I-7747, EU:C:2003:415..315
Apple Sales International and Apple Operations Europe v. Commission, Case T-101/17,
    [2017] OJ C 121/39 330
Arduino and Others v Compagnia Assicuratrice RAS SpA, Case C-35/99, [2002] ECR
    I-1529, EU:C:2002:97 112
Asnef-Equifax v. Asociación De Usuarios De Servicios Bancarios (AUSBANC), Case
    C-238/05, [2006] ECR I-11125, EU:C:2006:734 97–100
AstraZeneca v. Commission, Case C-457/10 P, EU:C:2012:770..191–3
Atlantic Container Line v. Commission, Joined Cases T-191 and T-212 to T-214/98, [2003]
    ECR II-3275, EU:T:2003:245 164
Bayer v. Commission, Case T-41/96, [2000] ECR II-3383, EU:T:2000:242.................................126
Bertelsmann AG and Sony Corporation of America v. Independent Music Publishers and
    Labels Association (Impala), Case C-413/06 P, [2008] ECR I-4951, EU:C:2008:392 264–5

Table of cases • **xvii**

Boeing/McDonnell Douglas, Commission Decision of 30 July 1997, Case COMP/M.877,
  [1997] OJ L 366/16 ....246–50, 255,
    265, 273
British Airways v. Commission, Case C-95/04 P, [2007] ECR I-2331, EU:C:2007:166 170,
    197–9
British Leyland Plc v. Commission, Case 226/84, [1986] ECR 3263, EU:C:1986:421 165–7
*Centre Belge d'Études de Marché-Télémarketing SA v. Compagnie Luxembourgeoise de
  Télédiffusion, SA*, Case 311/84, [1985] ECR 3261, EU:C:1985:394 299
Cipolla v. Fazari and Macrino v. Meloni, Joined Cases C-94 and C-202/04, [2006] ECR
  I-11421, EU:C:2006: 112, 115, 303–6
Cisco Systems v. Commission, Case T-79/12, EU:T:2013:635 252–3
Commission and France v. Ladbroke Racing Ltd, Joined Cases C-359 and C-379/95 P,
  [1997] ECR I-6265, EU:C:1997:531 ....306–8, 310
Commission and Spain v. Government of Gibraltar and United Kingdom, Joined Cases C-106
  and C-107/09 P, [2011] ECR I-11113, EU:C:2011:732 317
Commission v. DEI (Greek lignite), Case C-553/12 P, EU:C:2014:2083 293–6
Commission v. Denmark, Case 302/86, [1988] ECR 4607, EU:C:1988:421 118
Commission v. Greece, Case C-347/88,[1990] ECR I-4747, EU:C:1990:470 284–5
Commission v. Italy (CNSD), Case C-35/96, [1998] ECR I-3851, EU:C:1998:303 308–11
Compagnie Maritime Belge Transports SA v. Commission, Joined Cases C-395/96 and
  C-396/96 P, [2000] ECR I-1365, EU:C:2000:132 163
Competition Authority of Ireland v. Beef Industry Development Society Ltd (BIDS), Case
  C-209/07, [2008] ECR I-8637, EU:C:2008:643 62–6,
    74, 76, 93
Consorzio Industrie Fiammiferi, Case C-198/01, [2003] ECR I-8055, EU:C:2003:430 301–2,
    310
Consten and Grundig v. Commission, Joined Cases C-56/64-C-58/64, [1966] ECR 299,
  EU:C:1965:60 ....21–7, 125–6, 128
Costa v. ENEL, Case 6/64, [1964] ECR 585, EU:C:1964:66 282–3
Courage v. Crehan, Case C-453/99 [2001] ECR I–6297 15
Deutsche Börse/NYSE Euronext, Commission Decision of 1 February 2012, Case
  COMP/M.6166 ....243, 250–51, 273
Deutsche Börse v. Commission, Case T-175/12, EU:T:2015:148 243
Deutsche Grammophon Gesellschaft GmbH v. Metro-SB-Grossmärkte GmbH, Case 78/70,
  [1971] ECR 487, EU:C:1971:59 180
Deutsche Telekom AG v. Commission, Case C-280/08 P, [2010] ECR I-9555,
  EU:C:2010:603 224–8
Distillers Company Ltd v. Commission, Case C-30/78, [1980] ECR 229, EU:C:1980:186......127–8
Dole Food Company v. Commission, Case C-286/13, EU:C:2015:184 75
EDF v. Commission, Case C-124/10 P, EU:C:2012:318 314–15
EDP-Energias de Portugal SA v. Commission, Case T-87/05, [2005] ECR II-3745,
  EU:T:2005:333 268–9
EDP/ENI/GDP, Commission Decision of 9 December 2004, COMP/M.3440, [2005]
  OJ L 302/69 268–9
Eurocontrol, Case C-364/92 [1994] ECR I-43, EU:C:1994:7 18

European Night Services Ltd v. Commission, Cases T-374–375, 384 and 388/94, [1998]
  ECR II-3141, EU:T:1998:198 .... 82, 101–6
Expedia Inc. v. Autorité de la concurrence and Others, Case C-226/11, EU:C:2012:795 88
Facebook/WhatsApp, Commission Decision of 3 October 2014 in Case COMP/M.7217,
  [2014] OJ C 417/4 252
Fédération française des sociétés d'assurance (FFSA), Case C-244/94 [1995] ECR I–4013,
  EU:C:1995:392 19
Fédération nationale de la cooperation bétail et viande (FNCBV) v Commission, Joined Cases
  T-217/03 and T-245/03 [2006] ECR II-4987, EU:T:2006:391 20
FENIN v. Commission, Case C-205/03 P, [2006] ECR I-6295, EU:C:2006:453 296
France Telecom SA v. Commission, Case C-202/07 P, [2009] ECR I-2369, EU:C:2009:214
  (Wanadoo) 218–20
France Telecom SA v. Commission, Case T-340/03, [2007] ECR I-107, EU:T:2007:22 218–20
France v. Commission, Joined Cases C-68/94 and C-30/95, [1998] ECR I-1375,
  EU:C:1998:148 (Kali + Salz) 253–5, 257, 262
Franzen (Swedish alcohol monopoly), Case C-189/95, [1997] ECR I-05909, EU:C:1997:504
  284–90
GB-INNO-BM v ATAB, Case 13/77 [1977] ECR 2115 281
GB-INNO-BM v. Vereniging van de Kleinhandelaars in Tabak (INNO/ATAB), Case 13/77,
  [1977] ECR 2115, EU:C:1977:185 299–300
Gebrüder Reiff GmbH & Co. KG v. Bundesanstalt für den Güterfernverkehr, Case C-185/91,
  [1993] ECR I-5801, EU:C:1993:886 .... 300–301, 309
Gencor Ltd v Commission, Case T-102/96, [1999] ECR II-753, EU:T:1999:65 270–73
General Electric v. Commission (GE/Honeywell), Case T-210/01, [2005] ECR II-5575,
  EU:T:2005:456 .... 268–70, 273
General Motors v. Commission, Case C-551/03, EU:C:2006:229 165
GlaxoSmithKline Services Unlimited v. Commission, Case T-168/01, [2006] ECR II-2969,
  EU:T:2006:265 .... 30, 128–32
GlaxoSmithKline Services Unlimited v. Commission, Joined Cases C-501, C-513, C-515 and
  C-519/06 P [2009] ECR I-9291, EU:C:2009:610 .... 30, 128–32
Google, Commission Decision of 27 June 2017, Case COMP/ .... xxxiii–xxxvi,
  232–3
Groupement des cartes bancaires (CB) v. Commission, Case C-67/13 P, EU:C:2014:2204 ...... 14, 33,
  73–7
Groupement des cartes bancaires (CB) v. Commission, Case T-491/07 RENV, EU:T:
  2016:379 75
Hoffmann-La Roche v. Commission, Case 85/76, [1979] ECR 461, EU:C:1979:36 144,
  161–3, 194–6, 213
Hofner v. Macrotron GmbH, Case C-41/90, [1991] ECR I-1979, EU:C:1991:161 19,
  290–93, 295–6, 308
Huawei Technologies Co. Ltd v. ZTE Corp., Case C-170/13, EU:C:2015:477 192–3
Hutchison 3G Austria/Orange Austria, Commission Decision of 12 December 2012, Case
  COMP/M.6497, [2012] OJ C 224/8 256–7
Hutchison 3G UK/Telefonica Ireland, Commission Decision of 28 May 2014, Case
  COMP/M.6992, [2014] OJ C 264/2 257

Hutchison 3G UK/Telefonica UK, Commission Decision of 11 May 2016, Case
    COMP/M.7612, [2016] OJC 357/12 257
Imperial Chemical Industries Ltd v. Commission, Joined Cases C-48, 49, 51–57/69, [1972]
    ECR 619, EU:C:1972:70 .... 45–6, 48, 54, 56
IMS Health GmbH & Co., Case C-418/01, [2004] ECR I-5039, EU:C:2004:257 .... 184–7, 191
InnoLux Corp. v. Commission, Case C-231/14 P, EU:C:2015:451 60
Intel Corp. v. Commission, Case C-413/14P, EU:C:2017:632, and Case T-286/09,
    EU:T:2014:547 .... xxix–xxxii,
                                                                                                                            60, 201–4
Ireland v. Commission, Case T-778/16, [2017] OJ C 38/35 330
Irish Sugar v. Commission, Case C-497/99 P, EU:C:2001:393 164
Irish Sugar v. Commission, Case T-228/97, [1999] ECR II-2969, EU:T:1999:246 164
Istituto Chemioterapico Italiano Spa v. Commission, Joined Cases 6 and 7/73, [1974] ECR
    223, EU:C:1974:18 174–6
Italy v. Commission, Case 41/83, [1985] ECR 873, EU:C:1985:120 299
John Deere Ltd v. Commission, Case C-7/95 P, [1998] ECR I-3111, EU:C:1998:256 95–6
John Deere Ltd v. Commission, Case T-35/92, [1994] ECR II-957, EU:T:1994:259 95–6
Keck and Mithouard, Joined Cases C-267 and C-268/91, [1993] ECR I-6097,
    EU:C:1993:905 289
Klas Rosengren and Others, Case 170/04, [2007] ECR I-4071, EU:C:2007:313 290
Konkurrensverket v. TeliaSonera Sverige, Case C-52/09, [2011] ECR I-527, EU:C:2011:83 ... 228–32
Lundbeck v. Commission, Case T-472/13, EU:T:2016:449 76
MasterCard v. Commission, Case C-382/12 P, EU:C:2014:2201 .... 20, 82–8, 93
Masterfoods Ltd (Mars Ireland), Case C-344/98, [2000] ECR I-11369, EU:C:2000:689 151
Matra Hachette SA v. Commission, Case T-17/93, [1994] ECR II-595, EU:T:1994:89 329
MCI WorldCom/Sprint, Commission Decision of 28 June 2000 in Case COMP/M.1741
    [2003] OJ C 300/1 253
Merci Convenzionali Porto di Genova v. Siderurgica Gabrielli SpA, Case C-179/90, [1991]
    ECR I-5889, EU:C:1991:464 279–82
Métropole Télévision (M6) v. Commission, Case T-112/99, [2001] ECR II-2459,
    EU:T:2001:2015 76
Michelin v. Commission (Michelin I), Case 322/81, [1983] ECR 3461, EU:C: 1983:313 196
Michelin v. Commission, Case T-203/01, [2003] ECR II-4071, EU:T:2003:250 *(Michelin II)*
    .... 196–7, 199
Microsoft Corp. v. Commission, Case T-201/04, [2007] ECR II-3601, EU:T:2007:289
    .... 186–93, 208–11
Microsoft/Skype, Commission Decision of 7 October 2011 in Case COMP/M.6281,
    [2011] OJ C 341/2 252–3
Motorola/Enforcement of GPRS Standard Essential Patents, Commission Decisions of
    29 April 2014, Case COMP/AT.39985 192
Motosykletistiki Omospondia Ellados NPID (MOTOE), Case C-49/07 [2008] ECR I-4863,
    EU:C:2008:376 19
Musique Diffusion Française v. Commission, Joined Cases C-100/80 and C-103/80, [1983]
    ECR 1825, EU:C:1983:158 .... 27–8, 126
O2 (Germany) v. Commission, Case T-328/03, [2006] ECR II 1231, EU:T:2006:116 82

Ohra Schadeverzekeringen NV v. Netherlands, Case C-245/91, [1993] ECR I-5851,
EU:C:1993:887 300
Olympic/Aegean Airlines, Commission Decision of 26 January 2011 in Case
COMP/M.5830, [2012] OJ C 195/11 254
Oscar Bronner GmbH & Co. KG v. Mediaprint Zeitungs-und Zeitschriftenverlag GmbH & Co.,
Case C-7/97, [1998] ECR I-7791, EU:C:1998:569 176
Paint Graphos and Others, Joined Cases C-78 and C-80/08, [2011] ECR I-7611,
EU:C:2011:550 317
Pearle BV, Case C-345/02, [2004] ECR I-7139, EU:C:2004:448 316
*Pensii, Societate de Administrare a unui Fond de Pensii Administrat Privat SA v. Consiliul
Concurentei*, Case C-172/14, EU:C:2015:484 75
Piau v. Commission, Case T-193/02, [2005] ECR II-209, EU:T:2005:22 164
Pierre Fabre Dermo-Cosmétique v. Président de l'Autorité de la Concurrence, Case C-439/09,
[2011] ECR I-9419, EU:C:2011:649 152–5
Port of Rødby, Commission Decision 94/119/EC of 21 December 1993, [1994] OJ L
55/52 276–9
Post Danmark A/S v. Konkurrencerådet (Post Danmark I), Case C-209/10, EU:C:2012:172 14,
170, 220–23
Post Danmark A/S v. Konkurrencerådet (Post Danmark II), Case C-23/14, EU:C:2015:651 ...204–7,
223
Poucet and Pistre, Joined Cases C-159/91 and C-160/91 [1993] ECR I-637, EU:C:1993:63...... 19
Premier League and Karen Murphy, Joined Cases C-403 and C-429/08 [2011] ECR
I-9083, EU:C:2011:631 27
PreussenElektra AG v Schhleswag AG, Case C-379/98, [2001] ECR I-2099,
EU:C:2001:160 315–16
Radio Telefis Eireann v. Commission (Magill), Joined Cases C-241 and C-242/91 P, [1995]
ECR I-743, EU:C:1995:98 .... 181–4, 187, 191
Rambus, Case COMP/AT.38636, Summary Decision of 9 December 2009, [2010] OJ C
30/17 100–101
Régie des Postes v. Corbeau, Case C-320/91, [1993] ECR I-2533, EU:C:1993:198 295–6
Rewe-Zentral v. Bundesmonopolverwaltung Fur Branntwein (Cassis de Dijon), Case 120/78,
[1979] ECR 649, EU:C:1979:42 289
Ryanair/Aer Lingus, Commission Decision of 27 June 2007, Case COMP/M.4439,
[2008] OJ C 47/6 250–51
Ryanair Holdings v. Commission, Case T-342/07, [2010] ECR II-3457, EU:T:2010:280...... 250–51
SA Binon & Cie v. SA Agence et Messageries de la Presse, Case 243/83, [1995] ECR 2015,
EU:C:1985:284 136
Samsung/Enforcement of UMTS Standard Essential Patents, Commission Decision of 29
April 2014, Case COMP/AT.39939 192
Schöller Lebensmittel v. Commission, Case T-9/93, [1995] ECR II-1611, EU:T-1995:99 147–51
Sealink/B&I – Holyhead, Commission Decision of 11 June 1992 in Case IV/34.174,
[1992] 5 CMLR 255 173–4
SIA 'Maxima Latvija' v. Konkurences padome, Case C-345/14, EU:C:2015:784 75
Société Technique Minière (L.T.M.) v Maschinenbau Ulm GmbH (M.B.U.), Case C-56/65,
[1966] ECR 337. EU:C:1966:38 82

Sot. Lelos v. GlaxoSmithKline AEVE, Joined Cases C-468/06 to C-478/06 [2008] ECR
   I-7139, EU:C:2008:504 .... 30–31, 132–5
Stergios Delimitis v. Henninger Bräu AG, Case C-234/89, [1991] ECR I-935,
   EU:C:1991:91 144–7
Stichting Baksteen (Dutch Brickmakers, Commission Decision of 29 April 1994 in Case
   IV/34.456, [1994] OJ L 131/15) 67
Suiker Unie v. Commission, Joined Cases C-40–48, 50, 54–56, 111, 113–114/73, [1975]
   ECR 1663, EU:C:1975:174 47–8
*T-Mobile Netherlands BV and Others v Raad van bestuur van de Nederlandse
   Mededingingsautoritei*, Case C-8/08, [2009] ECR I-4529, EU:C:2009:343 72–3
Tele2 Polska, Case C-375/09 [2011] ECR I-3055, EU:C:2011:270 14
Telefonica Deutschland/E-Plus, Commission Decision of 2 July 2014 in COMP/M.7018,
   [2015] OJ C 86/5 257
TeliaSonera/Telenor, Commission Decision of 11 September 2015 in COMP/M.7419,
   [2015] OJ C 316/1 257
Tetra Laval BV v. Commission (Tetra/Sidel), Case C-12/03 P, [2005] ECR I-987,
   EU:C:2005:87 266–8
Tetra Pak International SA v Commission, Case C-333/94 P, [1996] ECR I–5951,
   EU:C:1996:436 .... 144, 208, 215, 218
Texas Instruments/Qualcomm, Press Release of 24 November 2009 in Case
   COMP/39.247, Memo/09/516 100–101
Tomra Systems ASA v. Commission, Case C-549/10 P, EU:C:2012:221 .... 199–200, 204
Toshiba v. Commission, Case C-373/14, EU:C:2016:26 75
United Brands Co. v. Commission, Case 27/76, [1978] ECR 207, EU:C:1978:22 167–9
Van den Bergh Foods Ltd, Commission Decision of 11 March 1998, Joined Cases
   IV/34.073, 34.395, 35.436, 98/531, [1998] OJ L 246/1 150–51
Van den Bergh Foods v. Commission, Case C-552/03 P [2006] ECR I-9091, EU:C:2006:607 151
Van den Bergh Foods v. Commission, Case T-65/98, [2003] ECR II-4653, EU:T:2003:281 151
Vodafone/Mannesmann, Commission Decision of 12 April 2000 in Case Comp/M.1795,
   [2000] OJ C 141/19 252–3
Volkswagen AG v. Commission, Case T-62/98 [2000] ECR II-2707, EU:T:2000:180 ..... 28–30, 126
Volvo AB v. Erik Veng (UK) Ltd, Case 238/87, [1988] ECR 6211, EU:C:1988:477 ..... 180–81, 184
Volvo/Scania, Commission Decision 15 March 2000 in Case COMP/M.1672, [2001] OJ
   L 143/74 242–3
W. Meng v. Germany, Case C-2/91, [1993] ECR I-5751, EU:C:1993:885 300
Wirtschaftsvereinigung Stahl and Others v. Commission, Case T-16/98, [2001] ECR II-1217,
   ECLI:EU:T: 2001:117 96–7
World Duty Free Group and Others, Joined Cases C-20/15 and C-21/15 P, EU:C:2016:981
   317–19
Wouters et Cie, Case C-309/99 [2002] ECR I-1527, EU:C:2002:98 .... 20, 113–15

Foreign Cases

Ireland
H.B. Ice-cream Ltd v. Masterfoods Ltd (trading as Mars Ireland) [1990] 2 IR 463 150

United Kingdom

Actavis/Hydrocortisone, CMA case, Statement of Objections on 16 December 2016 170
Pfizer/Flynn Pharma, CMA case CE/9742-13, 18 December 2015..170
Provimi Ltd v. Roche Products Ltd [2003] 2 All ER (Comm) 683 60

United States

Berkey Photo, Inc. v. Eastman Kodak Co. 603 F.2d 263, 294 (2d Cir.1979), cert. denied, 444
   U.S. 1093 (1980)..171
Brooke Group Ltd v. Brown & Williamson Tobacco Corp., 509 U.S. 209, 113 S.Ct. 2578, 125
   L.Ed.2d 168 (1993) 171, 179, 215–18
Business Electronics Corp. v. Sharp Electronics Corp 485 U.S. 717 (1988) 137, 139
California Retail Liquor Dealers Ass'n v. Midcal Aluminum, Inc., 445 U.S. 97, 100 S.Ct. 937,
   63 L.Ed.2d 233 (1980) 311
California v. American Stores Co., 495 U.S. 271, 110 S.Ct. 1853, 109 L.Ed.2d 240 (1990)...........239
California v. ARC America Corp., 490 U.S. 93, 109 S.Ct. 1661, 104 L.Ed.2d 86 (1989) 311
Camps Newfound/Owatonna, Inc. v. Town of Harrison, 520 U.S. 564, 589, 117 S.Ct. 1590,
   137 L.Ed.2d 852 (1997)...329
Citizen Publishing Co. v. United States, 394 U.S. 131, 89 S.Ct. 927, 22 L.Ed.2d 148
   (1969) 254
Continental T.V., Inc. v. GTE Sylvania Inc., 433 U.S. 36, 97 S.Ct. 2549, 53 L.Ed.2d 568
   (1977) 26–7, 138
Dr Miles Medical Co. v. John D. Park & Sons, 220 U.S. 373, 31 S.Ct. 376, 55 L.Ed. 502
   (1911) (overruled 2007) 136, 142
Eastman Kodak Co. v. Image Technical Services, 504 U.S. 451, 112 S.Ct. 2072, 119 L.Ed.2d
   265 (1992) 208
E.I. du Pont de Nemours & Co. v FTC, 729 F.2d 128 (2d Cir.1984)..164
Exxon Corp. v. Governor of Maryland, 437 U.S. 117, 98 S.Ct. 2207, 57 L.Ed.2d 91 (1978) 311
F. Hoffmann-La Roche v. Empagran S.A., 542 U.S. 155, 124 S.Ct. 2359, 159 L.Ed.2d 226
   (2004) 60
Hartford Fire Ins. Co. v. California, 509 U.S. 764, 796, 113 S.Ct. 2891, 125 L.Ed.2d 612
   (1993) 59
Hoover v. Ronwin, 466 U.S. 558, 104 S.Ct. 1989, 80 L.Ed.2d 590 (1984)..306
Illinois Tool Works Inc. v. Independent Ink, Inc., 547 U.S. 28, 126 S.Ct. 1281, 164 L.Ed.2d 26
   (2006) 208
Independent Service Organizations Antitrust Litigation (CSU v. Xerox), 203 F.3d 1322 (Fed.
   Cir. 2000), cert. denied, 531 U.S. 1143 (2001) 191
International Salt Co. v. United States, 332 U.S. 392, 68 S.Ct. 12, 92 L.Ed. 20 (1947)....................208
Interstate Circuit, Inc. v. United States, 306 U.S. 208, 59 S.Ct. 467, 83 L.Ed. 610 (1939) 48, 53
Jefferson Parish Hospital District No. 2 v. Hyde, 466 U.S. 2, 32, 104 S.Ct. 1551, 80 L.Ed.2d 2
   (1984) 208
Leegin Creative Products, Inc. v. PSKS, Inc., 551 U.S. 877, 127 S.Ct. 2705, 168 L.Ed.2d 623
   (2007) 27, 125, 136–43
Mannington Mills, Inc. v. Congoleum Corp., 595 F.2d 1287 (3rd Cir.1979) 59
Matsushita Electrical Industrial Co., Ltd v. Zenith Radio Corp., 475 U.S. 574, 106 S.Ct. 1348,
   89 L.Ed.2d 538 (1986) 48, 179

MCI Communications Corp. v. American Telephone & Telegraph Co., 708 F.2d 1081 (7th Cir.1983) 174
Motorola Mobility LLC v. AU Optronics Corp. 775 F.3d 816 (7th Cir. 2015), cert denied 60
National Society of Professional Engineers v. United States, 435 U.S. 679, 98 S.Ct. 1355, 55 L.Ed.2d 637 (1978) 118
Novell, Inc. v. Microsoft Corp, 731 F.3d 1064 (10th Cir. 2013) 191
Pacific Bell Telephone Co. v. linkLine Communications, In, 555 U.S. 438 (2009) 223–4
Polygram Holding, Inc. v. FTC 416 F.3d 29 (D.C. Cir. 2005) 77
Schwegmann Bros. v. Calvert Distillers Corp., 341 U.S. 384, 71 S.Ct. 745, 95 L.Ed. 1035 (1951) 311
Southern Motor Carriers Rate Conference, Inc. v. United States, 471 U.S. 48, 105 S.Ct. 1721, 85 L.Ed.2d 36 (1985)..311
State Oil Co v. Khan, 522 U.S. 3, 118 S.Ct 275, 139 L.Ed.2d 199 (1997) 137
Theatre Enterprises, Inc. v. Paramount Film Distributing Corp., 346 U.S. 537, 74 S.Ct. 257, 98 L.Ed. 273 (1954) 48
Timberlane Lumber Co. v. Bank of America, 549 F.2d 597 (9th Cir.1976).......................................59
Twombly v. Bell Atlantic Corp., 550 U.S. 544, 127 S.Ct. 1955, 167 L.Ed.2d 929 (2007) 48
United Haulers v. Oneida-Herkimer Solid Waste Mgmt. Authority, 550 U.S. 330, 127 S.Ct. 1786, 167 L.Ed.2d 655 (2007)..311
United States v. Aluminum Co. of America, 148 F.2d 416 (2d Cir.1945) 54, 58
United States v. American Telephone & Telegraph Co., 524 F.Supp. 1336, 1352 (D.D.C.1981) 174
United States v. Arnold, Schwinn & Co, 388 U.S. 365, 87 S.Ct. 1856, 18 L.Ed.2d 1249 (1967) (overruled 1977)..26
United States v. Dentsply Int'l Inc., 399 F.3d 181 (3d Cir. 2005), cert. denied, 546 U.S. 1089 (2006) 151
United States v. E.I. du Pont de Nemours and Co, 351 U.S. 377 (1956)..80
United States v. Microsoft Corp., 253 F.3d 34 (D.C. Cir. 2001)...179, 208
United States v. Socony-Vacuum Oil Co., Inc., 310 U.S. 150, 60 S.Ct. 811, 84 L.Ed. 1129 (1940) 48
United States v. Watchmakers of Switzerland Info. Center, 1963 (CCH) Trade Cas. ¶ 70 600 (S.D.N.Y.1962); 1965 (CCH) Trade Cas. ¶ 71 352 (S.D.N.Y.1965) 58
Utah Pie Co. v. Continental Baking Co., 386 U.S. 685, 87 S.Ct. 1326, 18 L.Ed.2d. 406 (1967)......232
Verizon Communications Inc. v. Law Offices of Curtis V. Trinko, 540 U.S. 398, 124 S.Ct. 872, 157 L.Ed.2d 823 (2004) 177–80, 191, 208
Virgin Atlantic Airways Ltd v. British Airways Plc, 257 F.3d 256 (2d Cir. 2001)..........................198–9
West Lynn Creamery v. Healy, 512 U.S. 186, 114 S.Ct. 2205, 129 L.Ed.2d 157 (1994).........311, 329

Introduction

Europe was balkanized at the end of World War II. Each nation's borders were economic frontiers, and the frontiers were barriers to trade. Economic nationalism divided Europe. The political economy of the nations also varied. Some had statist regimes, with a plethora of State-owned enterprises. Most had significant degrees of government regulation. The nations were inhospitable to foreign investment and high trade barriers in the form of quotas and tariffs kept out-of-state goods from flowing across the borders. The enterprises within each nation were plagued by inefficiencies and stagnation. Thus, European business lagged in a world on the brink of global trade and competition.

The Treaty establishing the European Economic Community of 1957 (subsequently the EC Treaty or 'ECT', and now the Treaty on the Functioning of the European Union or 'TFEU') was designed to foster peace among the nations and peoples of Europe by creating interdependences through the lifting of economic barriers and the achievement of one single market. The four freedoms of movement—goods, services, capital and people—were designed to eliminate State barriers to trade, investment, and the establishment of business. Competition policy was then tasked to ensure that business actors would not erect or re-erect barriers, exercise special privileges, or otherwise abuse their power.

With the traditional tariff and non-tariff barriers removed, competition policy became the trade-and-competition policy for the internal market. National anti-dumping laws were forbidden. State aids were subjected to rules of transparency and were tightly restricted. Commercial actors, public as well as private, were forbidden to abuse a dominant position or enter agreements with the object or effect of restricting competition. State monopolies were prohibited from discriminating against non-nationals, particularly so as not to impair imports or exports.

From the outset the Treaty mandated, as one of the specified activities necessary to carry out the purposes of the Community, 'the institution of a system insuring that competition in the common market is not distorted. . . .' (Article 3(f) ECT, subsequently Article 3(1)(g); ultimately moved to a clause in Protocol 27 by the Treaty of Lisbon).

Under the Treaty, competition policy is carried out by five sets of principles. First, free movement—the four freedoms—provides a basic framework. Second, Article 101 TFEU (formerly Article 81 ECT) prohibits undertakings from making anticompetitive agreements, and Article 102 TFEU (ex Article 82 ECT) prohibits dominant undertakings from abusing their dominance; these are the antitrust provisions of the EU Treaties. Third, public undertakings and undertakings to which Member States grant special or exclusive rights are, under Article 106 (ex Article 86 ECT), subject to the competition rules except to the extent that application of those rules would obstruct the performance of their public interest tasks. Fourth, since competition can be distorted not only by enterprises but also by State subsidies, Articles 107 to 109 (ex Articles 87 to 89 ECT) provide for the identification of proposed State aids and justification or elimination of them.

Fifth, recognizing that *States* may unduly obstruct trade and competition, the Treaty imposes obligations on the Member States in addition to the State aid regime. As noted, the Treaty prohibits the Member States from adopting trade-restraining measures; for example, Article 34, ex Article 28 ECT, prohibits quantitative restrictions on imports and measures of equivalent effect. Also, the Treaty requires Member States to 'progressively adjust any State monopolies of a commercial character' to assure no discrimination in procurement or marketing (Article 37, ex 31 ECT). In addition, the Treaty on European Union (or 'TEU') requires the Member States to 'facilitate the achievement of the Union's tasks' and abstain from measures that could jeopardize achievement of the Union's objectives (Article 4(3) TEU, ex Article 10 ECT). Accordingly, Member States are restricted in adopting anti-competitive legislation, although this constraint is importantly qualified by States' rights to adopt non-discriminatory regulation in pursuit of justifiable public ends.

The unitary quality of the EU's competition policy is greater than that of the competition policy of the US and of other nations and regions. In the US, policy regarding public restraints is more sharply separated from policy regarding private restraints, states retain more sovereign power to enact laws that have anti-competitive impacts, and there is no system disciplining state-granted subsidies.

***

This casebook presents a systematic, yet focused, collection of edited materials covering the whole spectrum of practices and situations falling within the scope of EU competition law, accompanied by questions and commentaries. It is distinctive by its condensed format, its emphasis on the discussion of substantive principles in their policy context and its numerous references to

US cases for comparative purposes. Written in plain language, it also includes various notes on the economics of antitrust and merger control, the objectives underlying the enforcement of competition principles at EU level, and jurisdictional issues arising in transnational cases. As a standalone resource adaptable to a variety of teaching formats, styles and levels, it is compatible with a wide range of academic traditions and suitable for other usages. In addition, it constitutes a unique reference deskbook for practitioners advising clients on EU competition matters, allowing them to keep key materials within reach and in a handy format.

Chapter 1 introduces the Treaty provisions directed towards market actors ('undertakings'); namely, Articles 101 and 102 TFEU. At the outset, the focus lies with the market-integrating aspects of the EU competition policy.

Chapter 2 considers a core anti-competitive restraint in the form of agreements among competitors that have no purpose except to eliminate competition among the competitors; that is, cartels, which most commonly include market-division, price-fixing and bid rigging. In discussing the law against cartels, Chapter 2 also introduces the economics of competition policy; and in connection with transnational cartels, it deals with jurisdiction and jurisdictional conflicts.

Aside from cartels, there are various other co-operations among competitors, many of which may improve production, distribution or economic or technological progress. Chapter 3 deals with these agreements, distinguishing permissible collaborations from forbidden ones under Article 101 TFEU.

Chapter 4 then addresses a related category of practices arising under Article 101 TFEU: agreements that impose vertical restraints. These are restraints in the course of distribution and licensing, including the licensing of technology. This chapter covers exclusionary and market-blocking restraints, and distribution of goods through selected outlets.

While Article 101 governs anti-competitive agreements, Article 102 TFEU governs the conduct of firms in a dominant position. This major provision of EU competition law—abuse of dominance—is the subject of Chapter 5. Thus Chapter 5 discusses: When does a firm have a dominant position, and when does conduct by that firm amount to a prohibited abuse?

The law of merger control is covered in Chapter 6. This chapter presents the important Merger Regulation, including merger analysis and notification under the merger control system, and conflict and coordination in world merger review.

Finally, Chapter 7 studies competition policy as it applies to actions and measures by the State and to private action authorized or encouraged by the State. European competition law applies to State measures in a number of ways. Public enterprises and State-granted monopolies are subject to competition principles. Member States are required to facilitate the achievement of the Union's tasks. All State aids must be reported and justified or eliminated. For private actors tasked by their State to take action that is anti-competitive, the umbrella of State protection is limited, especially when the action puts out-of-state Europeans on an unequal plane. Taken together with the positive freedoms of movement (the four freedoms), the European law principle that constrains State actions and measures harming trade and competition in the internal market, rounds the circle of European competition policy.

Generally, bear in mind that competition law and its enforcement form the fullest body of administrative law at EU level. In most other areas, the Member States are the principal agents for carrying out European law, which they are empowered and bound to do. In competition law, the Commission was the only significant administrator and enforcer of the law until May 2004, when powers of co-enforcement were devolved to Member States as part of a wide-ranging 'modernisation' of EU competition law enforcement. Accordingly, many of the principal judgements on rights of defence and other issues of procedure and process in the EU are competition cases, which increases the interest in this area and the importance of studying it.

Abuses of dominance: the *Intel* judgement of the Court of Justice

On 6 September 2017, the Court of Justice issued its long-awaited judgement in the appeal brought by Intel Corporation Inc. ('Intel') against a 2014 ruling of the General Court that upheld a Commission Decision finding Intel guilty of abuse of dominance as a result of various exclusionary practices directed at competing microprocessor supplier Advanced Micro-Devices ('AMD'). The practices in question included: (i) rebates granted to computer manufacturers Dell, Lenovo, HP and NEC (known as 'OEMs' for original equipment manufacturers), which were conditioned on the purchase of all or almost all of their x86 CPU microprocessors requirements from Intel; and (ii) direct payments made to HP, Acer and Lenovo to delay, cancel or restrict the marketing of certain products equipped with AMD microprocessors, which were referred to as 'naked restrictions' by the Commission.

The facts of the case and the judgement of the General Court are summarized and discussed in a specific note available on pp. 201–204 of this volume, which also presents the Opinion of Advocate General Wahl delivered on 20 October 2016 and is therefore a prerequisite in order to understand what follows. In support of its appeal, Intel put forward a number of pleas essentially challenging the General Court's assessment of the rebates in question, of the jurisdiction of the Commission, of the lack of recording of an interview conducted by the Commission over the course of its investigation, and of the amount of the €1.06 billion fine imposed by the Commission. The jurisdiction issue is discussed on p. 60. The remainder of this section relates to the Court of Justice's discussion of the legal framework governing the assessment of exclusivity requirements tied to rebates, and the extent to which these can be held abusive.

As such, the *Intel* judgement reflects the latest position of the Court of Justice on the treatment of pricing practices under Article 102 TFEU; by setting aside the controversial opinion of the General Court and acknowledging the need to 'further clarify' its own case-law, the Court set an important precedent.

CASE

Intel v. Commission (Case C-413/14 P)[1]

133   ... it must be borne in mind that it is in no way the purpose of Article 102 TFEU to prevent an undertaking from acquiring, on its own merits, the dominant position on a market. Nor does that provision seek to ensure that competitors less efficient than the undertaking with the dominant position should remain on the market.

134   Thus, not every exclusionary effect is necessarily detrimental to competition. Competition on the merits may, by definition, lead to the departure from the market or the marginalization of competitors that are less efficient and so less attractive to consumers from the point of view of, among other things, price, choice, quality or innovation.

135   However, a dominant undertaking has a special responsibility not to allow its behaviour to impair genuine, undistorted competition on the internal market.

136   That is why Article 102 TFEU prohibits a dominant undertaking from, among other things, adopting pricing practices that have an exclusionary effect on competitors considered to be as efficient as it is itself and strengthening its dominant position by using methods other than those that are part of competition on the merits. Accordingly, in that light, not all competition by means of price may be regarded as legitimate.

137   In that regard, the Court has already held that an undertaking which is in a dominant position on a market and ties purchasers—even if it does so at their request—by an obligation or promise on their part to obtain all or most of their requirements exclusively from that undertaking abuses its dominant position within the meaning of Article 102 TFEU, whether the obligation is stipulated without further qualification or whether it is undertaken in consideration of the grant of a rebate. The same applies if the undertaking in question, without tying the purchasers by a formal obligation, applies, either under the terms of agreements concluded with these purchasers or unilaterally, a system of loyalty rebates, that is to say, discounts conditional on the customer obtaining all or most of its requirements—whether the quantity of its purchases be large or small—from the undertaking in a dominant position.

138   However, that case-law must be further clarified in the case where the undertaking concerned submits, during the administrative procedure, on the basis of supporting evidence, that its conduct was not capable of restricting competition and, in particular, of producing the alleged foreclosure effects.

139   In that case, the Commission is not only required to analyse, first, the extent of the undertaking's dominant position on the relevant market and, second, the share of the

---

[1] EU:C:2017:632 (Grand Chamber).

CASE *(continued)*

market covered by the challenged practice, as well as the conditions and arrangements for granting the rebates in question, their duration and their amount; it is also [re]quired to assess the possible existence of a strategy aiming to exclude competitors that are at least as efficient as the dominant undertaking from the market.

140   The analysis of the capacity to foreclose is also relevant in assessing whether a system of rebates which, in principle, falls within the scope of the prohibition laid down in Article 102 TFEU, may be objectively justified. It has to be determined whether the exclusionary effect arising from such a system, which is disadvantageous for competition, may be counterbalanced, or outweighed, by advantages in terms of efficiency which also benefit the consumer. That balancing of the favourable and unfavourable effects of the practice in question on competition can be carried out in the Commission's decision only after an analysis of the intrinsic capacity of that practice to foreclose competitors which are at least as efficient as the dominant undertaking [so-called 'AEC test'].

141   If, in a decision finding a rebate scheme abusive, the Commission carries out such an analysis, the General Court must examine all of the applicant's arguments seeking to call into question the validity of the Commission's findings concerning the foreclosure capability of the rebate concerned.

142   In this case, while the Commission emphasized, in the decision at issue, that the rebates at issue were by their very nature capable of restricting competition such that an analysis of all the circumstances of the case and, in particular, an AEC test was not necessary in order to find an abuse of a dominant position (see, inter alia, paragraphs 925 and 1760 of that decision), it nevertheless carried out an in-depth examination of those circumstances, setting out, in paragraphs 1002 to 1576 of that decision, a very detailed analysis of the AEC test, which led it to conclude, in paragraphs 1574 and 1575 of that decision, that an efficient competitor would have had to offer prices which would not have been viable and that, accordingly, the rebate scheme at issue was capable of having foreclosure effects on such a competitor.

143   It follows that, in the decision at issue, the AEC test played an important role in the Commission's assessment of whether the rebate scheme at issue was capable of having foreclosure effects on as efficient competitors.

144   In those circumstances, the General Court was required to examine all of Intel's arguments concerning that test.

145   It held, however, in paragraphs 151 and 166 of the judgement under appeal, that it was not necessary to consider whether the Commission had carried out the AEC test in accordance with the applicable rules and without making any errors, and that it was also not necessary to examine the question whether the alternative calculations proposed by Intel had been carried out correctly. ...

CASE (continued)

147 Consequently, without it being necessary to rule on the second, third and sixth ground of appeal, the judgement of the General Court must be set aside, since, in its analysis of whether the rebates at issue were capable of restricting competition, the General Court wrongly failed to take into consideration Intel's line of argument seeking to expose alleged errors committed by the Commission in the AEC test.

[Eventually, the Court of Justice referred the case back to the General Court to determine whether the rebates in question are capable of restricting competition in view of the factual and economic evidence underpinning the Commission's assessment and the arguments put forward by Intel. The Intel 'saga' is therefore not over and the forthcoming judgement of the General Court should contain important findings on, e.g. the articulation of the AEC test.]

NOTES AND QUESTIONS

1. In *Intel*, the Court refers multiple times to the *Post Danmark 1* judgement but not a single time to *Post Danmark 2*. Why is it so, in your view, and what can be the implications? Draw the analogies and differences between Intel, on the one hand, and the two Post Danmark cases, on the other hand.
2. Does the Court effectively overrule Hoffman-la Roche and open the door to complete effects analysis? What does the judgement do to the dominant firm conduct that the Court simply presumes harms competition (or that the Court historically presumed not to harm competition, such as quantity rebates)?
3. What kind of 'supporting evidence' should be adduced and accepted in order to reverse the presumption of abuse and support the fact that an exclusivity requirement or loyalty rebate is not capable of restricting competition and of producing exclusionary effects? What should be the threshold to force the Commission into an effects analysis?
4. The Court seems to place exclusivity and loyalty rebates in the same basket of 'presumably abusive' restrictions. Does it make sense to establish a presumption of abuse in respect of these two practices, and to treat them together? Should differences be drawn between the two categories?
5. After the judgement, what is the likely status of the 'naked restrictions' in Intel? Can the undertaking introduce evidence that these too were not capable of harming competition? Or is there still some category of restraint that is just so bad (so likely to harm competition, so unlikely to have pro-market benefits) that it should not be allowed? What is this category?
6. What is the status of the AEC test after Intel? Is it now a mandatory part of the assessment of rebates and other pricing practices under Article 102 TFEU?
7. Does the judgement promote greater convergence in the analytical framework and sequence applicable under 101 and 102 TFEU? In particular, do you see analogies with *Cartes bancaires* (as suggested by A.G. Wahl)? Are the scope and strengths of the 'by object' category similar under 101 and 102, or do you see differences/weaknesses?
8. What is, in your view, the likely effect of the judgement on non-pricing cases (e.g. Google cases)?
9. What is, in your view, the overall likely effect of the judgement on the enforcement of Article 102 TFEU by the European Commission and NCAs?

Abuses of dominance: the *Google* decision (search)

On 27 June 2017, the Commission closed an investigation into Google's search services that had been on-going from at least November 2010, by imposing a record €2.42 billion fine for abuse of dominance. At the time of printing this volume, the public version of the Commission decision was not yet available. Excerpts from the Commission press release follow.

European Commission: press release

Antitrust: Commission fines Google €2.42 billion for abusing dominance as search engine by giving illegal advantage to own comparison shopping service.

...

Google's strategy for its comparison shopping service

... In 2004 Google entered the separate market of comparison shopping in Europe with a product that was initially called 'Froogle', re-named 'Google Product Search' in 2008 and since 2013 has been called 'Google Shopping'. It allowed consumers to compare products and prices online and find deals from online retailers of all types, including online shops of manufacturers, platforms (such as Amazon and eBay), and other re-sellers.

When Google entered comparison shopping markets with Froogle, there were already a number of established players. Contemporary evidence from Google shows that the company was aware that Froogle's market performance was relatively poor (one internal document from 2006 stated 'Froogle simply doesn't work').

... From 2008, Google began to implement, in European markets, a fundamental change in strategy to push its comparison shopping service. This strategy relied on Google's dominance in general internet search, instead of competition on the merits in comparison shopping markets:

- Google has systematically given prominent placement to its own comparison shopping service: when a consumer enters a query into the Google search engine in relation to which Google's comparison shopping service wants to show results, these are displayed at or near the top of the search results.

- Google has demoted rival comparison shopping services in its search results: rival comparison shopping services appear in Google's search results on the basis of Google's generic search algorithms. Google has included a number of criteria in these algorithms, as a result of which rival comparison shopping services are demoted. Evidence shows that even the most highly ranked rival service appears on average only on page four of Google's search results, and others appear even further down. Google's own comparison shopping service is not subject to Google's generic search algorithms, including such demotions.

As a result, Google's comparison shopping service is much more visible to consumers in Google's search results, whilst rival comparison shopping services are much less visible. ...

This means that by giving prominent placement only to its own comparison shopping service and by demoting competitors, Google has given its own comparison shopping service a significant advantage compared to rivals.

Breach of EU antitrust rules

Google's practices amount to an abuse of Google's dominant position in general internet search by stifling competition in comparison shopping markets. ...

- Today's Decision concludes that Google is dominant in general internet search markets throughout the European Economic Area (EEA), i.e. in all 31 EEA countries. It found Google to have been dominant in general internet search markets in all EEA countries since 2008, except in the Czech Republic where the Decision has established dominance since 2011. This assessment is based on the fact that Google's search engine has held very high market shares in all EEA countries, exceeding 90% in most. It has done so consistently since at least 2008, which is the period investigated by the Commission. There are also high barriers to entry in these markets, in part because of network effects: the more consumers use a search engine, the more attractive it becomes to advertisers. The profits generated can then be used to attract even more consumers. Similarly, the data a search engine gathers about consumers can in turn be used to improve results.
- Google has abused this market dominance by giving its own comparison shopping service an illegal advantage. It gave prominent placement in its search results only to its own comparison shopping service, whilst demoting rival services. It stifled competition on the merits in comparison shopping markets. ...

The effect of Google's illegal practices

... Since the beginning of each abuse, Google's comparison shopping service has increased its traffic 45-fold in the United Kingdom, 35-fold in Germany, 19-fold in France, 29-fold in the Netherlands, 17-fold in Spain and 14-fold in Italy.

Following the demotions applied by Google, traffic to rival comparison shopping services on the other hand dropped significantly. For example, the Commission found specific evidence of sudden drops of traffic to certain rival websites of 85% in the United Kingdom, up to 92% in Germany and 80% in France. These sudden drops could also not be explained by other factors. Some competitors have adapted and managed to recover some traffic but never in full. ...

Evidence gathered

In reaching its Decision, the Commission has gathered and comprehensively analysed a broad range of evidence, including:

1) contemporary documents from both Google and other market players;
2) very significant quantities of real-world data including 5.2 Terabytes of actual search results from Google (around 1.7 billion search queries);
3) experiments and surveys, analysing in particular the impact of visibility in search results on consumer behaviour and click-through rates;
4) financial and traffic data which outline the commercial importance of visibility in Google's search results and the impact of being demoted; and
5) an extensive market investigation of customers and competitors in the markets concerned (the Commission addressed questionnaires to several hundred companies).

Consequences of the Decision

The Commission Decision requires Google to stop its illegal conduct within 90 days of the Decision and refrain from any measure that has the same or an equivalent object or effect. In particular, the Decision orders Google to comply with the simple principle of giving equal treatment to rival comparison shopping services and its own service: Google has to apply the same processes and methods to position and display rival comparison shopping services in Google's search results pages as it gives to its own comparison shopping service.

It is Google's sole responsibility to ensure compliance and it is for Google to explain how it intends to do so. Regardless of which option Google chooses, the Commission will monitor Google's compliance closely and Google is under an obligation to keep the Commission informed of its actions (initially within 60 days of the Decision, followed by periodic reports).

Other Google cases

The Commission has already come to the preliminary conclusion that Google has abused a dominant position in two other cases which are still being investigated. These concern:

1) the Android operating system, where the Commission is concerned that Google has stifled choice and innovation in a range of mobile apps and services by pursuing an overall strategy on mobile devices to protect and expand its dominant position in general internet search; and
2) AdSense, where the Commission is concerned that Google has reduced choice by preventing third-party websites from sourcing search ads from Google's competitors.

The Commission also continues to examine Google's treatment in its search results of other specialized Google search services. Today's Decision is a precedent which establishes the framework for the assessment of the legality of this type of conduct. At the same time, it does not replace the need for a case-specific analysis to account for the specific characteristics of each market.

NOTES AND QUESTIONS

1. Reflect on the competitive effects of Google's strategy to expand beyond general internet search and to position and display favourably its other services, assuming the Commission's fact-finding is accurate. What should be sufficient, and what should be necessary, to prove harm to competition? What duties should Google have to its rivals in comparative search? What is a good remedy for this offence?
2. Does Google's expansion into comparison shopping and other services (e.g. maps) and the way these are displayed (e.g. with pictures and ratings) amount to an improvement of Google's search services? Does that expansion qualify as innovation? In the affirmative, should that innovation affect the analysis?
3. Google contends that its comparison shopping services compete with other large players, including Amazon (for a full statement, see https://www.blog.google/topics/google-europe/european-commission-decision-shopping-google-story/). Do you agree? Does it matter, and should it affect the analysis?
4. Google has appealed the Commission Decision (see Case T-612/17, *Google and Alphabet v. Commission*). In your view, what are Google's strongest grounds for appeal? Do you think that the subsequent *Intel* judgement of the Court of Justice could influence the review of the case, and to what extent? Consider critically the statement issued by prominent complainants in the Google case arguing that with the Intel judgement 'nothing changes for the Google appeal' (see http://fairsearch.org/the-intel-judgment-nothing-changes-for-the-google-appeal/).

1

The Treaty, objectives and the Single Market

Competition laws protect the dynamic process of competition. The process of competition rewards efficiency and inventiveness; it shakes out complacent and bad performers and induces the production and delivery of better goods and services and the provision of a range of goods and services at lower prices. It spurs innovation. It removes obstructions from the path of producers and it serves people in their capacity as consumers.

Every nation's competition law is a function of its context. Nowhere is this clearer than in the European Union, where the competition provisions are embedded in a Treaty with larger goals. Consider the European context, as framed in the European competition policy reports and statements by Competition Commissioners, below.

A. The objectives of EU competition policy

Competition law is a vital part of EU law. It is informed by many interrelated policies. In September 2014, looking forward to a newly constituted Commission on 1 November 2014, the then President-elect presented a mission letter to the Commissioner-elect in charge of competition outlining the objectives of her mandate and methodological considerations. Every year the Directorate-General for Competition of the European Commission also publishes a report on competition policy, which articulates the objectives of EU competition policy and States priorities. The following excerpts discuss the objectives of EU competition policy.

Mission Letter from The President of The Commission to the Competition Commissioner (2014)

Jean-Claude Juncker,
President-elect of the European Commission

Mission LetterBrussels, 10 September 2014

Margrethe Vestager
Commissioner for Competition

Dear Margrethe,

You are becoming a Member of the new European Commission at a particularly challenging time for the European Union. With the start of the new Commission, we have an exceptional opportunity, but also an obligation, to make a fresh start, to address the difficult geo-political situation, to strengthen economic recovery and to build a Europe that delivers jobs and growth for its citizens. * * *

I want the Commission as a whole to be more than the sum of its parts. I therefore want us to work together as a strong team, cooperating across portfolios to produce integrated, well-grounded and well-explained initiatives that lead to clear results. I want us to overcome silo mentalities by working jointly on those areas where we can really make a difference.
* * *

The Competition portfolio

You will be the Commissioner for Competition. You will, in particular, contribute to projects steered and coordinated by the Vice-President for Jobs, Growth, Investment and Competitiveness, the Vice-President for the Digital Single Market and the Vice-President for Energy Union. As a rule, you will liaise closely with the Vice-President for Jobs, Growth, Investment and Competitiveness in defining the general lines of our competition and State aid policies and the instruments of general scope related to them.

Competition policy is one of the areas where the Commission has exclusive competence and action in this field will be key to the success of our jobs and growth agenda. It should contribute to steering innovation and making markets deliver clear benefits to consumers, businesses and society as a whole. Every effort should be made to maximize the positive contribution of our competition policy in support of our overall priorities and to explain and demonstrate its benefits to citizens and stake holders at all levels.

During our mandate, I would like you to focus on the following:

- Mobilising competition policy tools and market expertise so that they contribute, as appropriate, to our jobs and growth agenda, including in areas such as the digital single market, energy policy, financial services, industrial policy and the fight against tax evasion. In this context, it will be important to keep developing an economic as well as a legal approach to the assessment of competition issues

and to further develop market monitoring in support of the broader activities of the Commission.
- Pursuing an effective enforcement of competition rules in the areas of antitrust and cartels, mergers and State aid, maintaining competition instruments aligned with market developments, as well as promoting a competition culture in the EU and world-wide.
- Maintaining and strengthening the Commission's reputation world-wide and promoting international cooperation in this area. * * *

Jean-Claude Juncker

Competition Commissioner Vestager accepted the mandate, affirming: 'Competition is not a lonely portfolio.'[1]

European Commission Report on Competition Policy (2015)

Strong and effective EU competition policy has always been a cornerstone of the European project. Now that sustaining the recovery and boosting economic growth are at the top of EU agenda, competition policy is more important than ever.

Competition policy keeps markets efficient and open. For European consumers, this translates into better market outcomes such as lower prices, better quality products and services, and greater choice. In addition, healthy competition gives companies fair chances to do business and to achieve their commercial goals, which in turn encourages growth, job creation and prosperity. When companies are able to compete on their own merits, businesses and households benefit from a wide range of good quality, innovative products and services at competitive prices. Increased competition also drives companies to invest and to become more efficient. These efficiency gains are then passed on to the wider economy. The ultimate aim of competition policy is to make markets work better – to the advantage of households and businesses.

At the beginning of his mandate, the President of the European Commission, Jean-Claude Juncker, said that his Commission will focus on the key challenges facing European society and the economy. Competition policy has an important role to

---

1 See H. Vane (2014), 'The end of the lonely portfolio?', *Global Competition Review*, **17** (10), 6. See also: M. Vestager, 'The values of competition policy', speech at CEPS Corporate Breakfast, 13 October 2015; M. Vestager, 'Competition is a consumer issue', speech to BEUC General Assembly, 13 May 2016; and M. Vestager, 'How competition supports innovation', speech at Regulation4Innovation, 24 May 2016 (all available at: ec.europa.eu/competition (accessed 31 May 2017)).

play in tackling those challenges. The work carried out in the field of competition in 2015 made a significant contribution to a number of Commission's key political priorities, namely boosting jobs, growth and investment, and creating a connected Digital Single Market, a resilient Energy Union, and a deeper and fairer single market. * * *

Speech by Commissioner
Margrethe Vestager
The Values of Competition Policy
CEPS, Brussels, 13 October 2015

I'm often asked about the values underpinning our competition policy. More specifically, people ask about the role of politics.

We can look at the politics of competition enforcement from three angles, starting from whether competition policy is based on political values and principles. The answer is, obviously, yes.

Keeping markets fair, level, and open is good for our economies and societies. It establishes a good environment for business in Europe where companies can generate wealth, create jobs, and invest in the future.

The second question is: Does competition enforcement relate to wider political priorities? And does it inform regulatory and other action taken to implement such priorities? Again, the answer is: Yes, it does.

The Juncker Commission is a political Commission with a clear set of objectives and the College of Commissioners plays as a team.

Competition policy – and I as Competition Commissioner – clearly have our own space in it. But there should be no doubt that I will do my part to help achieve the Commission's broader objectives.

The final question is: Is competition enforcement in individual cases politicized? Here the answer is a resounding No.

We enforce the law and serve the common European interest. We are committed to the principles of fairness, good administration, transparency and due process. There is simply no room to spare for political interference.

European Commission Report on Competition Policy (2013)

[T]he European Parliament's 2013 study on competition policy concluded: 'Competition plays a crucial role in promoting productivity and innovation as drivers of economic growth. This means that competition policy, which intensifies competition, will stimulate growth.'

It applies to all the instruments of competition policy. Antitrust enforcement can thwart dominant companies' attempts to keep new entrants away from the market and prevent them from competing effectively with them. It can also create the conditions for lower input prices for EU industry. Merger control can keep markets open and efficient. State aid policy protects the internal market from distortions and helps to steer public resources towards competitiveness-enhancing objectives.

In addition, competition and competition policy are part and parcel of the general conditions required for innovation to flourish. They provide incentives to innovative enterprises and start-ups, they encourage companies to become more efficient, and they promote subsidies designed to stimulate R&D and innovation.

Competition policy fosters competitiveness in a global context. Healthy competition in the Single Market prepares European companies to do business on global markets and succeed. It also underpins a modern industrial policy, as reflected in the Lisbon Treaty's provisions on industry (Article 173 TFEU) which states that action taken by the EU and the Member States shall be 'in accordance with a system of open and competitive markets.'

Furthermore, competition policy is the necessary counterpart of Single Market regulation. The impact of the regulatory measures on firms' strategies and investment can be undermined if Single-Market and competition rules are not properly enforced. * * *

Statement of Commissioner Joaquín Almunia on Launching Commission Consultation on Rules for Horizontal Cooperation Agreements
Excerpt from press release IP/10/489, 4 May 2010

Competition is one of the key tools for achieving a more competitive, connected, greener, knowledge based and inclusive society. Greater prosperity results from innovation and from using resources better, with knowledge as the key input. To make this transformation happen, Europe needs to use a number of tools, including competition, to drive companies to innovate and co-operate in efficiency enhancing projects.

European Commission Report on Competition Policy (2008)

Introduction

1. This year, for the first time, the Annual Report on Competition features a chapter focusing on a topic that is considered to be of particular importance in the field of competition policy. The topic chosen for this year is 'Cartels and consumers'. * * *

5. The fight against cartels is central to ensuring that the benefits of a properly functioning competition regime are offered to the final consumer in a given market for products or services. Cartels are amongst the most serious violation of competition law. They shield participants from competition, thus allowing them to raise prices, restrict output and divide markets. As a result, the money ends up in the wrong place, harming consumers through higher prices and leading to a narrower choice of products and services.

European Commission Report on Competition Policy (2006)
Foreword by then Competition Commissioner Neelie Kroes

The experience of the past fifty years of European integration shows that fair and undistorted competition in a single market works to the benefit of everyone in terms of prosperity, consumer choice, and sustainable employment.

'Free competition' is not an end in itself—it is a means to an end. When we strive to get markets working better, it is because competitive markets provide citizens with better goods and better services, at better prices. Competitive markets provide the right conditions for companies to innovate and prosper, and so to increase overall European wealth. More wealth means more money for governments to use to sustain the fabric of our societies and to guarantee social justice and a high-quality environment for generations to come.

When companies fix prices in markets like beer or elevators, customers pay higher prices and the economy at large picks up the bill. When companies abuse a dominant position, they not only exclude competitors but also dampen innovation since other companies know that however good their products are, they cannot compete on the merits. So our European anti-trust rules outlaw such behaviour throughout the Union, to the benefit of consumers.

European companies need to be able to take advantage of an open internal market, by creating efficiencies of scale and diversifying. Our merger control rules allow European champions to grow on their merits, developing into global players, provided that consumers are not harmed through reduced competition.

Our properly balanced State aids discipline prevents undue State intervention which would distort competition on the merits. . . .

The spirit and objectives underlying the European competition rules, and the need to enforce them effectively, remain as pertinent today as ever before. But of course the environment in which competition policy functions changes and develops over time.

European companies, employees and consumers are increasingly part of a global economy, and are having to adjust to reap the benefits globalization has to offer.

European competition policy—the rules and their enforcement—must play its part in supporting this process:

- by continuing to uphold a level playing field in our internal market, since free and fair competition at home allows European companies to learn from experience how to stand up to global competitive pressure . . .;
- by adapting to the realities of the day: in 2006 our ongoing State aid reform focused on the areas where limited amounts of aid can have most added value in terms of spurring on competitiveness and assisting change: training, regional cohesion, research, development and innovation . . .;
- by being better joined up: the mutual interaction of, for example, single market, consumer protection and trade policies with competition policy has never been more important. Sector inquiries and market monitoring are two tools we used in 2006 to identify remaining barriers to free competition—be they the result of business practices, regulation or other State action . . .;
- by working more beyond our European borders: increasing globalization also means more multi-jurisdictional mergers, anti-competitive conduct and even State subsidization across borders. International cooperation is vitally important for all modern competition authorities. Europe must continue to lead the way through day-to-day enforcement cooperation and bilateral and multilateral agreements. . . .

The European Commission remains firm in its resolve to ensure that European competition policy meets the challenge and continues to guarantee open and better functioning markets, not as a goal in itself, but as a means to help ensure that Europe is a net winner of globalization.

NOTES AND QUESTIONS

1. Describe in your own words the goals of the competition policy of the EU. Which of the following objectives do you think are most basic and should be preferred in the event of conflict or tension: consumer welfare, strength of European business, opportunity for small and medium-sized enterprises, market integration, market access, market liberalization, level playing field, fairness?
2. Is there a relationship of competition policy with the following? Explain.
   (a) the competitiveness of European businesses in world markets
   (b) growth
   (c) the environment
   (d) jobs
   (e) cohesion (e.g. lifting up the poorest Member States)
   (f) economic liberalization
   (g) cartels.

3. Are there advantages and/or disadvantages of linking competition policy with jobs, growth, investment and competitiveness? Of coordinating competition policy with the digital single market? With energy policy?
4. In the US, competition law (antitrust) does not incorporate non-competition objectives, at least not in theory. Since the 1980s, US antitrust law has pursued the related goals of consumer welfare and efficiency. Antitrust officials often claim that antitrust policy should influence other policies such as trade, but that other policies such as trade should not influence antitrust.
5. Do you observe differences in the rhetoric of US and of EU competition law policy? What differences? What are the advantages and disadvantages of couching competition law in a larger socio-political framework?

It would be a mistake to infer from the excerpts above that EU competition law is amorphous. It is actually quite well anchored, as we shall see.

B. Institutions and procedures

The enforcement of competition principles by the European Commission and in cooperation with the national competition authorities of the Member States ('NCAs') is governed by Regulation 1/2003 on the implementation of the rules on competition laid down in Articles [101] and [102] of the Treaty.[2] Another regulation governs merger control proceedings before the Commission and the interactions with NCAs in that context (Regulation 139/2004 on the control of concentrations between undertakings,[3] often referred to as the 'Merger Regulation'). See Chapter 6 for a discussion of merger control proceedings.

In a nutshell, antitrust cases for infringement of Articles 101 or 102 TFEU may be initiated by the Directorate-General for Competition of the Commission ('DG COMP'). The Commission has powers to investigate and to obtain documents by means of requests for information or inspections. After opening proceedings, the Commission issues a reasoned opinion (called a statement of objections or 'SO' in infringement cases), which describes the conduct involved and contains an assessment. The firms involved may then file written arguments, submit documents, and request a hearing, which is held before a hearing officer who rules on procedural matters.

The case handlers within the Directorate-General for Competition draft a preliminary decision. The draft is vetted within DG COMP and then by the Legal Service (lawyers to the various directorates of the Commission), by other relevant directorates of the Commission and by an advisory committee

---

2 [2003] O.J. L 1/1.
3 [2004] O.J. L 24/1.

of Member State representatives. The resulting revised draft decision is submitted to and ordinarily adopted by the College of Commissioners. The most common decisions adopted by the Commission include infringement decisions often imposing multi-million euros fines. Resolutions may also take the form of settlement decisions, wherein parties acknowledge the infringement, and commitment decisions, entailing the closure of cases without a finding of infringement but with commitments binding on the parties involved.

The firms involved and other persons with a special interest can seek annulment of any Commission decision before the EU General Court. Either party can then appeal the judgement to the EU Court of Justice, whose jurisdiction is then limited to points of law (not facts).

EU competition law cases may also be initiated, investigated and decided by national competition authorities according to applicable national procedures, and may be litigated by private parties in national courts (including in damages actions). In fact, a significant part of the EU competition case law arises from national courts' preliminary references to the EU Court of Justice. National competition authorities and national courts also enforce national competition provisions but are bound to ensure the consistency of the interpretation of such provisions with EU competition principles in cases affecting cross-border trade within the Union. Within the framework of the European Competition Network (or 'ECN'), the Commission and NCAs cooperate extensively in the enforcement of competition rules across the EU by exchanging information and sharing resources.

1. From Regulation 17/62 to Regulation 1/2003

In 1962, the Council adopted Regulation 17 to give the Commission the necessary powers to administer and enforce the Treaty provisions on competition and to give procedural rights to individuals. Regulation 17 remained in force until 2004, when it was replaced by Regulation 1/2003.

Regulation 17 empowered the Commission to carry out investigations, including surprise visits to search and copy documents ('dawn raids'), and to order the termination of infringements and the imposition of fines on undertakings.

Agreements, decisions and concerted practices within the scope of Article 101(1) had to be notified to the Commission, which could give a 'negative clearance'. That is, the Commission could certify that 'on the basis of the facts in its possession, there are no grounds under Article [101(1)] or Article [102] of the Treaty for action.' For agreements of a common and routine sort, such as exclusive distribution, the Commission adopted block exemptions. Agreements that complied with the block exemptions were automatically exempt and did not need to be notified.

By the late 1990s, the notification and prior approval system proved time-consuming, with little pay-off. It distracted the Commission from more important pursuits, such as cartels. Moreover, block exemptions had proliferated and their do's and don'ts were straightjacketing business transactions. Facing these and other constraints, chiefly the enlargement of the Union to ten new Member States, the Commission's Directorate-General for Competition undertook a programme of modernisation in the late 1990s. At the end of 2003, it adopted Regulation 1/2003, which, in 2004, replaced Regulation 17.

The introduction of Regulation 1/2003 was a dramatic event. It reflected significant procedural reform whereby powers would devolve to Member States. Member States would still be obliged to carry out EU law, and a new network of national authorities and DG Competition—the ECN—combined with continuing sharing of information about all relevant national court judgements, would assure consistency and coherence.[4]

Besides its institutional dimension, the modernisation process also included a substantive dimension to incorporate a more economic approach to the enforcement of EU competition law and a procedural dimension to introduce alternative 'negotiated' enforcement tools, including commitment and later settlement decisions.

2. The innovations brought about by Regulation 1/2003

In practice, Regulation 1/2003 devolved enforcement powers to the Member States with respect to agreements that restrict competition. It abolished the notification procedure and made Article 101(3) directly effective so that national competition authorities and national courts, as well as the Commission, could decide whether agreements fulfill the requirements of Article 101(3). This sharing of power lightened the Commission's workload, giving it time to consider more serious restraints of Union-wide interest.

Regulation 1/2003 established the following principles to coordinate the sharing of power in the enforcement of EU competition principles, among others:

---

4 Read Regulation 1/2003, which is available at: http://ec.europa.eu/competition/antitrust/legislation/regulations.html (accessed 31 May 2017).

1. Article 3 imposes two fundamental obligations on the courts and competition authorities of the Member States, to preserve the realm of EU law. First, where national competition law is applied to agreements and abusive practices that may affect trade between Member States, Article 3(1) imposes the obligation on national authorities and courts to apply Articles 101 and/or 102 concurrently with the national law. Second, Article 3(2) obliges the competition authorities and courts of the Member States not to invoke national law to prohibit agreements or concerted practices that may affect trade between Member States but that are not prohibited under EU competition law. Note that abuses of dominance are not in this category; Member States retain the power to prohibit abuses that may fall short of a Treaty violation.
2. The Commission retains its ability to deal with any case affecting trade between Member States. When it does so, it relieves national authorities of their competence to apply EU law in the particular case. Likewise, national courts and national competition authorities are precluded from adopting decisions that would run counter to a pre-existing Commission decision in the same case. In addition, Article 10 of Regulation 1/2003 equips the Commission with the sole power to adopt, on its own initiative and when the Union public interest so requires, ex ante decisions finding that a particular agreement or practice does not infringe Articles 101 or 102 TFEU. The Commission has not made use of that power so far but the Court of Justice has confirmed its exclusive nature and thus denied the ability of NCAs to adopt such a finding of inapplicability.[5]
3. In order to ensure the consistent application of EU competition law throughout the Union, Regulation 1/2003 creates mechanisms for information sharing and consultation among national competition authorities and DG COMP through the creation of the ECN—a robust network that has enhanced cooperation in handling cases, facilitated case allocation, and produced soft convergence of national laws and procedures. Also, national courts may ask the Commission for its support in the application of Articles 101 and 102 TFEU, and both national competition authorities and the Commission are empowered to make *amicus curiae* submissions before national courts. The Commission is equally entitled to publish opinions on any particular novel or unresolved questions for the application of Article 101 or 102.

Article 7 of Regulation 1/2003 incorporates the pre-existing fining power of the Commission and specifies that the Commission has power to impose

---

5 See Case C-375/09, *Tele2 Polska* [2011] ECR I-3055, EU:C:2011:270.

any remedy of a behavioural or structural nature that is proportionate to the infringement and necessary to bring it effectively to an end. Under Article 9, the Commission can accept commitments offered by companies to solve the competition issue identified after a preliminary assessment and close its investigation on that basis without a finding of infringement and imposing a fine.

Compared to Regulation 17, Regulation 1/2003 also confers additional investigative powers by empowering Commission officials to (i) seal premises for the period and to the extent necessary for their inspection, (ii) ask oral questions not linked to specific documents, and (iii) enter non-business premises when there is a reasonable suspicion that books and other records relevant for the inspection are being kept there.

Consider the virtues of Regulation 1/2003 in terms of devolution, empowerment, shared deliberation, cross-fertilization, coherence, and networking. What lessons might Regulation 1/2003 hold for other communities of nations facing multiple and sometimes overlapping systems of law?

As noted, instead of imposing a fine, the Commission can accept commitments under Article 9 of Regulation 1/2003. Consider the advantages of such a procedure for the Commission and defendants. Are there any risks? Consider the judgement of the EU General Court in the *Alrosa* case,[6] as reversed by the Court of Justice.[7]

Regulation 1/2003 governs the procedures and process for competition proceedings under EU law. Also relevant is a significant body of Court of Justice case law establishing rights of defence and articulating the bounds of legal privilege. These include the right of access to the Commission's investigation file, the right to be heard, the right not to incriminate oneself, the right not to be prosecuted twice for the same infringement (*ne bis in idem*), the right to a reasoned decision and the right to effective judicial review. The Commission codified many of these rights in Regulation 773/2004 on the conduct of proceedings by the Commission[8] and in notices and guidelines.

Note on the effects-based approach

As noted, the modernisation process also entailed a substantive dimension. Since the late 1990s and the completion of the single market, the rationality

---

6 Case T-170/06, *Alrosa Co. Ltd v. Commission* [2007] ECR II-2601, EU:T:2007:220.
7 Case C-441/07 P, [2010] ECR I-5949, EU:C:2010:377.
8 [2004] O.J. L 123/18.

underlying EU competition law enforcement progressively shifted from the protection of the freedom to trade of competitors to the promotion of a competitive process conducive to efficient outcomes and contributing as a result to the welfare of consumers. Initiated under the tenure of Commissioner Monti, that shift has since been affirmed in various policy documents issued by the Commission, including the Article 102 (formerly 82) Guidance Paper (further discussed in Chapter 5):

> 5. In applying Article 82 to exclusionary conduct by dominant undertakings, the Commission will focus on those types of conduct that are most harmful to consumers. Consumers benefit from competition through lower prices, better quality and a wider choice of new or improved goods and services. The Commission, therefore, will direct its enforcement to ensuring that markets function properly and that consumers benefit from the efficiency and productivity which result from effective competition between undertakings.
>
> 6. The emphasis of the Commission's enforcement activity in relation to exclusionary conduct is on safeguarding the competitive process in the internal market and ensuring that undertakings which hold a dominant position do not exclude their competitors by other means than competing on the merits of the products or services they provide. In doing so the Commission is mindful that what really matters is protecting an effective competitive process and not simply protecting competitors. This may well mean that competitors who deliver less to consumers in terms of price, choice, quality and innovation will leave the market.

The purpose of achieving efficient market outcomes leads naturally to (i) focus the analysis on the effects of particular commercial practices, rather than on hypothetical views as to the capability of such practices to affect competition, and (ii) articulate theories of harm relying on operative tests capable of balancing the pro- and anti-competitive effects of the practices in question. Hence, the substantive dimension of modernisation is often presented as a move towards an 'effects-based approach'. Alternatively, it is also referred to as a shift towards a 'more economic approach' to the enforcement of EU competition rules. This is because: (i) the basic premise of the effects-based approach is of an economic nature for it acknowledges that the most effective way to achieve allocative efficiency is to maximize individual utility; (ii) the observed rationality shift is also the result of a learning process and of an attempt to factor the evolution of the teachings of economics into the substance of norms; and (iii) the articulation of operative tests to substantiate the effects of particular practices has been made possible by the growing sophistication of tools of economic analysis.

The mutually reinforcing character of the different dimensions of the modernisation process—institutional, substantive and procedural—is also remarkable. Thus, the transition from a prior notification to an exception system for the review of cooperation agreements under Article 101 TFEU has effectively unlocked the analytical framework and allowed the move away from a strict bifurcated approach towards a more integrated balancing of the effects of the practice in question in the form of a structured rule-of-reason. That evolution has also had repercussions on the application of Article 102 TFEU, which now follows a similar pattern. Likewise, additional empirical evidence of the actual anti-competitive effects of certain practices has rendered certain practices almost unquestionably illegal, thereby allowing for expedited enforcement actions in the form of settlements. Conversely, practices with uncertain welfare effects can now be solved by means of commitments without entailing a finding of infringement.

Naturally, it takes time for any paradigmatic change to achieve a state of renewed consistency, and the move towards an effects-based approach has not been immune from cognitive dissonances requiring adjustments. For example, the tendency to rely on an extensive object category to establish infringements of Article 101 TFEU, with the potential of bypassing effects analysis, has been policed by the Court of Justice.[9] Conversely, the restrictive object category defined by the Court as entailing a rebuttable presumption of anti-competitive effects rooted in empirical findings accumulated over time, is compatible with a modern enforcement approach that needs to remain administrable and does not imply any normative view as to the robustness of markets.

The risk of double standards between the policy options favoured by the Commission and the law as stated by the Court of Justice is also a justifiable concern, and yet the Court has demonstrated openness to the teachings of modern economics underpinning the effects-based approach.[10] If the alignment between policy and law is still imperfect, there are at least good reasons to believe that a coherence is achievable. Finally, the emergence of the effects-based approach has given rise to some extreme views advocating either unreasonably high standards of proof or, in contrast, unreasonably wide understandings of the notion of restrictions of competition, in particular in the field of abuses of dominance.

---

9 Case C-67/13 P, *Groupement des cartes bancaires (CB) v. Commission*, EU:C:2014:2204 (excerpted in Chapter 3).
10 Case C-209/10, *Post Danmark I*, EU:C:2012:172 (excerpted in Chapter 5).

Although the effects-based system is not yet fully stabilized, it may lead to the articulation of a widely acceptable analytical framework relying on a structured rule-of-reason with screens based on structural market conditions, robust theories of harm, and proper consideration for efficiencies. In turn, that framework ought to be compatible with qualified object/per se rules based on empirically testable conditions. Still, when studying the materials contained in the following chapters, you should assess whether and to what extent they are compatible with the effects-based approach, and whether and to what extent the European courts are synchronized with the Commission. Reflect also on whether Member State authorities (NCAs) and courts are well positioned to handle economic analysis. Are they likely to do so in harmony with the European Commission and courts?

3. The private enforcement of EU competition law

Regulation 1/2003 governs public enforcement. The European system also contemplates private enforcement. In *Courage v. Crehan*,[11] a tenant pub that had accepted a beer-tying agreement (Mr Crehan) invoked the illegality of that agreement and requested damages while being sued for unpaid deliveries of beer. The suit was brought in a UK court. The brewer defended on the grounds that a party to an illegal agreement cannot contest the agreement. On an Article 267 reference, the Court of Justice held that not only is a party to an anti-competitive agreement not barred from suit (this may depend upon degree of complicity), but Articles 101 and 102 TFEU create rights for individuals that national courts must safeguard. 'The full effectiveness of Article [101] ... would be put at risk if it were not open to any individual to claim damages for loss caused to him by a contract or by conduct liable to restrict or distort competition', the Court said, and 'actions for damages before national courts can make a significant contribution to the maintenance of effective competition in the Community' (paras. 26–27). Member States thus have an obligation to provide effective procedural vehicles for private action.

There is no procedural vehicle for private actions within the European institutions but Court of Justice case law obliges the Member States to provide effective procedures under national law to ensure full compensation to victims caused by violations of EU law. Member State systems for private enforcement vary; some such as in the UK and Germany are strong, while others

---

11 Case C-453/99, *Courage v. Crehan* [2001] ECR I-6297.

are totally ineffective. The Commission Directorate-General for Competition undertook to develop a framework directive on private damage actions setting common standards and minimum requirements for Member State systems. A directive on 'certain rules governing actions for damages under national law for infringements of the competition law provisions of the Member States and of the European Union' was eventually approved on 26 November 2014.[12]

The directive provides that Member States must ensure victims of EU antitrust violations full compensation; that access to certain important evidence must be granted; that a final infringement decision of a national authority must constitute irrefutable proof of the infringement before courts of the same Member State and at least prima facie evidence before courts of other Member States; that indirect purchasers must be able to sue; that pass-on of over-charges must be a defence; and that multiple or punitive damages should not be available.

The directive does not mention class or collective actions. However, a 2013 Commission recommendation on 'common principles for injunctive and compensatory collective redress mechanisms in the Member States concerning violations of rights granted under EU law' urges Member States to authorize collective actions brought by non-profit representative entities (i.e., consumers associations or non-governmental organizations) with the requirement that plaintiffs joining the action opt in, not opt out.[13]

C. Introduction to Articles 101 and 102 TFEU

The Treaty contains rules prohibiting anti-competitive agreements and concerted practices (Article 101 TFEU) and rules regulating dominant firms' behaviour (Article 102 TFEU). Together with the control of State aids (according to Articles 107 to 109 TFEU) and with the Merger Regulation, these provisions form the heart of European competition policy.

After the EEC Treaty was adopted in 1957, it was necessary for the Council of the EU to adopt legislation to implement the competition provisions contained therein. The Council adopted the initial implementing measure in 1962. This was Regulation 17, which was replaced in 2004 with Regulation 1/2003.

In short, Article 101(1) declares that agreements that distort competition are incompatible with the common market; Article 101(2) declares

---

12 Directive 2014/104/EU [2014] O.J. L 349/1.
13 Directive 2014/104/EU and the recommendation on collective actions are available at: http://ec.europa.eu/competition/antitrust/actionsdamages/index.html (accessed 31 May 2017).

such agreements void; and Article 101(3) states that Article 101(1) may be declared inapplicable for agreements or practices that are economically progressive and benefit consumers. Article 102 prohibits abuses of a dominant position. The text of these provisions is set forth below, followed by a description of the current procedural regulation.

Article 101 TFEU, ex 81 ECT

1. The following shall be prohibited as incompatible with the common market: all agreements between undertakings, decisions by associations of undertakings and concerted practices which may affect trade between Member States and which have as their object or effect the prevention, restriction or distortion of competition within the common market, and in particular those which:

    (*a*) directly or indirectly fix purchase or selling prices or any other trading conditions;
    (*b*) limit or control production, markets, technical development, or investment;
    (*c*) share markets or sources of supply;
    (*d*) apply dissimilar conditions to equivalent transactions with other trading parties, thereby placing them at a competitive disadvantage;
    (*e*) make the conclusion of contracts subject to acceptance by the other parties of supplementary obligations which, by their nature or according to commercial usage, have no connection with the subject of such contracts.

2. Any agreements or decisions prohibited pursuant to this Article shall be automatically void.
3. The provisions of paragraph 1 may, however, be declared inapplicable in the case of:

    — any agreement or category of agreements between undertakings;
    — any decision or category of decisions by associations of undertakings;
    — any concerted practice or category of concerted practices;

    which contributes to improving the production or distribution of goods or to promoting technical or economic progress, while allowing consumers a fair share of the resulting benefit, and which does not:

    (a) impose on the undertakings concerned restrictions which are not indispensable to the attainment of these objectives;
    (b) afford such undertakings the possibility of eliminating competition in respect of a substantial part of the products in question.

Article 102 TFEU, ex 82 ECT

Any abuse by one or more undertakings of a dominant position within the common market or in a substantial part of it shall be prohibited as incompatible with the common market in so far as it may affect trade between Member States. Such abuse may, in particular, consist in:

(a) directly or indirectly imposing unfair purchase or selling prices or other unfair trading conditions;
(b) limiting production, markets or technical development to the prejudice of consumers;
(c) applying dissimilar conditions to equivalent transactions with other trading parties, thereby placing them at a competitive disadvantage;
(d) making the conclusion of contracts subject to acceptance by the other parties of supplementary obligations which, by their nature or according to commercial usage, have no connection with the subject of such contracts.

Note the examples of restrictive agreements or conduct in Article 101(1) TFEU and in Article 102 TFEU. Are they virtually identical? What is the major difference?

Restrictive agreements can be justified under Article 101(3) TFEU. Why doesn't Article 102 TFEU include a similar provision for abuses of dominance?

Note on the notion of undertaking

Articles 101 and 102 TFEU apply to 'undertakings'. The notion of undertakings therefore defines the scope *ratione personae* of the antitrust provisions of the Treaty. According to settled case law of the Court of Justice, any entity engaged in an economic activity, irrespective of its legal form and the way in which it is financed, must be considered as an undertaking, and any activity consisting in offering goods or services on a given market is an economic activity. In contrast, activities falling within the exercise of public powers are not of an economic nature. For example, air traffic control is not an activity of economic nature, according to the Court.[14] Still, the fact that an entity has a public law status, is vested with public powers or participates in regulatory processes does not, in itself, prevent it from being classified as an undertaking for the purposes of EU competition law in respect of the remainder of its economic activities. Thus the classification of an activity as falling within

---

14 Case C-364/92, *Eurocontrol* [1994] ECR I-43, EU:C:1994:7, para. 30.

the exercise of public powers or as an economic activity must be carried out separately for each activity exercised by any given entity.

What matters is therefore the nature of the activity in question, irrespective of the sector or the purpose sought. For example, the fact that an activity has a connection with sport does not hinder the application of the EU competition rules.[15] Likewise, employment procurement is an economic activity and public employment agencies involved in that activity are classified as undertakings.[16] Moreover, the fact that the offer of goods or services is made without profit motive does not prevent the relevant entity from being considered an undertaking, since that offer may exist in competition with that of other operators seeking to make a profit. This can be the case of a pension fund organized pursuant to rules set by public authorities and supplementing a basic compulsory scheme, in competition with insurance companies.[17] Non-profit-making associations offering goods or services on a given market may also find themselves in competition with one another. To the contrary, the Court of Justice has found that the management of a public social security system is not an economic activity insofar as the system is based on the principle of national solidarity and benefits thereof bear no relation to the amount of contributions; hence, the organizations operating such systems are not considered as undertakings within the meaning of Articles 101 and 102 TFEU.[18]

Article 101 TFEU also applies to decisions, including by-laws, of associations of undertakings. Associations of competitors can form breeding grounds for illegal conspiracies. For example, agreements to exchange information may be the tip of the iceberg of a price-fixing cartel. However, associations and societies often play useful functions that, rather than suppressing the market, help it work. They may undertake tasks that need to be done. The question is often whether some of the clauses and restrictions have gone too far; whether they have crossed the line from facilitating competition to suppressing it. This is often the nature of the inquiry in connection with collecting societies.

The Court of Justice has analyzed in various cases when an organization should be considered an association of undertakings (whose 'decisions' fall under Article 101 TFEU), and when it constitutes a single firm (whose decisions are deemed 'internal' and are therefore not caught by Article 101

---

15 Case C-49/07, *Motosykletistiki Omospondia Ellados NPID (MOTOE)* [2008] ECR I-4863, EU:C:2008:376, para. 22.
16 Case C-41/90, *Höfner and Elser* [1991] ECR I-1979, EU:C:1991:161, paras. 21–23.
17 Case C-244/94, *Fédération française des sociétés d'assurance (FFSA)* [1995] ECR I-4013, EU:C:1995:392, para. 22.
18 Joined Cases C-159/91 and C-160/91, *Poucet and Pistre* [1993] ECR I-637, EU:C:1993:63, paras. 18–19.

TFEU). In *MasterCard*,[19] the banks argued that after its 2007 initial public offering ('IPO'), MasterCard was no longer an association of undertakings but an independent firm that they no longer controlled. The Court disagreed. It found that MasterCard was created as an instrument of coordination between banks. Even after the IPO, the banks continued to exercise decision-making powers in relation to the operation of the payment system. Also, the banks and MasterCard retained a commonality of interest in setting the fees. Therefore, despite its change in form and control, MasterCard remained an association of undertakings and the banks could not avoid the application of Article 101 because of the IPO.

More generally, the notion of association of undertakings encompasses entities such as trade associations, professional regulatory bodies (including bar associations[20]), sports federations (e.g., soccer leagues engaging in the joint negotiation of broadcasting rights), cooperatives but also associations of associations of undertakings, such as federations of farming syndicates.[21]

Note the functional approach developed by the Court of Justice in drawing the contours of the notion of undertaking. What does it say about the scope of application of the competition provisions of the EU Treaties? The Union is sometimes regarded as unduly pro-market oriented. Does the definition of undertaking feed this perspective? Do you think wider exclusions from the notion of undertaking are warranted? If so, how would you design the exclusions, and based on what criteria?

D. Market integration and the blockage of imports

1. Overview

When business actors restrain the flow of trade over Member State lines, they may undermine market integration, harm competition, and violate Articles 101 and 102 TFEU. This section telescopes three categories of such restraints and concentrates on the third: vertical restraints blocking parallel imports.

First, competitors established in different Member States, feeling the heat of cross-border competition, might enter into a truce with their competitors, repartitioning the common market ('I take France, you take Germany'). In

---

19 Case C-382/12 P, *MasterCard v. Commission*, EU:C:2014:2201.
20 See Case C-309/99, *Wouters* [2002] ECR I-1527, EU:C:2002:98, para. 58.
21 Joined Cases T-217/03 and T-245/03, *Fédération nationale de la cooperation bétail et viande (FNCBV) v. Commission* [2006] ECR II-4987, EU:T:2006:391, para. 54.

an economic as well as an EU integration sense, this is the worst kind of restraint. Such an agreement frustrates competition and its benefits for consumers and the economy, and it counteracts the liberalizing effort to tear down barriers at Member State lines. Article 101 TFEU is applicable to such market-division cartels, which we deal with in Chapter 2.

Second, a dominant firm that has the power to do so might block competitors from entering 'its' Member State market. This is an equally harmful restraint. It keeps out competitors and makes it possible for the dominant firm to continue exercising monopoly power, and in doing so it undermines market integration. Without the help of the State, however, a firm, acting alone, does not normally have such power; and when a State confers an exclusive right, often this is in response to a 'public interest', as in the case of the Swedish alcohol monopoly (see Chapter 7). Market blockage by a dominant firm can be a serious abuse in violation of Article 102 in combination with Article 106 TFEU. Abuse of dominance is considered in Chapter 5.

Third, a producer might prevent or restrict its product from being shipped from one Member State to another either to protect its designated distributor from having to compete against the same-brand product shipped in from another distributor's territory, or to protect its profit margins where the product in the home State is price-controlled and shipment of the price-controlled product to a non-regulated State would undercut its profits and squeeze its investment in research. These restraints are vertical restraints; they are intra-brand restraints, and they are restraints against parallel imports.

The next section focuses on this latter form of restraint, first presenting the landmark case of *Consten and Grundig*, followed by notes on related distributor cases, and second presenting the contemporary case of *GlaxoSmithKline*, offering a limited relaxation of the rule of *Consten and Grundig*.

2. Parallel imports

a. *Consten and Grundig v. Commission*

Grundig, a manufacturer of radios, television sets, tape recorders, and dictating machines, appointed Consten to be its exclusive distributor in France. Consten and Grundig wanted Consten to be the only distributor of the Grundig products in France; thus, they wanted Consten to be able to exclude from France Grundig products put on the market in other Member States. To achieve this result they relied on French trademark law as well as the distribution contract. Since French case law held that only the owner of a trademark was entitled to enforce the trademark, the parties agreed that Consten should apply for and own the trademark GINT (Grundig International). Consten and Grundig agreed that if Consten should cease to be the distributor for Grundig in France, Consten would assign the mark to Grundig. Grundig made similar exclusive distribution and trademark arrangements with each of its distributors in the other EU countries.

Recall that, before the Treaty was adopted, the European nations had high tariffs and low quotas, which hindered the flow of goods across national borders. The Treaty required the Member States to remove the quotas and tariffs in the internal market. In the spring of 1961 when French quotas ended, the French discounter UNEF began purchasing GINT television sets, tape recorders, dictaphones and other electronic equipment from German wholesalers (who had also accepted export bans) and selling them in competition with Consten's dealers in France. Consten sued UNEF under French law for unfair competition and trademark infringement, alleging that UNEF knew that the sales to it were in breach of contract and that the sales by UNEF undermined Consten's contract. Thereupon, UNEF petitioned the Commission to declare the agreement between Consten and Grundig void under Article [101](2). Meanwhile, Regulation 17 came into effect, and Grundig filed a notification of its distribution agreement and sought an exemption under Article [101](3). In justification of the territorial division, Grundig argued that German buyers were familiar with its product and French buyers were not, and that the French market demanded a higher level of service and promotion than the German market. Moreover, it noted that Consten was responsible for guarantees, repair, customer service, accepting advance orders, maintaining stocks, and advertising in France. Grundig argued that cheap imports from Germany would undercut Consten's incentives to fulfill these duties, and that Consten's failure to fulfill its duties would undercut the brand's reputation and frustrate sales. Grundig depicted the market for electronics products as highly competitive, with prices dropping steadily even before UNEF's appearance on the French market.

The Commission refused to consider evidence of competition from competitors of Grundig, and denied Grundig's request for an exemption under Article [101](3). It observed that prices for Grundig products in France were substantially higher than prices for Grundig products in Germany. Consten and Grundig sued the Commission, seeking annulment of its decision.

The Advocate General, Karl Roemer, criticized the Commission for considering only competition among distributors of Grundig's products and not competition from competing brands. Advocate General Roemer said:

[I]t is not proper if the Commission proceeds in such a manner that from the very outset it considers *exclusively* the last-mentioned internal competition [intrabrand competition] and completely neglects in its considerations the competition with similar products [interbrand competition]. In fact, it is conceivable that the competition between different products or, to be more precise, between different producers is so severe as not to leave any room worth mentioning for what was called internal competition in a product (possibly with regard to price and service) . . . . Rightfully, it was . . . therefore incumbent on the Commission to make a survey of the entire competition situation . . . . Such a survey of the effects on the market would possibly have led to a result favourable for the plaintiffs . . . . Such more favourable result might have been possible in view of the relatively small share of Grundig in the French market for tape recorders and dictating machines (roughly 17 percent)—as far as we know, the Commission has not conducted any investigations concerning other products—or in view of the plaintiffs' allegation that the markets for television sets . . . and for transistor sets showed so severe a competition of various, and sometimes very strong producers of the Community and of third countries that it repeatedly became necessary to reduce the prices of Grundig sets considerably.

Because of the Commission's narrow concept of the term 'restraint of competition,' no such survey was made, and the Court of Justice in its proceeding cannot be obligated to make the survey itself belatedly. The only thing we can do in this situation is to find that the results which the Commission arrived at in the investigation of the criterion 'restraint of competition' must be deemed to lack a sufficient foundation and must for that reason be rejected. * * *

The Court of Justice disagreed. Here are excerpts from its judgement.

CASE

Consten and Grundig v. Commission (Cases 56–58/64)[22]

. . . [A]n agreement between producer and distributor which might tend to restore the national divisions in trade between Member States might be such as to frustrate the most fundamental objectives of the Community. The Treaty, whose preamble and content aim at abolishing the barriers between States, and which in several provisions gives evidence of a stern attitude with regard to their reappearance, could not allow undertakings to reconstruct

---

22 EU:C:1965:60.

> **CASE** *(continued)*
>
> such barriers. Article [101](1) is designed to pursue this aim, even in the case of agreements between undertakings placed at different levels in the economic process. ...
>
> The applicants and the German government maintain that since the Commission restricted its examination solely to Grundig products the decision was based upon a false concept of competition and of the rules on prohibition contained in Article [101](1), since this concept applies particularly to competition between similar products of different makes. ...
>
> The principle of freedom of competition concerns the various stages and manifestations of competition. Although competition between producers is generally more noticeable than that between distributors of products of the same make, it does not thereby follow that an agreement tending to restrict the latter kind of competition should escape the prohibition of Article [101](1) merely because it might increase the former.
>
> Besides, for the purpose of applying Article [101](1), there is no need to take account of the concrete effects of an agreement once it appears that it has as its object the prevention, restriction or distortion of competition.
>
> Therefore the absence in the contested decision of any analysis of the effects of the agreement on competition between similar products of different makes does not, of itself, constitute a defect in the decision.
>
> It thus remains to consider whether the contested decision was right in founding the prohibition of the disputed agreement under Article [101](1) on the restriction on competition created by the agreement in the sphere of the distribution of Grundig products alone. The infringement which was found to exist by the contested decision results from the absolute territorial protection created [by] the said contract in favour of Consten on the basis of French law. The applicants thus wished to eliminate any possibility of competition at the wholesale level in Grundig products in the territory specified in the contract essentially by two methods.
>
> First, Grundig undertook not to deliver even indirectly to third parties products intended for the area covered by the contract. The restrictive nature of that undertaking is obvious if it is considered in the light of the prohibition on exporting which was imposed not only on Consten but also on all the other sole concessionnaires of Grundig, as well as the German wholesalers. Secondly, the registration in France by Consten of the GINT trade mark, which Grundig affixes to all its products, is intended to increase the protection inherent in the disputed agreement, against the risk of parallel imports into France of Grundig products, by adding the protection deriving from the law on industrial property rights. Thus no third party could import Grundig products from other Member States of the Community for resale in France without running serious risks. ...

CASE (continued)

The situation as ascertained above results in the isolation of the French market and makes it possible to charge for the products in question prices which are sheltered from all effective competition. In addition, the more producers succeed in their efforts to render their own makes of product individually distinct in the eyes of the consumer, the more the effectiveness of competition between producers tends to diminish. Because of the considerable impact of distribution costs on the aggregate cost price, it seems important that competition between dealers should also be stimulated. The efforts of the dealer are stimulated by competition between distributors of products of the same make. Since the agreement thus aims at isolating the French market for Grundig products and maintaining artificially, for products of a very well-known brand, separate national markets within the Community, it is therefore such as to distort competition in the Common Market.

It was therefore proper for the contested decision to hold that the agreement constitutes an infringement of Article [101](1). No further considerations, whether of economic data (price differences between France and Germany, representative character of the type of appliance considered, level of overheads borne by Consten) or of the corrections of the criteria upon which the Commission relied in its comparisons between the situations of the French and German markets, and no possible favourable effects of the agreement in other respects, can in any way lead, in the face of abovementioned restrictions, to a different solution under Article [101](1) . . .

The applicants maintain more particularly that the criticized effect on competition is due not to the agreement but to the registration of the trade-mark in accordance with French law, which gives rise to an original inherent right of the holder of the trade-mark from which the absolute territorial protection derives under national law.

Consten's right under the contract to the exclusive use in France of the GINT trade-mark, which may be used in a similar manner in other countries, is intended to make it possible to keep under surveillance and to place an obstacle in the way of parallel imports. Thus, the agreement by which Grundig, as the holder of the trade-mark by virtue of an international registration, authorized Consten to register it in France in its own name tends to restrict competition. . . .

That agreement therefore is one which may be caught by the prohibition in Article [101](1). The prohibition would be ineffective if Consten could continue to use the trade-mark to achieve the same object as that pursued by the agreement which has been held to be unlawful.

[The Court did not interfere with the Commission's decision to deny an exemption under Article [101](3). It acknowledged that Consten, as Grundig's distributor in France, was required to perform various obligations such as to accept advance orders and to provide

CASE (continued)

warranty and after-sales service. The Court stated that territorial protection would give the parties to the agreement an advantage in *their* production and distribution activities. But, it said, to qualify for exemption the 'improvement must in particular show appreciable objective advantages of such a character as to compensate for the disadvantages which they cause in the field of competition', and must be indispensable. The argument that every 'improvement as conceived by the parties to the agreement must be maintained intact' . . . 'not only tends to weaken the requirement of indispensability but also among other consequences to confuse solicitude for the specific interests of the parties with the objective improvements contemplated by the Treaty.']

NOTES AND QUESTIONS

1. Is it true that the restraint resulted in isolation of the French market and meant that GINT TVs are sheltered from all competition? Why didn't the Court care?
2. How does the rule of *Consten and Grundig* increase market integration?
3. Why do you suppose that German prices were lower than French prices? Why might you want to know? Is the answer relevant to (a) whether the restraint is caught by Article 101(1); or (b) whether the restraint is entitled to an exemption under Article 101(3)?
4. Grundig appointed an exclusive distributor for each territory; Grundig agreed that it, itself, would not distribute GINT-brand product in the assigned territory; and each distributor agreed with Grundig to 'work' its territory. Thus far, these obligations are of the essence of an exclusive distribution agreement. The producer says to the distributor: I appoint you and you alone to distribute my product in this territory. This simple agreement does not fall within Article 101(1). Why?
5. The additional obligations on both Consten and Grundig are the key obligations in the case. What were these additional obligations and why were they of particular concern? Did they lessen competition to the harm of consumers?
6. Note the relationship between French trademark law and EU competition law. Which has the upper hand? Is the Court's answer consistent with Article 345 TFEU reserving to the Member States the right to define property within their States? Did the Court appropriately resolve the tension between free movement/competition principles and the right to exclusive control over one's intellectual property?
7. Under *Consten and Grundig*, can an agreement that absolutely eliminates parallel imports into a Member State ever be justified as essential for improvement of production or distribution? We will see below that allowances have been made at the margins.
8. The US once had a legal rule very similar to the rule of *Consten and Grundig*. Under *United States v. Arnold, Schwinn & Co.*,[23] a manufacturer/distributor agreement for imposition of absolute territorial restrictions on the distributor was held to be illegal on its face. Ten years later the US Supreme Court overruled *Schwinn*.[24] In *Sylvania* the Supreme Court observed that non-price restraints on distributors can improve the efficiency and competitiveness

---

23 388 U.S. 365, 87 S.Ct. 1856, 18 L.Ed.2d 1249 (1967) (overruled in 1977).
24 *Continental T.V., Inc. v. GTE Sylvania Inc.*, 433 U.S. 36, 97 S.Ct. 2549, 53 L.Ed.2d 568 (1977).

of the manufacturer, and it held that improvements in interbrand competition (e.g., competition between Sylvania and Sony TVs) can outweigh any harm from the decrease in intrabrand competition (i.e., competition among Sylvania's own distributors). Thirty years later the Court went much further, viewing preservation of interbrand competition as the goal of the Sherman Antitrust Act and ascribing no independent value to intrabrand competition.[25]

US law presumes that competition among producers (interbrand competition) is likely to force manufacturers to behave competitively and to assure that vertical restraints on distributors are efficient and procompetitive. It presumes that interbrand competition is likely to pressure manufacturers to distribute their products as efficiently as possible. Can *Consten and Grundig* be reconciled with this line of reasoning? Is the difference justified by context— the market integration goal of the EU?

b. Development of the rule against market partitioning

The rule of *Consten and Grundig* has remained a robust rule in the EU. A tight territorial restraint at Member State boundaries is considered a 'hard core' restraint. This does not rule out the possibility of an Article 101(3) justification but for air-tight restraints at nations' borders, justification is unlikely to be successful. For a more recent example involving broadcasters' territorial exclusivity for the retransmission of football games, see *Premier League and Karen Murphy*.[26] The sting of a rigid *Consten and Grundig* rule has been removed by a body of law that allows sellers to restrain a dealer's *active* solicitation of sales outside of its territory—a concept dealt with in Chapter 4 along with the vertical block exemption and vertical guidelines.

The next leading Court of Justice case after *Consten and Grundig* was *Pioneer*.[27] French, German and British distributors of Pioneer's high fidelity sound equipment agreed to stay out of one another's markets. The agreement, which Pioneer facilitated, aimed to keep low-priced British and German products out of the high-priced French market.

The firms contested the Commission decision on many grounds, including the level of fines, as to which the Court of Justice held:

---

25 See *Leegin Creative Leather Products, Inc. v. PSKS*, Inc., 551 U.S. 877, 127 S.Ct. 2705, 168 L.Ed.2d 623 (2007).
26 Joined Cases C-403 and C-429/08, *Premier League and Karen Murphy* [2011] ECR I-9083, EU:C:2011:631.
27 Cases 100–103/80, *Musique Diffusion Française v. Commission* [1983] ECR 1825, EU:C:1983:158 ('*Pioneer*').

104   According to the Commission, however, such a level is fully justified by the nature of the infringements. After 20 years of Community competition policy an appreciable increase in the level of fines is necessary, in its view, at least for types of infringement which have long been well defined and are known to those concerned, such as prohibitions on exports and imports. In fact those constitute the most serious infringements since they deprive consumers of all the benefits resulting from the elimination of customs duties and quantitative restrictions; they hinder the integration of the economies of the Member States and leave distributors and retailers in a position of subordination towards producers. Heavier fines are particularly necessary where, as in the present case, the principal aim of the infringement is to maintain a higher level of prices for consumers. The Commission states that many undertakings carry on conduct which they know to be contrary to Community law because the profit which they derive from their unlawful conduct exceeds the fines imposed hitherto. Conduct of that kind can only be deterred by fines which are heavier than in the past. * * *

107   [T]he Commission was right to classify as very serious infringements prohibitions on exports and imports seeking artificially to maintain price differences between the markets of the various Member States. Such prohibitions jeopardize the freedom of intra-Community trade, which is a fundamental principle of the Treaty, and they prevent the attainment of one of its objectives, namely the creation of a single market. * * *

In the 1990s, when the Italian lire was depressed, Volkswagen, maker of Volkswagens and Audis, tried to protect the German and Austrian dealers in its network from a shift of buyers to Italy. It entered into agreements with its subsidiaries and Italian dealers, imposing supply quotas and a bonus system designed to induce the Italian dealers to sell at least 85% of their available vehicles in Italy. The Commission severely fined Volkswagen for partitioning national markets. The Commission describes the case as follows, in the 1998 Competition Policy Report:

Opening-up of markets

68   The Commission has always kept a close eye on distribution agreements and their restrictive effects in so far as they hindered intra-Community trade. Some exclusive distribution agreements lead to the setting-up of watertight national distribution networks. In particular, clauses which prohibit distributors from supplying customers based outside the contract territory. In this way, national markets are artificially isolated from one another. The Commission considers that measures should be taken to combat this situation, not just in order to re-establish effective competition between economic operators but also in order to promote

market integration. In practice, the compartmentalization of national markets prevents price convergence within the Union and restricts access by consumers to the markets with the lowest prices. With the creation of the single currency, price differentials will be obvious because they will be expressed in euros. They will be increasingly viewed as unjustified by ordinary people, who will want to derive full benefit from economic and monetary union.

69   In 1998 the Commission clearly demonstrated its determination to promote the opening-up of markets, a prime example of this being the *Volkswagen* case [O.J. L 124, 23/4/98]. Since 1995 the Commission had received numerous complaints from European consumers, particularly from Germany and Austria, who had been confronted with various difficulties when attempting to buy new Volkswagen and Audi cars in Italy. These consumers wanted to benefit from the price differentials between their Member State and Italy, where prices were particularly advantageous. Following a series of inspections at the offices of Volkswagen AG, Audi AG and Autogerma SpA, which is a subsidiary of Volkswagen and the official importer for both makes in Italy, and at the offices of a number of Italian dealers, the Commission concluded that Europe's largest motor-manufacturing group had been pursuing a market-partitioning policy in the Union for about 10 years. Volkswagen AG had systematically forced its dealers in Italy to refuse to sell Volkswagen and Audi cars to foreign buyers, especially from Germany and Austria. The Commission fined Volkswagen ECU 102 million, the largest fine ever imposed on a single company.

The General Court confirmed the existence and gravity of the infringements, reducing the fine because the Commission had overstated the duration thereof.[28]

In what sense did the system of quotas and of bonuses based on sales in Italy 'partition markets'? Should Volkswagen have been able to protect its German and Austrian dealers from the siphoning off sales as a result of an unfavourable exchange rate?

In view of persistent price differentials of cars in different Member States, the Commission adopted a motor vehicle block exemption regulation, specifying restrictions that would be permissible or not. Eventually, the market for the sale of cars approximated the single market goals. The sale of parts, servicing and warranties, however, remained restricted. The Commission responded by adopting a specialized sector regulation and block exemption adopted and

---

28   Case T-62/98, *Volkswagen AG v. Commission* [2000] ECR II-2707, EU:T:2000:180.

later revised.[29] Read the regulation. What restrictions are allowed under the block exemption? What restrictions are not allowed? How important is the rule that qualified dealers with physical locations must be permitted to sell via the Internet?

In 2000, the Commission liberalized its policy on vertical restraints in general but it preserved as a hard-core restraint a restriction that absolutely prevents parallel imports from flowing over Member State lines. A somewhat revised block exemption regulation was adopted in 2010. See Chapter 4 below.

The policy disfavouring restraints on parallel imports and exports has been reaffirmed in more recent pharmaceutical cases, but with a nuance. In *GlaxoSmithKline v. Commission*,[30] the General Court allowed a possible exception in the context of the pharmaceutical industry, where price is often capped by State regulation and pharmaceutical companies claim that dual pricing (freedom to export at a higher price) is necessary to obtain sufficient profits for investment in innovation. In *Glaxo*, the Commission flatly prohibited a clause in Glaxo's distribution agreements providing that Glaxo would charge the distributors a certain higher price for sales of its medicines that were not subject to the Spanish price cap; thus, effectively, for sales outside of Spain. The General Court held that the Commission improperly failed to consider whether advantages to competition of dual pricing for in-state and out-of-state destined sales outbalanced the disadvantages to competition of dual pricing. The Court of Justice agreed that the Commission was required to seriously consider Glaxo's evidence on this point.[31]

A second *Glaxo* case arose in a Greek court. GlaxoSmithKline AEVE, a dominant firm, cut back the supply of medicines to its Greek wholesalers who bought the medicines not merely to distribute to the Greek (price-capped) market, as GSK desired, but to sell them into higher-priced States. The wholesalers sued GSK AEVE in the Greek court, which referred questions to the Court of Justice. The Court of Justice reaffirmed the strong principle against restraints on parallel imports. It held, nonetheless, that a dominant firm can limit orders to its wholesale customers to protect its commercial interests, but it can do so only to the extent that the limit is proportionate in view of the size of the national market and the firm's previous business rela-

---

29 See: http://ec.europa.eu/competition/sectors/motor_vehicles/legislation/legislation.html (accessed 31 May 2017).
30 Case T-168/01, *GlaxoSmithKline v. Commission*, EU:T:2006:265.
31 Case C-501/06 P, EU:C:2009:610.

tion with the wholesaler (e.g., the customary supply).[32] The Court of Justice expressed its continuing concern about parallel restraints as follows:

> 65 [T]he Court has held that an agreement between producer and distributor which might tend to restore the national divisions in trade between Member States might be such as to frustrate the objective of the Treaty to achieve the integration of national markets through the establishment of a single market. Thus on a number of occasions the Court has held agreements aimed at partitioning national markets according to national borders or making the interpenetration of national markets more difficult, in particular those aimed at preventing or restricting parallel exports, to be agreements whose object is to restrict competition within the meaning of that Treaty article.
>
> 66 In the light of the abovementioned Treaty objective as well as that of ensuring that competition in the internal market is not distorted, there can be no escape from the prohibition laid down in Article [102] for the practices of an undertaking in a dominant position which are aimed at avoiding all parallel exports from a Member State to other Member States, practices which, by partitioning the national markets, neutralize the benefits of effective competition in terms of the supply and the prices that those exports would obtain for final consumers in the other Member States.

Did GSK restrict supply or differentially raise the price of medicines to its Greek wholesalers partition markets? Divert the natural flow of trade? Undermine market integration? Increase GSK's market power? Hurt consumers? As to each, how? Did the Court weaken the rule of *Consten and Grundig* or simply articulate a narrow exception?

Conclusion

This chapter has stressed the market integration goal of EU competition law. The Single Market objective focuses European competition policy on openness of markets as a combined pro-competition and pro-integration goal. Is the principle of freedom of parallel imports and exports in tension with the goal of efficiency, or does it normally reinforce the goal of efficiency? Chapter 4 on vertical restraints explores this question further.

The following chapter (Cartels) highlights one point at which market integration and traditional competition goals incontestably converge:

---

32 See Joined Cases C-468/06 to C-478/06, *Sot. Lelos v. GlaxoSmithKline AEVE* [2008] ECR I-7139, EU:C:2008:504.

market-division cartels. Competitors divide markets at Member State boundaries, reinstating the economic borders that the Treaty removed. Even if you should question whether Grundig re-isolated France in an economic sense, you are not likely to question whether Nedchem and its quinine cartel co-conspirators tried to repartition Europe.

2
Cartels

Cartels are 'agreements and/or concerted practices between two or more competitors aimed at coordinating their competitive behaviour on the market and/or influencing the relevant parameters of competition through practices such as the fixing of purchase or selling prices or other trading conditions, the allocation of production or sales quotas, the sharing of markets including bid-rigging, restrictions of imports or exports and/or anti-competitive actions against other competitors.'[1] They are the classic example of anti-competitive agreements. Cartels are a scourge on consumers. They rob consumers of hundreds of millions of euros each year, often for products that are necessities of life. Accordingly, the Directorate-General for Competition of the European Commission allocates substantial resources to cartel enforcement.

Before embarking on the study of cartel law, re-read Article 101 TFEU. Note that Article 101(1) TFEU prohibits agreements that restrict competition by either object or effect. Cartels are prime examples of agreements that restrict competition by object because they 'may be considered so likely to have negative effects, in particular on the price, quantity or quality of the goods and services, that it may be considered redundant, for the purposes of applying Article [101(1)] TFEU, to prove that they have actual effects on the market.'[2]

In many Member States, cartels were an accepted business practice until effective enforcement of the cartel prohibition came into Europe with the EEC Treaty of Rome, therefore requiring a change in culture. The rule against hard core cartels is now notorious throughout most of the world, and enforcement against such cartels is a top priority of DG COMP.

Cartels are usually secret, sometimes carried out through trade associations, and often implemented by mechanisms that may give clues as to their

---

1 Commission Notice on immunity from fines and reduction of fines in cartel cases [2006] O.J. C 298/11, para. 1.
2 Case C-67/13 P, *Groupement des cartes bancaires (CB) v. Commission*, EU:C:2014:2204, para. 51.

existence. They usually take the form of agreements to fix prices or divide markets, i.e., to preserve domestic markets for domestic producers. Market division cartels seriously harm the market integration effort pursued at EU level. Also, they remove producers' incentives to perform at the highest level possible, thus undermining the goal of producing robust and competitive businesses, and they keep prices higher and performance lower, thus harming buyers.

Cartels may be nationwide, and therefore of special concern to an individual Member State, but in view of the tearing down of national barriers to trade in Europe, they are more likely to be trans-European; and in view of the lowering of global trade barriers, they are more and more commonly worldwide. Lower trade and non-trade barriers tend to beget cartels because firms that had enjoyed protection from competition by State barriers are suddenly confronted by competitive neighbours and often try to hold them back by agreement. World cartels today are often challenged by the US Department of Justice ('DOJ'), the European Commission, and authorities of many other countries. For example, in the 1990s, Asian and American producers of lysine, an amino acid used in animal foodstuffs for nutrition, fixed prices and sales quotas and carried on an extensive information exchange to support the price and quota fixing for sales worldwide including Europe. The cartel members were prosecuted criminally in the US, resulting in high fines and jail terms. In Europe the Commission brought proceedings (no criminal prosecution is available under EU law and the law applies to 'undertakings' not individuals) and levied fines against the US, Japanese and Korean conspirators totaling nearly €110 million.

Similarly, a worldwide vitamins conspiracy—this time led by the Swiss firm Hoffmann-La Roche—produced US prison terms and US and EU fines in 1999–2001. More recently, in 2010, the Commission fined six LCD panel producers almost €650 million for their participation in a price-fixing cartel that operated mainly from Taiwan. The same companies were criminally prosecuted by the DOJ in the US, leading to plea agreements, the collection of very large fines and significant prison sentences. Later on, the People's Republic of China's competition authority also prosecuted the same cartel and imposed multi-million RMB fines.

Cartel fines are often severe. In 2007, the Commission took action against a cartel in the elevator market. It imposed a fine of €479 million on ThyssenKrupp, and fines totalling €992 million on all members of the elevator cartel combined. In 2008, the Commission proceeded against a cartel in the automobile glass market. It fined Saint-Gobain, a repeat offender,

€896 million and assessed total fines against the members of the automobile glass cartel at more than €1.3 billion. In 2009, in the gas interconnection case, E.ON and GDF Suez were assessed €553 million each, for a total of €1.06 billion. The highest industry cartel fine imposed by the European Commission is the fine of €2.9 billion imposed on truck producers in 2016 for their participation in a 14-year conspiracy aimed to coordinate gross list prices and to pass on to customers the costs of compliance with emission rules; the case also lead to a record fine of €1.008 billion levied against Daimler alone. Cartel fines are regularly adjusted upon review by the EU General Court but very rarely annulled in their entirety.

Detection of cartels is difficult. The task has been greatly aided by leniency or amnesty programmes. Leniency programmes not only help uncover specific cartels but also, in general, destabilize cartels, sowing seeds of mistrust among the cartel members. The leniency policy of the European Commission grants total immunity to cartel members who are the first to provide sufficient information to launch an inspection against an undetected cartel, and it grants a reduction of fines to others who provide additional information to establish the cartel, its gravity and duration. The benefit of immunity or reduction in fine is conditioned on the full and continuous cooperation of the informants with the Commission investigation.[3]

The following sections begin with a short explanation of the economics of competition and of cartels, followed by a presentation of cartel cases. The cases concern factual as well as legal analysis, particularly regarding proof of the existence of the cartel. Many cartel cases also raise jurisdictional questions: To what extent does the Treaty reach foreign firms that conspire abroad and harm the European market? The chapter closes with a discussion of cartel defenses; in particular, it asks whether there is such a thing as a crisis cartel defence?

A. Cartels and the economics of competition

Certain basic economic principles undergird competition law. Moreover, economics can be applied to help a society achieve many of its goals more directly and at lower cost.

Many analysts assume that a system of free enterprise with competition law exists only to obtain a more efficient allocation of resources or only to

---

[3] The policy is described at: http://ec.europa.eu/competition/cartels/leniency/leniency.html (accessed 1 June 2017).

prevent price rises to consumers, and that competition law has exactly and only this goal. This is not necessarily the case. Competition law may have other goals as well. In the EU, these goals include market integration, openness and access, control of dominance, and competitiveness (the growth of efficient, dynamic and responsive firms for the sake of economic strength in world markets). Pursuit of many of the goals tends to produce allocative efficiency or prevent consumer price-rises; thus the goals may share common ground. But sometimes goals other than efficiency (in its various forms) may be in tension with efficiency goals, and a society may choose them nonetheless. In either event, it is important to understand the basic principles of the economics of competition law in the service of efficiency.

Firms with sustained market power may have an incentive to act inefficiently, both in the sense of letting costs rise and in the sense of using their power to exploit buyers. Firms with monopoly power may have the incentive to preserve their monopolies by striking down competitors or blocking them from markets. Firms that have grown to a monopoly or dominant size under conditions of free enterprise may have achieved their positions by competition on the merits. To preserve incentives to excel as well as to preserve a firm's organic efficiencies, we may wish to control a dominant firm's anti-competitive behaviour and to work on other fronts to reduce barriers, rather than to strike down the structure itself. This is the approach of the EU to dominant firms, as reflected in Article 102, as we will discuss in Chapter 5.

This chapter deals largely with the less ambiguous economic problem of cartels. In connection with cartels, the efficiency and non-efficiency goals of competition policy converge. A rule against cartels serves goals of efficiency, fairness, and market integration.

Here, then, is a brief introduction to market economics.

In a system of perfect competition, there would be a number of sellers, a number of buyers, and perfect market information available to all. The sellers, competing among themselves for business, would be induced to make and provide what their customers want. To do so they would aspire to be inventive and progressive and to minimize costs. The pressures of competition would keep prices near costs. The producers would make and provide as much product as the buyers wanted and were willing to pay for at cost or more. Consumers would be sovereign.

The same responsiveness would be observed even in a market of few sellers if there were no significant barriers to entry into the market and if entry were very quick and easy. In that case, potential competitors would (in theory, for barriers are seldom so inconsequential) provide the same pressures as actual competitors. Also, in theory, sophisticated and powerful buyers could provide the same pressures on sellers to behave competitively, especially if the buyers were in a position to enter the market themselves or to finance entry by others if they were not satisfied with the performance of the existing sellers. Further, in high-technology markets marked by rapid changes in technology (new economy markets), the threat of breakthrough innovations by potential competitors may provide a pressure inducing responsiveness to even a dominant firm.

If all markets in the world were characterized by effective competition—with efficient and fully responsive sellers—competition itself would allocate resources to the production and distribution of all goods and services in the proportions buyers demand. The fullest possible production would then be squeezed out of the world's scarce resources. Demand would remain a function of the existing distribution of wealth, however, for the distribution of wealth influences what people choose to buy.

Real markets deviate substantially from the ideal. Still, competition tends to produce an efficient allocation of resources, push cost downwards, incentivize innovation, and help intermediate buyers and ultimately consumers get what they want, and at a price more or less near cost (including a reasonable return on investment). Competition is one of the most important mechanisms that society relies on to produce efficiency and serve consumers.

Competition also tends to keep markets free and open, and thereby to provide opportunities for entrepreneurs and small and medium-sized firms. Likewise, competition is a product of freedom of enterprise. It fosters diversity and pluralism, and it provides rewards based on merit. Therefore, competition both reflects and tends to support democratic institutions. Finally, forces of competition know no artificial divisions, such as national borders. If the French as well as the Germans demand sugar and the sugar is produced in Germany, the market will drive sugar across national lines. In that sense, competition is market integrating. Competition policy combined with the free movement principle is to the EU what the free enterprise ethic combined with the interstate commerce clause of the US Constitution is to the US.

While competition and freedom to compete on the merits serve all of the above objectives, private firms can sometimes restrain competition and thereby undermine the objectives of competition policy. The most obvious way in which firms can restrain competition and harm consumers is by forming a cartel. The classic form of cartel is a price-fixing or market division agreement by all significant firms in the market. In theory, parties to a price-fixing agreement could agree to charge a high price and not to compete on price. If buyers have no good substitutes and barriers to entry are high, the conspirators would have the power to raise prices considerably above the competitive price (i.e., considerably higher than the cost of efficient firms including a reasonable return on investment). The cartel members would naturally be able to sell less at this higher price. They would have to prevent increases in production, for extra production would drive the price back down. Accordingly, the cartel members would hold back output, and they would exploit the buyers who remain in the market. Essentially the same thing would happen if the parties agree to divide markets; each would become the monopolist in its market and would raise prices; buyers would demand less of the goods at the supracompetitive prices, and the firms would reduce output.

This phenomenon may be depicted graphically as follows (Figure 2.1).

The demand curve (D) slopes downwards. The base line represents the quantity demanded at a given price. The vertical line at the left represents the price. Less is demanded as price rises. Therefore higher price yields lower quantity/output. If the firms' cost is 10 (the competitive price), and upon forming a cartel their profit-maximizing price is 15 (the monopoly price), given the depicted demand function, the cartel members would reduce production from 140 units to 100 units. They would make more money by

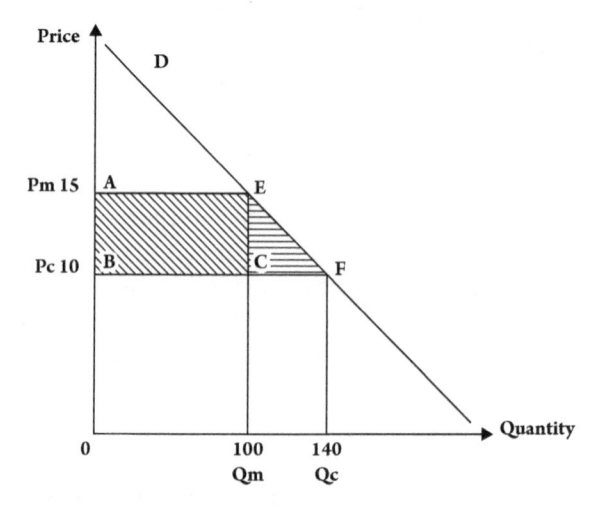

Figure 2.1 The effects of market power: dead weight loss and wealth transfer

producing less because of their ability to exploit the remaining customers. Society loses. Triangle CEF is called the dead weight or welfare loss. People wanted to buy the amount depicted by the triangle, and they were willing to buy it at cost or more, but this amount was never produced. Rectangle ABCE represents the product sold at the extra-high price, and it represents a wealth transfer. Under conditions of competition buyers would have kept the money represented by rectangle ABCE. The cartel empowered the sellers to extract this surplus from the buyers.

As noted, cartelists can use mechanisms other than price fixing to achieve the same ends. They can allocate territories so that each becomes a monopolist in its own territory. They can allocate customers, creating monopoly power over specific customer segments. Or they can parcel out production quotas—one of the devices used by the OPEC (oil) cartel of the oil-producing nations. Setting quotas as a means of limiting output is the other side of the price-fixing coin. By setting a high price, the quantity demanded will fall. By setting quotas, the collaborators create scarcity and the price will rise. Several devices can be used in tandem. Cartelists often fix prices and then set quotas (or agree on market shares), to avoid squabbling about who gets to enjoy the high price. Moreover, if no member can sell more than a fixed quota, it will not be able to cheat on its co-conspirators (i.e., secretly violate its obligations) by selling more goods at a lower price.

The above presented the static effect of cartels; that is, a cartel will normally cause the price of a known good, produced in known ways, to be higher and output to be lower than under conditions of independent decision-making. Cartels also have a negative dynamic effect. If firms have agreed not to compete and do not anticipate rivalry, they tend to let costs rise and their incentives to innovate to find new and better ways of satisfying their customers are muted. This effect is called x-inefficiency.

The objectives of the cartel can sometimes be achieved through means short of conspiracy. If a market is highly concentrated (i.e., there are few firms) and incumbents are insulated by barriers to entry—especially if the sellers are relatively similar to one another in cost structure and the product is homogeneous—the price and output moves of the incumbents may be relatively transparent to one another. The price that will maximize the profits of each is likely to be approximately the same for all. No firm would charge a price higher than the common price because it would be out-competed and it would lose its sales. None would venture to charge a lower price because competition would break out and all producers would be worse off: they would sell approximately the same quantity of goods but at a lower price.

As a result, unless legal risks are sufficiently great, the firms may find it both possible and profitable to form a cartel, and they may be able to achieve cartel effects—higher price, lower output, lower dynamism—even without an explicit agreement.

In an oligopolistic market (one comprised of few firms), firms may coordinate their actions by price leadership and signalling devices. Also, they may coordinate by staying within their own traditional territories. A territorial strategy has often been employed by firms in Europe, where national markets were historically isolated by trade barriers. French firms feared that if they began to sell in Germany, German firms, in retaliation, would dump their products on the French market, and vice versa. Patterns of mutual deference or spheres of influence developed, reinforcing oligopoly behavior. The more concentrated the market, the less need there was for an explicit agreement, because the result could be achieved without one.

Since merging is one way of reducing the number of players in a market, and the fewness of players makes coordination easier, mergers that result in high concentration may produce cartel-like effects (known as 'coordinated effects'); i.e. the firms left in the market may adopt cooperative rather than competitive modes of interaction. Mergers, however, are integrative and may produce synergies and efficiencies, while cartels are virtually always inefficient and are by definition formed to suppress competition. Therefore the law treats cartels much more harshly than it treats mergers.

B. Proof of cartels

The most powerful and tempting way for firms to control the market is to join with one another, that is, to collaborate rather than to compete. Accordingly, all antitrust or competition laws prohibit certain combinations or concerted practices. In the Treaty, the prohibition is contained in Article 101 TFEU. While it is not always clear whether a collaboration harms competition, cartels are by nature agreements that harm competition.

The cases typically involve both basic and complex questions of fact and law. For example, as to the facts: Did the parties agree not to compete? Can an agreement be inferred from the firms' behaviour and from facts about the market? As to the law: May the parties justify their agreement by showing that it did not harm competition or that it had no effect on consumers?

Cartel cases involving quinine, dyestuffs, cement and sugar were formative cases in the development of EU competition law. As you will see in the

Quinine case below, much of the analysis concerns whether the Commission and court could infer from the facts that the firms had a cartel agreement. Consider also, as you read the *Quinine* case, what the firms did to help the formation of a cartel, to make it work and to make it stable. What characteristics about the market and its structure made it more or less likely for a cartel to work? What evidence was the give-away that the cartel continued to operate after 1962?

Quinine is probably the earliest case of trans-Atlantic agency cooperation in prosecuting an international cartel.

1. The *Quinine* case

CASE

ACF Chemiefarma v. Commission (Case 41/69) ('*Quinine*')[4]

[Nedchem and five other Dutch firms, and Boehringer and Buchler, both German firms, produced quinine and quinidine, ingredients used to manufacture drugs to treat malaria and heart disease. In 1958, they entered into a series of agreements to reserve their home markets for themselves and to fix prices and quotas for exports to all other countries. After the German Federal Cartel Office discovered the cartel, Nedchem and Boehringer concluded a new agreement that excluded deliveries within the EU from the arrangement. In March 1960, Nedchem, the two German firms, and French and British producers of quinine and quinidine concluded a new export cartel agreement. The new agreement excluded sales into EU Member States, set quotas for exports to non-member nations, and reserved certain markets outside of the common market for specified cartel members. It also provided for equalization of quantities to be sold by members if quotas were exceeded or not reached and provided that no cartel member could cooperate in the production or sale of quinine or quinidine outside of the common market with firms not participating in the agreement. Each party agreed to supply the others with information about where, to whom, and how much they sold, on the basis of which Nedchem would equalize the quantities to be sold by each.

In April 1960, two gentlemen's agreements were drawn up among the parties—though never signed—which extended the provisions of the export agreements to sales within the common market and reserved home markets. The French parties agreed not to manufacture synthetic quinidine, and all parties agreed that non-compliance with the gentlemen's agreement would

---

4 [1970] ECR 661, EU:C:1970:71.

CASE *(continued)*

terminate the written export agreement and vice versa. The agreements were supplemented by a pool agreement for bark to make quinine. The parties would jointly purchase this critical raw material through Nedchem. Nedchem would buy stockpile surpluses of bark from the US' General Services Administration, allocate the bark among the cartel members, and receive a 2% commission from the members.

In 1962, Regulation 17 went into effect, giving the Commission the powers necessary to enforce the then equivalent to Article 101 TFEU. Also in 1962, a dispute arose regarding the bark pool, and the parties claimed that they abandoned their gentlemen's agreement shortly thereafter.

In 1963–64, the US, needing quinine to save the lives of sick American soldiers in Vietnam, became suspicious of the existence of an international quinine cartel as a result of Nedchem's purchases of large quantities of the US bark stockpile. The Department of Justice conducted extensive investigations (eventually resulting in civil and criminal cases under the US Sherman Antitrust Act ('Sherman Act')), and in 1967 it shared information with the European Commission. The Commission and national authorities began investigations into whether and to what extent the gentlemen's agreements were being applied in the common market after 1962. The Commission found that violations continued until February 1965, and imposed fines.]

115   The defendant bases its view that the gentlemen's agreement was continued until February1965 on documents and declarations emanating from the parties to the agreement the tenor of which is indistinct and indeed contradictory so that it is impossible to conclude whether those undertakings intended to terminate the gentlemen's agreement at their meeting on 29 October 1962.

116   The conduct of the undertakings in the common market after 29 October 1962 must therefore be considered in relation to the following four points: sharing out of domestic markets, fixing of common prices, determination of sales quotas and prohibition against manufacturing synthetic quinidine.

Protection of the Producers' Domestic Markets

117   The gentlemen's agreement guaranteed protection of each domestic market for the producers in the various Member States.

118   After October 1962 when significant supplies were delivered on one of those markets by producers who were not nationals, as for example in the case of sales of quinine and quinidine in France, there was a substantial alignment of prices conformingto French domestic prices which were higher than the export prices to third countries.

CASE *(continued)*

119   It does not appear that there were alterations in the insignificant volume of trade between the other Member States referred to by the clause relating to domestic protection in spite of considerable differences in the prices prevailing in each of those States.

120   The divergences between the domestic legislation of those States cannot by itself explain those differences in price or the substantial absence of trade.

121   Obstacles which might arise in the trade in quinine and quinidine from differences between national legislation governing pharmaceutical products under trademark cannot relevantly be invoked to explain those facts.

122   The correspondence exchanged in October and November 1963 between the parties to the export agreement with regard to the protection of domestic markets merely confirmed the intention of those undertakings to allow this state of affairs to remain unchanged.

123   This intention was subsequently confirmed by Nedchem during the meeting of the undertakings concerned in Brussels on 14 March 1964.

124   From those circumstances it is clear that with regard to the restriction on competition arising from the protection of the producers' domestic markets the producers continued after the meeting on 29 October 1962 to abide by the gentlemen's agreement of 1960 and confirmed their common intention to do so.

125   The applicant maintains that owing in particular to the shortage of raw materials the sharing out of domestic markets, as emerges from the exchange of letters of October and November 1963, had no effect on competition in the Common Market.

126   Despite the scarcity of raw materials and an increase in the demand for the products in question, as the contested decision finds, a serious threat of shortage nevertheless emerged only in 1964 as a result of the interruption of Nedchem's supplies from the American General Service Administration.

127   On the other hand, such a situation cannot render lawful an agreement the object of which is to restrict competition in the Common Market and which affects trade between the Member States.

128   The sharing out of domestic markets has as its object the restriction of competition and trade within the Common Market.

129   The fact that, if there were a threatened shortage of raw materials, such an agreement might in practice have had less influence on competition and on international trade

CASE *(continued)*

than in a normal period in no way alters the fact that the parties did not terminate their activities.

130   Furthermore, the applicant has furnished no conclusive evidence capable of proving that it had ceased to act in accordance with the agreement before the date of expiry of the export agreement.

131   Consequently, the submissions concerning that part of the decision relating to the continuation of the agreement on the protection of the producers' domestic markets until the beginning of February 1965 are unfounded.

Joint Fixing of Sales Prices

132   With regard to the joint fixing of sales prices for the markets which were not shared out, that is to say, the Belgo-Luxembourg Economic Union and Italy, the gentlemen's agreement provided for the application to such sales of the current prices for exports to third countries fixed by mutual agreement, in accordance with the export agreement. * * *

134   If, as the defendant maintains, the parties to the export agreement continued until February 1965 to apply their current export prices to supplies to the above-mentioned Member States, it would follow that they continued to abide by that part of the gentlemen's agreement relating to the joint fixing of sales prices.

135   With regard to the period from November 1962 to April 1964, the figures supplied by the defendant show a substantial and constant identity between the current prices fixed for export within the framework of the agreement and the prices maintained by the undertakings concerned, including the applicant, for their sales in unprotected domestic markets in the Community.

136   Where such prices deviate from the scale of export prices they do so in terms of rebates or increases corresponding generally to those agreed on under the gentlemen's agreement.

137   The applicant had supplied no evidence capable of proving that this argument is unfounded.

138   Moreover the increase in prices of 15%, which was jointly decided upon on 12 March 1964 under the export agreement which led Nedchem to withdraw its opposition, was uniformly applied—although that undertaking would have preferred to continue to fix lower prices—with regard to supplies to Italy, Belgium and Luxembourg also.

> **CASE** *(continued)*
>
> 139 These circumstances show that with regard to sales prices the parties to the export agreement continued after October 1962 to act in the Common Market as if the gentlemen's agreement of 1960 were still in force. * * *

2. The *Dyestuffs* case

Enterprises in all six of the original Member States, and ICI in the UK, were charged with fixing the prices of dyestuffs and dividing markets. The Commission brought proceedings in 1972, the year before the UK joined the EU. ICI sought dismissal on jurisdictional grounds; but ICI had subsidiaries in the EU, and the Court of Justice held the parent and subsidiaries to be one economic entity with sufficient presence in Europe. See, for jurisdictional aspects, section E below.

Ten large producers supplied 80% of the dyestuffs market. The basic pattern of behaviour was one of price leadership, with one firm announcing its intention to increase prices by a stated percentage, often to take effect at a specified later date. The competitors usually followed suit, often announcing within two or three days their intention to raise prices by the same percentage.

The dyestuff companies argued that the Commission had proved no agreement or concertation; it had merely shown oligopoly behaviour (the tendency of oligopolists to act interdependently even without agreement because of the structure of the market). The Commission disagreed, and the Court of Justice upheld the Commission's decision. Here is an excerpt; while reading it, keep in mind that the law has become more demanding on proof of agreement, as you will see in the *Wood Pulp* case below. Consider: Was conspiracy a better story than mere interdependence or any other unilateral action?

CASE

Imperial Chemical Industries Ltd v. Commission (Cases 48, 49, 51–57/69) (*'Dyestuffs'*)[5]

66   Although parallel behaviour may not by itself be identified with a concerted practice, it may however amount to strong evidence of such a practice if it leads to conditions of competition which do not correspond to the normal conditions of the market, having regard to the nature of the products, the size and number of the undertakings, and the volume of the said market. * * *

109   ... [A]lthough parallel conduct in respect of prices may well have been an attractive and risk-free objective for the undertakings concerned, it is hardly conceivable that the same action could be taken spontaneously at the same time, on the same national markets and for the same range of products.

110   Nor is it any more plausible that the increases of January 1964, introduced on the Italian market and copied on the Netherlands and Belgo-Luxembourg markets, which have little in common with each other either as regards the level of prices or the pattern of competition, could have been brought into effect within a period of two to three days without prior concertation. * * *

118   Although every producer is free to change his prices, taking into account in so doing the present or foreseeable conduct of his competitors, nevertheless it is contrary to the rules on competition contained in the Treaty for a producer to cooperate with his competitors, in any way whatsoever, in order to determine a coordinated course of action relating to a price increase and to ensure its success by prior elimination of all uncertainty as to each other's conduct regarding the essential elements of that action, such as the amount, subject-matter, date and place of the increases.

119   In these circumstances and taking into account the nature of the market in the products in question, the conduct of the applicant, in conjunction with other undertakings against which proceedings have been taken, was designed to replace the risks of competition and the hazards of competitors' spontaneous reactions by cooperation constituting a concerted practice prohibited by Article [101](1) of the Treaty. * * *

---

5   [1972] ECR 619, EU:C:1972:70.

3. The *Sugar Cartel* case

The *Sugar Cartel* case was the last of the formative cartel judgements.[6] Among other things, various sugar producers from the Netherlands, Belgium and Germany allegedly entered into understandings and practices to coordinate their behaviour in order to moderate the impact of overproduction of sugar in Belgium and to restrain the Belgian dealers from exporting large amounts of Belgian sugar to the Netherlands. The firms denied that they had formed a cartel. Further, they argued that the sugar market was so highly regulated by national quotas and an EU-wide intervention purchase price that it was impossible for private parties to distort trade. The Court disagreed on both counts, noting that the government regulation left 'a residual field of competition'. It found a multitude of serious infringements. The case is well known for its definition of the word 'concert':

> 172 SU and CSM submit that since the concept of 'concerted practices' presupposes a plan and the aim of removing in advance any doubt as to the future conduct of competitors, the reciprocal knowledge which the parties concerned could have of the parallel or complementary nature of their respective decisions cannot in itself be sufficient to establish a concerted practice; otherwise every attempt by an undertaking to react as intelligently as possible to the acts of its competitors would be an offence.
>
> 173 The criteria of coordination and cooperation laid down by the caselaw of the Court, which in no way require the working out of an actual plan, must be understood in the light of the concept inherent in the provisions of the Treaty relating to competition that each economic operator must determine independently the policy which he intends to adopt on the common market including the choice of the persons and undertakings to which he makes offers or sells.
>
> 174 Although it is correct to say that this requirement of independence does not deprive economic operators of the right to adapt themselves intelligently to the existing and anticipated conduct of their competitors, it does however strictly preclude any direct or indirect contact between such operators, the object or effect whereof is either to influence the conduct on the market of an actual or potential competitor or to disclose to such a competitor the course of conduct which they themselves have decided to adopt or contemplate adopting on the market.

---

6 Cases 40–48, 50, 54–56, 111, 113–114/73, *Suiker Unie v. Commission* [1975] ECR 1663, EU:C:1975:174 ('*Sugar Cartel*').

NOTES AND QUESTIONS

1. In *Quinine*, consider the evidence (esp. paras. 118–124)—which was only circumstantial—from which the Court concluded that the gentlemen's agreements continued after 1962. Did the facts raise an inference that the agreements continued in force? How strong was the alternative inference that, after 1962, the parties had no agreement with respect to sales in the Community; that each one simply chose to follow past patterns of behaviour and hoped that its export partners would do so too? Does the latter scenario constitute concerted action under *Quinine*? *Dyestuffs*? *Sugar Cartel*? In the 1970s and 1980s, the law was still evolving; the issue of proof of concerted action was to come before the Court once again in *Wood Pulp* below.

2. In an important American case, motion picture distributors changed their pattern of behaviour in a sudden, dramatic, uniform, and exploitative way. Moreover, the change in behaviour was profitable if all firms did the same thing; but if only one of them had raised its prices, it would have priced itself out of the market. As the Supreme Court concluded, it would strain credulity to believe that each firm acted independently. The Supreme Court[7] upheld the lower court's finding of conspiracy under Section 1 of the Sherman Act.[8] But the Supreme Court has also held that mere conscious parallelism is not equivalent to a combination or conspiracy and therefore does not constitute a violation of the Sherman Act.[9] The Court has dismissed cases of parallel action that can be explained just as plausibly by independent or interdependent action.[10]

3. Note how the quinine export cartel tended to facilitate a domestic (European) cartel. Note also how the parties used various devices that helped to make the cartel work. For example, by pooling raw material purchases in the early years of the agreement and by designating one of their members—Nedchem—to be their purchasing agent and to allocate the raw material in accordance with assigned quotas, the firms could police their own cartel agreement and be sure that no one cheated by producing too much. Likewise, as a result of sharing extensive information with one another, cheating from their agreement would become obvious, and cheating was explicitly punishable by expulsion from both cartels. Finally, the agreement not to produce synthetic quinine by the French, who were selling at a particularly high price in France, tended to keep off the market a substitute product that could have undermined the cartel by driving down the cartel price.

4. After the *Quinine* case, can firms defend their conduct on grounds that their agreement had no effect because market forces overwhelmed their attempt to raise prices (i.e., they tried to run a cartel, but they failed)? Can they successfully argue that an aborted cartel had no effect on trade between Member States? Should 'no effect' be a defence? Why or why not?[11]

5. Why was the quinine export agreement as such of no interest to the Court? What is the scope of EU law with respect to export cartels selling to destinations outside of the European Union? Consult the language of Article 101 TFEU.

---

7 *Interstate Circuit, Inc. v. United States*, 306 U.S. 208, 59 S.Ct. 467, 83 L.Ed. 610 (1939).
8 Section 1 of the Sherman Act (15 U.S.C. § 1) provides in relevant part:
   Every contract, combination in the form of trust or otherwise, or conspiracy, in restraint of trade or commerce among the several States, or with foreign nations, is declared to be illegal.
9 *Theatre Enterprises, Inc. v. Paramount Film Distributing Corp.*, 346 U.S. 537, 74 S.Ct. 257, 98 L.Ed. 273 (1954).
10 See *Twombly v. Bell Atlantic Corp.*, 550 U.S. 544, 127 S.Ct. 1955, 167 L.Ed.2d 929 (2007); *Matsushita Electrical Industrial Co., Ltd v. Zenith Radio Corp.*, 475 U.S. 574, 106 S.Ct. 1348, 89 L.Ed.2d 538 (1986).
11 See *United States v. Socony-Vacuum Oil Co., Inc.*, 310 U.S. 150, 60 S.Ct. 811, 84 L.Ed. 1129 (1940) (lack of effect is not a defence to a cartel violation under US law).

Like EU law, US antitrust law excludes from its scope export cartels that hurt foreigners only.[12] Is this good policy? From the point of view of worldwide free movement and efficiency? From the point of view of sovereignty of nations?

4. The *Wood Pulp* case

US, Canadian, Finnish, Swedish and Norwegian firms shipped wood pulp to the EU. The Commission found that the US, Canadian and Finnish firms concerted on prices, and imposed large fines. The companies sought annulment of the Commission decision before the Court of Justice. They asserted lack of jurisdiction by reason of extraterritoriality. Also, they claimed that there was not sufficient evidence from which the Commission could derive concert of action. The *Sugar Cartel* judgement, excerpted above, was the common referent for the definition of concertation.

CASE

Ahlström Osakeyhtiö v. Commission (Cases C-89, 104, 114, 116–117, 125–129/85) ('*Wood Pulp*')[13]

[The Commission brought proceedings against 40 wood pulp producers from the US, Canada and Finland and three of their trade associations for concerting on price announcements and on price. The producers made quarterly price announcements sometimes simultaneously and sometimes nearly so. Prices were almost always quoted in dollars, a practice that both increased the transparency of the producers' intentions to one another and assured that shifts in exchange rates in the various Member States would have no impact. Prices and price changes tended to be uniform. The Commission found, for example:

> that the prices announced by the Canadian and US producers were the same from the first quarter of 1975 to the third quarter of 1977 and from the first quarter of 1978 to the third quarter of 1981, that the prices announced by the Swedish and Finnish producers were the same from the first quarter of 1975 to the second quarter of 1977 and from the third quarter of 1978 to the third quarter of 1981 and, finally, that the prices of all the producers were the same from the first quarter of 1976 to the second quarter of 1977 and from the third quarter of 1979 to the third quarter of 1981.

The Commission determined that the pulp producers had engaged in concerted conduct in violation of Article 101.

---

12 See the Foreign Trade Antitrust Improvements Act of 1982, codified in the Sherman Act as Section 7A (15 U.S.C. § 6a).
13 [1993] ECR I-1307, EU:C:1993:120.

CASE *(continued)*

The Court of Justice annulled most of the Commission's decision.]

A.   *Quarterly price announcements as the infringement*

59   According to the Commission's first hypothesis, it is the system of quarterly price announcements in itself which constitutes the infringement of art. [101] of the Treaty.

60   First, the Commission considers that that system was deliberately introduced by the pulp producers in order to enable them to ascertain the prices that would be charged by their competitors in the following quarters. The disclosure of prices to third parties, especially to the press and agents working for several producers, well before their application at the beginning of a new quarter, gave the other producers sufficient time to announce their own, corresponding, new prices before that quarter and to apply them from the commencement of that quarter.

61   Secondly, the Commission considers that the implementation of that mechanism had the effect of making the market artificially transparent by enabling producers to obtain a rapid and accurate picture of the prices quoted by their competitors. * * *

63   According to the court's judgement in *Suiker Unie* . . ., a concerted practice refers to a form of co-ordination between undertakings which, without having been taken to the stage where an agreement properly so-called has been concluded, knowingly substitutes for the risks of competition practical co-operation between them. In the same judgement, the court added that the criteria of co-ordination and co-operation must be understood in the light of the concept inherent in the provisions of the Treaty relating to competition that each economic operator must determine independently the policy which he intends to adopt on the common market.

64   In this case, the communications arise from the price announcements made to users. They constitute in themselves market behaviour which does not lessen each undertaking's uncertainty as to the future attitude of its competitors. At the time when each undertaking engages in such behaviour, it cannot be sure of the future conduct of the others.

65   Accordingly, the system of quarterly price announcements on the pulp market is not to be regarded as constituting in itself an infringement of art. [101](1) of the Treaty.

B.   *Concertation on announced prices as the infringement*

66   In the second hypothesis, the Commission considers that the system of price announcements constitutes evidence of concertation at an earlier stage . . . . [T]he Commission states that, as proof of such concertation, it relied on the parallel conduct of the pulp producers

CASE (continued)

in the period from 1975 to 1981 and on different kinds of direct or indirect exchange of information. * * *

70   Since the Commission has no documents which directly establish the existence of concertation between the producers concerned, it is necessary to ascertain whether the system of quarterly price announcements, the simultaneity or near-simultaneity of the price announcements and the parallelism of price announcements as found during the period from 1975 to 1981 constitute a firm, precise and consistent body of evidence of prior concertation.

71   In determining the probative value of those different factors, it must be noted that parallel conduct cannot be regarded as furnishing proof of concertation unless concertation constitutes the only plausible explanation for such conduct. It is necessary to bear in mind that, although art. [101] of the Treaty prohibits any form of collusion which distorts competition, it does not deprive economic operators of the right to adapt themselves intelligently to the existing and anticipated conduct of their competitors. * * *

(a)   *System of price announcements* * * *

74   In their pleadings, on the other hand, the applicants maintain that the system is ascribable to the particular commercial requirements of the pulp market. * * *

76   The experts [appointed by the Court] observe first that the system of announcements at issue must be viewed in the context of the long-term relationships which existed between producers and their customers and which were a result both of the method of manufacturing the pulp and of the cyclical nature of the market. In view of the fact that each type of paper was the result of a particular mixture of pulps having their own characteristics and that the mixture was difficult to change, a relationship based on close co-operation was established between the pulp producers and the paper manufacturers. Such relations were all the closer since they also had the advantage of protecting both sides against the uncertainties inherent in the cyclical nature of the market: they guaranteed security of supply to buyers and at the same time security of demand to producers.

77   The experts point out that it is in the context of those long-term relationships that, after the Second World War, purchasers demanded the introduction of that system of announcements. Since pulp accounts for between 50–75 per cent of the cost of paper, those purchasers wished to ascertain as soon as possible the prices which they might be charged in order to estimate their costs and to fix the prices of their own products. However, as those purchasers did not wish to be bound by a high fixed price in the event of the market weakening, the announced price was regarded as a ceiling price below which the transaction price could always be renegotiated.

> **CASE** *(continued)*
>
> 78   The explanation given for the use of a quarterly cycle is that it is the result of a compromise between the paper manufacturers' desire for a degree of foreseeability as regards the price of pulp and the producers' desire not to miss any opportunities to make a profit in the event of a strengthening of the market.
>
> 79   The US dollar was, according to the experts, introduced on the market by the North American producers during the 1960s. That development was generally welcomed by purchasers who regarded it as a means of ensuring that they did not pay a higher price than their competitors.
>
> *(b)   Simultaneity or near-simultaneity of announcements*
>
> 81   According to the applicants, the simultaneity or near-simultaneity of the announcements—even if it were established—must instead be regarded as a direct result of the very high degree of transparency of the market. Such transparency, far from being artificial, can be explained by the extremely well-developed network of relations which, in view of the nature and the structure of the market, have been established between the various traders. * * *
>
> 83   First, . . . a buyer was always in contact with several pulp producers. One reason for that was connected with the paper-making process, but another was that, in order to avoid becoming overdependent on one producer, pulp buyers took the precaution of diversifying their sources of supply. With a view to obtaining the lowest possible prices, they were in the habit, especially in times of falling prices, of disclosing to their suppliers the prices announced by their competitors.
>
> 84   Secondly, it should be noted that most of the pulp was sold to a relatively small number of large paper manufacturers. Those few buyers maintained very close links with each other and exchanged information on changes in prices of which they were aware.
>
> 85   Thirdly, several producers who made paper themselves purchased pulp from other producers and were thus informed, in times of both rising prices and falling prices, of the prices charged by their competitors. That information was also accessible to producers who did not themselves manufacture paper but were linked to groups that did.
>
> 86   Fourthly, that high degree of transparency in the pulp market resulting from the links between traders or groups of traders was further reinforced by the existence of agents established in the Community who worked for several producers and by the existence of a very dynamic trade press. * * *
>
> 88   Finally, it is necessary to add that the use of rapid means of communications, such as the telephone and telex, and the very frequent recourse by the paper manufacturers to very well-

CASE *(continued)*

informed trade buyers meant that, notwithstanding the number of stages involved—producer, agent, buyer, agent, producer—information on the level of the announced prices spreads within a matter of days, if not within a matter of hours on the pulp market. * * *

Conclusions

126   Following that analysis, it must be stated that, in this case, concertation is not the only plausible explanation for the parallel conduct. To begin with, the system of price announcements may be regarded as constituting a rational response to the fact that the pulp market constituted a long-term market and to the need felt by both buyers and sellers to limit commercial risks. Further, the similarity in the dates of price announcements may be regarded as a direct result of the high degree of market transparency, which does not have to be described as artificial. Finally, the parallelism of prices and the price trends may be satisfactorily explained by the oligopolistic tendencies of the market and by the specific circumstances prevailing in certain periods. Accordingly, the parallel conduct established by the Commission does not constitute evidence of concertation.

NOTES AND QUESTIONS

1. In para. 64 the Court says that the system of quarterly price announcements 'does not lessen each undertaking's uncertainty as to the future attitude of its competitors.' Why not? Argue for the Commission that the system lessens uncertainty. Would this interpretation change the outcome?
2. In para. 71 the Court declares that parallel conduct cannot furnish proof of concertation 'unless concertation constitutes the only plausible explanation for such conduct.' Why such a heavy burden? If agreement was the most probable explanation of the parallel price moves, should the Court have drawn an inference of a concerted practice?
3. The buyers desired advance price information. Does that explain the quarterly price announcements? Does it explain the virtual simultaneity of the price announcements? Does it explain the uniform price rises?
4. Consider, once again, the definition of 'concertation'. When you read the excerpts from the *Sugar Cartel* case, did you infer that oligopolistic interdependence was to be treated as concertation? What do you now believe is the relationship between oligopolistic interdependence and concertation under EU law?

    In the US, the Supreme Court has similarly moved from a soft test for proof of 'combination' or 'concert' to a demanding standard that puts a significant burden on the plaintiff. Compare *Interstate Circuit* with *Matsushita*, p. 48 at notes 7 and 10 above. What are the policy reasons for a rigorous standard of proof?
5. Observe the conundrum of oligopoly behaviour. A few firms in a high-barrier market may be able to mimic the effects of a cartel without an explicit agreement or even an understanding. Should this phenomenon be relevant to a judicial construction of the word 'concert'?

C. World cartels and offshore cartels: jurisdiction, comity, and cooperation

1. Effects, sovereignty, and restraint

A conspiracy in one country may harm consumers in another country, or in the world.

The US was the pioneer of the 'effects' doctrine, under which US law catches offshore anti-competitive conduct targeted at Americans. This is the holding of *United States v. Aluminum Co. of America* ('*Alcoa*').[14] For many years, some of the US' trading partners, and particularly the UK, adamantly opposed application of the effects doctrine to their nationals, labelling the doctrine an affront to their sovereignty.

But as years went by, other nations began to feel the threat of offshore anti-competitive acts targeted at their nation, and some form of the effects doctrine became necessary self-protection.

The first major European Court case on point was the dyestuffs cartel, *Imperial Chemical Industries Ltd v. Commission*, above. ICI, a UK company, was part of the dyestuffs cartel. The UK had not yet joined the EU. ICI sought dismissal for lack of jurisdiction. The Commission rejected ICI's argument, and applied the effects test. On appeal, the Court of Justice side-stepped the controversy surrounding the effects doctrine. ICI had subsidiaries in the Union, and, the Court said, ICI exercised 'decisive influence' over them. Therefore, the parent and its subsidiaries were one economic unit. The Court said, at para. 130:

> By making use of its power to control its subsidiaries established in the [Union], the applicant was able to ensure that its decision was implemented on that market.

The question of jurisdiction over offshore actors arose in a starker form in *Wood Pulp* below. Not all of the alleged conspirators had subsidiaries in Europe. Sixteen years had passed since *Dyestuffs*. Globalization had increased nations' vulnerability to offshore cartels.

US, Finnish, Swedish and Canadian firms exported wood pulp into the common market, themselves or through export associations. Many years before, to facilitate exports, the US had enacted the Webb-Pomerene Act

---

14 148 F.2d 416 (2d Cir.1945). (See Notes and Questions below.)

of 1918. The US wood pulp firms were members of a Webb-Pomerene Association, and the Webb-Pomerene Act exempted the exporters and their association from the US antitrust laws except to the extent that their conduct harmed competition in the US.

The European Commission charged the wood pulp firms and two of their export associations with fixing the price of wood pulp that was being sold to buyers in the EU. The Commission found infringements and imposed fines. The firms sued for annulment, on grounds that included lack of jurisdiction. The jurisdictional issue reached the Court of Justice before the question of proof of the cartel, treated above. Assume for purposes of the jurisdictional matter that there was in fact a cartel agreement.

CASE

Ahlström Osakeyhtiö v. Commission (Cases C-89, 104, 114, 116–117, 125–129/85) ('Wood Pulp')[15]

3   [T]he Commission set out the grounds which in its view justify the Community's jurisdiction to apply Article [101] of the Treaty to the concertation in question. It stated first that all the addressees of the decision were either exporting directly to purchasers within the Community or were doing business within the Community through branches, subsidiaries, agencies or other establishments in the Community. It further pointed out that the concertation applied to the vast majority of the sales of those undertakings to and in the Community. Finally it stated that two-thirds of total shipments and 60% of consumption of the product in question in the Community had been affected by such concertation. The Commission concluded that: 'The effect of the agreements and practices on prices announced and/or charged to customers and on resale of pulp within the EEC was therefore not only substantial but intended, and was the primary and direct result of the agreements and practices.' * * *

6   All the applicants which have made submissions regarding jurisdiction maintain first of all that by applying the competition rules of the Treaty to them the Commission has misconstrued the territorial scope of Article [101]. They note that in its judgement of 14 July 1972 in Case 48/69 (*ICI v. Commission* [1972] ECR 619) the Court did not adopt the 'effects doctrine' but emphasized that the case involved conduct restricting competition within the common market because of the activities of subsidiaries which could be imputed to the parent companies. The applicants add that even if there is a basis in Community law for applying

---

15   [1993] ECR I-1307, EU:C:1993:120.

CASE *(continued)*

Article [101] to them, the action of applying the rule interpreted in that way would be contrary to public international law which precludes any claim by the Community to regulate conduct restricting competition adopted outside the territory of the Community merely by reason of the economic repercussions which that conduct produces within the Community.

7 The applicants which are members of the KEA [Kraft Export Association] further submit that the application of Community competition rules to them is contrary to public international law in so far as it is in breach of the principle of non-interference. They maintain that in this case the application of Article [101] harmed the interest of the United States in promoting exports by United States undertakings as recognized in the Webb Pomerene Act of 1918 under which export associations, like the KEA, are exempt from United States anti-trust laws.

8 Certain Canadian applicants also maintain that by imposing fines on them and making reduction of those fines conditional on the producers giving undertakings as to their future conduct the Commission has infringed Canada's sovereignty and thus breached the principle of international comity. * * *

Territorial Scope of Article [101] and Public International Law

(a) *The Individual Undertakings*

11 In so far as the submission concerning the infringement of Article [101] of the Treaty itself is concerned, it should be recalled that that provision prohibits all agreements between undertakings and concerted practices which may affect trade between Member States and which have as their object or effect the restriction of competition within the common market.

12 It should be noted that the main sources of supply of wood pulp are outside the Community, in Canada, the United States, Sweden and Finland and that the market therefore has global dimensions. Where wood pulp producers established in those countries sell directly to purchasers established in the Community and engage in price competition in order to win orders from those customers, that constitutes competition within the common market.

13 It follows that where those producers concert on the prices to be charged to their customers in the Community and put that concertation into effect by selling at prices which are actually coordinated, they are taking part in concertation which has the object and effect of restricting competition within the common market within the meaning of Article [101] of the Treaty.

14 Accordingly, it must be concluded that by applying the competition rules in the Treaty in the circumstances of this case to undertakings whose registered offices are situated outside the

CASE *(continued)*

Community, the Commission has not made an incorrect assessment of the territorial scope of Article [101].

15   The applicants have submitted that the decision is incompatible with public international law on the grounds that the application of the competition rules in this case was founded exclusively on the economic repercussions within the common market of conduct restricting competition which was adopted outside the Community.

16   It should be observed that an infringement of Article [101], such as the conclusion of an agreement which has had the effect of restricting competition within the common market, consists of conduct made up of two elements, the formation of the agreement, decision or concerted practice and the implementation thereof. If the applicability of prohibitions laid down under competition law were made to depend on the place where the agreement, decision or concerted practice was formed, the result would obviously be to give undertakings an easy means of evading those prohibitions. The decisive factor is therefore the place where it is implemented.

17   The producers in this case implemented their pricing agreement within the common market. It is immaterial in that respect whether or not they had recourse to subsidiaries, agents, sub-agents, or branches within the Community in order to make their contacts with purchasers within the Community.

18   Accordingly, the Community's jurisdiction to apply its competition rules to such conduct is covered by the territoriality principle as universally recognized in public international law.

19   As regards the argument based on the infringement of the principle of non-interference, it should be pointed out that the applicants who are members of KEA have referred to a rule according to which where two States have jurisdiction to lay down and enforce rules and the effect of those rules is that a person finds himself subject to contradictory orders as to the conduct he must adopt, each State is obliged to exercise its jurisdiction with moderation. The applicants have concluded that by disregarding that rule in applying its competition rules the Community has infringed the principle of non-interference.

20   There is no need to enquire into the existence in international law of such a rule since it suffices to observe that the conditions for its application are in any event not satisfied. There is not, in this case, any contradiction between the conduct required by the United States and that required by the Community since the Webb Pomerene Act merely exempts the conclusion of export cartels from the application of United States anti-trust laws but does not require such cartels to be concluded. * * *

CASE *(continued)*

22   As regards the argument relating to disregard of international comity, it suffices to observe that it amounts to calling in question the Community's jurisdiction to apply its competition rules to conduct such as that found to exist in this case and that, as such, that argument has already been rejected.

23   Accordingly it must be concluded that the Commission's decision is not contrary to Article [101] of the Treaty or to the rules of public international law relied on by the applicants.

(b) KEA

24   According to its Articles of Association, KEA is a non-profit-making association whose purpose is the promotion of the commercial interests of its members in the exportation of their products and it serves primarily as a clearing-house for its members for information regarding their export markets. KEA does not itself engage in manufacture, selling or distribution.

25   It should further be pointed out that within KEA a number of groups have been formed, including the Pulp Group, to cover the different sectors of the pulp and paper industry. Under Article 1 of the by-laws of KEA, undertakings may only join KEA by becoming a member of one of those groups. Article 2 of the by-laws provides that the groups enjoy full independence in the management of their affairs. * * *

27   It is apparent from the foregoing that KEA's price recommendations cannot be distinguished from the pricing agreements concluded by undertakings which are members of the Pulp Group and that KEA has not played a separate role in the implementation of those agreements.

28   In those circumstances the decision should be declared void in so far as it concerns KEA.

NOTES AND QUESTIONS

1. Since the 1940s, US courts have exercised 'effects' jurisdiction; that is, if foreigners acted, even abroad, with the intent to affect US commerce and they caused a reasonably direct effect on US commerce, the US courts were said to have subject matter jurisdiction and the Sherman Act applied.[16] US courts could not, however, require foreign firms acting in their home territory to do what their home government forbade, or to abstain from doing what their home government required, for such an order would interfere impermissibly with the sovereignty of the foreign State.[17]

---

16 *United States v. Aluminum Co. of America*, 148 F.2d 416 (2d Cir.1945).
17 See *United States v. Watchmakers of Switzerland Info. Center*, 1963 (CCH) Trade Cas. ¶ 70 600 (S.D.N.Y.1962); 1965 (CCH) Trade Cas. ¶ 71 352 (S.D.N.Y.1965) (judgement revised to apply only to conduct that operated outside of Switzerland).

In the 1960s and 1970s, applications of the *Alcoa* doctrine were criticized by various nations, especially Great Britain, whose nationals were sued for treble damages in US courts as members of world cartels that had targeted American buyers. In response to the criticism and to threats of retaliation by trading partners, US courts developed balancing principles. They stated that courts either lack jurisdiction or should refrain from exercising jurisdiction if foreign nations' and foreign nationals' interests in non-application of US law outbalanced the US' interest in enforcement.[18]

In 1993 the US Supreme Court decided its first antitrust extraterritoriality case in a quarter of a century. Lloyds of London reinsurers had agreed in London with Americans, and some had agreed in London only among themselves, to reduce the coverage of reinsurance policies that they would offer on the US market. When sued, these British defendants moved to dismiss, asserting that the US court lacked jurisdiction or that comity considerations required dismissal. They claimed that their conduct was lawful where performed (in the UK), and that in view of the UK regulatory policy, which conferred the right of self-regulation on Lloyds of London members, a conflict existed that required dismissal of the case against them by the US court. The Supreme Court disagreed. It noted that there was no direct conflict, for the UK law did not require (or encourage) the London firms to boycott the American insurers. In this context, the Court stated:

> [I]t is well established by now that the Sherman Act applies to foreign conduct that was meant to produce and did in fact produce some substantial effect in the United States.[19]

Is there any difference between the holding of *Hartford* and the holding of *Wood Pulp*? Has the EU essentially adopted the effects test?

2. Would the outcome of *Wood Pulp* have been the same if the producers sold 'FOB New York' without knowledge that the wood pulp was being shipped directly into the EU? Should the rules of jurisdiction be the same regardless whether the sale and transfer of title took place in New York or the Netherlands? Is the harm to competition within the European Union the same in either case? Are the sovereignty interests of the affected countries the same?[20]

3. In *Wood Pulp*, why did the Court declare void the Commission's decision against KEA? What would the result have been if there were no sector groups within KEA and if KEA's price recommendations were autonomous and distinct from joint actions of its members? Was the jurisdictional decision regarding KEA harder than the jurisdictional decision regarding the individual producers?

4. In 1982, the US Congress, responding especially to concerns of American business that US antitrust law was following them into foreign markets especially for their export collaborations, adopted the Foreign Trade Antitrust Improvements Act ('FTAIA'). The FTAIA cut back or clarified the reach of the Sherman Act in matters involving foreign commerce, principally to protect US sellers from Sherman Act challenges for impacts of their activity abroad. The statute carves out import commerce, which remains subject to pre-existing rules supporting effects jurisdiction. As to all other commerce with foreign nations, the statute provides that the Sherman Act shall not apply unless:

(1) such conduct has a direct, substantial and reasonably foreseeable effect—

    (A) on [domestic] trade or commerce . . . or (B) on export trade or commerce . . . [and]

---

18 *Timberlane Lumber Co. v. Bank of America*, 549 F.2d 597 (9th Cir.1976); *Mannington Mills, Inc. v. Congoleum Corp.*, 595 F.2d 1287 (3rd Cir.1979).
19 *Hartford Fire Ins. Co. v. California*, 509 U.S. 764, 796, 113 S.Ct. 2891, 125 L.Ed.2d 612 (1993).
20 See, for a theory of jurisdiction, E. Fox (2000), 'National law, global markets, and Hartford: Eyes wide shut', *Antitrust L.J.*, **68**, 73.

(2) such effect gives rise to a claim under [the Sherman Act], other than this section. . . .

For actions based on (1)(B), the statute expressly applies only to injury to export business in the US.

Paragraph (2) apparently meant only that the FTAIA itself did not create a substantive cause of action. But the US Supreme Court construed the paragraph to mean that conspiracies abroad are not within the reach of the Sherman Act unless the US effect of the conduct ('such effect') 'gives rise to' the particular plaintiff's Sherman Act claim.[21]

Since buyers abroad are normally injured by the price fixing, not its US effect, *Empagran* might significantly limit the reach of the Sherman Act, especially in an increasingly integrated world in which firms do business through global value chains and US consumers suffer from input cartels consummated abroad.[22]

UK courts have been more generous in hosting out-of-state claimants suing out-of-state cartelists—at least when the out-of-staters are European. A German company that bought price-fixed vitamins in Germany from Roche Germany was allowed to sue the cartelists (British, German, Swiss and French) in the UK[23] pursuant to Regulation 44/2001 on jurisdiction and the recognition and enforcement of judgements in civil and commercial matters.[24]

5. The EU courts tend to adopt a broad interpretation of the effects doctrine when establishing theirs and the Commission's jurisdiction. For example, in the LCD panel cartel case, the Court of Justice rejected InnoLux's argument that taking into account its sales of finished products in the European Economic Area ('EEA'), in calculating the fine, when those products incorporate LCD panels that were the subject of internal sales outside of the EEA, exceeded the Commission's territorial jurisdiction. The Court considered rather that the Commission had jurisdiction to apply Article 101 TFEU to the cartel at issue, since the cartel participants had implemented the cartel, which was worldwide, in the EEA by making direct sales in the EEA of LCD panels to independent third-party undertakings.[25]

Outside of the field of cartels, in the case initiated by the European Commission against Intel under Article 102 TFEU for strategies to block Intel's rival AMD from gaining traction in launching its new chip, the General Court held it immaterial that a major customer, Lenovo, procured its chips for delivery in China, and another major customer, Acer, sourced its chips in Taiwan.[26] Intel appealed that finding but the Court of Justice affirmed, thereby contradicting the opinion of the Advocate General.[27] In essence, the Court held that the Commission's jurisdiction is established under the (qualified) effects test when 'it is foreseeable that the conduct in question will have an immediate and substantial effect in the European Union' (para. 49). Because foreseeable in this context means 'probable' (para. 51), sales of chips delivered to, for example, Lenovo in China, could fall within the EU's jurisdiction since Lenovo notebooks could then be sold in the EU. Moreover, the Court found that even negligible sales outside the EU could satisfy the 'substantial' criterion because they were part of a broader strategy aimed at foreclosing AMD's access to important sales channels, i.e., that it is requisite to consider the effects of the conduct in question as a whole without fragmenting it.

---

21 *F. Hoffmann-La Roche v. Empagran S.A.*, 542 U.S. 155, 124 S.Ct. 2359, 159 L.Ed.2d 226 (2004).
22 See *Motorola Mobility LLC v. AU Optronics Corp.* (7th Cir. Nov. 26, 2014), dismissing a claim by Motorola for overcharges on liquid crystal display panels price fixed in East Asia, incorporated into cell phones by Motorola subsidiaries in China, and shipped to Motorola-US.
23 *Provimi Ltd v. Roche Products Ltd* [2003] 2 All ER (Comm) 683.
24 [2001] O.J. L 12/1, now Regulation 1215/2012/EU [2012] O.J. L 351/1.
25 Case C-231/14 P, *InnoLux Corp. v. Commission*, EU:C:2015:451, para. 73.
26 Case T-286/09, *Intel Corp. v. Commission*, EU:T:2014:547, para. 221 et seq.
27 Case C-413/14 P, *Intel Corp. v. Commission*, EU:2017:632 (Grand Chamber).

2. Cooperation, and seeds of a global regime

The EU, the US, and other trading partners recognize the need for cooperation and coordination. Europe and the US cooperate formally and informally on many matters. They have a working group on mergers, and their staffs cooperate in vetting mergers of common interest to the extent consistent with confidentiality obligations. Often the merger partners waive confidentiality so that the merger can be dealt with more expeditiously. Confidentiality obligations are a significant impediment to cooperation in cartel investigations.

The EU has entered into a number of bilateral agreements for cooperation on competition policy. It entered into a cooperation agreement with the US effective in 1991 wherein the parties promised to notify and confer regarding intended antitrust action that may adversely affect the important interests of the other (negative comity). In 1998, the US and the EU strengthened a commitment to inform the other when anti-competitive activities harming their citizens were occurring on the soil of the other. In specified circumstances, each undertook to consider withholding its own enforcement while the notified jurisdiction was taking action to cure the violation (positive comity). The numerous EU bilateral antitrust agreements are linked to the DG COMP website.[28]

The EU has advocated a world competition agreement within the framework of the World Trade Organization ('WTO'), starting with building blocks of cooperation; commitments of transparency, due process, and technical assistance to developing countries; and a substantive commitment of nations to enact and maintain an anti-cartel law.[29] The proposal faced preliminary opposition from the US and from developing countries. After revisions, it became an agenda item on the Ministerial Declaration of the Doha trade round of the World Trade Organization (2001). Caught in the crossfire of a dispute on agricultural subsidies, the competition item of the Doha agenda was withdrawn, and it is unlikely to reappear on a WTO agenda for some years.

The Directorate-General for Competition of the European Commission is a founding member of the International Competition Network ('ICN'), a virtual network of the antitrust authorities of the world formed in 2001 to discuss a range of practical and policy competition issues, formulate and disseminate best practices, and promote convergence.[30] DG COMP is active

---

28 At: http://ec.europa.eu/competition/international/legislation/legislation.html (accessed 1 June 2017).
29 See Commission, Communication to the Council: Towards an International Framework of Competition Rules, COM (96) 284 final.
30 See: http://www.internationalcompetitionnetwork.org (accessed 1 June 2017).

in most working groups, including one on cartels. In the absence of international law, the ICN has become the major world forum for international cooperation and convergence on competition issues, and the European Commission is a major player.[31]

D. May cartels be justified? Crisis cartels

Whole industries may fall into crises of overcapacity. Should the competitors be allowed to combine, in order to lift themselves out of the crisis?

The Irish beef industry faced such a crisis. The Irish government requested the industry to agree to a plan of rationalization, and, in response, all of the principal Irish beef processors, accounting for 93% of the Irish industry, formed an association and entered into a rationalization agreement. The Irish Competition Authority challenged the agreement in the *BIDS* case below. The Irish court sided with the Irish government and the industry, finding that the industry was in survival mode and it needed to be rationalized; the rationalization would save costs and help to restore the industry to efficiency and competitiveness; and that no credible evidence had been adduced to show that the agreement would restrict or distort competition or hurt consumers.

The Irish court made a reference to the EU Court of Justice for a ruling on the interpretation of Article 101 TFEU.

CASE

Competition Authority of Ireland v. Beef Industry Development Society Ltd (Case C-209/07) ('*BIDS*')[32]

11   Having informed BIDS . . . that it considered the BIDS arrangements [to reduce crisis overcapacity in the Irish beef industry] contrary to Article [101(1) TFEU], the Competition Authority applied to the High Court, for an order restraining BIDS and Barry Brothers from giving effect to them.

---

31 For a restated EU perspective on cooperation in competition law enforcement and substantive convergence, see Commissioner Vestager, 'Working together to support fair competition worldwide', speech at the UCL Jevons Institute Conference, 3 June 2016.
32 [2008] ECR I-8637, EU:C:2008:643.

CASE (continued)

12   ...[T]he High Court dismissed that application. It held that the agreement between BIDS and Barry Brothers did not fall under the prohibition laid down in Article [101(1) TFEU] but nor did it satisfy the requirements for exemption laid down in Article [101(3) TFEU].

13   The Competition Authority appealed against that decision to the Supreme Court, which decided to stay the proceedings and to refer the following question to the Court of Justice for a preliminary ruling:

where it is established to the satisfaction of the court that:

(a) there is overcapacity in the industry for the processing of beef which, calculated at peak throughput, would be approximately 32%;
(b) the effect of this excess capacity will have very serious consequences for the profitability of the industry as a whole over the medium term;
(c) while... the effects of surplus requirements have not been felt to any significant degree as yet, independent consultants have advised that, in the near term, the overcapacity is unlikely to be eliminated by normal market measures, but over time the overcapacity will lead to very significant losses and ultimately to processors and plants leaving the industry;
(d) processors of beef representing approximately 93% of the market for the supply of beef of that industry have agreed to take steps to eliminate the overcapacity and are willing to pay a levy in order to fund payments to processors willing to cease production, and

the said processors, comprising 10 companies, form a corporate body ('the society') for the purpose of implementing an arrangement with the following features:

— [goers] killing and processing 420 000 animals per annum, representing approximately 25% of active capacity would enter into an agreement with [stayers] to leave the industry and to abide by the following terms;
— goers would sign a two year non-compete clause in relation to the processing of cattle on the entire island of Ireland;
— the plants of goers would be decommissioned;
— land associated with the decommissioned plants would not be used for the purposes of beef processing for a period of five years;
— compensation would be paid to goers in staged payments by means of loans made by the stayers to the society;
— a voluntary levy would be paid to the society by all stayers at the rate of EUR 2 per head of the traditional percentage kill and EUR 11 per head on cattle kill above that figure;
— the levy would be used to repay the stayers' loans; levies would cease on repayment of the loans;

CASE (continued)

— the equipment of goers used for primary beef processing would be sold only to stayers for use as back-up equipment or spare parts or sold outside the island of Ireland;
— the freedom of the stayers in matters of production, pricing, conditions of sale, imports and exports, increase in capacity and otherwise would not be affected,

and that it is agreed that such an agreement is liable, for the purpose of application of Article [101(1) TFEU], to have an appreciable effect on trade between Member States, is such arrangement to be regarded as having as its object, as distinct from effect, the prevention, restriction or distortion of competition within the common market and therefore, incompatible with Article [101](1) of the Treaty [on the Functioning of the European Union]?

The question referred for a preliminary ruling

14   By its question, the national court asks, in essence, whether agreements with features such as those of the BIDS arrangements are to be regarded, by reason of their object alone, as being anti-competitive and prohibited by Article [101(1) TFEU] or whether, on the other hand, it is necessary, in order to reach such a conclusion, first to demonstrate that such agreements have had anti-competitive effects.

15   It must be recalled that, to come within the prohibition laid down in Article [101(1) TFEU], an agreement must have 'as [its] object or effect the prevention, restriction or distortion of competition within the common market'. . . .

16   In deciding whether an agreement is prohibited by Article [101(1) TFEU], there is therefore no need to take account of its actual effects once it appears that its object is to prevent, restrict or distort competition within the common market. . . .

17   The distinction between 'infringements by object' and 'infringements by effect' arises from the fact that certain forms of collusion between undertakings can be regarded, by their very nature, as being injurious to the proper functioning of normal competition. * * *

19   . . . BIDS submits that [its] arrangements do not come within the category of infringements by object, but should, on the contrary, be analysed in the light of their actual effects on the market. It argues that the BIDS arrangements, first, are not anti-competitive in purpose and, second, do not entail injurious consequences for consumers or, more generally, for competition. It states that the purpose of those arrangements is not adversely to affect competition or the welfare of consumers, but to rationalise the beef industry in order to make it more competitive by reducing, but not eliminating, production overcapacity.

20   That argument cannot be accepted.

CASE (continued)

21   In fact, to determine whether an agreement comes within the prohibition laid down in Article [101(1) TFEU], close regard must be paid to the wording of its provisions and to the objectives which it is intended to attain. In that regard, even supposing it to be established that the parties to an agreement acted without any subjective intention of restricting competition, but with the object of remedying the effects of a crisis in their sector, such considerations are irrelevant for the purposes of applying that provision. Indeed, an agreement may be regarded as having a restrictive object even if it does not have the restriction of competition as its sole aim but also pursues other legitimate objectives. It is only in connection with Article [101(3) TFEU] that matters such as those relied upon by BIDS may, if appropriate, be taken into consideration for the purposes of obtaining an exemption from the prohibition laid down in Article [101(1) TFEU].

22   BIDS argues, in addition, that the concept of infringement by object should be interpreted narrowly. Only agreements as to horizontal price-fixing, or to limit output or share markets, agreements whose anti-competitive effects are so obvious as not to require an economic analysis come within that category.... * * *

32   The matters brought to the Court's attention show that the BIDS arrangements are intended to improve the overall profitability of undertakings supplying more than 90% of the beef and veal processing services on the Irish market by enabling them to approach, or even attain, their minimum efficient scale. In order to do so, those arrangements pursue two main objectives: first, to increase the degree of concentration in the sector concerned by reducing significantly the number of undertakings supplying processing services and, second, to eliminate almost 75% of excess production capacity.

33   The BIDS arrangements are intended therefore, essentially, to enable several undertakings to implement a common policy which has as its object the encouragement of some of them to withdraw from the market and the reduction, as a consequence, of the overcapacity which affects their profitability by preventing them from achieving economies of scale.

34   That type of arrangement conflicts patently with the concept inherent in the ... Treaty provisions relating to competition, according to which each economic operator must determine independently the policy which it intends to adopt on the common market. Article [101(1) TFEU] is intended to prohibit any form of coordination which deliberately substitutes practical cooperation between undertakings for the risks of competition.

35   In the context of competition, the undertakings which signed the BIDS arrangements would have, without such arrangements, no means of improving their profitability other than by intensifying their commercial rivalry or resorting to concentrations. With the BIDS

CASE *(continued)*

arrangements it would be possible for them to avoid such a process and to share a large part of the costs involved in increasing the degree of market concentration as a result, in particular, of the levy of EUR 2 per head processed by each of the stayers.

36   In addition, the means put in place to attain the objective of the BIDS arrangements include restrictions whose object is anti-competitive.

37   As regards, in the first place, the levy of EUR 11 per head of cattle slaughtered beyond the usual volume of production of each of the stayers, it is, as BIDS submits, the price to be paid by the stayers to acquire the goers' clientele. However, it must be observed, as did the Advocate General . . ., that such a measure also constitutes an obstacle to the natural development of market shares as regards some of the stayers who, because of the dissuasive nature of that levy, are deterred from exceeding their usual volume of production. That measure is likely therefore to lead to certain operators freezing their production.

38   As regards, secondly, restrictions imposed on the goers as regards the disposal and use of their processing plants, the BIDS arrangements also contain, by their very object, restrictions on competition since they seek to avoid the possible use of those plants by new operators entering the market in order to compete with the stayers. As the Competition Authority pointed out in its written observations, since the investment necessary for the construction of a new processing plant is much greater than the costs of taking over an existing plant, those restrictions are obviously intended to dissuade any new entry of competitors throughout the island of Ireland.

39   Finally, the fact that those restrictions, as well as the non-competition clause imposed on the goers, are limited in time is not such as to put in doubt the finding as to the anti-competitive nature of the object of the BIDS arrangements . . . . [S]uch matters may, at the most, be relevant for the purposes of the examination of the four requirements which have to be met under Article [101(3) TFEU] in order to escape the prohibition laid down in Article [101(1) TFEU].

40   In the light of the foregoing considerations, the reply to the question referred must be that an agreement with features such as those of the standard form of contract concluded between the 10 principal beef and veal processors in Ireland, who are members of BIDS, and requiring, among other things, a reduction of the order of 25% in processing capacity, has as its object the prevention, restriction or distortion of competition within the meaning of Article [101(1) TFEU] . . . . * * *

NOTES AND QUESTIONS

1. What was the purpose of the agreement? Was BIDS' purpose to address the crisis of overproduction of beef in Ireland by reducing overcapacity, thereby resuscitating the industry and making it more competitive? Assume that BIDS and the Irish government thought there was a good chance that the plan would succeed. Is such an agreement caught by Article 101(1) TFEU as a restraint by object? Should it be?
2. BIDS maintained in the Irish court that, if caught by Article 101(1) TFEU, the agreement should be exempted under Article 101(3) TFEU. This issue was not before the European Court, but assume that it was. What would the Court decide? Does the text of Article 101(3) TFEU provide any clues?
3. In *Dutch Brickmakers*,[33] the European Commission exempted, under Article 101(3) TFEU, a rationalization agreement by brickmakers who were plagued by overcapacity. The brickmakers agreed to reduce surplus capacity over a limited period of time while not making any agreement on prices. This case is exceptional.

    The wisdom of allowing judicial or administrative authorization of crisis or restructuring cartels is much debated. US law makes no allowance for crises, on the theory that market solutions are better than private solutions, and a crisis justification for cartels would weaken the clear rule of law. Germany and the UK once allowed authorization of crisis cartels in the public interest. They have revised their laws to mirror Article 101 TFEU. Until 1999, Japanese law allowed authorization of depression and rationalization cartels. This authorization was repealed.[34] In some jurisdictions, however, the law provides the possibility of a public interest defence that might allow the authority to approve such a cartel.[35]
4. The European Commission's antitrust fining guidelines[36] contain a section F entitled 'Ability to pay', which reads as follows:

    > In exceptional cases, the Commission may, upon request, take account of the undertaking's inability to pay in a specific social and economic context. It will not base any reduction granted for this reason in the fine on the mere finding of an adverse or loss-making financial situation. A reduction could be granted solely on the basis of objective evidence that imposition of the fine as provided for in these Guidelines would irretrievably jeopardise the economic viability of the undertaking concerned and cause its assets to lose all their value.

    Which concern does this section aim to address? What are the risks involved in applying that section, or in the absence thereof? In what context do you think the Commission has made use of that section?
5. See Chapter 7 for an account of the European Competition Commissioner's role in responding to the urgent public needs in the financial crisis of 2008–09, presenting competition as part of the solution, not part of the problem.

* * *

As noted, cartels form the most blatant breaches of competition law principles in the EU and worldwide. According to the Commission, '[s]uch

---

33 *Stichting Baksteen*, Case IV/34.456, [1994] O.J. L 131/15 ('*Dutch Brickmakers*').
34 See Anti-Monopoly Law of Japan, § 24(3), Law No. 54, 1947, as amended.
35 See Anti-Monopoly Law of the People's Republic of China (2008), Article 15.
36 Available at: http://ec.europa.eu/competition/antitrust/legislation/fines.html (accessed 1 June 2017).

practices are among the most serious violations of Article [101 TFEU].'[37] However, the scope of Article 101 TFEU encompasses a wide range of agreements between firms beyond cartels, which require a careful analysis and balancing of their actual or likely effects before reaching a finding of infringement. The following two chapters discuss successively agreements either between competitors (horizontal) or between businesses located at different levels in the supply chain (vertical).

---

[37] Commission Notice on immunity from fines and reduction of fines in cartel cases [2006] O.J. C 298/11, para. 1.

3
Horizontal restraints

A. Agreements among competitors: general

Chapter 2 dealt with hardcore cartels: agreements among competitors specifically designed to lessen the competition among them. There are many other kinds of collaborations among competitors, often designed for legitimate purposes, such as sharing risks and creating synergies, getting market information, setting standards to facilitate trade, and protecting the environment.

Read Article 101 TFEU again. Consider the structure of paragraphs 101(1), (2) and (3). Note that Article 101(1) TFEU prohibits agreements that may affect trade between Member States that 'have as their object or effect' the 'prevention, restriction or distortion of competition'. Article 101(2) declares such agreements void. Article 101(3) declares that 101(1) may be declared inapplicable if the agreement (1) contributes to improving production or distribution or promoting technical or economic progress, (2) allows consumers a fair share of the benefits, (3) does not impose unnecessary restrictions (any restrictions must be 'indispensable to the attainment of [the above] objectives'), and (4) does not give the firms concerned the possibility to eliminate competition in a substantial part of the market.

In cases in which a cartel agreement (e.g. competitors' price-fixing or market allocation) is established, few of the nuances of Article 101 TFEU come into play. Cartels are designed to distort competition and empirical evidence suggests that they do have this effect unless the cartel members' predictions and expectations go awry; as a result, they can virtually never be justified because by their nature they suppress competition, hold back efficiency and progress, and harm consumers.

In contrast, when considering agreements among competitors other than hard core cartels and vertical agreements (agreements between buyers and suppliers, see Chapter 4), the following issues arise:

1. What does 'prevent, restrict or distort' competition mean, such that a restraint is caught by Article 101(1) and needs examination under 101(3)?
2. When may or must Article 101(1) be declared inapplicable by reason of Article 101(3) and who must prove what, under Article 101(3)? This concept is often translated into: When is an agreement entitled to an 'exemption'? But note: this use of the word 'exemption' is very particular. It does not or does not usually mean that anti-competitive agreements can be exempted because of some higher public interest. It means that agreements caught by the wide net of Article 101(1) can be shown to be pro-competitive, efficient, or technically progressive; if they fulfil the four conditions of Article 101(3) they are not proscribed.

Note on the notion of '(block) exemption'

Under the now superseded Regulation 17/62, as noted in the Introduction, parties whose agreements were caught by Article 101(1) were obliged to file them with the Commission. The Commission could grant a negative clearance; i.e., an opinion that the agreement was not caught by Article 101(1); or could grant an exemption—usually for a term of years and with conditions; or it could deny an exemption. From the time the agreement was notified until such a time as the Commission denied an exemption, the agreement was considered not to be void under Article 101(2) and the Commission could impose no fines for that period. The Commission became overwhelmed with notifications of agreements, most of which were routine and posed no antitrust problem. To alleviate the literally mounting burden, the Commission began to issue block exemption regulations in areas of frequent contracting, declaring the subject agreements exempt from notification and automatically entitled to an Article 101(3) exemption if they contained certain mandatory or allowed clauses (white list) and contained no prohibited clauses (black list). Most of the block exemptions that were issued covered vertical agreements of specified sorts. A few—notably specialization agreements and research and development agreements—covered agreements between competitors (horizontal).

Although firms could seek individual exemptions, the process took time and effort, and if the agreement was in an area subject to a block exemption, it was convenient for the firms to get the benefit of the ready-made exemption. Therefore they usually tailored their agreement to fit the requirements of the block exemption. Eventually, the Commission came to recognize the straightjacket-effect of the block exemptions, which were formalistic and overly detailed. At the same time, the Commission's Directorate-General for Competition was moving towards effects-based analysis rather than formalistic rules, and was also recognizing the extent to which the notification and clearance procedure, in a context in which exemption authority lay solely within the Commission, was overwhelming it and distorting priorities. Accordingly, the Commission proposed and the Council legislated dramatic changes. Regulation 1/2003 superseded Regulation 17 in May 2004. Article 101 TFEU in its entirety was declared directly effective, meaning that Article 101(1)–(3) is effectively part of national law and national authorities and national courts, as well as the Commission, can declare agreements compatible with Article 101. The notification and clearance procedure was abolished. The Commission withdrew some block exemptions and reviewed others, retaining some in order to give guidance and greater certainty.

Analysis moved away from a formalistic approach. The question became, for the most part, not whether certain clauses were present or absent, but whether the agreement was likely to promote competition and benefit consumers, or to harm competition and consumers. Still, the structure of Article 101—first spreading a wide net to catch all agreements that may distort, prevent or restrict competition, and then requiring their justification—would continue to play a role in analysis, including the assignment of burdens of proof or burdens of producing evidence.

The following section B, examines materials that testify of the analysis used to determine whether a cooperation or collaboration falls within Article 101(1) and, if so, whether it is entitled to an exemption because of net positive effects on competition (including efficiency and innovation). Section C then considers whether and when non-competition/efficiency/innovation objectives may be admissible. Finally, section D discusses specific horizontal block exemptions.

B. The reach of Article 101(1)

Modernisation entailed the devolution of powers to Member State courts and authorities, more effects-based economic analysis, and commensurately a move away from the bifurcated analysis encapsulated in the structure of Article 101 TFEU, lightening the line between Article 101(1) and (3) in favour of an integrated analysis. An integrated analysis would ask: Does this agreement create or is it a use of market power likely to harm consumers and the functioning of the market? If the agreement has some anti-competitive aspects, does it have outbalancing pro-competitive or efficiency/innovation aspects? Can the anti-competitive aspects be eliminated without destroying the pro-competitive ones? However, the Treaty is unchanged and according to the structure of Article 101 TFEU one still must ask in the first place: Does this agreement fall within Article 101(1)?

Until the late 1990s, the European Commission and courts treated agreements between or among significant competitors as almost perfunctorily falling within Article 101(1). That approach has been modified and eventually codified in guidelines on the applicability of Article 101 TFEU to horizontal co-operation agreements (the '2011 Horizontal Guidelines'). The guidelines cover a variety of horizontal practices, including information exchange, joint R&D, purchasing, production and commercialization agreements, as well as standardization. Read the 2011 Horizontal Guidelines.[1]

According to the 2011 Horizontal Guidelines, '[a]rticle 101(1) prohibits agreements the object or effect of which is to restrict competition' (para. 23). As a result, the initial question relates to whether an agreement entails a threshold case of object or effect of harm to competition. There are special cases on labour and the professions that place certain subject matters beyond the reach of Article 101(1), for policy reasons and despite some harm to competition, but these are exceptional and consequently discussed at the end of this chapter. Thus, generally, to fall within Article 101(1), an agreement must either have the *object* of distorting or restricting competition or the *effect* of affecting negatively the parameters of competition such as price, output, innovation, and the variety and quality of goods or services. If an agreement is a restriction by object, there is no need to prove effects; logically, the starting point in the analysis is therefore whether the agreement in question falls within the object category.

1. 'By object' restrictions

By definition, cartels have the object to harm competition, and thus are caught automatically. But what agreements beyond cartels are caught? The Court of Justice has entertained this question in various cases over recent years.

In *T-Mobile Netherlands*,[2] which involved an instance of information exchange between mobile telephony operators in the Netherlands, the Court of Justice significantly expanded the concept of 'by object' restriction. On preliminary reference, the Court held that 'in order for a concerted practice to be regarded

---

1 At: http://ec.europa.eu/competition/antitrust/legislation/horizontal.html (accessed 2 June 2017).
2 Case C-8/08, *T-Mobile Netherlands BV and Others v. Raad van bestuur van de Nederlandse Mededingingsautoriteit* [2009] ECR I-4529, EU:C:2009:343.

as having an anti-competitive object, it is sufficient that it has the potential to have a negative impact on competition ... the concerted practice must simply be capable in an individual case, having regard to the specific legal and economic context, of resulting in the prevention, restriction or distortion of competition within the common market' (para. 31). While showing some hesitations, the Court repeated that language in following cases such as *Allianz Hungaria*,[3] which pertained to an agreement between two insurance companies and auto repair shops, dealers and an association of car dealers specifying costs that would be covered by the insurance and increasing coverage in accordance with the number of policies sold. The uncertainty generated by *T-Mobile Netherlands*' equation between 'by object' restriction and the mere capability of distorting competition was subsequently alleviated in *Cartes Bancaires*, a judgement rendered by the Court of Justice on appeal from a General Court judgement upholding a Commission decision.

CASE

Groupement des Cartes Bancaires (CB) v. Commission (Case C-67/13 P)[4]

[Cartes Bancaires Group ('CB') is a French association of banks that manages a system for bank card payments and withdrawal. The system makes it possible for the members to use their cards at any merchant or ATM belonging to any member. Banks provide two types of services related to payment cards. They issue cards to consumers and provide acquiring services to merchants, allowing them to accept cards. Typically, the issuing side is more profitable than the acquiring one. According to CB, there was a risk that banks would free ride and concentrate too much on issuing cards, while neglecting acquiring services. To correct this bias, CB required members to pay fees and submit to other rules that aimed to equalize the revenues from issuing and acquiring functions and balance the banks' incentives. According to the Commission, however, this fee and the other contemplated measures were designed to keep prices artificially high and to deter entry. The Commission found that CB's conduct altogether was a restriction by object. The Court of Justice disagreed. In analysing the conditions for finding a restriction by object it held:]

49   ... [I]t is apparent from the Court's case-law that certain types of coordination between undertakings reveal a sufficient degree of harm to competition that it may be found that there

---

3 Case C-32/11, *Allianz Hungária Biztosító Zrt. and Others v. Gazdasági Versenyhivatal*, EU:C:2013:160.
4 EU:C:2014:2204.

CASE *(continued)*

is no need to examine their effects [citing *BIDS* (the Irish beef case, Chapter 2 above), and *Allianz Hungaria*].

50   That case-law arises from the fact that certain types of coordination between undertakings can be regarded, by their very nature, as being harmful to the proper functioning of normal competition . . . .

51   Consequently, it is established that certain collusive behaviour, such as that leading to horizontal price-fixing by cartels, may be considered so likely to have negative effects, in particular on the price, quantity or quality of the goods and services, that it may be considered redundant, for the purposes of applying Article 81(1) EC, to prove that they have actual effects on the market . . . Experience shows that such behaviour leads to falls in production and price increases, resulting in poor allocation of resources to the detriment, in particular, of consumers.

52   Where the analysis of a type of coordination between undertakings does not reveal a sufficient degree of harm to competition, the effects of the coordination should, on the other hand, be considered and, for it to be caught by the prohibition, it is necessary to find that factors are present which show that competition has in fact been prevented, restricted or distorted to an appreciable extent . . .

53   According to the case-law of the Court, in order to determine whether an agreement between undertakings or a decision by an association of undertakings reveals a sufficient degree of harm to competition that it may be considered a restriction of competition 'by object' within the meaning of Article 81(1) EC, regard must be had to the content of its provisions, its objectives and the economic and legal context of which it forms a part. When determining that context, it is also necessary to take into consideration the nature of the goods or services affected, as well as the real conditions of the functioning and structure of the market or markets in question . . .

57   . . . when the General Court defined the concept of the restriction of competition 'by object' within the meaning of that provision, it did not refer to the settled case-law of the Court of Justice mentioned in paragraphs 49 to 52 of the present judgement, thereby failing to have regard to the fact that the essential legal criterion for ascertaining whether coordination between undertakings involves such a restriction of competition 'by object' is the finding that such coordination reveals in itself a sufficient degree of harm to competition.

58   Secondly, in the light of that case-law, the General Court erred in finding . . . that the concept of restriction of competition by 'object' must not be interpreted 'restrictively'. The concept of restriction of competition 'by object' can be applied only to certain types of

Horizontal restraints · 75

> **CASE** *(continued)*
>
> coordination between undertakings which reveal a sufficient degree of harm to competition that it may be found that there is no need to examine their effects, otherwise the Commission would be exempted from the obligation to prove the actual effects on the market of agreements which are in no way established to be, by their very nature, harmful to the proper functioning of normal competition.

NOTES AND QUESTIONS

1. Did *Cartes Bancaires* restore clarity to the question of what is a restraint by object and what is a restraint by effect? What is the effect of this judgement on *T-Mobile* and *Allianz Hungaria*? Does the mere 'potential to have a negative impact on competition' suffice to qualify an agreement as a restriction 'by object'? Would/should the agreement in *Allianz Hungaria* be treated as 'by effect'? Does *Cartes Bancaires* now rule out any effects analysis in determining whether a restraint is 'by object'?

    On remand, the General Court found that the measures introduced by CB to balance the banks' incentives to invest in the network's issuing and acquiring functions still amounted to an infringement 'by effect' within the meaning of Article 101(1) TFEU.[5]

2. The Court of Justice's reasoning in *Cartes Bancaires* has since then been reproduced and applied consistently in cases such as *ING Pensii*[6] (involving client-sharing agreements between companies managing private pension funds) and *Maxima Latvija*[7] (involving an agreement between shopping mall lessors and an anchor store containing a clause that grated the latter a veto right over the lessor's ability to lease to third-party competitors) but also in judgements rendered on appeal against Commission decisions in *Dole v. Commission*[8] (involving an information sharing scheme between importers of bananas) or *Toshiba v. Commission*[9] (involving an agreement between producers of power transformers based in the European Economic Area and Japan not to compete in each other's markets).

3. Prior to *Cartes Bancaires*, it was observed that one of the paradoxical consequences of modernisation and the turn to a so-called 'effects-based' approach to competition law enforcement, was the systematic reliance of the Commission on the 'object' category when finding an infringement of Article 101 TFEU, even beyond cartel cases. What explanations would you give to this tendency? In view of *Cartes Bancaires*, is there necessarily a conflict between favouring an effects-based enforcement and relying on a 'by object' category? If appropriate, how would you reconcile these two concepts?[10]

---

5 Case T-491/07, *RENV*, EU:T:2016:379, paras. 157 et seq.
6 Case C-172/14, *ING Pensii, Societate de Administrare a unui Fond de Pensii Administrat Privat SA v. Consiliul Concurenței*, EU:C:2015:484.
7 Case C-345/14, *SIA 'Maxima Latvija' v. Konkurences padome*, EU:C:2015:784.
8 Case C-286/13, *Dole Food Company v. Commission*, EU:C:2015:184.
9 Case C-373/14, *Toshiba v. Commission*, EU:C:2016:26.
10 For a discussion, see D. Gerard (2012), 'The effects-based approach under Article 101 TFEU and its paradoxes: Modernisation at war with itself?' in D. Waelbroeck and J. Bourgeois (eds), *Ten Years of Effects-based Approach in EU Competition Law Enforcement*, Brussels: Bruylant, p. 17.

4. On 8 September 2016, the General Court upheld the Commission's finding that agreements entered into between drug originator Lundbeck and generic companies amounted to 'by object' restrictions of competition.[11] These agreements aimed to settle disputes about possible infringements of Lundbeck's intellectual property ('IP') rights relating to the marketing of anti-depressant citalopram. In essence, the agreements entailed payments by Lundbeck and the delaying of generic market entry; hence the term 'pay-for-delay' coined to describe these arrangements. It was the first time that the Commission prosecuted such arrangements so that the 'by object' qualification was particularly contentious.[12]

The Commission's main argument was that the size of the payments made by Lundbeck was so significant that it did not reflect the parties' assessment of the strength of their respective rights but rather amounted to a 'buying-off of competition', with effects similar to that of collusive market-sharing and output-limiting agreements, chiefly higher prices for consumers. The General Court agreed notably because, in its view, the defence of Lundbeck's patents in court could not, even in the most favourable scenario, have led to the same negative consequences for consumers.

Do you see any weaknesses in the Court's analogy between 'pay-for-delay' settlements and market sharing cartels? The Commission relied on the *BIDS* case to support its 'by object' qualification (see above, p. 62); was that appropriate? Generally, is the size of the 'reverse payment' a suitable or determinative indicator? Lundbeck argued that the size of the payment reflected the asymmetry of risks between the parties; do you agree? Does it matter that the generic companies were not actual but potential competitors when the agreements were entered into?

5. A related question is whether the Commission is required, or even authorized, to weigh competitive benefits against competitive harms in determining whether an agreement is caught by Article 101(1). Is it? Consider the case of *Métropole TV*. Does it still reflect proper analysis?

In *Métropole TV*,[13] six major firms in the French TV sector formed a satellite TV joint venture, TPS, which entered the market dominated by Canal+. The applicants argued that they were entitled to negative clearance (the then available declaration of not being caught by Article 101(1)), rather than exemption, of a clause providing that certain channels were to be broadcast exclusively on TPS. Their argument depended upon the availability of rule-of-reason analysis under Article 101(1). The General Court rejected this approach, holding that the clause was caught by Article 101(1) because it restricted competition; the competitors of TPS were denied access to programs considered attractive to numerous French viewers. The positive effects had to be weighed under Article 101(3). That solution was reproduced in the Commission horizontal guidelines, which still consider that '[t]he balancing of restrictive and pro-competitive effects is conducted exclusively within the framework laid down by Article 101(3)' (para. 20).

6. The proper application of Article 101 is of particular interest to the Member States, for Article 3(2) of Regulation 1/2003[14] provides that if an agreement, decision or concerted practice capable of affecting trade between Member States is not prohibited by Article 101, it cannot be prohibited by national competition law.

7. In the US, the structure of analysis takes a somewhat different form. If the agreement is clearly

---

11 Case T-472/13, *Lundbeck v. Commission*, EU:T:2016:449, para. 332 et seq.
12 Commission Decision of 19 June 2013 in Case AT.39226 – *Lundbeck*.
13 Case T-112/99, *Métropole Télévision (M6) v. Commission* [2001] ECR II-2459, EU:T:2001:2015, esp. para. 74.
14 Regulation 1/2003/EC of 16 December 2002 on the implementation of the rules on competition laid down in Articles 81 and 82 of the Treaty [2002] O.J. L 1/1.

anti-competitive (usually meaning price-raising) and clearly without pro-competitive virtue, it may be condemned on its face ('per se'). If the agreement does not meet this threshold but still, from economic learning and experience, the anti-competitive impact seems obvious, the burden shifts to the defendant to explain why the restraint is unlikely to harm consumers or how it is likely to offer offsetting competitive benefits. But if the competitive harm is more ambiguous, the plaintiff must offer a market analysis and demonstrate how the agreement is likely to create or enhance market power, to the detriment of consumers. *Polygram Holding, Inc. v. FTC*[15] offers a helpful statement and analysis.

2. 'By effect' restrictions

In *Cartes Bancaires*, the Court of Justice limited the scope of 'by object' restrictions to those categories of agreements (or specific features thereof) whose negative effects on competition can be presumed because 'experience has shown that they lead to falls in production and price increases, resulting in poor allocation of resources to the detriment, in particular, of consumers' (para. 51), i.e., that they have the effect of harming competition. In turn, the qualification of a particular agreement as falling within a 'by object' category requires an analysis of 'the content of its provisions, its objectives and the economic and legal context of which it forms a part', and 'consideration for the nature of the goods or services affected, as well as the real conditions of the functioning and structure of the market or markets in question' (para. 53). Conversely, when a particular agreement does not fall within a 'by object' category, the effects thereof must be considered and, for it to be caught by Article 101(1), 'it is necessary to find that factors are present which show that competition has in fact been prevented, restricted or distorted to an appreciable extent' (para. 52).

The notion of anti-competitive effect constitutes therefore the cornerstone of the notion of restriction of—or 'harm to'—competition, and thus of the scope of Article 101(1), whether it needs to be established or can be presumed. But what is anti-competitive effect and how do you establish it? The 2011 Horizontal Guidelines indicate that the determinative factor is whether the agreement in question enables the parties to 'maintain, gain or increase market power' and is thereby 'likely to give rise to negative market effects with respect to prices, output, product quality, product variety or innovation' (para. 3). In other words, an agreement would be deemed to have an anti-competitive effect and to harm competition if it enables the parties to acquire (or strengthen their pre-existing) market power thereby modifying their incentive and ability (and that of third-party competitors) to profitably raise prices or reduce output, including by degrading product/service quality, reducing variety or hampering innovation.

---

15 416 F.3d 29 (D.C. Cir. 2005).

Conceptually, the first step therefore entails a determination of the (lack of) market power of the parties to the agreement in question, which is traditionally defined as the ability to profitably maintain prices above or output below competitive levels for a period of time (and generally to impose commercial terms) because of a lack of sufficient competitive constraints. As such, market power is a question of degree and the degree of market power required for finding a restriction of competition under Article 101 is lower than for a finding of dominance under Article 102, which is a level of substantial market power. In practice, establishing market power requires identifying firms that currently operate on the same market as the parties to the agreement at issue. To that end, defining the relevant market is decisive.

Note on market definition

Most competition decisions and judgements in the field of antitrust (Articles 101 and 102 TFEU) or merger control involve market definition. In 1997, the Commission issued a Notice on the definition of the relevant market.[16] Excerpts follow.

> The main purpose of market definition is to identify in a systematic way the competitive constraints that the undertakings involved face. The objective of defining a market in both its product and geographic dimension is to identify those actual competitors of the undertakings involved that are capable of constraining their behaviour and of preventing them from behaving independently of an effective competitive pressure. It is from this perspective, that the market definition makes it possible, inter alia, to calculate market shares that would convey meaningful information regarding market power for the purposes of assessing dominance or for the purposes of applying Article [101]. * * *
>
> Relevant product markets are defined as follows:
>
> 'A relevant product market comprises all those products and/or services which are regarded as interchangeable or substitutable by the consumer, by reason of the products' characteristics, their prices and their intended use.'
>
> Relevant geographic markets are defined as follows:
>
> 'The relevant geographic market comprises the area in which the undertakings concerned are involved in the supply and demand of products or services, in which

---

16 The Notice can be found at: http://eur-lex.europa.eu/legal-content/EN/ALL/?uri=CELEX:31997Y1209(01) (accessed 2 June 2017).

the conditions of competition are sufficiently homogeneous and which can be distinguished from neighbouring areas because the conditions of competition are appreciably different in those areas'. * * *

Competitive constraints

Firms are subject to three main sources of competitive constraints: demand substitutability, supply substitutability and potential competition. From an economic point of view, for the definition of the relevant market, demand substitution constitutes the most immediate and effective disciplinary force on the suppliers of a given product, in particular in relation to their pricing decisions. A firm or a group of firms cannot have a significant impact on the prevailing conditions of sale, such as prices, if its customers are in a position to switch easily to available substitute products or to suppliers located elsewhere. Basically, the exercise of market definition consists in identifying the effective alternative sources of supply for the customers of the undertakings involved, both in terms of products/services and geographic location of suppliers. * * *

The assessment of demand substitution entails a determination of the range of products which are viewed as substitutes by the consumer. One way of making this determination can be viewed, as a thought experiment, postulating a hypothetical small, non-transitory change in relative prices and evaluating the likely reactions of customers to that increase [usually referred to as the SSNIP test for Small but Significant Non-transitory Increase in Price]. The exercise of market definition focuses on prices for operational and practical purposes, and more precisely on demand substitution arising from small, permanent changes in relative prices. This concept can provide clear indications as to the evidence that is relevant to define markets.

Conceptually, this approach implies that starting from the type of products that the undertakings involved sell and the area in which they sell them, additional products and areas will be included into or excluded from the market definition depending on whether competition from these other products and areas affect or restrain sufficiently the pricing of the parties' products in the short term.

The question to be answered is whether the parties' customers would switch to readily available substitutes or to suppliers located elsewhere in response to an hypothetical small [but significant] in the range 5%–10%, permanent relative price increase in the products and areas being considered. If substitution would be enough to make the price increase unprofitable because of the resulting loss of sales, additional substitutes and areas are included in the relevant market. This would be done until the set of products and geographic areas is such that small, permanent increases in relative prices would be profitable. * * *

> Generally, and in particular for the analysis of merger cases, the price to take into account will be the prevailing market price. This might not be the case where the prevailing price has been determined in the absence of sufficient competition. In particular for investigation of abuses of dominant positions, the fact that the prevailing price might already have been substantially increased will be taken into account.* * *

To define a market, one normally starts with the smallest plausible market hypothesis, i.e., one seeks to define an area wherein, if there were only one firm, that firm—the hypothetical monopolist—could exploit its customers, raising price and lowering output, without fear that other suppliers would simply fill the slack. Thus, if the parties to an agreement (or the putative dominant firm) are global producers and marketers of fresh fruits and vegetables, the starting point would be to focus on the product involved in the agreement, such as bananas, not all fruits (let alone all fruits and vegetables). Bananas are a distinctive soft fruit, so a key question is how many people readily substitute other fruit for bananas. If in all significant geographic areas a critical mass of people switch readily or would do so if banana prices were to increase, a banana producer/importer would not have market power.

There can of course be various difficulties in assessing substitutability and cross-elasticity between products/services and thus in defining relevant product or geographic markets in a particular case, including the availability of the necessary data or evidence. In practice, even though markets must be defined based on the facts prevailing at the relevant time and in the relevant geography, some difficulties may be alleviated by the existence of a large body of precedents defining markets across many industries. Still, it is a fact that the hypothetical monopolist or SSNIP test may not deliver the right outcome in certain circumstances. Consider, for example, a dominant undertaking that is already charging a monopoly price so that customers would stop buying from it at all if it were to raise price further. If a SSNIP test is applied in these circumstances, it would have the effect of unduly broadening the scope of the relevant market because buyers are already at the point where they would cease purchasing the dominant product and turn to another solution if prices were to increase (this is known as the 'Cellophane Fallacy' in reference to a famous error made by the US Supreme Court in *United States v. EI du Pont de Nemour and Co.*[17]).

---

17 351 US 377 (1956).

To learn more about market definition and its difficulties, you may want to watch the tutorial prepared by the International Competition Network (known as the 'ICN', which is the hub of the global competition law enforcement community) or read the transcript thereof.[18]

Once markets are defined, the examination of market power will focus on the competitive constraints (or lack thereof) exercised by existing competitors, potential entrants and buyers on the ability of firms parties to an agreement (or a single firm in the case of Article 102) to dictate market terms. To that end, market shares are often relied upon as a starting point, even though they are insufficient as such to support a determinative finding of market power or dominance, because they reflect a preference for the supplier in question on the part of a larger or narrower segment of demand and the related (in)ability to profitably forego supplies in case of price increase. For example, the EU block exemptions and associated guidelines on horizontal and vertical agreements rely on market share thresholds (in the range of 20–30%) to define 'safe harbours' based on the presumption that if the parties have a low combined (or individual in the case of vertical agreements) market share, the agreement in question is unlikely to give rise to restrictive effects on competition within the meaning of Article 101 TFEU (see also the note on agreements of minor importance ('de minimis') at the end of this section). Generally, to refine your understanding of market power and how it is determined in practice, you may also want to watch the ICN tutorial on this topic or read the transcript thereof.[19]

In turn, the assessment of anti-competitive effects will turn on whether the agreement in question has had or is likely to have an adverse impact on prices, output or other parameters of competition such as innovation, as a result of a reduction of competition between the parties or with third parties. This will typically depend on several factors pertaining to the agreement itself—such as the substance, scope and duration of its terms—and to the market context, including characteristic features of the parties—e.g, their costs structure, the relative importance of the activities covered by the agreement, the closeness of competition between them—and the incentives and abilities of (potential) competitors and customers to respond to the implementation of the said agreement. Likewise, anti-competitive effects may derive directly from the agreement itself or from indirect consequences thereof by, e.g., increasing the likelihood of coordination among the parties.

---

18 Available at: http://www.internationalcompetitionnetwork.org/about/steering-group/outreach/icncurriculum/marketdef.aspx (accessed 2 June 2017).
19 Available at: http://www.internationalcompetitionnetwork.org/about/steering-group/outreach/icncurriculum/marketpower.aspx (accessed 2 June 2017).

Practically, the assessment of the actual or potential effects of a particular agreement on competition (or of a possible abuse under Article 102 TFEU, or of a concentration in the case of merger control), including the identification of the relevant parameters supporting a 'theory of harm' to competition, requires building a counterfactual scenario: What would be or have been the competitive dynamics on the market in the absence of that agreement?[20] If the agreement is only envisaged, the point of reference would be the *status quo ante*, adjusted for likely future events. If the agreement has already been implemented, a likely *ex-ante* scenario will need to be established based on comparators, adjusted for exogenous factors. In both cases, economic models can assist in simulating market outcomes in the absence of the agreement and likely future/past events will need to be supported by evidence so that they represent 'a real, concrete possibility'.[21] At this point, however, efficiency gains generated by the agreement are not supposed to be factored into the analysis for they will be assessed under Article 101(3) TFEU.

CASE

MasterCard v. Commission (Case C-382/12 P)[22]

[On the same day as the *Cartes Bancaires* judgement, the Court of Justice ruled on the appeal brought by MasterCard against a Commission decision finding that MasterCard's multilateral interchange fees ('MIF') for cross-border payment card transactions infringed Article 101 TFEU.[23] MasterCard is a worldwide payment organization grouping several thousand banks issuing cards and/or acquiring merchants, all bound by network rules and a number of joint decisions (MasterCard being considered as an association of undertakings pursuant to Article 101 TFEU). The MIF was a fee ranging between 0.4 and 1.20% of the transaction value (+€0.05) levied on each payment at a retail outlet, which was eventually charged by customers' banks (the 'issuing' banks) to the merchant's bank (the 'acquiring' banks) thereby inflating the base on which acquiring banks charged merchants for accepting payment cards. In fact, the MIF accounted for a large part of the final price businesses paid for accepting MasterCard's payment cards. The Commission concluded that MasterCard's MIF inflated the cost of card acceptance by retailers and of retail consumer prices without leading to proven efficiencies; it gave MasterCard six months to withdraw the fees. The Commission equally

---

20 See, originally, Case 56/65, *Société Technique Minière (L.T.M.) v. Maschinenbau Ulm GmbH (M.B.U.)*, EU:C:1966:38, pp. 249–250; more recently, Case T-328/03, *O2 (Germany) v. Commission*, EU:T:2006:116, paras. 68–69 and 71.
21 Joined Cases T-374/94, T-375/94, T-384/94 and T-388/94, *European Night Services v. Commission* [1998] ECR II-3141, EU:T:1998:198, paras. 114–115.
22 EU:C:2014:2201.
23 Commission Decision of 19 December 2007 in Case COMP/34.579 – *MasterCard I*.

CASE *(continued)*

concluded that MIFs were not illegal as such but that it would accept such fees only where there is evidence that they bring innovation to the system and benefit all users.

The decision defined the relevant markets by distinguishing between an upstream 'system/network market' and downstream markets for 'issuing' payment card (customers side) and 'acquiring' payment card transactions (merchants side). In defining the 'acquiring' market, the Commission relied mainly on product characteristics and past switching behaviour rather than on the results of a SSNIP test because of a significant risk of *cellophane fallacy*:

> 287   In this case the risk of a *cellophane fallacy* is significant for several reasons. Pricing in the issuing and acquiring markets is largely determined by collectively set interchange fees. Also, the concentration in the acquiring business is high in most EEA countries, potentially allowing acquirers to charge supra-competitive prices. Thus, a survey with merchants in these markets asking whether they would cancel a card if the fees were raised by a small but sustainable [amount] can be expected to lead to exaggerated results. . . .

On the issuing side, the Commission concluded that payment card related services were part of market separate from other payment means, including cash, checks and bank transfers. Both issuing and acquiring markets were considered national in scope. The decision also underlined that: '[t]he primary focus for analysing whether there is an appreciable effect on competition is the position and importance of the parties on the market taking into account the market structure' including, e.g., the network effects of MasterCard's cards business.

The Commission went on to assess the effects of the MIF, as follows:

> 408   The assessment of MasterCard's MIF as a restriction of competition is based on its restrictive effects on competition in the acquiring markets. In the absence of a bilateral agreement [between the issuing and acquiring banks], the multilateral rule fixes the level of the interchange fee rate for all acquiring banks alike, thereby inflating the base on which acquiring banks set charges to merchants. Prices set by acquiring banks would be lower in the absence of the multilateral rule and in the presence of a rule that prohibits ex post pricing.

In practice, the Commission conducted different quantitative analyses to establish that the MIF constituted a floor for the merchant fees charged by acquiring banks. It equally relied on evidence from several merchants that the MIF hampered price competition between acquiring banks. Subsequently, the Commission found that: (i) inter-system competition (between, e.g., MasterCard and Visa or domestic payment card systems) generated upward pressures on interchange fees (due to issuing banks' incentive to promote the cards with the higher interchange level thus bringing them most revenue) thereby amplifying and aggravating the distortions of competition in the acquiring markets; (ii) inter-system

> **CASE** *(continued)*
>
> competition did not sufficiently constrain MasterCard in maintaining a high level of interchange fees; and (iii) MIF was not subject to constraints from acquirers or merchants (based, e.g., on an analysis of merchants' demand elasticity) so that members of the MasterCard payment organization collectively held market power over merchants and their customers.
>
> The Commission further considered whether any restriction deriving from the MasterCard MIF was directly related and necessary for operating its payment card system, i.e., whether it was ancillary to a legitimate operation compatible with Article 101 TFEU. In that framework, the decision examined at length a 'counterfactual hypothesis' based on whether: (i) banks could cooperate in an open payment card system without the MIF; and (ii) less restrictive means than the MasterCard MIF would have allowed banks to co-operate as well. Both questions were answered in the affirmative:
>
>> 648 . . . a MIF and its restrictive effects on price competition between acquiring banks are not objectively necessary for the co-operation of banks in the MasterCard payment organization and for the viability of the scheme.
>
> In closing its assessment under Article 101(1), the Commission found that the MasterCard MIF appreciably restricted competition in most EEA Member States because of:
>
>> 650. . .
>>
>> (i) the substantial economic impact of the MIF within the EEA;
>> (ii) the strong position of MasterCard on the relevant markets, in particular due to network effects;
>> (iii) the fact that the MIF is part of a network of inter-related agreements that together have a reinforced cumulative effect; and
>> (iv) the fact that the MIF is a collective price agreement that determines to a significant degree prices for cross-border and domestic transactions in the downstream acquiring markets and allows MasterCard's members to exploit their market power.
>
> MasterCard appealed the Commission decision before the General Court, which confirmed it, and subsequently before the Court of Justice. With respect to whether the MasterCard MIF fell within the framework of Article 101(1) TFEU, one of the main grounds of appeal related to the counterfactual analysis relied upon in the Commission's effects analysis. The Court of Justice stated as follows:]
>
> 161 As regards [the] criticism . . . that, in assessing whether a decision has a restrictive effect on competition, the Commission should have considered what the actual

CASE (continued)

'counterfactual hypothesis' would have been in the absence of the MIF, it should be noted that the Court of Justice has repeatedly held that in order to determine whether an agreement is to be considered to be prohibited by reason of the distortion of competition which is its effect, the competition in question should be assessed within the actual context in which it would occur in the absence of the agreement in dispute. As the General Court rightly held, . . . the same applies in the case of a decision of an association of undertakings within the meaning of Article [101 TFEU].

162   Nevertheless, it is apparent . . . that, in order to assess the competitive effects of the MIF, the General Court relied on 'the premise of a MasterCard system operating without a MIF — solely on the basis of a rule prohibiting *ex post* pricing', that is to say, on the same 'counterfactual hypothesis' it applied in order to examine whether the MIF could be regarded as an ancillary restriction . . ., in relation to the MasterCard payment system.

163   . . . the same 'counterfactual hypothesis' is not necessarily appropriate to conceptually distinct issues. Where it is a matter of establishing whether the MIF have restrictive effects on competition, the question whether, without those fees, but by the effect of prohibiting *ex post* pricing, an open payment system such as the MasterCard system could remain viable is not, in itself, decisive.

164   By contrast, the Court should, to that end, assess the impact of the setting of the MIF on the parameters of competition, such as the price, the quantity and quality of the goods or services. Accordingly, it is necessary, in accordance with the settled case-law . . ., to assess the competition in question within the actual context in which it would occur in the absence of those fees.

165   In that regard, the Court of Justice has already had occasion to point out that, when appraising the effects of coordination between undertakings in the light of Article [101 TFEU], it is necessary to take into consideration the actual context in which the relevant coordination arrangements are situated, in particular the economic and legal context in which the undertakings concerned operate, the nature of the goods or services affected, as well as the real conditions of the functioning and the structure of the market or markets in question.

166   It follows from this that the scenario envisaged on the basis of the hypothesis that the coordination arrangements in question are absent must be realistic. From that perspective, it is permissible, where appropriate, to take account of the likely developments that would occur on the market in the absence of those arrangements.

167   In the present case, however, the General Court did not in any way address the likelihood, or even plausibility, of the prohibition of *ex post* pricing if there were no MIF,

> **CASE** *(continued)*
>
> in the context of its analysis of the restrictive effects of those fees. In particular, it did not . . . address the issue as to how — taking into account in particular the obligations to which merchants and acquiring banks are subject . . . —the issuing banks could be encouraged, in the absence of MIF, to refrain from demanding fees for the settlement of bank card transactions.
>
> 168 Admittedly, . . . the General Court was not obliged, in the context of the examination of the ancillary nature . . . of the MIF, to examine whether it was likely that the prohibition of *ex post* pricing would occur in the absence of such fees. Nevertheless, . . . the situation is different in the separate context of establishing whether the MIF have restrictive effects on competition.
>
> 169 In those circumstances, it is correctly submitted in the present case that, in relying on the single criterion of economic viability, . . . to justify taking into consideration the prohibition of *ex post* pricing in the context of its analysis of the effects of the MIF on competition, and by failing therefore to explain in the context of that analysis whether it was likely that such a prohibition would occur in the absence of MIF otherwise than by means of a regulatory intervention, the General Court made an error of law.
>
> 170 It should be noted, however, that if the grounds of a decision of the General Court disclose an infringement of EU law but its operative part is shown to be well founded on other legal grounds, such infringement is not one that should bring about the annulment of that decision and it is appropriate to carry out a substitution of grounds.
>
> 171 That is the case here. The appellants' arguments before the General Court in relation to the objective necessity of the MIF, . . ., which is not contested in the present appeal, were based in essence on the claim that, without MIF, acquirers would be put at the mercy of issuers, who would be able to determine the level of the interchange fee unilaterally, since merchants and acquirers would be bound to accept the transaction.
>
> 172 In . . . the judgement under appeal, the General Court correctly considered, . . . that the Commission was fully entitled to conclude that 'the possibility that some issuing banks might hold up acquirers . . . could be solved by a network rule that is less restrictive of competition than MasterCard's current solution that, by default, a certain level of interchange fees applies. The alternative solution would be a rule that imposes a prohibition on *ex post* pricing on the banks in the absence of a bilateral agreement between them'.
>
> 173 It follows from this that, . . . the only other option presenting itself at first instance as enabling the MasterCard system to operate without MIF was in fact the hypothesis of a system operating solely on the basis of a prohibition of *ex post* pricing. In those

Horizontal restraints · 87

> **CASE** *(continued)*
>
> circumstances, that prohibition may be regarded as a 'counterfactual hypothesis' that is not only economically viable in the context of the MasterCard system but also plausible or indeed likely, given that there is nothing in the judgement under appeal to suggest, and it is common ground, that it was not in any way claimed before the General Court that MasterCard would have preferred to let its system collapse rather than adopt the other solution, that is to say, the prohibition of *ex post* pricing.
>
> 174 Consequently, even though the General Court wrongly considered that the economic viability of the prohibition of *ex post* pricing in the context of the MasterCard system was sufficient, by itself, to justify taking that prohibition into consideration in the analysis of the effects of the MIF on competition, in the circumstances of the present case, . . . the General Court was entitled to rely in its analysis of the restrictive effects of the MIF on the same 'counterfactual hypothesis' it had used in the context of its analysis of the objective necessity of those fees, albeit for reasons other than those stated by the General Court in . . . the judgement under appeal. In those circumstances, the error of law established in paragraph 169 of the present judgement has no bearing on the analysis of the restrictive effects carried out by the General Court on the basis of the 'counterfactual hypothesis' in question.

NOTES AND QUESTIONS

1. The Court of Justice offered a clear reminder of the centrality of the counterfactual method in establishing 'by effect' restrictions under Article 101(1) TFEU. In *MasterCard*, the Commission had not expressly relied on the counterfactual method to establish a restriction of competition but had rather done so to assess whether the applicable MIF could be deemed ancillary to the operation of the payment system put in place under MasterCard's umbrella, which was not problematic as such. In the present case, that methodological flaw did not have consequences but can you think of other circumstances in which it would? What are the conceptual differences between the assessment of the restrictive character of provisions of an agreement and of the ancillary nature of these provisions?

   In the Guidelines on the application of Article 101(3) TFEU (see section C below), the Commission states as follows: 'In Community competition law the concept of ancillary restraints covers any alleged restriction of competition which is directly related and necessary to the implementation of a main non-restrictive transaction and proportionate to it. If an agreement in its main parts, for instance a distribution agreement or a joint venture, does not have as its object or effect the restriction of competition, then restrictions, which are directly related to and necessary for the implementation of that transaction, also fall outside Article [101](1) . . . . It follows that the ancillary restraints test is similar to the test [for establishing a restriction of competition]. However, the ancillary restraints test applies in all cases where the main transaction is not restrictive of competition. It is not limited to determining the impact of the agreement on [. . .] competition' (para. 29).

2. The centrality of the counterfactual method is directly associated with the move towards a systematic 'effects-based approach' in EU competition law enforcement. In the field of

abuses of dominance under Article 102 TFEU, the Commission recently grounded the assessment of the exclusionary character of unilateral practices in such counterfactual. According to the 2009 Dominance Guidance Paper (as discussed in Chapter 5, section C(2) below): 'This assessment will usually be made by comparing the actual or likely future situation in the relevant market (with the dominant undertaking's conduct in place) with an appropriate counterfactual, such as the simple absence of the conduct in question or with another realistic alternative scenario, having regard to established business practices' (para. 21). Likewise, when assessing the competitive effects of a concentration, 'the Commission compares the competitive conditions that would result from the notified merger with the conditions that would have prevailed without the merger' (Horizontal Merger Guidelines, para. 9, discussed in Chapter 6 below). In turn, the counterfactual method is central to the articulation of well-developed theories of harm to competition in antitrust or merger control cases.

At this point, should you wish to deepen your understanding of the notions of 'competitive effects' and 'effects-based approach' to competition policy and enforcement, consider watching the ICN tutorial on this topic or read the transcript thereof.[24]

3. In MasterCard, the Court of Justice also blamed the General Court for not examining whether the counterfactual scenario relied upon by the Commission was 'realistic', 'likely' or even 'plausible'. In your view, are these terms synonymous or do they refer to different evidentiary standards? If they connote different standards, what do each of these standards entail? Should the Court of Justice have drawn a difference between them? In principle, could it make a difference to rely on one or the other standard, and how?

Note on agreements of minor importance ('de minimis')

Irrespective of whether it results from an agreement between competitors (horizontal) or between non-competitors (vertical), a restriction of competition needs to be 'appreciable' to be caught by Article 101(1) TFEU, meaning that an agreement falls outside of Article 101 if it has 'only an insignificant effect on the market.'[25] When is then a restraint so insignificant that it is below the threshold of Article 101 TFEU? That question is governed by the Commission Notice on agreements of minor importance which do not appreciably restrict competition under Article 101(1) of the Treaty on the Functioning of the European Union ('De Minimis Notice').[26] The Notice provides, in part:

---

24 Available at: http://www.internationalcompetitionnetwork.org/about/steering-group/outreach/icncurriculum/effects.aspx (accessed 2 June 2017).
25 Case C-226/11, *Expedia Inc. v. Autorité de la concurrence and Others*, EU:C:2012:795, para. 16.
26 Available at: http://eur-lex.europa.eu/legal-content/EN/TXT/?uri=CELEX:52014XC0830(01) (accessed 2 June 2017).

De Minimis Notice[27]

* * *

3. In this Notice the Commission indicates, with the help of market share thresholds, the circumstances in which it considers that agreements which may have as their effect the prevention, restriction or distortion of competition within the internal market do not constitute an appreciable restriction of competition under Article 101 of the Treaty. This negative definition of appreciability does not imply that agreements between undertakings which exceed the thresholds set out in this Notice constitute an appreciable restriction of competition. Such agreements may still have only a negligible effect on competition and may therefore not be prohibited by Article 101(1) of the Treaty.

4. Agreements may also fall outside Article 101(1) of the Treaty because they are not capable of appreciably affecting trade between Member States. This Notice does not indicate what constitutes an appreciable effect on trade between Member States. Guidance to that effect is to be found in the Commission's Notice on effect on trade, in which the Commission quantifies, with the help of the combination of a 5% market share threshold and a EUR 40 million turnover threshold, which agreements are in principle not capable of appreciably affecting trade between Member States. Such agreements normally fall outside Article 101(1) of the Treaty even if they have as their object the prevention, restriction or distortion of competition. * * *

8. The Commission holds the view that agreements between undertakings which may affect trade between Member States and which may have as their effect the prevention, restriction or distortion of competition within the internal market, do not appreciably restrict competition within the meaning of Article 101(1) of the Treaty:

(a) if the aggregate market share held by the parties to the agreement does not exceed 10% on any of the relevant markets affected by the agreement, where the agreement is made between undertakings which are actual or potential competitors on any of those markets (agreements between competitors); or

(b) if the market share held by each of the parties to the agreement does not exceed 15% on any of the relevant markets affected by the agreement, where the agreement is made between undertakings which are not actual or potential competitors on any of those markets (agreements between non-competitors).

9. In cases where it is difficult to classify the agreement as either an agreement between competitors or an agreement between non-competitors the 10% threshold is applicable. * * *

---

27 [2014] O.J. C 291/1.

> 11. [T]his Notice does not cover agreements which have as their object the prevention, restriction or distortion of competition within the internal market. The Commission will thus not apply the safe harbour created by the market share thresholds set out in points 8, 9, and 11 to such agreements. For instance, as regards agreements between competitors, the Commission will not apply the principles set out in this Notice to, in particular, agreements containing restrictions which, directly or indirectly, have as their object: a) the fixing of prices when selling products to third parties; b) the limitation of output or sales; or c) the allocation of markets or customers. Likewise, the Commission will not apply the safe harbour created by those market share thresholds to agreements containing any of the restrictions that are listed as hardcore restrictions in any current or future Commission block exemption regulation, which are considered by the Commission to generally constitute restrictions by object.

* * *

In 2014, the Commission sought to provide guidance on restrictions of competition 'by object' excluded from the scope of the De Minimis Notice.[28] This document offers a broad restatement of the Commission's views about the scope of 'by object' agreements and includes various references to relevant cases decided by the EU courts in that area. Importantly, the Commission underlines in introduction that: 'The types of restrictions that are considered to constitute restrictions "by object" differ depending on whether the agreements are entered into between actual or potential competitors or between non-competitors (for example between a supplier and a distributor). In the case of agreements between competitors (horizontal agreements), restrictions of competition by object include, in particular, price fixing, output limitation and sharing of markets and customers. As regards agreements between non-competitors (vertical agreements), the category of restrictions by object includes, in particular, fixing (minimum) resale prices and restrictions which limit sales into particular territories or to particular customer groups.' The guidance then addresses successively horizontal 'by object restrictions', distinguishing between price-fixing, market sharing and output restrictive practices, and vertical 'by object' restrictions, with a focus on territorial/customer sales restrictions and resale price maintenance.

As we proceed to examine the requirements of Article 101(3), consider how the question—what is caught by Article 101(1)?—may still have significance despite modernisation and the direct effectiveness of Article 101 in its

---

28 See the Commission Staff Working Document – Guidance on restrictions of competition 'by object' for the purpose of dining which agreements may benefit from the De Minimis Notice, as revised in 2015, at: http://ec.europa.eu/competition/antitrust/legislation/de_minimis_notice_annex_en.pdf (accessed 2 June 2017).

entirety. Once an agreement is caught by Article 101(1), the undertakings have the burden to justify under Article 101(3). Note the four necessary conditions for the justification, specified in the Treaty. If the agreement is caught by Article 101(1), in particular as a 'by object' restriction, can the undertakings prevail by showing that the agreement did not in fact restrict competition? Or is restriction of competition conclusively presumed, and does the undertaking thus need to prove offsetting pro-competitive or pro-efficiency effects?

C. Article 101(3): Effects of the agreement on competition, efficiency, innovation

1. Introduction and guidelines

If an agreement falls within Article 101(1), it must, to be valid, satisfy the four conditions of Article 101(3), namely: (1) contribute to improving production or distribution of goods or promoting technical or economic progress (identified in Commission guidelines as 'efficiency gains'); (2) allow consumers a fair share of benefits; (3) not impose restrictions indispensable to the attainment of the above objectives, and (4) not afford the undertakings the possibility to eliminate competition in respect of a substantial part of the products concerned.

In 2004, the Commission issued Guidelines on the application of Article 101(3) of the Treaty.[29] The Guidelines were motivated by the need to give guidance to the Member States' authorities and courts, which would be applying Article 101(3) for the first time. The Guidelines state:

> 13   The objective . . . of Article 101 is to protect competition on the market as a means of enhancing consumer welfare and of ensuring an efficient allocation of resources. Competition and market integration serve these ends since the creation and preservation of an open single market promotes an efficient allocation of resources throughout the Community for the benefit of consumers.

The 2004 Guidelines go on to state that they present an analytical framework and methodology based on 'the economic approach'. '[R]eflected in Article [101(3)] . . . is the assessment of the positive economic effects of restrictive agreements' (paras. 5 and 32).

---

29   These are available at: http://ec.europa.eu/competition/antitrust/legislation/art101_3_en.html (accessed 2 June 2017).

The 2004 Guidelines identify certain principles as follows:

3.1 General principles

40   Article [101](3) of the Treaty only becomes relevant when an agreement between undertakings restricts competition within the meaning of Article [101] (1). In the case of non-restrictive agreements there is no need to examine any benefits generated by the agreement.

41   Where in an individual case a restriction of competition within the meaning of Article [101](1) has been proven, Article [101](3) can be invoked as a defence. According to Article 2 of Regulation 1/2003 the burden of proof under Article [101](3) rests on the undertaking(s) invoking the benefit of the exception rule. Where the conditions of Article [101](3) are not satisfied the agreement is null and void, cf. Article [101](2). However, such automatic nullity only applies to those parts of the agreement that are incompatible with Article [101], provided that such parts are severable from the agreement as a whole. If only part of the agreement is null and void, it is for the applicable national law to determine the consequences thereof for the remaining part of the agreement.

42   According to settled case law the four conditions of Article [101](3) are cumulative, i.e. they must all be fulfilled for the exception rule to be applicable. If they are not, the application of the exception rule of Article [101](3) must be refused. The four conditions of Article [101](3) are also exhaustive. When they are met the exception is applicable and may not be made dependent on any other condition. Goals pursued by other Treaty provisions can be taken into account to the extent that they can be subsumed under the four conditions of Article [101] (3). * * *

47   Any claim that restrictive agreements are justified because they aim at ensuring fair conditions of competition on the market is by nature unfounded and must be discarded. The purpose of Article [101] is to protect effective competition by ensuring that markets remain open and competitive. The protection of fair conditions of competition is a task for the legislator in compliance with Community law obligations and not for undertakings to regulate themselves. * * *

NOTES AND QUESTIONS

1. According to the 2004 Guidelines, are non-competition justifications admissible? What do you learn from para. 42?
2. What does the Commission mean by agreements 'aim[ing to] ensur[e] fair competition' (para. 47)? Give an example. Why is such an agreement the antithesis of a pro-competitive agreement?

3. Read the Commission's Amicus Curiae brief to the Irish Court in the *Irish Beef* case[30] (discussed in Chapter 2 above). You will recall that the case concerned an agreement between slaughterhouses to reduce capacity at the behest of the Irish government to solve a crisis of over-capacity. On preliminary reference, the Court of Justice found that the agreement was a restriction of competition by object. The case was sent back to the Irish Court to determine whether the agreement should be exempted under Article 101(3) TFEU.

Did the Commission indicate whether it thought the agreement should be exempted? Which criteria would be the most difficult for the parties to satisfy?

Should an economic crisis justify a more lenient approach to justifications in order to help companies survive the crisis?

4. Since the publication of the Article 101(3) guidelines, there have been very few cases at EU level discussing in depth the application of the four conditions of Article 101(3) TFEU. Can you hypothesize why it is so? What do you make of the fact that, according to the Article 101(3) guidelines, 'Article [101(3)] . . . does not distinguish between agreements that restrict competition by object and agreements that restrict competition by effect' (para. 20)? For illustration purposes, consult Commission Decision of 19 December 2007 in Case COMP/34.579 – *MasterCard* (referred to above at p. 82).

* * *

The tension between Article 101(1) and 101(3) TFEU inherent to the bifurcated structure of that provision is particularly apparent from the analysis of agreements or decisions of associations of undertakings—which may be by-laws of associations—that are designed to foster efficiency or innovation. These tend to fall into two categories: (1) loose agreements, such as exchanges of information and standard-setting decisions; and (2) tighter agreements, which contemplate integration of the participating entities, such as joint ventures or alliances. The tightest joint ventures are concentrations covered by the Merger Regulation, which are discussed in Chapter 6.

2. Loose agreements

a. *Agreements to exchange information*

Economics teaches that information (knowledge of the market) is good. It helps sellers understand supply and demand; it helps them determine the efficient amount to produce, and where, to whom, and how much to sell. Similarly it helps buyers understand the efficient amount of goods or services to buy and the lowest price at which they can buy. Information helps make markets work.

---

30 Available at: http://ec.europa.eu/competition/court/amicus_curiae_2010_bids_en.pdf (accessed 2 June 2017).

But in highly concentrated, high-barrier markets where firms have incentives to behave cooperatively, the sharing of market information can have outbalancing negative qualities. Oligopolists' knowledge of the sensitive business details of one another can help them coordinate and stabilize prices upwards. When firms are few, aggregated data can be more easily disaggregated. Moreover, when the information is obtained as the result of agreement among the firms, the danger signals are compounded: firms are not likely to give their sensitive information (e.g. cost, output, forecasts) to a competitor if they expect the data to be used against them. They are more likely to share the information if they can expect cooperation in lessening competition.

Often, when market conditions point to a negative (price-raising) effect, one suspects that the data sharing agreement is meant to facilitate a cartel; for, as we saw in Chapter 2, cartelists need to know the most sensitive information about one another to find a joint profit-maximizing price, and they need to police their cartel agreement to prevent defection. Information sharing supports both tasks.

Note on John Deere Ltd v. Commission

The Agricultural Engineers Association was a trade association of producers and importers of agricultural tractors in the UK. It had some 200 members, and was open to membership by all other agricultural tractor companies. The market was oligopolistic; the four largest firms accounted for almost 80% of sales. The firms' market shares were stable and entry barriers were high. The product was homogeneous. The association organized an exchange of information among its members (who accounted for 88% of sales) based on the information contained in registration forms that were required to be filed by the UK. The data revealed great detail of sales and market shares, broken down by year, quarter, month and week, and by country, region, county, and dealer territory, and made it possible to identify not only the sales of each producer but also the imports and exports between dealer territories.

The information exchanged did not directly concern prices, and there was no evidence that the information exchange was designed in support of a cartel. Indeed, there was no claim that the *object* of the agreement was to harm trade or competition; and the Commission was unable to establish that the agreement, which was in force for 20 years, produced an actual anticompetitive effect (higher prices).

The Commission found that the information exchange agreement was caught by Article 101(1) and was not entitled to an exemption. The General Court

Horizontal restraints · **95**

agreed. It upheld Commission findings that the data exchange (1) disadvantaged non-members, who would not have the benefit of the information exchanged; (2) produced *potential* anti-competitive effects among members, by providing a forum for facilitating a high price policy; and (3) made it possible for each participating manufacturer to monitor *its* dealers' sales and thus made 'it possible for [manufacturers] to confer absolute territorial protection on each of their dealers.'[31] Further, the association did not show that the restrictions on competition resulting from the agreement were indispensable, 'particularly with regard to the objectives of contributing to economic progress and equitable distribution of the benefits' (para. 105). The Court of Justice affirmed.[32] It rejected John Deere's arguments, among others, that Article 101(1) does not prohibit purely potential effects on competition, and that the General Court improperly inferred harm to competition from high concentration without any evidence of higher prices or changes in the pattern of trade.

John Deere was the first prohibition by the Commission and the Court of a pure information exchange of non-price information; that is, an information exchange not as part of a cartel.

NOTES AND QUESTIONS

1. Were the Court and Commission correct? How is such an agreement 'exclusionary' to non-members? How does the exchange of sales information harm competition among members? Do you suspect that the members shared sales data to compete or to lessen competition? Do you believe that this exchange of information chilled parallel imports, i.e., kept each producer's product within each of its dealer's territories and thus kept the producer's product from competing with itself? Could this have been a device to help the producers cartelize? Which of the possible effects would most concern you if you were a competition authority?
2. In *T-Mobile Netherlands* (discussed above), representatives of the five big mobile telephone operators 'held a meeting . . . [on 13 June 2001 at which] they discussed . . . the reduction of standard dealer remunerations for postpaid subscriptions [commissions to their agents for distributing their product to consumers], which was to take effect on or about 1 September 2001'. They shared confidential information in their discussions (para. 12). When challenged, the firms argued that their conversations had no effect on consumer prices. The Dutch court made a preliminary reference. The Court of Justice held that, for a concerted practice to have an anti-competitive object, 'it is sufficient that it has the potential to have a negative impact on competition'. In the case of an anti-competitive object, it is not necessary that there be an anti-competitive effect, which 'can only be of relevance for determining the amount of any fine and assessing any claim for damages' (paras. 30, 31). 'Article [101] . . . is designed to protect not only the immediate interests of individual competitors or consumers but also to protect the structure of the market and thus competition as such' (para. 38).

---

31 Case T-35/92, *John Deere Ltd v. Commission* [1994] ECR II-957, EU:T:1994:259, para. 96.
32 Case C-7/95 P, *John Deere Ltd v. Commission* [1998] ECR I-3111, EU:C:1998:256.

Does this mean that the information exchange agreement was automatically caught by Article 101(1)? Do you think that it was merely a benign or procompetitive agreement to exchange information and thus get knowledge? Or was it a thinly-veiled attempt to ratchet down commissions payable to the agents?

3. In *Dole Food Company v. Commission* (discussed above),[33] banana producers engaged in bilateral communications relating to price-setting factors before setting their weekly quotation prices. They discussed the factors relevant to the setting of their quotation prices and shared price trends and indications for the coming week. The Court of Justice held that the exchange was a violation by object. It made it possible for the competitors to reduce uncertainty. Accordingly, the Commission did not have to prove effects; nor did it have to prove a direct link between the practice and consumer prices. Do you think the competitors shared the information to coordinate or to compete? In your opinion, what was the key factual element that determined the Commission's analysis, as upheld by the General Court and the Court of Justice?

Note on Wirtschaftsvereinigung Stahl[34]

On 26 November the Commission adopted a decision under Article 65 of the ECSC Treaty [the counterpart to Article 101 in the now-expired Coal and Steel Community Treaty] prohibiting an information exchange system notified by Wirtschaftsvereinigung Stahl, the German steel industry association. The system, which had not been implemented, provided for the exchange between association members of sensitive, recent and individualised data on supplies of more than 40 steel products in the various Member States, broken down by steel quality. The exchange would also have concerned the breakdown by consumer sector and the market shares of member companies on the German market. The leading German steel producers were to have participated in the system. * * *[35]

The notified information exchange agreement would have restricted competition between the parties (in the concentrated markets) by increasing market transparency to such a degree that any independent competitive action on the part of one company would have been noticed immediately by its competitor, which would have been able to take suitable retaliatory measures such as systematically canvassing customers or offering temporary or local selective discounts. This increased transparency would thus have been liable to deter companies from trying to increase their market shares, a fundamental competitive activity. In addition, the frequency of the exchange, i.e. monthly, and the freshness of the data exchanged (one month old) would

---

33 On appeal from T-588/08, EU:T:2013:130 and Commission Decision of 15 October 2008 in Case COMP/39.188 – *Bananas*.

34 Case T-16/98, *Wirtschaftsvereinigung Stahl and Others v. Commission* [2001] ECR II-1217, ECLI:EU:T:2001:117.

35 Excerpt from European Commission Report on Competition Policy (1997), p. 127, available at: http://ec.europa.eu/competition/publications/annual_report/1997/broch97_en.pdf (accessed 2 June 2017).

have reduced considerably the time during which a company could have derived any benefit from behaving competitively.

The decision is consistent with the Commission's practice, which has been upheld by the General Court (citing *John Deere*), of viewing as anti-competitive any systems involving the exchange of sensitive, recent and individualised data on a concentrated market in homogeneous products.

* * *

What was the principal harm feared from the steel industry's information exchange? In which case—tractors or steel—is the concern of cartel-like or cooperative pricing behaviour stronger?

CASE

Asnef-Equifax v. Asociación De Usuarios De Servicios Bancarios (Case C-238/05)[36]

[Financial institutions in Spain agreed to exchange information about solvency of customers and lateness of payment. They planned to establish a register for such information. The Spanish competition authority authorized the register for five years on condition that the register be available to all financial institutions on a non-discriminatory basis and that it not disclose the information it contained on lenders. Ausbanc, an association of bank users, sought an annulment in a Spanish court. It alleged that the register would facilitate a boycott against poor credit risks. The Spanish court made an Article 267 reference to the Court of Justice regarding applicability and treatment under Article 101 TFEU. The court identified the various questions of fact regarding economic and legal context that the national court would have to decide, and it gave considerable guidance both as to when Article 101(1) would apply and when the Article 101(3) criteria would be satisfied.]

55 ... [R]egisters such as the one at issue in the main proceedings, by reducing the rate of borrower default, are in principle capable of improving the functioning of the supply of credit. As the Advocate General observed, ... if, owing to a lack of information on the risk of borrower default, financial institutions are unable to distinguish those borrowers who are more likely to default, the risk thereby borne by such institutions will necessarily be increased and they will tend to factor it in when calculating the cost of credit for all borrowers, including those less likely to default, who will then have to bear a higher cost than they would

---

36 [2006] ECR I-11125, EU:C:2006:734.

CASE *(continued)*

if the institutions were in a position to evaluate the probability of repayment more precisely. In principle, registers such as that mentioned above are capable of reducing such a tendency.

56   Furthermore, by reducing the significance of the information held by financial institutions regarding their own customers, such registers appear, in principle, to be capable of increasing the mobility of consumers of credit. In addition, those registers are apt to make it easier for new competitors to enter the market.

57   Nonetheless, whether or not there is in the main proceedings a restriction of competition within the meaning of Article [101(1) TFEU] depends on the economic and legal context in which the register exists, and in particular on the economic conditions of the market as well as the particular characteristics of the register.

58   In that regard, first of all, if supply on a market is highly concentrated, the exchange of certain information may, according in particular to the type of information exchanged, be liable to enable undertakings to be aware of the market position and commercial strategy of their competitors, thus distorting rivalry on the market and increasing the probability of collusion, or even facilitating it. On the other hand, if supply is fragmented, the dissemination and exchange of information between competitors may be neutral, or even positive, for the competitive nature of the market. In the present case, it is common ground, . . . that the referring court premissed its reference for a preliminary ruling on the existence of 'a fragmented market', which it is for that court to verify.

59   Secondly, in order that registers such as that at issue in the main proceedings are not capable of revealing the market position or the commercial strategy of competitors, it is important that the identity of lenders is not revealed, directly or indirectly. In the present case, it is apparent from the decision for referral that the Tribunal de Defensa de la Competencia imposed on Asnef-Equifax, which accepted it, a condition that the information relating to lenders contained in the register not be disclosed.

60   Thirdly, it is also important that such registers be accessible in a nondiscriminatory manner, in law and in fact, to all operators active in the relevant sphere. If such accessibility were not guaranteed, some of those operators would be placed at a disadvantage, since they would have less information for the purpose of risk assessment, which would also not facilitate the entry of new operators on to the market.

61   It follows that, provided that the relevant market or markets are not highly concentrated, that the system does not permit lenders to be identified and that the conditions of access and use by financial institutions are not discriminatory, an information exchange system such as the register is not, in principle, liable to have the effect of restricting competition within the meaning of Article [101(1) TFEU].

CASE *(continued)*

62 While in those conditions such systems are capable of reducing uncertainty as to the risk that applicants for credit will default, they are not, however, liable to reduce uncertainty as to the risks of competition. Thus, each operator could be expected to act independently and autonomously when adopting a given course of conduct, regard being had to the risks presented by applicants. Contrary to Ausbanc's contention, it cannot be inferred solely from the existence of such a credit information exchange that it might lead to collective anti-competitive conduct, such as a boycott of certain potential borrowers.

63 Furthermore, since, as the Advocate General observed, . . . any possible issues relating to the sensitivity of personal data are not, as such, a matter for competition law, they may be resolved on the basis of the relevant provisions governing data protection. In the main proceedings, it is apparent from the documents before the Court that, under the rules applicable to the register, affected consumers may, in accordance with the Spanish legislation, check the information concerning them and, where necessary, have it corrected, or indeed deleted.

The applicability of Article [101(3) TFEU]

64 Only if the referring court finds, in the light of the considerations set out at paragraphs 58 to 62 of this judgement, that there is indeed in the dispute before it a restriction of competition within the meaning of Article [101(1)] will it be necessary for that court to carry out an analysis by reference to Article [101(3)] in order to resolve that dispute.

65 The applicability of the exemption provided for in Article [101(3)] is subject to the four cumulative conditions laid down in that provision. . . .

66 It is clear from the documents before the Court, and in particular from the second question referred by the national court, that that court seeks an answer from the Court in respect of, in particular, the second of those conditions, which provides that consumers are to be allowed a fair share of the profit resulting from the agreement, decision or practice in question. The national court asks, in essence, whether, where all consumers do not derive a benefit from the register, the register might nonetheless benefit from the exemption provided for in Article [101(1)].

67 Apart from the potential effects described at paragraphs 55 and 56 of this judgement, registers such as the one at issue in the main proceedings are capable of helping to prevent situations of overindebtedness for consumers of credit as well as, in principle, of leading to a greater overall availability of credit. In the event that the register restricted competition within the meaning of Article [101(1)], those objective economic advantages might be such as to offset the disadvantages of such a possible restriction. It would be for the national court, if necessary, to verify that.

> **CASE** *(continued)*
>
> 68 Admittedly, in principle it is not inconceivable that, as Ausbanc suggests, certain applicants for credit will, owing to the existence of such registers, be faced with increased interest rates, or even be refused credit.
>
> 69 However, without its being necessary to decide whether such applicants would nonetheless benefit from a possible credit discipline effect or from protection against overindebtedness, that circumstance cannot in itself prevent the condition that consumers be allowed a fair share of the benefit from being satisfied.
>
> 70 Under Article [101(3)], it is the beneficial nature of the effect on all consumers in the relevant markets that must be taken into consideration, not the effect on each member of that category of consumers.
>
> 71 Moreover, as follows from paragraphs 55 and 67 of this judgement, registers such as the one at issue in the main proceedings are, under favourable conditions, capable of leading to a greater overall availability of credit, including for applicants for whom interest rates might be excessive if lenders did not have appropriate knowledge of their personal situation. * * *

Read the paragraphs of the 2011 guidelines on horizontal co-operation agreements that apply to exchange of information.[37] Apply them to *John Deere, T-Mobile*, the German steel exchange, and *Asnef-Equifax*.

b. Standard setting

Standard-setting organizations are regarded as increasingly important in facilitating innovation, particularly in information technologies such as for mobile phones. It has become common for holders of IP rights to commit to disclose their IP while standards are being created, and, if the standard incorporates their IP, to commit to license it on fair, reasonable, and non-discriminatory terms ('FRAND' terms).

In high-profile cases involving Rambus and Qualcomm, the Commission suspected the undertaking of staging a patent ambush: advocating a standard incorporating the firm's IP, failing to disclose the IP, and charging high royalties after the standard is adopted. The *Rambus* case resulted in a commitment

---

37 At: http://ec.europa.eu/competition/antitrust/legislation/horizontal.html, at section 2 (accessed 2 June 2017).

decision, and the *Qualcomm* case was dropped for failure of proof of wrongdoing.[38]

Obviously drawing from these experiences, the Commission has included standard-setting in its 2011 guidelines on horizontal co-operation agreements. The guidelines specify conditions under which standard-setting agreements will not give rise to competition concerns.[39] Many of the FRAND cases arise under Article 102 TFEU, where a holder of an essential patent that it has agreed to license seeks an injunction against an infringing use by a willing licensee. For a discussion of these cases, see Chapter 5 below.

3. Tighter agreements

Firms may form joint ventures and alliances to share risks and areas of expertise and thus to create synergies. These are pro-competitive properties. The combination can, however, also have some anti-competitive aspects. For example, it might combine important competitors in a concentrated market, and the partners might otherwise be in a position to continue their competition against one another. Also, the partners might incorporate unnecessary or unreasonably restrictive ancillary restrictions, such as certain exclusive dealing that lessens outsiders' access. In the rare case, a joint venture might be an essential facility that outsiders cannot duplicate and that outsiders must be able to access to compete effectively.

The principal judgement on pro-competitive and anti-competitive effects of joint ventures is *European Night Services*. Here are excerpts from the judgement regarding Article 101(3).

CASE

European Night Services Ltd v. Commission (Cases T-374–375, 384 and 388/94)[40]

[Four railway firms—the railway companies of Britain ('BR'), Germany ('DB'), the Netherlands ('NS'), and France ('SNCF')—agreed to form a joint venture, European Night

---

38 See Commission Decision of 9 December 2009 in Case COMP/38.636 – *Rambus*, and Commission Decision of 24 November 2009 in Case COMP/39.247 – *Texas Instruments/Qualcomm*.
39 See link at: http://ec.europa.eu/competition/antitrust/legislation/horizontal.html (accessed 2 June 2017).
40 [1998] ECR II-3141, EU:T:1998:198.

CASE (continued)

Services ('ENS'), to provide overnight passenger rail services between the UK and the continent by way of the Channel Tunnel. They filed their agreements with the Commission, seeking a negative clearance or an exemption under the regulation applying competition rules to rail transport. The Commission found, as the relevant markets, the market for the transport of business travellers (for whom air travel, among other things, is a substitute) and the market for the transport of leisure travellers (for whom car travel, among other things, is a substitute). It made no reference in its decision to market shares of ENS or any competing operators, but later referred to data in the parties' notification to contend that a conservative estimate of ENS' market share was 7% to 8%. The Commission denied a negative clearance and granted an exemption for a period of eight years on condition that the parent companies supply equivalent services on the same terms to any international grouping of railways and any transport operator wishing to compete with ENS in the Channel Tunnel. The railways appealed, contending that the Commission had not shown grounds for application of Article [101(1) TFEU], that ENS' market share was less than 5% on most routes and in any case was insignificant, and that in any event the conditions imposed by the Commission were disproportionate and improper and the term of exemption was too short. On the last two points, the General Court said:]

As to the Commission's requirement that the parent railroads supply to competitors of ENS the same necessary services that they supply to ENS

205 According to paragraph 79 of the contested decision, the aim of [requiring ENS to supply services to competitors] is that of 'preventing the restrictions of competition from going beyond what is indispensable'. * * *

207 ... [E]ven if the Commission had made an adequate and correct assessment of the restrictions of competition in question, it would be necessary to consider whether it was a proper application of Article [101] (3) to impose on the notifying parties the condition that train paths, locomotives and crews must be supplied to third parties on the same terms as to ENS, on the ground that they are necessary or that they constitute essential facilities, as discussed by the parties in their pleadings and at the hearing. * * *

209 ... [W]ith regard to an agreement such as that in the present case, setting up a joint venture, which falls within Article [101](1) of the Treaty, the Court considers that neither the parent undertakings nor the joint venture thus set up may be regarded as being in possession of infrastructure, products or services which are 'necessary' or 'essential' for entry to the relevant market unless such infrastructure, products or services are not 'interchangeable' and unless, by reason of their special characteristics—in particular the prohibitive cost of and/or time reasonably required for reproducing them—there are no viable alternatives available to potential competitors of the joint venture, which are thereby excluded from the market.

CASE (continued)

210   The question whether the Commission could validly regard the supply of (a) train paths, (b) locomotives and (c) crews to ENS by its parent undertakings as necessary or essential services which had to be made available to third parties on the same terms as to ENS and whether, in so doing, it provided a valid statement of reasons for its decision must be examined in the light of the above considerations and by analogy with the case law . . . . Finally, that examination will also serve as the basis for determining whether the Commission made a correct analysis of the alleged restrictions of competition with regard to third parties arising out of the special relationship between the parent undertakings and ENS.

211   With regard, first, to train paths, [the Commission's decision is based on a false premise because it erroneously treated ENS as a transport operator].

212   With regard, second, to the supply of locomotives, as pointed out above, locomotives cannot be regarded as necessary or essential facilities unless they are essential for ENS's competitors, in the sense that without them they would be unable either to penetrate the relevant market or to continue operating on it. However, since the decision defined the relevant market as the market for the transport of business travellers and the market for the transport of leisure travellers, both of which are intermodal, and since ENS's market share does not exceed 7 per cent to 8 per cent according to the Commission, or 5 per cent according to the notification of the parties, on either of those intermodal markets, it cannot be accepted that a possible refusal by the notifying undertakings to supply ENS's competitors with special locomotives for the Channel Tunnel could have the effect of excluding such competitors from the relevant market as thus defined. It has not been demonstrated that an undertaking having such a small market share can be in a position to exert any influence whatever on the functioning or structure of the market in question.

213   Only if the market under consideration were the completely different, intramodal, market for business and leisure travel by rail, on which the railway undertakings currently hold a dominant position, could a refusal to supply locomotives possibly have an effect on competition. However, it was not that intramodal market which was finally considered relevant by the Commission, but the intermodal market. . . .***

215   As the applicants have argued, the contested decision does not contain any analysis demonstrating that the locomotives in question are necessary or essential. More specifically, it is not possible to conclude from reading the contested decision that third parties cannot obtain them either directly from manufacturers or indirectly by renting them from other undertakings. Nor has any correspondence between the Commission and third parties, demonstrating that the locomotives in question cannot be obtained on the market, been produced before the Court. As the applicants have stated, any undertaking wishing to operate the same rail services as ENS through the Channel Tunnel may freely purchase or rent the locomotives in question on the market. . . .

> **CASE** *(continued)*
>
> 216 ... [T]he Commission has ... merely asserted that ... only the notifying undertakings actually possess such locomotives. That argument cannot, however, be accepted. The fact that the notifying undertakings have been the first to acquire the locomotives in question on the market does not mean that they are alone in being able to do so.
>
> 217 Consequently, the Commission's assessment of the necessary or essential nature of the special locomotives designed for the Channel Tunnel and, thus, the obligation imposed on the parent undertakings to supply such locomotives to third parties are vitiated by an absence or, at the very least, an insufficiency of reasoning.
>
> 218 For the same reasons, the obligation imposed on the parent undertakings also to supply train crews for special locomotives for the Channel Tunnel to third parties is similarly vitiated by an absence or an insufficiency of reasoning.
>
> 219 Consequently, the contested decision is vitiated by an absence or, at the very least, an insufficiency of reasoning in so far as it requires the applicants to supply to third parties in competition with ENS the same 'necessary services' as it supplies to ENS. * * *
>
> 221 As regards, first, access to infrastructure (train paths), it is true that access for third parties may in principle be hindered when it is controlled by competitors; nevertheless, the obligation of railway undertakings which are also infrastructure managers to grant such access on fair and non-discriminatory terms to international groupings competing with ENS is explicitly provided for and guaranteed by Directive 91/440. The ENS agreements therefore cannot, by definition, impede access to infrastructure by third parties. As regards the supply to ENS of special locomotives and crew for the Channel Tunnel, the mere fact of its benefitting from such a service could impede access by third parties to the downstream market only if such locomotives and crew were to be regarded as essential facilities. Since ... they cannot be categorised as such, the fact that they are to be supplied to ENS under the operating agreements for night rail services cannot be regarded as restricting competition *vis-à-vis* third parties. That aspect of the Commission's analysis of restrictions of competition *vis-à-vis* third parties is therefore also unfounded.
>
> *As to duration of the exemption granted*
>
> 222 The applicants emphasise that the ENS agreements relate to a major long-term investment and that the return on the project is dependent on the securing of advantageous 20-year financing for the purchase of the specialised rolling stock, so that the limitation of the exemption to eight years is inadequate. . . .* * *
>
> 230 ... [E]ven if it is assumed that the Commission's assessment of the restrictions on competition in the contested decision was adequate and correct, the Court considers that

CASE *(continued)*

the duration of an exemption granted under Article [101](3) of the Treaty—or, as here, Article 5 of Regulation 1017/68—and Article 53(3) EEA must be sufficient to enable the beneficiaries to achieve the benefits justifying such exemption, namely, in the present case, the contribution to economic progress and the benefits to consumers provided by the introduction of new high-quality transport services . . . . Since, moreover, such progress and benefits cannot be achieved without considerable investment, the length of time required to ensure a proper return on that investment is necessarily an essential factor to be taken into account when determining the duration of an exemption, particularly in a case such as the present, where it is undisputed that the services in question are completely new, involve major investments and substantial financial risks and require the pooling of know-how by the participating undertakings.

231 The consideration set out in . . . the decision, that 'the duration of the exemption will therefore depend inter alia on the period for which it can reasonably be supposed that market conditions will remain substantially the same,' cannot, therefore, be regarded as decisive, on its own, for determining the duration of the exemption, without also taking account of the length of time necessary to enable the parties to achieve a satisfactory return on their investment.

232 However, the contested decision does not contain any detailed assessment of the length of time required to achieve a return on the investments in question under conditions of legal certainty, in the light, in particular, of the fact that the parties have entered into financial commitments covering a period of 20 years for the purchase of the special rolling stock. . . . ***

234 Consequently, the Commission's decision to limit the duration of the exemption granted for the ENS agreements is in any event vitiated by an absence of reasoning. ***

[T]he contested decision must be annulled.

NOTES AND QUESTIONS

1. Was ENS a pro-competitive joint venture? Why? Should the joint venture have an obligation under Article 101 TFEU to give competitors access to the tunnel (had it not been provided by agreement)? What was the Court's concern with imposing conditions on the joint venture? Was it well taken?
2. If, in *ENS*, the market was rail travel and the joint venturers were the only firms that possessed locomotives fit to travel through the Channel Tunnel, would the Commission's requirement that the joint venturers supply locomotives to third parties on the same terms as they supply ENS withstand scrutiny?

3. Today, after modernisation, *ENS* would not seek a negative clearance or exemption. It would simply, after consulting its lawyers, proceed with the venture. If the Commission, a national authority in an affected Member State, or a private party that considered itself harmed, brought proceedings, would the analysis differ? Would the outcome differ? Note that, under the old Regulation 17, if an agreement fell within Article 101(1) but was justified under Article 101(3), the Commission was likely to impose conditions and would limit any exemption to a term of years. Is the system under Regulation 1/2003 superior?

4. Relationship to innovation and competitiveness

Consider the following two matters, as summarized by the Commission in its 1996 Competition Policy Report,[41] both of which involve strategic alliances—i.e., synergistic joint ventures that enable the partners to enter new markets and expand their capabilities.

Atlas/GlobalOne

On 17 July [1996] the Commission authorized the Atlas project, a joint venture between Deutsche Telekom AG (DT) and France Télécom (FT) aimed at providing telecommunications services to large users in Europe. The services provided by Atlas include network services, outsourcing and very small aperture satellite (VSAT) services. The Commission also authorized the proposed GlobalOne joint venture, an alliance between Atlas and Sprint Corporation (Sprint) for the supply of the above services worldwide. Within GlobalOne, the parties will provide the same services as within Atlas, together with traveller services and telecommunications services to other telecommunications organizations (TOs).

In the relevant markets, the services provided to corporate users raise important issues to do with competition in the EEA. This is the case, for example, with the market for the transmission of data via terrestrial networks. DT and FT have market shares there well in excess of 70% in Germany and France respectively, buttressed by a legal monopoly over the supply of infrastructure. In addition, the Atlas project provided for the elimination of a competitor of DT in Germany, namely FT's local subsidiary, Info AG.

In the course of the proceeding, France and Germany first of all undertook to liberalize the alternative infrastructures by introducing a system under which licences would be granted to any operator meeting certain technical requirements, thereby making competitors less dependent on the networks of FT and DT.

---

[41] European Commission Competition Policy Report (1996), at p. 121, available at: http://ec.europa.eu/competition/publications/annual_report/1996/en.pdf (accessed 2 June 2017).

The Commission made the Atlas/GlobalOne authorization conditional on the granting of the first two infrastructure licences in France and Germany.

DT and FT have postponed the transfer of their domestic data transmission networks to the joint venture pending full liberalization of infrastructure services in France and Germany. FT has undertaken to sell Info AG. This modified contractual framework, coupled as it is with strict conditions and obligations, will help to ensure that the two projects satisfy an increasingly urgent demand and compete with the few telecommunications services providers existing at world level without, however, resulting in any elimination of competition. * * *

Iridium

The Commission, by formal decision, gave the green light to the creation of Iridium, a company led by the US corporation Motorola, which intends to provide from the last quarter of 1998 global digital wireless communications services using a constellation of 66 low earth orbit (LEO) satellites, to be launched and placed in orbit during the next 24 months. Services will include mobile voice telephony, paging and basic data services (such as facsimile) and will be provided via portable hand-held (dual mode or single mode) telephones, vehicle-mounted telephones, pagers and other subscriber equipment.

Apart from Motorola, Iridium is owned by 16 strategic investors including a number of telecommunication services providers and equipment manufacturers from around the world. Two European companies figure among those strategic investors: Stet (Italy; 3.8%) and Vebacom (Germany; 10%). Each of the two has its own gateway service territory covering different parts of Europe and the associated exclusive right to construct and operate a gateway within its respective territory.

In the decision, the creation of Iridium has been concluded to fall outside the scope of both Article [101(1) TFEU] and Article 53(1) of the EEA [European Economic Area] Agreement. In this respect, it was concluded that none of the strategic investors could be reasonably expected to separately assume the very high level of investments required (nearly USD 5 billion) and the very high risk of technical and commercial failure associated with such a new system. In addition, no investor has all the necessary licences to operate such a system.

Satellite systems like Iridium (commonly referred to as S-PCS systems) are expected to complement wireless terrestrial mobile technologies (such as GSM) in areas where those terrestrial technologies have failed to penetrate (i.e. rural parts of the developed world and both urban and rural parts of lower income countries) or where terrestrial roaming is not available because of incompatible technologies.

In addition, S-PCS systems are expected to act as a complement and even a substitute for the public switched fixed telephone network, enhancing service coverage in remote areas of low population density and/or where the terrestrial infrastructure is very poor.

The same conclusion as to the inapplicability of the competition rules of both the [TFEU] and the EEA Agreement was reached in respect of several ancillary restraints; namely as regards the distribution of the Iridium services and the pricing policies which Iridium may suggest as guidelines to gateways investor operators.

NOTES AND QUESTIONS

1. Did Iridium restrict or distort competition? Were its members competitors, or potential competitors?
2. How did the agreement of Atlas and GlobalOne restrict competition? How did the Commission counteract the problems? How did the Commission use the occasion to impose conditions that would increase competition?
3. Describe the Commission's approach towards innovation and competitiveness.

D. Article 101(1) and (3): public policy and non-competition goals

The Commission's guidelines on the application of Article 101(3) TFEU state that an agreement falls within Article 101(1) if it restricts competition, and that an Article 101(3) exemption is available only if it has offsetting pro-competitive (including efficiency and innovation) effects. What if the agreement is intended to pursue an important public policy objective? Are there any exceptions from the principle stated in the Article 101(3) guidelines?

1. Labour

CASE

Albany International BV and Textile Industry Pension Funds (Case C-67/96)[42]

[The Netherlands maintains a pension system. A compulsory statutory scheme entitles the whole population to receive a basic pension, calculated by reference to the statutory minimum wage. This amount, however, is quite limited.

---

42 [1999] ECR I-5751, EU:C:1999:430.

CASE *(continued)*

Industry sectors are covered by supplementary pensions managed by collective schemes negotiated in the context of collective worker-employer agreements. The law requires employers in the sector to be affiliated with the sectoral fund, subject to satisfying conditions for exemption.

Albany International BV was a textile company. It was not party to the collective agreement. It provided its own supplementary coverage through an insurer of its choice; it sought and was denied an exemption from the statutory scheme, and it refused to pay its mandatory contributions to the statutorily designated fund, the Textile Industry Trade Fund. When sued for arrears, it challenged the Dutch law's requirement of compulsory affiliation, and the collective agreement providing for the designated fund, as contrary to Article 3(1)(g) EC (now in Protocol 27), Article 4(3) TEU, and, Articles 101, 102 and 106 TFEU.[43] Questions were referred to the Court of Justice.]

47   Albany contends that the request by management and labour to make affiliation to a sectoral pension fund compulsory constitutes an agreement between the undertakings operating in the sector concerned, contrary to Article [101](1) of the Treaty.

48   Such an agreement, in its view, restricts competition in two ways. First, by entrusting the operation of a compulsory scheme to a single manager, it deprives the undertakings operating in the sector concerned of the possibility of affiliation to another pension scheme managed by other insurers. Second, that agreement excludes the latter insurers from a substantial part of the pension insurance market.

49   The effects of such an agreement on competition are 'appreciable' because it affects the entire Netherlands textile sector. They are aggravated by the cumulative effect of making affiliation to pension schemes compulsory in numerous sectors of the economy and for all undertakings in those sectors.

50   Moreover, such an agreement affects trade between Member States in so far as it concerns undertakings which engage in cross-frontier business and deprives insurers established in other Member States of the opportunity to offer a full pension scheme in the Netherlands either by virtue of cross-frontier services or through branches or subsidiaries.

---

43 Article 3(1)(g) EC required 'a system ensuring that competition in the internal market is not distorted'; Article 4(3) TEU requires the Member States to 'facilitate the achievement of the Union's tasks'; Article 106 TFEU requires public and state-privileged undertakings to abstain from measures inconsistent with the non-discrimination mandate and the competition rules and to comply with the competition rules as long as compliance does not obstruct their performance of public tasks. The interaction of these provisions is further dealt with in Chapter 7.

CASE *(continued)*

51   Therefore, according to Albany, by creating a legal framework for, and acceding to a request from, the two sides of industry to make affiliation to the sectoral pension fund compulsory, the public authorities favoured or furthered the implementation and operation of agreements between undertakings operating in the sectors concerned which are contrary to Article [101] (1) of the Treaty, thereby infringing Articles [3(1)(g) ECT, 4(3) TEU and 101 TFEU].

52   It is necessary to consider first whether a decision taken by the organisations representing employers and workers in a given sector, in the context of a collective agreement, to set up in that sector a single pension fund responsible for managing a supplementary pension scheme and to request the public authorities to make affiliation to that fund compulsory for all workers in that sector is contrary to Article [101] of the Treaty. * * *

54   . . . [I]t is important to bear in mind that, under Article [3(1)(g) and (j)] of the EC Treaty, the activities of the Community are to include not only a 'system ensuring that competition in the internal market is not distorted' but also 'a policy in the social sphere'. Article 2 of the EC Treaty provides that a particular task of the Community is 'to promote throughout the Community a harmonious and balanced development of economic activities' and 'a high level of employment and of social protection'.[44]

55   In that connection, Article 118 of the EC Treaty[45] . . . provides that the Commission is to promote close cooperation between Member States in the social field, particularly in matters relating to the right of association and collective bargaining between employers and workers.

56   Article 118b of the EC Treaty adds that the Commission is to endeavour to develop the dialogue between management and labour at European level which could, if the two sides consider it desirable, lead to relations based on agreement.

57   Moreover, Article 1 of the Agreement on social policy (OJ 1992 C 191, p. 91) states that the objectives to be pursued by the Community and the Member States include improved living and working conditions, proper social protection, dialogue between management and labour, the development of human resources with a view to lasting high employment and the combatting of exclusion.

58   Under Article 4(1) and (2) of the Agreement, the dialogue between management and labour at Community level may lead, if they so desire, to contractual relations, including

---

44 Now substantially incorporated into Article 3(3) TEU.
45 Article 118 EC has been repealed. Social rights are protected in Article 3(3) TEU and in the Charter of Fundamental Rights of the European Union, annexed to and part of the Treaties.

CASE (continued)

agreements, which will be implemented either in accordance with the procedures and practices specific to management and labour and the Member States, or, at the joint request of the signatory parties, by a Council decision on a proposal from the Commission.

59 It is beyond question that certain restrictions of competition are inherent in collective agreements between organizations representing employers and workers. However, the social policy objectives pursued by such agreements would be seriously undermined if management and labour were subject to Article [101](1) of the Treaty when seeking jointly to adopt measures to improve conditions of work and employment.

60 It therefore follows from an interpretation of the provisions of the Treaty as a whole which is both effective and consistent that agreements concluded in the context of collective negotiations between management and labour in pursuit of such objectives must, by virtue of their nature and purpose, be regarded as falling outside the scope of Article [101](1) of the Treaty.

61 The next question is therefore whether the nature and purpose of the agreement at issue in the main proceedings justify its exclusion from the scope of Article [101](1) of the Treaty.

62 First, like the category of agreements referred to above which derive from social dialogue, the agreement at issue in the main proceedings was concluded in the form of a collective agreement and is the outcome of collective negotiations between organisations representing employers and workers.

63 Second, as far as its purpose is concerned, that agreement establishes, in a given sector, a supplementary pension scheme managed by a pension fund to which affiliation may be made compulsory. Such a scheme seeks generally to guarantee a certain level of pension for all workers in that sector and therefore contributes directly to improving one of their working conditions, namely their remuneration.

64 Consequently, the agreement at issue in the main proceedings does not, by reason of its nature and purpose, fall within the scope of Article [101](1) of the Treaty.

NOTES AND QUESTIONS

1. Albany articulated a number of ways in which the requirement of compulsory affiliation harmed competition: it could not choose its own insurer; it could get a better rate from its own insurer, which was likely to be more efficient than a monopolist fund; insurers—including non-Dutch insurers—would be deprived of access to the market. Indeed the Court, finding the

sectoral pension fund to be an undertaking, observed that the fund was engaged in economic activity in competition with insurance companies, and that its pursuit of a social objective through cross-subsidization of risks ('manifestations of solidarity') could render its services less competitive than comparable services (see paras 84–86). See also paras 97–98: competition was restricted; firms might otherwise provide their workers with a superior scheme. Why wouldn't these effects bring the agreement within Article 101(1), leaving the question of overriding social benefits for analysis under Article 101(3), if social benefits were an admissible justification?

2. Did the Court simply, in effect, grant an exemption to bona fide labour agreements? Was this a good idea?

In the US, Section 6 of the Clayton Act[46] grants an antitrust exemption to agreements among workers (e.g., collaboration under the auspices of labour unions). 'The labour of a human being is not a commodity or article of commerce.' The courts have expanded the exemption to cover bona fide labour negotiations, including by employers, and the resulting collective bargaining agreements. This is called the non-statutory labour exemption.

3. After *Albany*, and in view of the Court's invocation of the social aspects of the Treaty, how would you expect the Commission and Court to treat agreements other than collective bargaining agreements that promise benefits to jobs and workers? Can benefits to workers and the economy be balanced against harms to competition as aspects of economic progress under Article 101(3) TFEU?

2. The liberal professions

The Court of Justice has decided important cases on the regulation of the liberal professions and its effect on competition. See *Wouters* (immediately below), *Arduino*[47] and *Cipolla* and *Macrino*.[48] *Arduino* and *Cipolla* concern mandatory fee schedules for Italian lawyers. The Court has ruled that the State can authorize self-regulation by a professional body setting mandatory minimum fees as long as the State retains the decision-making powers and establishes sufficient control mechanisms.

Commission Reports of 2004 and 2005 observe a trend of Member States to deregulate, and they find that countries with little regulation of the liberal professions serve consumers no less well than countries with significant regulation of the professions.[49]

---

46 15 U.S.C. § 17.
47 Case C-35/99, *Arduino and Others v. Compagnia Assicuratrice RAS SpA* [2002] ECR I-1529, EU:C:2002:97.
48 Cases C-94/04 and 202/04, *Cipolla* and *Macrino* [2006] ECR I-11421, EU:C:2006:758.
49 The reports are available at http://ec.europa.eu/competition/sectors/professional_services/reports/reports.html (accessed 2 June 2017).

CASE

Wouters et Cie (Case C-309/99)[50]

[This judgement arises out of the request for a preliminary ruling referred to the Court by the Netherlands Council of State in the framework of proceedings initiated by Wouters and other members of the Bar seeking to set aside the decisions of the Amsterdam and Rotterdam Bar prohibiting them from practicing law in full partnership with accountants. Those decisions were adopted pursuant to the Regulation on Joint Professional Activity adopted by the Bar of the Nederlands in 1993 ('the 1993 Regulation'). The 1993 Regulation prohibits members of the Bar to 'assume or maintain any obligations which might jeopardize the free and independent exercise of their profession, including . . . the relationship of trust between lawyer and client' and to 'enter into or maintain any professional partnership unless the primary purpose of each partner's respective profession is the practice of the law'. Wouters and his colleagues claimed that the decisions of the Amsterdam and Rotterdam Bar, as well as the 1993 Regulation, were incompatible with the Treaty provisions on competition, right of establishment and freedom to provide services.]

Question 1(a)

56 The question to be determined is whether, when it adopts a regulation such as the 1993 Regulation, a professional body is to be treated as an association of undertakings or, on the contrary, as a public authority.

[The Court answered that the bar is to be treated as an association of undertakings.] * * *

Question 2

73 By its second question the national court seeks, essentially, to ascertain whether a regulation such as the 1993 Regulation which, in order to guarantee the independence and loyalty to the client of members of the Bar who provide legal assistance in conjunction with members of other liberal professions, adopts universally binding rules governing the formation of multi-disciplinary partnerships, has the object or effect of restricting competition within the common market and is likely to affect trade between Member States. * * *

84 The prohibition at issue in the main proceedings prohibits all contractual arrangements between members of the Bar and accountants which provide in any way for shared decision-making, profit-sharing or for the use of a common name, and this makes any form of effective partnership difficult. * * *

---

50 EU:C:2002:98.

CASE *(continued)*

86   It appears to the Court that the national legislation in issue in the main proceedings has an adverse effect on competition and may affect trade between Member States.

87   As regards the adverse effect on competition, the areas of expertise of members of the Bar and of accountants may be complementary. Since legal services, especially in business law, more and more frequently require recourse to an accountant, a multi-disciplinary partnership of members of the Bar and accountants would make it possible to offer a wider range of services, and indeed to propose new ones. Clients would thus be able to turn to a single structure for a large part of the services necessary for the organisation, management and operation of their business (the 'one-stop shop' advantage).

88   Furthermore, a multi-disciplinary partnership of members of the Bar and accountants would be capable of satisfying the needs created by the increasing interpenetration of national markets and the consequent necessity for continuous adaptation to national and international legislation.

89   Nor, finally, is it inconceivable that the economies of scale resulting from such multi-disciplinary partnerships might have positive effects on the cost of services.

90   A prohibition of multi-disciplinary partnerships of members of the Bar and accountants, such as that laid down in the 1993 Regulation, is therefore liable to limit production and technical development within the meaning of Article [101](1)(b) of the Treaty. * * *

97   However, not every agreement between undertakings or every decision of an association of undertakings which restricts the freedom of action of the parties or of one of them necessarily falls within the prohibition laid down in Article [101](1) of the Treaty. For the purposes of application of that provision to a particular case, account must first of all be taken of the overall context in which the decision of the association of undertakings was taken or produces its effects. More particularly, account must be taken of its objectives, which are here connected with the need to make rules relating to organisation, qualifications, professional ethics, supervision and liability, in order to ensure that the ultimate consumers of legal services and the sound administration of justice are provided with the necessary guarantees in relation to integrity and experience. . . . It has then to be considered whether the consequential effects restrictive of competition are inherent in the pursuit of those objectives.

98   Account must be taken of the legal framework applicable in the Netherlands, on the one hand, to members of the Bar and to the Bar of the Netherlands, which comprises all the registered members of the Bar in that Member State, and on the other hand, to accountants. * * *

102   [The members of the Bar] should be in a situation of independence vis-à-vis the public authorities, other operators and third parties, by whom they must never be influenced. They must

CASE (continued)

furnish, in that respect, guarantees that all steps taken in a case are taken in the sole interest of the client.

103 By contrast, the profession of accountant is not subject, in general, and more particularly, in the Netherlands, to comparable requirements of professional conduct. * * *

105 . . . The Bar of the Netherlands was entitled to consider that members of the Bar might no longer be in a position to advise and represent their clients independently and in the observance of strict professional secrecy if they belonged to an organisation which is also responsible for producing an account of the financial results of the transactions in respect of which their services were called upon and for certifying those accounts. * * *

107 A regulation such as the 1993 Regulation could therefore reasonably be considered to be necessary in order to ensure the proper practice of the legal profession, as it is organised in the Member State concerned. * * *

NOTES AND QUESTIONS

1. Describe the harm to competition likely to result from the bar's regulatory rule.
2. Would a similar self-regulatory restraint be caught by Article 101(1) TFEU if imposed by non-professionals, or by non-lawyers? May accountants agree that accounting firms may not combine with economists' firms? May plumbing firms agree not to allow their members to be electricians or contractors?
3. Why is the lawyers' restraint not subject to examination under Article 101(3) TFEU? Analyse the bar rule under Article 101(3). Does it satisfy the conditions?
4. In *Cipolla* and *Macrino*, Italy set a mandatory minimum fee schedule for lawyers based on a schedule prepared by a lawyers' association. The minimum fee requirement disadvantaged out-of-state lawyers (among others) in their attempts to compete by discounting. The Court of Justice acknowledged that the measure restrained cross-border services, but held that the restraint could be justified if it met overriding requirements relating to the public interest such as protection of consumers and administration of justice, and if the restraint was proportional to the objective. What is the measure's probable effect on consumers (clients)? What is the public interest in setting a minimum fee? Do you think a public interest concern can outweigh the harm to consumers? Is *Cipolla* consistent with the principles of Article 61 TFEU (Member States may not impair free movement of services based on nationality or residence)? With the combination of Article 4(3) TEU (Member State duty of loyalty to facilitate the tasks of the Union), and Articles 61, 101, and 102 TFEU? See Chapter 7 as to the permissibility of the State restraint.
5. In the US, lawyers may not lawfully agree among themselves that no law firm will integrate with an accountants' or economists' firm. But lawyers (bar associations) may and do propose that State courts adopt such a rule; and State courts typically mandate the separation as a 'rule of ethics'. State court rules are State action and are not subject to antitrust. Is mandated separation of lawyer/economist/accountant firms wise, efficient, good for clients?

3. The environment and competitiveness

EU policy supports environmental measures and the integration of environmental concerns into the various Community policies (see Article 3(3) TEU). In its 1998 Competition Policy Report,[51] the Commission summarized as follows its activity regarding competition and the environment:

> 129 At the Cardiff European Summit, the Member States recalled the provisions of the Treaty of Amsterdam [Article 6] stipulating that Community policies should take account of environmental protection with a view to achieving sustainable development, an approach which was endorsed at the Vienna Summit. In its XXVth Report on Competition Policy, the Commission spelt out its position regarding implementation of the Community competition rules in the environmental field. In particular, it stated: 'When the Commission examines individual cases, it weighs up the restrictions of competition arising out of an agreement against the environmental objectives of the agreement, and applies the principle of proportionality in accordance with Article [101](3). In particular, improving the environment is regarded as a factor which contributes to improving production or distribution or to promoting economic or technical progress.' In that connection, 1998 was marked by four cases reflecting the Commission's commitment to take a positive approach to environmental issues in its competition analyses.
>
> 130 The Commission approved the agreement signed by the European Association of Consumer Electronics Manufacturers (EACEM) and 16 of its members, all major manufacturers of television sets and video cassette recorders. This agreement is a voluntary commitment to reduce the electricity consumption of this equipment when it is in stand-by mode. The Commission exempted the agreement under Article [101](3) on the ground that the energy-saving and environmental benefits of the scheme clearly represented technical and economic progress and, by their nature, would be passed on to consumers. The energy saving could amount to 3.2 TWh a year from 2005. This reduction in energy consumption will have a significant impact in terms of the management of energy resources, reductions in CO_2 emissions and, accordingly, measures to counter global warming. The Commission also ascertained that the scheme would not eliminate competition in the affected markets and that its restrictive effect was essential to achieving its full benefits.
>
> 131 The Association of European Automobile Manufacturers (ACEA) has undertaken, on behalf of its members, to reduce CO_2 emissions from passenger

---

51 Available at: http://ec.europa.eu/competition/publications/annual_report/1998/en.pdf (accessed 2 June 2017).

cars. This effort is in line with the Community policy of reducing CO_2 emissions into the atmosphere. ACEA has set a reduction target of 25% by 2008. The Commission and the Member States will monitor the efforts made to achieve that target. The Commission also took the view that this agreement between European automobile manufacturers did not infringe the competition rules. ACEA determines an average reduction target for all its members, but each of them is free to set its own level, which will encourage them to develop and introduce new CO_2-efficient technologies independently and in competition with one another. Accordingly, ACEA's voluntary agreement does not constitute a restriction of competition and is not caught by Article [101](1).

132   [EUCAR is the European Council for Automotive Research and Development. It consists of Opel, BMW (including Rover), Mercedes, Fiat, Ford PSA, Porsche, Renault, VW and Volvo.] In the *EUCAR* case, the Commission adopted a favourable stance on a cooperation agreement between Europe's leading motor manufacturers which is designed to boost research in the [European] motor industry, particularly on environmental issues. Most of the projects that will be developed involve experimental research on, for example, limiting noise or emission pollution caused by motor vehicles. The products obtained from this research may not be directly usable in a specific type of vehicle. The Commission therefore took the view that the research was at the pre-competitive stage and that the agreements did not infringe Community law.

133   Finally, the Commission approved the membership agreements of Valpak, a non-profit-making, industry-led compliance scheme operating in the United Kingdom which has been set up to discharge the packaging waste recovery and recycling obligations of its members. The legal framework set up in the United Kingdom to implement the [EU] directive [on packaging waste] provides scope for competition in the market for compliance-scheme services which seek to fulfil recovery and recycling obligations on behalf of a business. While Valpak is currently the largest compliance scheme operating in the United Kingdom, other competing schemes exist and have notified their arrangements to the Commission.

134   Following its examination of Valpak's membership agreements, the Commission concluded that the agreements restricted competition within the meaning of Article [101](1) because they obliged businesses wishing to join the scheme to transfer the totality of their obligations in all packaging materials. This 'all or nothing' approach, which transposes a regulatory provision, restricts the extent to which Valpak and other schemes will be able to compete against one another on a material-specific basis. The Commission went on to consider whether the notified arrangements could benefit from exemption under Article [101](3). In view of the emerging nature of the market and the likelihood that Valpak and other schemes

would be obliged to invest in the United Kingdom's collection and/or reprocessing infrastructure in order to meet their members' obligations in the future, the Commission concluded that an 'all or nothing' approach was necessary, at least in the short term, if schemes such as Valpak were to succeed in securing sufficient funding to allow the necessary investment to take place. The Commission informed Valpak at the same time that it reserved the right to reexamine the case after three years.

NOTES AND QUESTIONS

1. Consider, with respect to each agreement described above, the possible harm to competition. Is each agreement caught by Article 101(1)? Do you agree with the Commission's analysis regarding when an exemption is necessary?
2. A Danish recycling law limited bottle types for beer and soft drinks sold in Denmark, creating an obstacle to out-of-state beer and soft drink sellers. The limitation of bottle types—to those most commonly used in Denmark—facilitated recycling and helped protect the environment.[52] Suppose the restraint was imposed by agreement among the Danish beverage makers and their retailers, rather than by the legislature of Denmark. Analyse the agreement. Does it fall within Article 101(1) TFEU? Does it satisfy the conditions of Article 101(3)? Suppose the Danish beverage makers make a convincing case that the proliferation of non-recyclable bottles will impose serious costs on the environment. How should the Commission make the trade-off between free movement, competition and the environment?
3. May the European beef processors agree not to supply beef to wholesalers or retailers that sell beef injected with hormones?
4. Under US antitrust law, an agreement that has anti-competitive aspects can be justified only by outbalancing procompetitive aspects.[53] Even if competitive price-bidding by professional engineers would cause engineers to cut corners and design unsafe buildings, the engineers may not decide to ban price-bidding. Regulation should specify minimum safety standards for building designs. How would each of the above agreements described in the Competition Policy Report fare under US law? Which is the better approach—that of the US or of the EU? Or are they effectively the same?

CECED
Commission Decision, Case IV/F-1/36.718[54]

[Almost all producers and importers of washing machines in Europe entered into an agreement designed to reduce energy consumption and thereby to reduce polluting emissions from washing machines. The agreement was notified to the Commission by their trade association, the European Council of Domestic Appliance Manufacturers ('CECED'). Under the agreement, the producers and importers agreed to stop producing for, and importing into, the EU the least energy efficient washing machines, designated as categories D to G by a Commission Directive. Categories D to G represented 10–11% of all washing machines sold in the EU, and

---

52 See Case 302/86, *Commission v. Denmark* [1988] ECR 4607, EU:C:1988:421.
53 *National Society of Professional Engineers v. United States*, 435 U.S. 679, 98 S.Ct. 1355, 55 L.Ed.2d 637 (1978).
54 [2000] O.J. L 187/47.

comprised a significant proportion of the sales of some of the agreeing manufacturers. Energy efficiency was an import focus of advertising and sales. The market was fragmented. The agreeing manufacturers accounted for more than 95% of the market.

The Commission granted a short (less than one-year) exemption, stating, as to the four conditions of Article 101(3) TFEU:]

— The agreement objectively contributes to technical and economic progress, by focusing production on more efficient machines. Such benefits would be unlikely or would occur less quickly without the agreement.
— Consumers derive benefits at the same time individually and for society as a whole: likely higher purchase costs of more efficient washing machines are quickly compensated by savings in electricity bills; the agreement contributes to [EU] environmental objectives and the benefits very largely exceed potential cost increases triggered as a result of the agreement. Even if individual purchasers were not to derive the financial benefits that they actually attain, the magnitude of environmental benefits is such that the net contribution to society's economic welfare would still be positive.
— The restrictions of competition are indispensable to attaining those benefits. Consumers do not sufficiently take external costs into account in their purchase decisions. The application of a minimum efficiency ratio mitigates this market failure. Alternatives such as public awareness campaigns or application of ecolables would be complementary, rather than substitutable to the agreement.
— The agreement does not eliminate competition. Various technical means to improve energy efficiency of washing machines are economically available to all manufacturers; competition remains also on important purchase criteria such as prices, technical effectiveness, brand image etc.; finally, 90% of sales of washing machines are not directly concerned.

NOTES AND QUESTIONS

1. Are you confident that consumer benefits of the washing machine agreement outweigh costs? What about the consumers who prefer the low price, or other features of machines that happen to fall within categories D to G, and who prefer not to be altruistic?
2. What is the significance of the fact that some of the collaborating manufacturers made D-to-G machines? Would the agreement be more suspect if none of them did? Even so, can we trust these producers to set the standard in the public interest?
3. Suppose you represent a Canadian manufacturer whose washing machines are low priced, offer features householders love, and fall within category D. Your client's machines are relatively new, and its European fortunes—and market share—are fast rising. It is suddenly faced with a private European boycott. Your client and its loyal European consuming public consider a suit to annul the Commission decision granting exemption. Frame your analysis of the anti-competitive effects of the CECED agreement. Review each of the four requirements for exemption. Which are most vulnerable? What are your odds of winning in court?

4. If the EU wanted energy standards that excluded machines in categories D to G, why did it not adopt legislation setting an energy efficiency floor that excluded those categories?
5. Might the Commission exemption constitute a blockage of market access to exporters from other nations in violation of the General Agreement on Tariffs and Trade ('GATT')? Article XI of the GATT prohibits states from imposing quantitative restrictions on imports. Article XX provides a derogation for a State measure necessary for health and safety; this must be backed up by scientific evidence.
6. Having in mind the cases involving labour, the liberal professions, the environment, and competitiveness, comment on how the Community seeks to blend its competition enforcement with other public policy goals. Has it achieved a wise balance? Is it wise to try to achieve a balance? Are non-competition justifications admissible? Why do you think the Commission did not want the Member States to apply non-competition offsets to competition harms?

E. Block exemptions

As noted at the outset of the chapter, there are two important block exemptions on horizontal cooperation: research and development, and specialization. The Commission last updated these block exemptions in 2010.

1. Research and development

Research and development ('R&D') lies at the core of innovation, competition, and competitiveness. The R&D block exemption singles out cooperative research and development for protection. The block exemption is contained in Commission Regulation 1217/2010.[55]

Of course not all R&D agreements fall within Article 101(1) TFEU. Collaborations between small enterprises are normally not caught. Moreover, collaboration on pure R&D even by large firms generally does not fall within Article 101(1) unless the parties agree not to carry out R&D in the same field.

Pursuant to Article 101(3) TFEU, the regulation declares exempt joint R&D and joint exploitation of its results, and necessary ancillary restraints including agreement not to carry out independently or with third parties R&D in the same or a closely related field, as long as the parties' market share does not exceed 25% and the agreement does not include blacklisted clauses. Moreover, to qualify for block exemption: (1) each party must have access to the results in order to further its research; (2) the parties must grant each other access to any pre-existing know-how that is indispensable for the

---

55 Regulation 1217/2010/EU of 14 December 2010 on the application of Article 101(3) of the Treaty on the Functioning of the European Union to certain categories of research and development agreements [2010] O.J. L 335/36, available at: http://ec.europa.eu/competition/antitrust/legislation/horizontal.html (accessed 2 June 2017).

granting of the results; (3) the supplying partner, in the event of specialization not entailing joint distribution, must fulfil orders for supplies from other partners; and (4) in the event of joint exploitation, the results must be IP-protected and must be sufficiently important; they must 'be indispensable for the manufacture of the contract products or the application of the contract technologies' (Article 3(4)). The regulation contains a blacklist of clauses that disqualify agreements from exemption (Article 5).

In the same year that the EU adopted its first block exemption for joint R&D, the US Congress enacted the National Cooperative Research Act ('NCRA') of 1984, which was amended in 1993.[56] The US Congress feared that the antitrust laws were chilling R&D, especially in view of the fact that successful private plaintiffs in US antitrust lawsuits are entitled to three times the damages they suffer ('treble damages'). The NCRA states that research joint ventures shall be judged under a rule of reason in view of all relevant market facts and shall not be condemned per se. Also, the Act provides a notification procedure. If a transaction is notified and is later found to lessen competition, the parties can be assessed compensatory damages but not treble damages. This protection applies to the production phase of a research joint venture but only if the principal production facilities are in the US and the controlling persons are American or from a country with equally favourable antitrust treatment. (Is this consistent with GATT obligations of non-discrimination?) A notified transaction may be enjoined if it is found to be anti-competitive. The NCRA applies equally to large and small firms.

Would you expect the European block exemption to encourage R&D? Would you expect the US statute to encourage research and development?

2. Specialization

The specialization block exemption is provided by Commission Regulation 1218/2010.[57]

At the outset, the Commission contemplated reciprocal specialization: one firm made product *A*, the other made complementary product *B*; they would each agree to supply their specialty product to the other, and they would each agree not to manufacture the product that was the specialty

---

56 15 U.S.C.A. § 4301.
57 Regulation 1218/2010/EU of 14 December 2010 on the application of Article 101(3) of the Treaty on the Functioning of the European Union to certain categories of specialization agreements [2010] O.J. L 335/43, available at: http://ec.europa.eu/competition/antitrust/legislation/horizontal.html (accessed 2 June 217).

of the other. More recently, firms began to adopt unilateral specialization: A outsources from B; B agrees to manufacture and supply to A all of its needs of an input; A agrees to cease its production of that input. The 2010 block exemption covers reciprocal specialization and unilateral specialization between competitors. The regulation recites that specialization agreements generally contribute to improving production or distribution because they enable firms to concentrate on the manufacture of certain products and thus to operate more efficiently and supply goods more cheaply.

The specialization regulation declares exempt agreements for specialization, including ancillary restraints necessary for their implementation, where the combined market shares do not exceed 20%, except for agreements containing blacklisted provisions. The exemption also applies where the parties agree to exclusive purchase or supply in the context of specialization or joint production, or the parties do not separately distribute the objects of specialization but provide for joint distribution or distribution by a non-competitor (Article 2(3)). The exemption does not apply to agreements that have as their object price fixing to third parties, limiting output or sales, or allocating markets or customers (Article 4).

Why is it necessary for competitors, seeking to achieve the efficiency benefits of specialization, to promise to stay out of the manufacturing market of the other? In the US, this aspect of specialization agreements would normally be regarded as a cartel-like violation of the law unless the parties could show that the commitment was necessary to make the joint venture work.

* * *

The study of horizontal co-operation agreements has allowed for a discussion of Article 101(3) and of the interplay between Article 101(1) and 101(3) TFEU, in a way that cartels did not. It also permitted to substantiate the 'economic approach' underlying the analytical framework developed in the Article 101(3) guidelines, which echoes the shift to effects-based analysis that the Commission initiated in the late 1990s, as noted in Chapter 1. Often presented as the substantive leg of the modernisation process, that type of analysis was originally introduced in relation to vertical agreements, the area to which the next chapter is devoted.

4

Vertical restraints

A. Vertical restraints and their effects

Vertical restraints are restraints in the course of distributing a product or service, or in the course of bringing technology and its commercial applications to market. They involve 'agreement or concerted practice entered into between two or more undertakings each of which operates, for the purposes of the agreement or the concerted practice, at a different level of the production or distribution chain, and relating to the conditions under which the parties may purchase, sell or resell certain goods or services.'[1]

In distribution agreements, a producer might instruct its distributor where or to whom to sell the product, and at what price. Since a producer offers a particular kind or brand of product, the restraints that a producer imposes on its distributors are called intrabrand restraints. Intrabrand restraints may help a producer get to market more efficiently, e.g., by giving the distributor a stronger incentive to work its territory and by preventing 'free riders' (who do not invest in the territory) from 'skimming the cream' off the top of the demand primed by the designated distributor's investment. If the restraints are cost-effective and if the brands in the market compete robustly against one another, the interbrand competition may ensure that consumers receive the benefits of the restraints.

However, intrabrand restraints may also help the producer *exploit* the consumer. For example, in a concentrated, high-barrier market, the restraints may help the few producers coordinate their prices; or they may help an individual producer that has market power extract more money from consumers. They may also suppress innovation in the methods and systems of distribution,

---

[1] Regulation 330/2010/EU on the application of Article 101(3) TFEU to categories of vertical agreements and concerted practices [2010] O.J. L 102/1, Article 1(a).

such as the Internet. Moreover, vertical restraints may be procured by powerful distributors to help form a distributor cartel. For these reasons, resale price fixing agreements that set minimum prices, resale price maintenance ('RPM'), are regarded as a hardcore restraint in the EU (although justification is possible) and in many other jurisdictions. Economists, however, point out that RPM can be an efficient business strategy to induce distributors to provide more service. In view of efficient uses of RPM that may increase interbrand competition, the US eventually abandoned its nearly century-old per se rule against RPM agreements (see below the discussion on the *Leegin* case).

Other vertical restraints include exclusive selling ('I will sell to you alone and not to your competitors'), exclusive buying (single branding or requirements contracts), selective distribution, franchising, tying contracts, and export restrictions. Technology licensing restrictions are also a form of vertical restraint.

Historically, the EU has developed a particular approach towards vertical restraints influenced by the objective of integrating the common market. At the heart of that approach lie concerns such as whether intrabrand restraints that prevent parallel imports can calcify price differentials among Member States and undermine the market integration goal. But the corollary concern is whether prohibiting those restraints may equally undermine the efficiency goal. Hence, vertical restraints raise the question of the possible existence of a tension between integration and efficiency.

Note on the effect of modernisation

Until the final years of the 1990s, vertical restraints were regarded in the EU with great suspicion. This was especially true of restraints that could tend to keep a seller's product from crossing Member State borders, for the restraint then had a market integration dimension as well.

Several block exemptions were adopted, in particular on exclusive distribution, exclusive purchasing and franchising, designed not only to give more certainty to business but also to regulate and generally suppress vertical restraints. The area became rule-bound with a heavy hand, rather than concept or theory-driven. The effect was not unlike the effect and treatment in the US through the 1960s and early 1970s, where, too, vertical restraints were treated with much suspicion; for example, they were regarded as schemes by powerful producers to rein in the autonomy of their distributors, thereby also depriving consumers of the benefits that more autonomous distributors would bring; or as schemes to fence out rivals.

In the US a sea-change came in the late 1970s and continued to evolve through the 2006 term of the US Supreme Court when, in *Leegin*, it overturned the per se rule against agreements that fix resale prices.[2] As illustrated by *Leegin*, the contemporary US perspective is hospitable towards vertical restraints, regarding them as a normally efficient means to get to market and seldom capable of aggrandizing market power.

In the EU the inhospitality perspective lasted until the late 1990s when the Directorate-General for Competition rethought the appropriate analysis of vertical restraints and, in 1997, published a green paper which proposed a more economic, more sympathetic, and less restrictive approach. Block exemptions were liberalized in 2000 and again in 2010. Less restrictive block exemptions were regarded as a wise methodology to give guidance and more certainty.[3]

The remainder of this chapter consists of a discussion of the EU courts' case law on parallel imports and exports, exclusive purchasing, tying and other foreclosures, selective distribution, franchising, before turning in more detail to the study of the existing block exemptions. As you read the cases, be aware of their dates of decision; particularly whether they were decided before June 1999, when the notification process was abolished for vertical restraints. Consider how the earlier cases might be decided under modern economic concepts, influenced as always by the market integration goals. Remember that the process of notification and individual exemption is a mode of the past; but still, agreements must be analysed under the Treaty provisions, Article 101(1) and (3).

B. Is there an agreement within Article 101(1)?

Normally a vertical agreement will fall within Article 101(1) if the restraint is not de minimis and the restraint has an impact on intrabrand competition (see *Consten and Grundig*, discussed again below) or interbrand competition. This will be especially so where the supplier imposes obligations on its distributor not to buy from its competitors, or imposes customer, territory or price restraints or requires a tie-in, unless the restraints are objectively

---

2 *Leegin Creative Products, Inc. v. PSKS, Inc.*, 551 U.S. 877, 127 S.Ct. 2705, 168 L.Ed.2d 623 (2007).
3 The relevant block exemption and accompanying guidelines can be found at: http://ec.europa.eu/competition/antitrust/legislation/vertical.html (accessed 5 June 2017).

necessary, for example, to penetrate a market or to guard against a health or safety hazard.

Would proof that robust interbrand competition would protect consumer welfare take the agreement out of Article 101(1)? Why might this point still matter despite elimination of the notification requirement?

An important battleground is whether an agreement is present at all, for unilateral conduct does not fall within Article 101 TFEU. In *Bayer v. Commission* ('*Adalat*'),[4] Bayer as producer of the cardio-vascular-treating drug Adalat, faced several Member States with widely varying price ceilings. The controlled price in France and Spain was 40% lower than in the UK. Certain wholesale customers of Bayer France and Bayer Spain increased their orders disproportionately, clearly to take advantage of the higher profits in the UK. In response, Bayer France and Bayer Spain limited fulfilment of orders to the quantities expected to be demanded in the territory. Allegedly, the wholesalers acquiesced in the *de facto* export ban in order to continue receiving supplies. The Commission found that the conduct was concerted and violated Article 101(1) TFEU. It imposed a fine of €3 million euros. The General Court annulled the decision, however, concluding that there was no 'common intention' between Bayer and the wholesalers. It said:

> 71 Th[e] case law shows that a distinction should be drawn between cases in which an undertaking has adopted a genuinely unilateral measure, and thus without the express or implied participation of another undertaking, and those in which the unilateral character of the measure is merely apparent. Whilst the former do not fall within Article [101](1) of the Treaty, the latter must be regarded as revealing an agreement between undertakings and may therefore fall within the scope of that article. That is the case, in particular, with practices and measures in restraint of competition which, though apparently adopted unilaterally by the manufacturer in the context of its contractual relations with its dealers, nevertheless receive at least the tacit acquiescence of those dealers.

C. Parallel imports and exports, and dual pricing

The first vertical restraint case to reach the Court was *Consten and Grundig*,[5] as discussed in Chapter 1. Reread the case at p. 23 above, and the excerpts from the *Pioneer* and *Volkswagen* cases following it.

---

4 Case T-41/96, *Bayer v. Commission* [2000] ECR II-3383, EU:T:2000:242.
5 Joined Cases 56 and 58/64, *Consten and Grundig* [1966] ECR 299, EU:C:1966:41.

Note on *Distillers Company Ltd v. Commission*

Distillers Company Ltd ('DCL'), the world's largest seller of Scotch whiskey, established 38 subsidiaries producing spirits in the UK. It accounted for approximately 70% of all gin sales in the UK, 30% to 50% of Scotch whiskey in the UK, and lower percentages on the Continent.

DCL imposed the following conditions of sale:

(a) '[T]he various allowances, rebates and discounts are designed to meet the particular requirements of the home trade and customers are only entitled to them when the goods are in fact consumed within the UK.'
(b) 'Accordingly, if you wish to buy for export to other Common Market countries you must indicate this on your order and purchase must be made at the gross price.'
(c) '... If ... a customer obtains or claims any home trade allowances, rebates or discounts in respect of goods which he has bought and any of those goods turn up in any country outside the UK, the right is reserved for all companies in the DCL group to sell thereafter to such customer only at the gross price.'

The punitive measures were to be applicable in the following circumstances:

> When a DCL subsidiary has a reasonable belief that any quantity of goods bought by the purchaser from any DCL subsidiary has been or will be consumed outside the United Kingdom;

> even when the exports are made by a subsequent purchaser;

> regardless of the quantity ordered, until and to the extent that the purchaser produces evidence satisfactory to the selling DCL subsidiary company that the goods will be consumed in the United Kingdom.

When investigated by the Commission, DCL claimed that its dual pricing was justified by the following facts: In the UK its brands were very well known, prices were depressed by price controls, and DCL sold directly to very large and powerful brewery groups that had retail outlets and that demanded very low prices. Outside of the UK, the brands were unknown. Moreover, France banned advertisements, and some countries imposed discriminatory taxes. DCL had to invest significant additional amounts of money for promotion on the Continent if it was to sell there at all.

The Commission declared that DCL's price agreements would not be granted an exemption under Article 101(3) because the dual pricing system interfered with parallel imports and isolated the UK market. Distillers then withdrew Johnnie Walker Red Label and Dimple Haig whiskeys from sale in the UK, stating that it could not make sales at the higher price in the UK and it could not cover promotion costs if it sold at the lower price on the Continent. It announced a new brand to replace Johnnie Walker. DCL sued for annulment of the Commission's decision. The Court of Justice held, simply, that the legal effect of DCL's failure to notify the price terms was that the price terms could not be exempted.[6]

NOTES AND QUESTIONS

1. Could Consten and Grundig meet the requirements of Article 101(3) TFEU today? Would the evidence of interbrand competition be excluded today?

    Consten and Grundig is generally understood as a market integration case. Imposing tight territorial restrictions at Member State lines is anathema to the market integration principle of the EU. Should it be? Might such territorial assignments and allocations increase the efficiency of distribution? Note that the vertical block exemption (Regulation 330/2010, as discussed below), applicable for under 30% market shares, recognizes the efficiency of territorial assignments and generally allows them as long as distributors may accept unsolicited bids from outside of the territory. Thus, distributors can be subject to active restraints (not to solicit actively outside of the territory), but not to passive restraints.

2. Did DCL's price agreements 'isolate' the UK market? How? Would DCL be likely to satisfy Article 101(3) TFEU today?

3. *GlaxoSmithKline* put a dent in the unwavering EU rule against restraints of parallel imports.

CASE

GlaxoSmithKline Services Unlimited v. Commission (Case T-168/01) (Spanish price ceiling)[7]

[Spanish legislation capped the price of pharmaceuticals sold to pharmacies and hospitals and covered by Spanish reimbursement rules. GlaxoSmithKline ('GSK'), a major pharmaceutical producer, made agreements with its wholesalers that for all other products (i.e. pharmaceuticals not for the domestic market), GSK would charge a price set by objective economic factors, and that this would be the price that GSK had initially proposed to the Spanish government as the reimbursement price plus a cost-of-living adjustment (clause 4 of the General Sales Conditions). The Commission found that the clause violated Article 101

---

6 Case 30/78, *Distillers Company Ltd v. Commission* [1980] ECR 229, EU:C:1980:186.
7 [2006] ECR II-2969, EU:T:2006:265 (upheld in Joined Cases C-501, C-513, C-515 and C-519/06 P [2009] ECR I-9291, EU:C:2009:610).

CASE *(continued)*

TFEU. In so holding, the Commission discounted GSK's arguments and evidence as to the virtues and advantages of Clause 4. GSK petitioned the General Court to annul the Commission's decision.]

295   In the light of the structure of GSK's arguments and also of the discussion of that point during the administrative procedure, the Decision could not avoid examining, first of all, whether parallel trade led to a loss in efficiency for the pharmaceutical industry in general, and for GSK in particular. . . .

296   However, a comparison of the evidence provided by GSK with the other evidence invoked by the Commission in the Decision clearly reveals that in the medicines sector the effect of parallel trade on competition is ambiguous, since the gain in efficiency to which it is likely to give rise for intrabrand competition, the role of which is limited by the applicable regulatory framework, must be compared with the loss in efficiency to which it is likely to give rise for interbrand competition, the role of which is central.

297   In those circumstances, the Commission could not refrain from examining, second, whether Clause 4 of the General Sales Conditions could enable GSK's capacity for innovation to be reinstated and thus could give rise to a gain in efficiency for interbrand competition.

298   That, moreover, formed the very core of the prospective analysis which the Commission was under a duty to carry out in order to respond to GSK's request for an exemption. According to the consistent case-law cited . . ., it is necessary to determine whether the agreement prohibited on account of the disadvantage which it represents for competition (Article [101(1)]) presents an advantage of such a kind as to offset that disadvantage (Article [101(3)]).

299   The Commission was therefore still required to examine GSK's arguments relating to the advantages expected of Clause 4 of the General Sales Conditions. In that regard, recital 156 to the Decision, the only recital susceptible of attesting to an examination on that point, indicates essentially:

> '[I]t is a matter of discretion for pharmaceutical companies to decide how much they wish to invest in R&D. Any savings they might hypothetically make by preventing parallel trade would therefore not automatically lead to higher R&D investments. It is conceivable that these savings might merely be added to the companies' profits. Obviously, the generation of extra profits alone cannot justify an exemption. In this regard, GSK's argument would mean that the first condition for [the application of Article [101(3)] would be fulfilled for every agreement that could be said to contribute to an increase in the revenues of a firm engaged in R&D. The condition would in any case be meaningless, since it is in the nature of any agreement restricting competition to be likely to increase a firm's earnings.'

CASE (continued)

300 However, GSK did not claim that the creation of additional profits would in itself justify an exemption. On the contrary, it maintained that parallel trade prevented it from making the profits necessary for the optimum financing of its R&D, that Clause 4 of the General Sales Conditions would enable it to increase its revenues and that it would have every interest, in the light of the fierce interbrand competition, of the central role played by innovation in that competition and of the methods of financing R&D, in investing a part of this surplus in R&D in order to overtake its competitors or to ensure that it would not be overtaken by them. In other words, it claimed that its General Sales Conditions should be exempted because they would have not merely the immediate effect of increasing its revenues, but above all the secondary effect of increasing its capacity for innovation. Furthermore, it maintained that that advantage must be compared with the fact that, when it was obtained by parallel traders, that surplus did not constitute an advantage, because, not being obliged to engage in genuine competition among themselves, the parallel traders reduced prices only to the extent necessary to attract retailers and therefore kept most of that surplus for themselves, as GSK again submitted at the hearing.

301 The Commission could not merely reject those arguments outright on the ground that the advantage described by GSK would not necessarily be achieved, as it did at recital 156 to the Decision, but was required, in accordance with the case-law, also to examine, as specifically as possible, in the context of a prospective analysis, whether, in the particular circumstances of the case and in the light of the evidence submitted to it, it seemed more likely that the advantages described by GSK would be achieved or, on the contrary, that they would not. It was not entitled to consider, in a peremptory manner and without providing proper arguments, that the factual arguments and the evidence submitted by GSK must be regarded as hypothetical, as it maintained most recently at the hearing. * * *

303 It follows from the foregoing that the Decision is vitiated by a failure to carry out a proper examination, as the Commission did not validly take into account all the factual arguments and the evidence pertinently submitted by GSK, did not refute certain of those arguments even though they were sufficiently relevant and substantiated to require a response, and did not substantiate to the requisite legal standard its conclusion that it was not proved, first, that parallel trade was apt to lead to a loss in efficiency by appreciably altering GSK's capacity for innovation and, second, that Clause 4 of the General Sales Conditions was apt to enable a gain in efficiency to be achieved by improving innovation.

The balancing exercise * * *

306 . . . [T]he Commission's finding that Clause 4 of the General Sales Conditions restricts competition is well founded only in so far as it finds that Clause 4 has the effect of depriving

CASE *(continued)*

final consumers of medicines reimbursed by a national sickness insurance scheme of the advantage which they would have derived, in regard to prices and costs, from the participation of the Spanish wholesalers in intrabrand competition on the markets of destination of the parallel trade from Spain.

307 Consequently, the Commission's conclusion that there is no need to carry out a balancing exercise, which would show in any event that the advantage associated with Clause 4 does not offset the disadvantage which it represents for competition, cannot be upheld. The Commission was required, first, to conduct an appropriate examination of GSK's factual arguments and evidence, in order to be in a position to carry out, second, the complex assessment necessary in order to weigh up the disadvantage and the advantage associated with Clause 4 of the General Sales Conditions.

Conclusion

308 It follows from the foregoing that the Commission could not lawfully conclude that, as regards the existence of a contribution to the promotion of technical progress, GSK had not demonstrated that the first condition for the application of Article [101(3)] was satisfied. In those circumstances, there is no need to examine GSK's arguments relating to a contribution to the improvement of the distribution of medicines.

c) Evidence of the advantage being passed on to the consumer, of the indispensability of Clause 4 of the General Sales Conditions and of the absence of the elimination of competition * * *

315 . . . In effect, the fact that Clause 4 of the General Sales Conditions prevents the limited pressure which might exist, owing to parallel trade from Spain, on the price and the cost of medicines in the geographic markets of destination must be related to the facts, put forward by GSK and not disputed by the Commission, that competition by innovation is very fierce in the sector and that competition on price exists in another form, although by law it emerges only when, upon expiry of the patent, manufacturers of generic medicines are able to enter the market. In those circumstances, it was still necessary . . . to assess what form of competition must be given priority with a view to ensuring the maintenance of effective competition sought by Article 3(1)(g) EC [now in a protocol] and Article [101].

4.   *Conclusion* * * *

317 Accordingly, the Decision must be annulled in so far as, in Article 2, it rejects GSK's request for an exemption.

NOTES AND QUESTIONS

1. On reconsideration, what must the Commission establish, or decide on the basis of sufficient evidence, to deny the exemption? What must GSK establish to entitle it to an exemption? Is the Commission well placed to conduct the balancing exercise?
2. Is *GSK* a small or large wedge in the door of allowing restraints on parallel imports if justified by (imperative?) considerations of efficiency and innovation? Is the holding likely to be limited to pharmaceuticals?

    A related case arose in Greece, wherein GSK's Greek subsidiary, GSK AEVE, cut back the supply of medicines to wholesalers who sold into higher-priced export markets. The wholesalers sued. GSK AEVE justified on grounds of the Greek price-capping legislation; the claim that the trans-shipping wholesalers, not the consumer, profit from parallel imports/exports; and the claim that GSK AEVE had to stem the tide of low-priced exports for the sake of its investments in R&D. The Greek court referred questions to the Court of Justice. The Court, applying Article 102, confirmed the strong principle against restraints on parallel trade but allowed an exception.

CASE

Sot. Lelos KAI SIA EE v. GlaxoSmithKline AEVE (Joined Cases C-468 to C-478/06)[8]

52 The first thing to consider is GSK AEVE's argument that parallel trade in any event brings only few financial benefits to the ultimate consumers.

53 In that connection, it should be noted that parallel exports of medicinal products from a Member State where the prices are low to other Member States in which the prices are higher open up in principle an alternative source of supply to buyers of the medicinal products in those latter States, which necessarily brings some benefits to the final consumer of those products.

54 It is true, as GSK AEVE has pointed out, that, for medicines subject to parallel exports, the existence of price differences between the exporting and the importing Member States does not necessarily imply that the final consumer in the importing Member State will benefit from a price corresponding to the one prevailing in the exporting Member State, inasmuch as the wholesalers carrying out the exports will themselves make a profit from that parallel trade.

55 Nevertheless, the attraction of the other source of supply which arises from parallel trade in the importing Member State lies precisely in the fact that that trade is capable of offering the same products on the market of that Member State at lower prices than those applied on the same market by the pharmaceuticals companies.

---

[8] [2008] ECR I-7139, EU:C:2008:504.

CASE *(continued)*

56 As a result, even in the Member States where the prices of medicines are subject to State regulation, parallel trade is liable to exert pressure on prices and, consequently, to create financial benefits not only for the social health insurance funds, but equally for the patients concerned, for whom the proportion of the price of medicines for which they are responsible will be lower. At the same time, as the Commission notes, parallel trade in medicines from one Member State to another is likely to increase the choice available to entities in the latter Member State which obtain supplies of medicines by means of a public procurement procedure, in which the parallel importers can offer medicines at lower prices.

57 Accordingly, without it being necessary for the Court to rule on the question whether it is for an undertaking in a dominant position to assess whether its conduct vis-à-vis a trading party constitutes abuse in the light of the degree to which that party's activities offer advantages to the final consumers, it is clear that, in the circumstances of the main proceedings, such an undertaking cannot base its arguments on the premiss that the parallel exports which it seeks to limit are of only minimal benefit to the final consumers. * * *

65 In relation to the application of Article [101] of the . . . Treaty, the Court has held that an agreement between producer and distributor which might tend to restore the national divisions in trade between Member States might be such as to frustrate the objective of the Treaty to achieve the integration of national markets through the establishment of a single market. Thus on a number of occasions the Court has held agreements aimed at partitioning national markets according to national borders or making the interpenetration of national markets more difficult, in particular those aimed at preventing or restricting parallel exports, to be agreements whose object is to restrict competition within the meaning of that Treaty article. * * *

67 Although the degree of price regulation in the pharmaceuticals sector cannot therefore preclude the Community rules on competition from applying, the fact nonetheless remains that, when assessing, in the case of Member States with a system of price regulation, whether the refusal of a pharmaceuticals company to supply medicines to wholesalers involved in parallel exports constitutes abuse, it cannot be ignored that such State intervention is one of the factors liable to create opportunities for parallel trade.

68 Furthermore, in the light of the Treaty objectives to protect consumers by means of undistorted competition and the integration of national markets, the Community rules on competition are also incapable of being interpreted in such a way that, in order to defend its own commercial interests, the only choice left for a pharmaceuticals company in a dominant position is not to place its medicines on the market at all in a Member State where the prices of those products are set at a relatively low level. * * *

CASE (continued)

70   In that respect, and without it being necessary to examine the argument raised by GSK AEVE that it is necessary for pharmaceuticals companies to limit parallel exports in order to avoid the risk of a reduction in their investments in the research and development of medicines, it is sufficient to state that, in order to appraise whether the refusal by a pharmaceuticals company to supply wholesalers involved in parallel exports constitutes a reasonable and proportionate measure in relation to the threat that those exports represent to its legitimate commercial interests, it must be ascertained whether the orders of the wholesalers are out of the ordinary.

71   Thus, although a pharmaceuticals company in a dominant position, in a Member State where prices are relatively low, cannot be allowed to cease to honour the ordinary orders of an existing customer for the sole reason that that customer, in addition to supplying the market in that Member State, exports part of the quantities ordered to other Member States with higher prices, it is nonetheless permissible for that company to counter in a reasonable and proportionate way the threat to its own commercial interests potentially posed by the activities of an undertaking which wishes to be supplied in the first Member State with significant quantities of products that are essentially destined for parallel export.

72   In the present cases, the orders for reference show that, in the disputes which gave rise to those orders, the appellants in the main proceedings have demanded not that GSK AEVE should fulfil the orders sent to it in their entirety, but that it should deliver them quantities of medicines corresponding to the monthly average sold during the first 10 months of 2000. In six of the 11 actions in the main proceedings, the appellants asked for those quantities to be increased by a certain percentage, which was fixed by some of them at 20%.

73   In those circumstances, it is for the referring court to ascertain whether the abovementioned orders are ordinary in the light of both the previous business relations between the pharmaceuticals company holding a dominant position and the wholesalers concerned and the size of the orders in relation to the requirements of the market in the Member State concerned. * * *

76   . . . [A] producer of pharmaceutical products must be in a position to protect its own commercial interests if it is confronted with orders that are out of the ordinary in terms of quantity. Such could be the case, in a given Member State, if certain wholesalers order from that producer medicines in quantities which are out of all proportion to those previously sold by the same wholesalers to meet the needs of the market in that Member State.

77   In view of the foregoing, the answer to the questions referred should be that Article 102 must be interpreted as meaning that an undertaking occupying a dominant position on the relevant market for medicinal products which, in order to put a stop to parallel exports

CASE (continued)

carried out by certain wholesalers from one Member State to other Member States, refuses to meet ordinary orders from those wholesalers is abusing its dominant position. It is for the national court to ascertain whether the orders are ordinary in the light of both the size of those orders in relation to the requirements of the market in the first Member State and the previous business relations between that undertaking and the wholesalers concerned. * * *

? NOTES AND QUESTIONS

1. Did GSK AEVE's constraint on supply to the wholesaler/exporters harm market integration? How? Did it have positive as well as negative effects for consumers (people needing medications)? Does the rule of the case tend to limit the negative effects (higher prices in a neighbouring State) while freeing up pro-competitive aspects (more innovation, made possible by sales at market price or above)? Or is the rule calibrated to something else entirely, such as fairness to traditional customers?
2. How will the rule of the case make a difference—to the conduct of GSK AEVE, to consumers, to likelihood of innovation?

D. Resale price maintenance: Europe, and a view from the US

Like Europe, the US took a sceptical stance towards vertical restraints for many years, believing that they impaired the give-and-take dynamic of the competition process and thus harmed powerless market actors and consumers. US antitrust law condemned, per se, agreements between a manufacturer and a distributor as to the price, customers or territories at which, to whom, or where the distributor must sell.

The Chicago School revolution began to take root in the late 1970s and found particularly fertile ground after the election of Ronald Reagan in 1980. One centrepiece claim of Chicago was the perversity of inhospitality towards vertical restraints. Chicago School theorists saw vertical restraints as a way to realize efficiencies and compete in interbrand markets. If a number of producers occupied a market and there was no conspiracy among them, each one would have the incentive to design its distribution system in a way most likely to get to market efficiently and to sell the most it could of its product. No one could get market power by a vertical restraint. Indeed, even if there were few producers (but no cartel) or a monopoly producer with the power to charge a supra-competitive price, each would take its profit from its first sale (e.g., to wholesalers) and still would have the incentive to design its distribution system in order to serve consumers efficiently. After the Chicago

School revolution began, the Supreme Court overturned the vertical per se rules, one by one. By 2007, there was only one remaining per se rule against a vertical distribution restraint—the nearly century-old rule against minimum resale price maintenance agreements.[9] This rule was challenged in *Leegin*, as discussed below.

Meanwhile, Europe and many other jurisdictions, as well as states of the US, likewise condemned RPM agreements. In Europe they were held to fall categorically into Article 101(1) because they have the object to restrict competition (albeit intrabrand competition). They are recognized as a hardcore violation in the vertical block exemption regulation and vertical guidelines. They may be entitled to an Article 101(3) exemption in particular instances, as in the case of newspaper and periodical distribution where RPM constitutes 'the sole means of supporting the financial burden resulting from the taking back of unsold copies . . . if the latter practice constitutes the sole method by which a wide selection of newspapers and periodicals can be made available to readers. . . .' The decision-maker 'must take account of those factors . . .'.[10]

In the US, the eyes turned to *Leegin*.

CASE

Leegin Creative Leather Products, Inc. v. PSKS, Inc.[11]

[Leegin was a small designer, producer and distributor of leather accessories, including belts it sold under the brand name 'Brighton'. It sold its products across the US in more than 5000 retail stores.

PSKS, which operates Kay's Kloset, was a women's apparel store in Lewisville, Texas. It bought the Brighton brand from Leegin in 1995. While it bought from many other manufacturers as well, Brighton was its most important brand.

In 1997, Leegin established a policy of not selling to retailers who sold Brighton goods below its suggested prices. It explained that it thought consumers were 'perplexed by promises of product quality and support of product which we believe is lacking in . . . larger stores.'

---

9 *Dr Miles Medical Co. v. John D. Park & Sons*, 220 U.S. 373, 31 S.Ct. 376, 55 L.Ed. 502 (1911).
10 Case 243/83, *SA Binon & Cie v. SA Agence et Messageries de la Presse* [1995] ECR 2015, EU:C:1985:284, paras. 44–46.
11 551 U.S. 877, 127 S.Ct. 2705, 168 L.Ed.2d 623 (2007).

CASE (continued)

Consumers are further confused by the ever popular sale, sale, sale, etc.' Leegin wanted to 'break away from the pack by selling [at] specialty stores' that offer consistently great quality merchandise and support.

PSKS pledged to adhere to the suggested prices, but later marked down its Brighton line by 20% to compete with nearby retailers. Leegin demanded that PSKS stop discounting, and when PSKS refused, Leegin stopped supplying its belts to PSKS. PSKS sued. At trial, in view of *Dr Miles*, the district court excluded Leegin's proffer of testimony regarding the pro-competitive effect of its pricing policy. The jury found that Leegin had entered into vertical resale price agreements, and returned a verdict for PSKS, amounting as trebled to a judgement of nearly $4 million.

The Court granted certiorari to determine whether resale price maintenance should continue to be per se illegal.]

JUSTICE KENNEDY * * *

Resort to *per se* rules is confined to restraints, like those mentioned [competitor price-fixing or market division], 'that would always or almost always tend to restrict competition and decrease output.' *Business Electronics*, [485 U.S.] at 723. To justify a *per se* prohibition a restraint must have 'manifestly anticompetitive' effects, and 'lack . . . any redeeming virtue,' . . . * * *

The reasons upon which *Dr. Miles* relied do not justify a *per se* rule. As a consequence, it is necessary to examine, in the first instance, the economic effects of vertical agreements to fix minimum resale prices, and to determine whether the *per se* rule is nonetheless appropriate.

A
* * *

The justifications for vertical price restraints are similar to those for other vertical restraints. Minimum resale price maintenance can stimulate interbrand competition—the competition among manufacturers selling different brands of the same type of product—by reducing intrabrand competition—the competition among retailers selling the same brand. The promotion of interbrand competition is important because 'the primary purpose of the antitrust laws is to protect [this type of] competition.' *Khan*, 522 U.S., at 15. A single manufacturer's use of vertical price restraints tends to eliminate intrabrand price competition; this in turn encourages retailers to invest in tangible or intangible services or promotional efforts that aid the manufacturer's position as against rival manufacturers. Resale price

CASE (continued)

maintenance also has the potential to give consumers more options so that they can choose among low-price, low-service brands; high-price, high-service brands; and brands that fall in between.

Absent vertical price restraints, the retail services that enhance interbrand competition might be underprovided. This is because discounting retailers can free ride on retailers who furnish services and then capture some of the increased demand those services generate. Consumers might learn, for example, about the benefits of a manufacturer's product from a retailer that invests in fine showrooms, offers product demonstrations, or hires and trains knowledgeable employees. Or consumers might decide to buy the product because they see it in a retail establishment that has a reputation for selling high-quality merchandise. If the consumer can then buy the product from a retailer that discounts because it has not spent capital providing services or developing a quality reputation, the high-service retailer will lose sales to the discounter, forcing it to cut back its services to a level lower than consumers would otherwise prefer. Minimum resale price maintenance alleviates the problem because it prevents the discounter from undercutting the service provider. With price competition decreased, the manufacturer's retailers compete among themselves over services.

Resale price maintenance, in addition, can increase interbrand competition by facilitating market entry for new firms and brands. '[N]ew manufacturers and manufacturers entering new markets can use the restrictions in order to induce competent and aggressive retailers to make the kind of investment of capital and labour that is often required in the distribution of products unknown to the consumer.' *GTE Sylvania*, [433 U.S.] at 55.... New products and new brands are essential to a dynamic economy, and if markets can be penetrated by using resale price maintenance there is a procompetitive effect.

Resale price maintenance can also increase interbrand competition by encouraging retailer services that would not be provided even absent free riding. It may be difficult and inefficient for a manufacturer to make and enforce a contract with a retailer specifying the different services the retailer must perform. Offering the retailer a guaranteed margin and threatening termination if it does not live up to expectations may be the most efficient way to expand the manufacturer's market share by inducing the retailer's performance and allowing it to use its own initiative and experience in providing valuable services....

B

While vertical agreements setting minimum resale prices can have procompetitive justifications, they may have anticompetitive effects in other cases; and unlawful price fixing, designed solely to obtain monopoly profits, is an ever present temptation. Resale price maintenance may, for example, facilitate a manufacturer cartel. An unlawful cartel will seek

CASE *(continued)*

to discover if some manufacturers are undercutting the cartel's fixed prices. Resale price maintenance could assist the cartel in identifying price-cutting manufacturers who benefit from the lower prices they offer. Resale price maintenance, furthermore, could discourage a manufacturer from cutting prices to retailers with the concomitant benefit of cheaper prices to consumers.

Vertical price restraints also 'might be used to organize cartels at the retailer level.' A group of retailers might collude to fix prices to consumers and then compel a manufacturer to aid the unlawful arrangement with resale price maintenance. In that instance the manufacturer does not establish the practice to stimulate services or to promote its brand but to give inefficient retailers higher profits. Retailers with better distribution systems and lower cost structures would be prevented from charging lower prices by the agreement. . . .

A horizontal cartel among competing manufacturers or competing retailers that decreases output or reduces competition in order to increase price is, and ought to be, *per se* unlawful. To the extent a vertical agreement setting minimum resale prices is entered upon to facilitate either type of cartel, it, too, would need to be held unlawful under the rule of reason. This type of agreement may also be useful evidence for a plaintiff attempting to prove the existence of a horizontal cartel.

Resale price maintenance, furthermore, can be abused by a powerful manufacturer or retailer. A dominant retailer, for example, might request resale price maintenance to forestall innovation in distribution that decreases costs. A manufacturer might consider it has little choice but to accommodate the retailer's demands for vertical price restraints if the manufacturer believes it needs access to the retailer's distribution network. A manufacturer with market power, by comparison, might use resale price maintenance to give retailers an incentive not to sell the products of smaller rivals or new entrants. As should be evident, the potential anticompetitive consequences of vertical price restraints must not be ignored or underestimated.

C

Notwithstanding the risks of unlawful conduct, it cannot be stated with any degree of confidence that resale price maintenance 'always or almost always tend[s] to restrict competition and decrease output.' *Business Electronics* . . . . As the [*per se*] rule would proscribe a significant amount of procompetitive conduct, these agreements appear ill suited for *per se* condemnation. * * *

Respondent also argues the *per se* rule is justified because a vertical price restraint can lead to higher prices for the manufacturer's goods . . . . Respondent is mistaken in relying on pricing

> **CASE** (continued)
>
> effects absent a further showing of anticompetitive conduct.... For, as has been indicated already, the antitrust laws are designed primarily to protect interbrand competition, from which lower prices can later result. The Court, moreover, has evaluated other vertical restraints under the rule of reason even though prices can be increased in the course of promoting procompetitive effects. And resale price maintenance may reduce prices if manufacturers have resorted to costlier alternatives of controlling resale prices that are not *per se* unlawful.
>
> Respondent's argument, furthermore, overlooks that, in general, the interests of manufacturers and consumers are aligned with respect to retailer profit margins....
>
> * * *
>
> Resale price maintenance, it is true, does have economic dangers. If the rule of reason were to apply to vertical price restraints, courts would have to be diligent in eliminating their anticompetitive uses from the market. This is a realistic objective, and certain factors are relevant to the inquiry. For example, the number of manufacturers that make use of the practice in a given industry can provide important instruction. When only a few manufacturers lacking market power adopt the practice, there is little likelihood it is facilitating a manufacturer cartel, for a cartel then can be undercut by rival manufacturers. Likewise, a retailer cartel is unlikely when only a single manufacturer in a competitive market uses resale price maintenance. Interbrand competition would divert consumers to lower priced substitutes and eliminate any gains to retailers from their price-fixing agreement over a single brand. Resale price maintenance should be subject to more careful scrutiny, by contrast, if many competing manufacturers adopt the practice....
>
> The source of the restraint may also be an important consideration. If there is evidence retailers were the impetus for a vertical price restraint, there is a greater likelihood that the restraint facilitates a retailer cartel or supports a dominant, inefficient retailer. If, by contrast, a manufacturer adopted the policy independent of retailer pressure, the restraint is less likely to promote anticompetitive conduct....
>
> As a final matter, that a dominant manufacturer or retailer can abuse resale price maintenance for anticompetitive purposes may not be a serious concern unless the relevant entity has market power. If a retailer lacks market power, manufacturers likely can sell their goods through rival retailers....
>
> The rule of reason is designed and used to eliminate anticompetitive transactions from the market. This standard principle applies to vertical price restraints. A party alleging injury from a vertical agreement setting minimum resale prices will have, as a general matter, the

CASE *(continued)*

information and resources available to show the existence of the agreement and its scope of operation. As courts gain experience considering the effects of these restraints by applying the rule of reason over the course of decisions, they can establish the litigation structure to ensure the rule operates to eliminate anticompetitive restraints from the market and to provide more guidance to businesses. . . .* * *

JUSTICE BREYER, joined by JUSTICES STEVENS, SOUTER and GINSBURG, dissenting: [After noting information that prices go up when minimum resale pricing is allowed, citing a study showing a 19% to 27% price rise during the period of fair trading laws, and cataloguing possible harms and benefits of resale price maintenance:] * * *

The case before us asks which kind of approach the courts should follow where minimum resale price maintenance is at issue. Should they apply a per se rule (or a variation) that would make minimum resale price maintenance always (or almost always) unlawful? Should they apply a 'rule of reason'? Were the Court writing on a blank slate, I would find these questions difficult. But, of course, the Court is not writing on a blank slate, and that fact makes a considerable legal difference. * * *

The upshot is, as many economists suggest, sometimes resale price maintenance can prove harmful; sometimes it can bring benefits. . . . But before concluding that courts should consequently apply a rule of reason, I would ask such questions as, how often are harms or benefits likely to occur? How easy is it to separate the beneficial sheep from the antitrust goats? * * *

Economic discussion, such as the studies the Court relies upon, can *help* provide answers to these questions, and in doing so, economics can, and should, inform antitrust law. But antitrust law cannot, and should not, precisely replicate economists' (sometimes conflicting) views. That is because law, unlike economics, is an administrative system the effects of which depend upon the content of rules and precedents only as they are applied by judges and juries in courts and by lawyers advising their clients. And that fact means that courts will often bring their own administrative judgement to bear, sometimes applying rules of *per se* unlawfulness to business practices even when those practices sometimes produce benefits. . . .

I have already described studies and analyses that suggest (though they cannot prove) that resale price maintenance can cause harms with some regularity—and certainly when dealers are the driving force. But what about benefits? How often, for example, will the benefits to which the Court points occur in practice? I can find no economic consensus on this point. There is a consensus in the literature that 'free riding' takes place. But 'free riding' often takes place in the economy without any legal effort to stop it. Many visitors to California take free rides on the Pacific Coast Highway. We all benefit freely from ideas, such as that of creating the first supermarket. Dealers often take a 'free ride' on investments that others have made in

> **CASE** *(continued)*
>
> building a product's name and reputation. The question is how often the 'free riding' problem is serious enough significantly to deter dealer investment.
>
> To be more specific, one can easily *imagine* a dealer who refuses to provide important presale services, say a detailed explanation of how a product works (or who fails to provide a proper atmosphere in which to sell expensive perfume or alligator billfolds), lest customers use that 'free' service (or enjoy the psychological benefit arising when a high-priced retailer stocks a particular brand of billfold or handbag) and then buy from another dealer at a lower price. Sometimes this must happen in reality. But does it happen often? We do, after all, live in an economy where firms, despite *Dr. Miles*' *per se* rule, still sell complex technical equipment (as well as expensive perfume and alligator billfolds) to consumers. * * *
>
> All this is to say that the ultimate question is not whether, but *how much*, 'free riding' of this sort takes place. And, after reading the briefs, I must answer that question with an uncertain 'sometimes.' . . .
>
> How easily can courts identify instances in which the benefits are likely to outweigh potential harms? My own answer is, *not very easily*. For one thing, it is often difficult to identify *who*—producer or dealer—is the moving force behind any given resale price maintenance agreement . . . . For another thing, as I just said, it is difficult to determine just when, and where, the 'free riding' problem is serious enough to warrant legal protection. * * *
>
> I recognize that scholars have sought to develop check lists and sets of questions that will help courts separate instances where anticompetitive harms are more likely from instances where only benefits are likely to be found. But applying these criteria in court is often easier said than done. The Court's invitation to consider the existence of 'market power,' for example, invites lengthy time-consuming argument among competing experts, as they seek to apply abstract, highly technical, criteria to often ill-defined markets. And resale price maintenance cases, unlike a major merger or monopoly case, are likely to prove numerous and involve only private parties. One cannot fairly expect judges and juries in such cases to apply complex economic criteria without making a considerable number of mistakes, which themselves may impose serious costs. . . .
>
> Are there special advantages to a bright-line rule? Without such a rule, it is often unfair, and consequently impractical, for enforcement officials to bring criminal proceedings. And since enforcement resources are limited, that loss may tempt some producers or dealers to enter into agreements that are, on balance, anticompetitive.
>
> . . . The question before us is not what should be the rule, starting from scratch. We here must decide whether to change a clear and simple price-related antitrust rule that the courts have applied for nearly a century. * * *

Meanwhile, while the US Supreme Court considered and reversed the US ban on resale price maintenance agreements, the European Commission was re-examining its treatment of vertical restraints including RPM. In 2010, it issued a revised block exemption and vertical guidelines.[12] Read Regulation 330/2010 containing the block exemption. You will note that the regulation exempts vertical agreements where the seller occupies less than 30% of the market and the buyer accounts for less than 30% of purchases, unless the agreement contains a hardcore restriction. Minimum RPM is a hardcore restriction. It could theoretically get an individual exemption under Article 101(3), but this would be rare. Become familiar with the block exemption and the vertical guidelines that relate to RPM. (See Guidelines on Vertical Restraints, point 2.10, paras. 223–229.)

NOTES AND QUESTIONS

1. In the US *Leegin* case, who has the stronger argument, Justice Kennedy or Justice Breyer?
2. Under US law, 'rule of reason' entails analysis of the market facts to determine whether the undertaking is likely to get or increase market power, harming consumers, as a result of the challenged conduct or practice. The Court, per Justice Kennedy, said: 'just' raising price is not equivalent to harm to consumers. The higher price might mean more service or more demand. (Is this perspective accepted in Europe?) In some cases, rule of reason analysis can involve shortcuts; e.g., if the challenged conduct is usually harmful a presumption might be applied, and the conduct might be declared illegal unless the undertaking comes forward with an efficiency justification. This is called a structured rule of reason. If you were to suggest a structured rule of reason for RPM, what would that rule be? Is your proposed rule likely to be acceptable to Justice Kennedy?
3. Consider the US Court's assertions: protecting interbrand competition is 'the primary purpose of the antitrust laws'; higher prices are irrelevant 'absent a further showing of anticompetitive conduct'.
4. Compare the European block exemption and guidelines with the US *Leegin* case. What different perceptions do you observe about the possible harms and possible benefits of RPM? Is the structure of analysis, including burdens of proof, likely to lead to different results? What would be the outcome of the *Leegin* case (agreement not to discount a minor brand of fine belts) in each jurisdiction—US after trial, and EU?

The above sections looked at distribution restraints of the sort that constrain the choices of chosen distributors as to the price at which they must sell or the customers to whom or territories in which they may sell. Other vertical restraints require exclusive buying or selling, force the distributor to buy unwanted items or to buy only from designated sellers, foreclose outsiders from entering the distribution network, or, as in franchising, combine several of the above restraints to foster uniformity. As you read cases decided before approximately the year 2000, and especially cases denying or conditioning

---

12 Accessible at: *http://ec.europa.eu/competition/antitrust/legislation/vertical.html* (accessed 5 June 2017).

exemptions, consider whether those cases accord with the new economic approach, which would protect consumers and the market from uses of market power. Note that cases of exclusionary conduct entail many of the same concepts as do abuse of dominance cases under Article 102 TFEU. Indeed, if the undertaking is dominant, an anti-competitive exclusionary agreement can be condemned under both Articles 101 and 102 TFEU.

E. Single branding (exclusive purchasing), tying and related foreclosures

A producer or other seller of a product may wish to obligate its distributor or other buyers to buy the product, or a portion of its needs, only from the seller, or to buy a second product from the seller. For example, in *Hoffmann-La Roche*, p. 194 below, vitamin producer Merck contracted with the dominant vitamin producer Hoffmann-La Roche to buy from Roche its needs of vitamin B_6 in excess of its own manufacturing capacity. And in *Tetra Pak*, p. 218 below, the dominant supplier of aseptic cartons for milk and juice required buyers to buy, also, their needs of non-aseptic cartons. In both cases the Court condemned the restraints as abuses of dominance in violation of Article 102 TFEU on the grounds that they 'deprive[d] the purchaser of or restrict[ed] his possible choices of sources of supply and ... den[ied] other producers access to the market' (quoting from *Hoffmann-La Roche*).

Exclusive, single-branding, requirements or tie-in contracts may also be caught by Article 101(1) TFEU. Under what conditions? How and when can they be justified under Article 101(3) TFEU?

CASE

Stergios Delimitis v. Henninger Bräu AG (Case C-234/89)[13]

[Stergios Delimitis rented a pub from Henninger Bräu, agreeing to sell only Henninger Bräu beer in the pub. Asserting that the contract violated Article 101 TFEU and was void, Delimitis failed to pay rent, and Henninger deducted the rent from Delimitis' rental deposit. Delimitis sued for return of the rent. Henninger relied on the contract, which presumably was not intended to harm competition but reflected the brewery's desire for an assured outlet for its beer and Delimitis' desire for the premises and an assured supply.

---

13 [1991] ECR I-935, EU:C:1991:91.

CASE (continued)

The national court sought a preliminary ruling on whether the contract was caught by Article 101(1) TFEU and if so whether it fell within the then block exemption on exclusive purchasing. The Court of Justice set forth the following framework for determining whether exclusive contracts that are part of a network of similar contracts have the effect, if not the object, of 'preventing, restricting or distorting competition':]

15 ... [I]t is necessary to analyse the effects of a beer supply agreement, taken together with other contracts of the same type, on the opportunities of national competitors or those from other Member States, to gain access to the market for beer consumption or to increase their market share and, accordingly, the effects on the range of products offered to consumers.
* * *

18 [The relevant market is] the national market for beer distribution in premises for the sale and consumption of drinks.

19 In order to assess whether the existence of several beer supply agreements impedes access to the market as so defined, it is further necessary to examine the nature and extent of those agreements in their totality, comprising all similar contracts tying a large number of points of sale to several national producers. The effect of those networks of contracts on access to the market depends specifically on the number of outlets thus tied to national producers in relation to the number of public houses which are not so tied, the duration of the commitments entered into, the quantities of beer to which those commitments relate, and on the proportion between those quantities and the quantities sold by free distributors.

20 The existence of a bundle of similar contracts, even if it has a considerable effect on the opportunities for gaining access to the market, is not, however, sufficient in itself to support a finding that the relevant market is inaccessible, inasmuch as it is only one factor, amongst others, pertaining to the economic and legal context in which an agreement must be appraised. The other factors to be taken into account are, in the first instance, those also relating to opportunities for access.

21 In that connection it is necessary to examine whether there are real concrete possibilities for a new competitor to penetrate the bundle of contracts by acquiring a brewery already established on the market together with its network of sales outlets, or to circumvent the bundle of contracts by opening new public houses. For that purpose it is necessary to have regard to the legal rules and agreements on the acquisition of companies and the establishment of outlets, and to the minimum number of outlets necessary for the economic operation of a distribution system. The presence of beer wholesalers not tied to producers who are active on the market is also a factor capable of facilitating a new producer's access to that market since he can make use of those wholesaler's sales networks to distribute his own beer.

CASE (continued)

22   Secondly, account must be taken of the conditions under which competitive forces operate on the relevant market. In that connection it is necessary to know not only the number and the size of producers present on the market, but also the degree of saturation of that market and customer fidelity to existing brands, for it is generally more difficult to penetrate a saturated market in which customers are loyal to a small number of large producers than a market in full expansion in which a large number of small producers are operating without any strong brand names. . . .

23   If an examination of all similar contracts entered into on the relevant market and the other factors relevant to the economic and legal context in which the contract must be examined shows that those agreements do not have the cumulative effect of denying access to that market to new national and foreign competitors, the individual agreements comprising the bundle of agreements cannot be held to restrict competition within the meaning of Article [101](1) of the Treaty. They do not, therefore, fall under the prohibition laid down in that provision.

24   If, on the other hand, such examination reveals that it is difficult to gain access to the relevant market, it is necessary to assess the extent to which the agreements entered into by the brewery in question contribute to the cumulative effect produced in that respect by the totality of the similar contracts found on that market. Under the Community rules on competition, responsibility for such an effect of closing off the market must be attributed to the breweries which make an appreciable contribution thereto. Beer supply agreements entered into by breweries whose contribution to the cumulative effect is insignificant do not therefore fall under the prohibition under Article [101](1). * * *

27   The reply to be given to the first three questions is therefore that a beer supply agreement is prohibited by Article [101](1) of the Treaty, if two cumulative conditions are met. The first is that, having regard to the economic and legal context of the agreement at issue, it is difficult for competitors who could enter the market or increase their market share to gain access to the national market for the distribution of beer in premises for the sale and consumption of drinks. The fact that, in that market, the agreement in issue is one of a number of similar agreements having a cumulative effect on competition constitutes only one factor amongst others in assessing whether access to that market is indeed difficult. The second condition is that the agreement in question must make a significant contribution to the sealing-off effect brought about by the totality of those agreements in their economic and legal context. The extent of the contribution made by the individual agreement depends on the position of the contracting parties in the relevant market and on the duration of the agreement.

NOTES AND QUESTIONS

1. *Delimitis* was considered a break-through judgement, prior to which single-branding contracts with significant producers were deemed almost automatically caught by Article 101(1) TFEU and thus were in need of justification.
2. What do you suppose was Delimitis' theory of the case—and its theory of antitrust harm?

CASE

Schöller Lebensmittel v. Commission (Case T-9/93)[14]

[Langnese-Iglo, a subsidiary of Unilever, and Schöller Lebensmittel were the leading firms in Germany in the sale of ice cream; particularly impulse-buying ice cream. Each, separately, had a network of agreements with the sellers requiring that the retailers purchase ice cream only from it, or supplying freezers 'free' and requiring that the retailer use the freezer only for the supplier's ice cream and not for the ice cream of competitors.

Mars, a French manufacturer of ice cream bars, was trying to pierce the German impulse ice cream market. Finding the two firms' supply contracts to be road blocks to market access, Mars complained to the Commission. The Commission brought proceedings against each. The Commission withdrew a comfort letter that it had previously given to Schöller and decided both the question of applicability of Article 101(1) TFEU and the question of entitlement of the applicants to an individual exemption.

In *Schöller*, the Court first examined whether the contested supply agreements had an appreciable effect on competition. It found 'that the applicant holds a strong position in the relevant market'; it held 'more than 25 per cent' in the traditional trade, and, by its agreements, tied more than 10% of the sales outlets. Combined with Langnese's contracts, the tied portion of the market exceeded 30%.]

83   With respect to [other] factors, the Commission has drawn attention to the existence of additional substantial barriers to access to the market, both in the grocery trade and in the traditional trade. . . . [A]ccess to the market for new competitors is made more difficult by the existence of a system under which a large number of freezer cabinets are lent by the applicant to retailers both in the grocery trade and in the traditional trade . . ., the retailers being obliged to use them exclusively for the applicant's products.

84   The Court considers that the Commission was right to treat that factor as contributing to making access to the market more difficult. The necessary consequence of that situation is

---

14   See also Case T-7/93, *Langnese-Iglo v. Commission* [1995] ECR II-1533, EU:T:1995:98, as upheld in Case C-279/95 P, [1998] ECR I-5609, EU:C:1998:447.

CASE *(continued)*

that any new competitor entering the market must either persuade the retailer to exchange the freezer cabinet installed by the applicant for another, which involves giving up the turnover in the products from the previous supplier, or to persuade the retailer to install an additional freezer cabinet, which may prove impossible, particularly because of lack of space in small sales outlets. Moreover, if the new competitor is able to offer only a limited range of products, as in the case of the intervener, it may prove difficult for it to persuade the retailer to terminate its agreement with the previous supplier. * * *

86   . . . [T]he Court considers that examination of all the similar agreements concluded on the market and of other aspects of the economic and legal context in which they operate . . . shows that the exclusive purchasing agreements concluded by the applicant are liable appreciably to affect competition within the meaning of Article [101](1) of the Treaty.

87   In view of the strong position occupied by the applicant in the relevant market and, in particular, its market share, the Court considers that the agreements contribute significantly to the closing-off of the market.

88   In view of all the foregoing, the Court considers that the Commission was right to conclude that the contested agreements give rise to an appreciable restriction of competition in the relevant market. * * *

139   In considering whether the Commission was right to refuse to grant an individual exemption, it must first be borne in mind that an individual exemption decision may be granted only if, in particular, the four conditions laid down by Article [101](3) of the Treaty are all met by the agreement in question, with the result that an exemption must be refused if any of the four conditions is not met. * * *

143   . . . Although it is apparent . . . that exclusive purchasing agreements lead in general to an improvement in distribution, in that they enable the supplier to plan the sale of his goods with greater precision and for a longer period and ensure that the reseller's requirements will be met on a regular basis for the duration of the agreement, and even if it is assumed that it would be necessary for the applicant, for reasons of cost, to terminate supplies to certain small sales outlets if it were obliged to give up supplies to them on an exclusive basis, the Commission considers nevertheless that the contested agreements do not give rise to objective and specific advantages for the public interest such as to compensate for the disadvantages which they cause in the field of competition.

144   In support of that argument, the Commission states, first, that, in view of the strong position on the market held by the applicant, the contested agreements do not . . . have the effect of intensifying competition between different brands of products. The Commission

CASE (continued)

rightly took the view that the network of agreements at issue constitutes a major barrier to access to the market, with the result that competition is restricted.

145   ... [It is clear] that the Commission considered that supplies to any small sales outlets abandoned by the applicant, for reasons of costs, would be taken over either by other suppliers, for example small local producers, or by independent dealers selling several ranges of products. Moreover, the Commission points out that the applicant itself recognised that it continues to supply even very small sales outlets, whose annual turnover hovers around 300 German marks, in those cases where their geographical situation is favourable.

146   Against that background, it must be borne in mind that the intervener, Mars, stated that it is wholly exceptional for impulse products to be distributed using a transport system owned by the producers. The parties agree that it is only in Germany, Denmark and Italy that undertakings in the Unilever group, including Langnese, have concluded exclusive agreements covering sales outlets.

147   Although the applicant claims that it would be obliged, for reasons of cost, to cease supplying a number of small sales outlets if it had to give up its exclusive purchasing agreements, the Court considers that it has not provided any evidence to show that such a situation would be liable to jeopardise regular supplies of impulse ice-cream to the territory as a whole and, in particular, that the small sales outlets concerned would not subsequently be supplied by other suppliers or wholesalers, simply as a consequence of the unrestricted competition which would then prevail. Nor has the applicant produced any convincing evidence of the special conditions in Germany which made it necessary to create an ice-cream distribution system belonging to the producers. The Court therefore considers that the applicant has not shown that the Commission committed a manifest error of assessment in considering that the contested agreements did not fulfil the first condition laid down by Article [101](3) of the Treaty....***

NOTES AND QUESTIONS

1. Is an impulse ice cream market in Germany plausible? If Schöller supplied the entire market, could it probably raise its prices to a supra-competitive level without losing so many customers (to packaged ice cream or something else) that the price rise would not be worth it? (Assume that the answer is affirmative as you proceed to analyse the problem.)
2. Did Schöller have market power? Is market power important to the decision? Should it be?
3. What were the effects of the exclusivity and freezer clauses on competitors? On potential competitors? On consumers? Which effects are most important?
4. What were the efficiencies of the exclusive supply contracts? Of the 'free' freezer arrangements? How, in your view, do the efficiencies balance against the anti-competitive aspects of the agreements? What was the Court's view?

5. What was the strongest case for granting the exemption? Was the Commission right to deny it?
6. If you were Mars and if you could not expect the European Commission to grant you relief from your competitors' exclusivity and freezer clauses, what strategies would you adopt?
7. If Schöller and Langnese withdrew the exclusivity obligation and offered retailers the choice of (a) freezers for sale at market price, (b) freezers for rent at market price, or (c) freezers 'free' with an obligation to use only the supplier's ice cream in the freezer, would the new arrangement be permissible? What if virtually all of the retailers chose option (c)?[15]
8. The Irish court took an entirely different view of the freezer arrangement and its effects. Masterfoods (Mars) had been enlisting numerous retailers in Ireland to stock and display Mars bars in their freezers. HB Ice-cream (of the Unilever family) ('HB'), the dominant impulse ice cream seller in Ireland, sought to enforce its exclusive contracts with the retailers. In 1992, it persuaded an Irish court to permanently restrain Mars from inducing breach of HB's contracts. The Irish court, per Judge Lynch, analysed the contracts as follows:

> I think that a breach of paragraph (e) [distorting competition by imposing unrelated obligations] does not arise at all in this case. The contracts in question are bailments of freezers whether they be on loan or hire. The terms objected to relate to the very basis of the contract of bailment, namely, the purpose for which the goods (the freezers) are bailed to the bailee (the retailer). The freezers are bailed to the bailees for the purpose of storing, selling and advertising HB ice cream products only. Those terms are not supplementary obligations nor by their nature or according to commercial usage do they not have an essential connection with the contracts of bailment. They do. It would seem that none of the particular breaches set out in paragraphs (a) to (e) of Article [101](1) apply: certainly, none clearly apply to the facts of Article [101] if it was reasonably clear that there was a contravention of the general intention of the article. Is it reasonably likely that these contracts of bailment of freezers may affect trade between Member States of the European Community and may prevent, restrict or distort competition within the common market? I am not satisfied that Mars has made out a sufficient prima facie or serious case to that effect.[16]

Masterfoods complained to the European Commission about the exclusivity clauses and the Irish court injunction. The Commission, after finding that 40% of sales outlets in Ireland were tied up by the exclusivity clause, held:

> [T]he exclusivity provision in the freezer-cabinet agreement concluded between HB and retailers in Ireland, for the placement of cabinets in retail outlets which have only one or more freezer cabinets supplied by HB for the stocking of single-wrapped items of impulse ice cream, and not having a freezer cabinet either procured by themselves or provided by another ice-cream manufacturer constitutes an infringement of Article [101](1) of the Treaty. ***

> HB's inducement to retailers in Ireland to enter into freezer-cabinet agreements subject to a condition of exclusivity by offering to supply them with one or more freezer cabinets for the stocking of single-wrapped items of impulse ice cream and to maintain the

---

15 See Commission Decision of 4 September 1998 in Cases IV/34.073, 34.395, 35.436, 98/531 – *Van den Bergh Foods Ltd* (subsidiary of Unilever).
16 *H.B. Ice-cream Ltd v. Masterfoods Ltd* (trading as Mars Ireland) [1990] 2 IR 463.

cabinets, free of any direct charge, constitutes an infringement of Article [102] of the Treaty.[17]

Meanwhile, the Irish Supreme Court stayed the Irish appeal and asked the European Court of Justice whether its obligation of sincere cooperation (Article 4(3) TEU) required it to stay the Irish case pending the disposition of Van den Bergh's appeal. The Court of Justice responded in the affirmative, holding that Ireland could not maintain a judgement inconsistent with the Community disposition of the same issue.[18]

On its appeal from the Commission decision, Van den Bergh stressed that the retailers were free to terminate their contract with HB or to install freezers not belonging to HB; and it argued that their freedom to do so meant that there was no foreclosure. The General Court responded that the retailers had little incentive to exercise this freedom, and seldom did. It noted also the unique circumstances of the market, including the limited space in the retail stores and the popularity of HB's ice cream, and concluded that the Commission did not err in finding that the clause produced a sufficiently high degree of foreclosure to constitute an infringement.[19]

9. The 2010 Guidelines on Vertical Restraints[20] cover the range of exclusionary agreements. Read again the block exemption, and read the framework for analysis of individual cases (Vertical Guidelines, paras. 96–127) and the analysis of single-branding (paras. 129–150), exclusive distribution (paras. 151–167), exclusive supply (paras. 192–202), and tying (paras. 214–222). Applying the guidelines, would you come to any different conclusions in the cases above? If you need more facts, specify what facts you would need.

10. US law tends to examine more sceptically, first, the market power of the seller, and second, the feared inability of outsiders to reach the market efficiently notwithstanding exclusivity clauses. Also, US courts would tend to perceive the freezer clause more sympathetically, as a good deal for the retailer. But if the undertaking had significant market power and if its exclusive contract requirements excluded efficient outsiders such that the price of the product (impulse ice cream) was artificially increased, the clause would be likely to offend US law also.[21]

11. Look at the guidelines' treatment of Internet freedoms and restrictions. See Vertical Guidelines, paras. 51–54 and 64. Are the lines drawn in the appropriate place? Consider, for example, that sending of unsolicited promotional emails to specified customers outside of an assigned territory is an 'active' sale. An agreement may prohibit such a practice and still qualify for the block exemption. Requiring exclusive distributors to reroute web customers to the distributor in their territory would involve a lost opportunity for a 'passive' sale, and would be prohibited. But, without losing eligibility for the exemption, sellers can restrict sales to distributors with brick-and-mortar outlets, who then can sell on the Internet, and the sellers can block online sales of their goods by distributors without brick-and-mortar outlets. Are the Internet provisions appropriately protective of brand owners' needs to guard against free riders? Or too restrictive of the freedom of eBay and its ilk to give good deals to consumers?

---

17 Commission Decision of 11 March 1998 in Cases IV/34.073, 34.395, 35.436, 98/531 – *Van den Bergh Foods Ltd* (subsidiary of Unilever).
18 Case C-344/98, *Masterfoods Ltd (Mars Ireland)* [2000] ECR I-11369, EU:C:2000:689.
19 Case T-65/98, *Van den Bergh Foods v. Commission* [2003] ECR II-4653, EU:T:2003:281, as upheld in Case C-552/03 P [2006] ECR I-9091, EU:C:2006:607.
20 At: http://ec.europa.eu/competition/antitrust/legislation/vertical.html (accessed 5 June 2017).
21 See, e.g., *United States v. Dentsply Int'l Inc.*, 399 F.3d 181 (3d Cir. 2005), cert. denied, 546 U.S. 1089 (2006).

> **CASE**
>
> ## Pierre Fabre Dermo-Cosmétique v. Président de l'Autorité de la Concurrence (Case C-439/09)[23]
>
> 36 The selective distribution contracts at issue stipulate that sales of cosmetics and personal care products by the Avène, Klorane, Galénic and Ducray brands must be made in a physical space, the requirements for which are set out in detail, and that a qualified pharmacist must be present.
>
> 37 According to the referring court, the requirement that a qualified pharmacist must be present at a physical sales point *de facto* prohibits the authorised distributors from any form of internet selling.
>
> 38 As the Commission points out, by excluding *de facto* a method of marketing products that does not require the physical movement of the customer, the contractual clause considerably reduces the ability of an authorised distributor to sell the contractual products to customers outside its contractual territory or area of activity. It is therefore liable to restrict competition in that sector. * * *
>
> 42 Although it is for the referring court to examine whether the contractual clause at issue prohibiting *de facto* all forms of internet selling can be justified by a legitimate aim, it is for the Court of Justice to provide it for this purpose with the points of interpretation of European Union law which enable it to reach a decision. . . .
>
> 43 It is undisputed that, under Pierre Fabre Dermo-Cosmétique's selective distribution system, resellers are chosen on the basis of objective criteria of a qualitative nature, which are laid down uniformly for all potential resellers. However, it must still be determined whether the restrictions of competition pursue legitimate aims in a proportionate manner in accordance with the considerations set out at paragraph 41 of the present judgement.
>
> 44 In that regard, it should be noted that the Court, in the light of the freedoms of movement, has not accepted arguments relating to the need to provide individual advice to the customer and to ensure his protection against the incorrect use of products, in the context of non-prescription medicines and contact lenses, to justify a ban on internet sales. . . .

---

22 [2011] ECR I-9419, EU:C:2011:649.

Vertical restraints · **153**

CASE *(continued)*

45   Pierre Fabre Dermo-Cosmétique also refers to the need to maintain the prestigious image of the products at issue.

46   The aim of maintaining a prestigious image is not a legitimate aim for restricting competition and cannot therefore justify a finding that a contractual clause pursuing such an aim does not fall within Article 101(1) TFEU.

47   In the light of the foregoing considerations, . . . Article 101(1) TFEU must be interpreted as meaning that, in the context of a selective distribution system, a contractual clause requiring sales of cosmetics and personal care products to be made in a physical space where a qualified pharmacist must be present, resulting in a ban on the use of the internet for those sales, amounts to a restriction by object within the meaning of that provision where, following an individual and specific examination of the content and objective of that contractual clause and the legal and economic context of which it forms a part, it is apparent that, having regard to the properties of the products at issue, that clause is not objectively justified.

The possibility of a block exemption or an individual exemption

48   If it is established that an agreement or contractual clause restricts competition within the meaning of Article 101(1) TFEU, it will be for the referring court to examine whether the conditions in paragraph 3 of that article are met.

49   The possibility for an undertaking to benefit, on an individual basis, from the exception provided for in Article 101(3) TFEU derives directly from the Treaty. It is not contested in any of the observations submitted to the Court. That possibility is also open to the applicant in the main proceedings.

50   However, in that regard, given that the Court does not have sufficient information before it to assess whether the selective distribution contract satisfies the conditions in Article 101(3) TFEU, it is unable to provide further guidance to the referring court. * * *

[The Court then analyses the position under the block exemption that was applicable at the time of the decision of the French Competition Authority.[24]]

53   [I]t follows from Article 4(c) of Regulation No 2790/1999 that the exemption is not to apply to vertical agreements which directly or indirectly, in isolation or in combination with

---

23   Regulation 2790/1999/EC of 22 December 1999 on the application of Article 81(3) of the Treaty to categories of vertical agreements and concerted practices [1999] O.J. L336/21.

CASE *(continued)*

other factors under the control of the parties, have as their object the restriction of active or passive sales to end users by members of a selective distribution system operating at the retail level of trade, without prejudice to the possibility of prohibiting a member of the system from operating out of an unauthorised place of establishment.

54   A contractual clause such as the one at issue in the main proceedings, prohibiting *de facto* the internet as a method of marketing, at the very least has as its object the restriction of passive sales to end users wishing to purchase online and located outside the physical trading area of the relevant member of the selective distribution system.

55   According to Pierre Fabre Dermo-Cosmétique, the ban on selling the contractual products via the internet is equivalent however to a prohibition on operating out of an unauthorised establishment. It submits that, since the conditions for exemption laid down at the end of the provision, cited in paragraph 53, are thus met, Article 4 does not apply to it.

56   It should be pointed out that, by referring to 'a place of establishment', Article 4(c) of Regulation No 2790/1999 concerns only outlets where direct sales take place. The question that arises is whether that term can be taken, through a broad interpretation, to encompass the place from which internet sales services are provided.

57   As regards that question, it should be noted that, as an undertaking has the option, in all circumstances, to assert, on an individual basis, the applicability of the exception provided for in Article 101(3) TFEU, thus enabling its rights to be protected, it is not necessary to give a broad interpretation to the provisions which bring agreements or practices within the block exemption.

58   Accordingly, a contractual clause, such as the one at issue in the main proceedings, prohibiting *de facto* the internet as a method of marketing cannot be regarded as a clause prohibiting members of the selective distribution system concerned from operating out of an unauthorised place of establishment within the meaning of Article 4(c) of Regulation No 2790/1999.

59   In the light of the foregoing considerations . . . Article 4(c) of Regulation No 2790/1999 must be interpreted as meaning that the block exemption provided for in Article 2 of that regulation does not apply to a selective distribution contract which contains a clause prohibiting *de facto* the internet as a method of marketing the contractual products. However, such a contract may benefit, on an individual basis, from the exception provided for in Article 101(3) TFEU where the conditions of that provision are met.

Vertical restraints · 155

NOTES AND QUESTIONS

1. A ban on online sales cannot benefit from the block exemption because it restricts passive sales. Is that the case here? Did the Court discuss how passive sales could occur? Were prices higher in France than they were elsewhere in Europe?
2. Under *Pierre Fabre*, it appears risky to completely ban online sales, even though an individual exemption under Article 101(3) TFEU remains theoretically possible. What other strategies could a manufacturer use to limit or control sales on the Internet?
3. *Pierre Fabre* concerned not a Commission decision, but a decision of the French Competition Authority.[24] National authorities have become more active in enforcing competition law in vertical agreements, particularly for online sales.

Re-read para. 54 of the Vertical Guidelines and then read the following press release of the German Competition Authority (the Bundeskartellamt). Is there a conflict between the two approaches? What interests does the German Competition Authority protect?

Adidas Abandons Ban on Sales Via Online Market Places
2 July 2014

The Bundeskartellamt has closed its proceedings against adidas AG (adidas) after the company amended its conditions for online sales in such a way that they comply with competition law.

Adidas operates a selective distribution system which only allows authorised retailers to sell adidas products to consumers. The conditions for online sales, which were introduced in 2012, included a far-reaching prohibition for retailers to sell via the large online market places eBay and Amazon Marketplace, as well as other platforms such as Rakuten.de, Yatego.de, Hitmeister.de and meinPaket.de. The Bundeskartellamt had initiated proceedings after it had received numerous complaints by sports retailers.

Andreas Mundt, President of the Bundeskartellamt: 'The trading possibilities offered by the Internet create new challenges for both manufacturers and retailers. In this dynamic market environment, it is our task to keep markets and opportunities open for the benefit of retailers and consumers. It goes without saying that manufacturers can select their distributors according to certain quality requirements. However, both under European and German competition law they are prohibited from largely eliminating a principal distribution channel such as the web. Our proceedings against adidas and also against ASICS (which have not yet been concluded) serve as test cases because currently a number of brand manufacturers

---

24 See Decision of the Conseil de la concurrence n.08-D-25 of 29 October 2008.

are contemplating similar measures. We welcome the fact that adidas now allows its authorised retailers not only to operate their own online shops but also to operate shops at online market places. Not least because of declining customer numbers, this is particularly important for small and medium-sized sports retailers who want to expand their customer base. Consumers will also directly benefit from the amended conditions of sale.'

After extensive investigations at sporting goods manufacturers and German retailers, adidas was informally notified that its ban on sales via online market places and the restrictions imposed on authorised retailers with regard to search engine advertising gave cause for serious competition concerns. In response to this, adidas submitted an amended version of its conditions of sale for e-commerce, in which it completely abandoned its ban on sales via online market places. It also clarified that all authorised retailers are free to use adidas brand-related terms as search words for search engine advertising such as Google AdWords.

F. Block exemptions: history and reform

As soon as Regulation 17 became effective in 1962 as the first regulation implementing Articles 101 and 102, thousands of notifications of distribution agreements began flooding the Commission's Directorate-General for Competition, which was obliged to examine each to determine whether an exemption should issue. The Commission responded to the unmanageable workload, as well as the opportunity to give guidance, by adopting its first block exemption regulation ('BER'), Commission Regulation 67/67,[25] regarding agreements for the exclusive distribution of goods and agreements for the licensing of intellectual property. The Commission issued superseding BERs as well as new specialized ones for patents, know-how, and motor vehicle distribution. The BERs provided detailed roadmaps of what parties must, could, and must not do in order to have the benefit of exemption without filing a notification and seeking an individual exemption.

Business firms organized entire distribution systems to conform with the block exemptions, since analysis of restraints outside of the block exemptions was uncertain. Eventually, the system of detailed block exemptions came under severe criticism. They were formalistic. They straightjacketed business transactions. They were not united by any economic or other theory.

---

25 Regulation 67/67/EEC of the Commission of 22 March 1967 on the application of Article 85 (3) of the Treaty to certain categories of exclusive dealing agreements [1967] O.J. 57/849.

Vertical restraints · **157**

The Commission launched an intensive re-examination of its treatment of vertical restraints and in particular the block exemptions. In 1997, it issued an influential green paper, which included economic analysis recognizing the efficiency properties of most vertical restraints. At the conclusion of the long process of re-examination and in the years thereafter, important changes were made. First, the Council amended Regulation 17 (later replaced by Regulation 1/2003[26]) to exempt all vertical agreements from the requirement that they be notified in order to secure an exemption effective from the date of the agreement.[27]

Second, the Commission and Council liberalized the block exemptions, eliminating much detail. They issued a general vertical block exemption and guidelines for analysis of agreements falling outside of the block exemption, culminating in the revised general vertical block exemption and guidelines of 2010, referenced above.

Two specific vertical BERs that still remain concern technology transfer and motor vehicles.

A revised motor vehicle block exemption regulation and guidelines were issued in May 2010.[28] The block exemption applies to agreements between motor vehicle manufacturers and their authorized dealers, repairers and spare part distributors. The legislation acknowledges that strong competition now exists in the sale of new vehicles, while impediments continue in the repair, maintenance and spare parts markets. To come within the block exemption, an agreement must not have as its object, among other things: (i) the restriction of sales of spare parts to independent repairers by members of the selective distribution system of a vehicle manufacturer; (ii) the restriction on suppliers of spare parts to sell such parts, repair tools, diagnostic or other equipment to selectively authorized or independent repairers, distributors or end users; or (iii) the restriction of the ability of a manufacturer of spare parts to put its trademark visibly on components used for initial assembly of motor vehicles or spare parts. To get advantage

---

27 Regulation 1/2003/EC of 16 December 2002 on the implementation of the rules on competition laid down in Articles 81 and 82 of the Treaty [2002] *O.J.* L 1/1.
28 Regulation 1216/99/EC of 10 June 1999 amending Regulation No 17: first Regulation implementing Articles 81 and 82 of the Treaty [1999] *O.J.* L 148/5.
29 Regulation 461/2010/EU of 27 May 2010 on the application of Article 101(3) of the Treaty on the Functioning of the European Union to categories of vertical agreements and concerted practices in the motor vehicle sector [2010] *O.J.* L 129/52; *Supplementary guidelines* on vertical restraints in agreements for the sale and repair of motor vehicles and for the distribution of spare parts for motor vehicles [2010] *O.J.* C 138/16.

158 · EU competition law

of the block exemption, manufacturers must not have more than 30% of the market.[29]

A revised technology transfer block exemption ('TTBER'), effective in May 2014, covers patents, know-how, design rights, and software copyrights.[30] The regulation contains a list of hardcore prohibitions. For obtaining the benefit of the block exemption, it imposes a cap of 20% for licensing between competitors and 30% for licensing between non-competitors. Analysis outside of the block exemption is explained in accompanying guidelines.[31,32]

? NOTES AND QUESTIONS

1. Do you agree with the Commission's characterizations and analysis? Would you have formulated any categories or analysis differently? In what respect?
2. Applying the modernized analysis to the facts of the following cases, consider whether the restraints fall clear of Article 101(1), if not whether they come within the vertical block exemption, and if not whether they probably would be justified under the framework of the Vertical Guidelines:
   - *Consten and Grundig*
   - *Pioneer*
   - *Delimitis*
   - *Schöller*
   - *Masterfoods*
   - *Leegin*, if it occurred in Europe.

* * *

Since the review of the Vertical BER and guidelines, the Commission has essentially left the enforcement of Article 101 TFEU in the area of vertical restraints to national competition authorities and national courts, which retain the ability to seek guidance by means of preliminary references to the EU Court of Justice. The consequence has been the development of varying standards across Member States on, e.g., evidentiary requirements to establish the existence of RPM. However, it is expected that the Commission's ongoing e-commerce sector inquiry will somewhat revive its enforcement practice in the area of vertical restraints.

---

30 The regulation and guidelines are available at: http://ec.europa.eu/competition/sectors/motor_vehicles/legislation/legislation.html (accessed 5 June 2017).
31 Regulation 316/2014/EU of 21 March 2014 on the application of Article 101(3) of the Treaty on the Functioning of the European Union to categories of technology transfer agreements [2014] O.J. L 93/17.
32 Guidelines on the application of Article 101 of the Treaty on the Functioning of the European Union to technology transfer agreements [2014] O.J. C 89/3.
33 The regulation and guidelines are available at: http://ec.europa.eu/competition/antitrust/legislation/transfer.html (accessed 5 June 2017).

5

Abuses of dominance

Article 102 TFEU (formerly Article 82 EC) forbids the abuse of a dominant position. It provides:

Article 102

Any abuse by one or more undertakings of a dominant position within the internal market or in a substantial part of it shall be prohibited as incompatible with the internal market in so far as it may affect trade between Member States.

Such abuse may in particular consist in:

(a) directly or indirectly imposing unfair purchase or selling prices or other unfair trading conditions;
(b) limiting production, markets or technical development to the prejudice of consumers;
(c) applying dissimilar conditions to equivalent transactions with other trading parties, thereby placing them at a competitive disadvantage;
(d) making the conclusion of contracts subject to acceptance by the other parties of supplementary obligations which, by their nature or according to commercial usage, have no connection to the subject of such contracts.

At the time, the drafters of Article 86 (the original EEC Treaty number) drew upon the law of West Germany and also the law of the US. German law has long prohibited market-dominant enterprises from abusing their single-firm or group dominance by hindering competitors or exploiting or discriminating against buyers or sellers.[1] Section 2 of the US Sherman Antitrust Act ('Sherman Act') also provides that no person shall 'monopolize, or attempt to monopolize, or combine or conspire with any other person or persons, to monopolize . . .'.[2]

---

[1] Act Against Restraints of Competition § 19.
[2] 15 U.S.C. § 2.

US antitrust law was adopted at the time of the industrial revolution in response to a distrust of 'big business' and a fear of excessive concentration of private power.[3] German cartel law was adopted at the end of World War II in connection with American aid under the Marshall Plan. By safeguarding freedom of trade, the German law was designed to diffuse power and to prevent the ascendancy of another Nazi regime. The law was welcomed by the Freiburg School, which espoused a 'social market economy'.[4]

Among the Western European nations, however, distrust of big business was not the problem in the 1950s. Europe was a continent of many small nations, each isolated by high trade barriers. Private business firms were normally operating below efficient scale. Consolidations, particularly cross-border consolidations, were welcomed in order to increase efficiency and integrate the common market. When adopted in 1957, Article 86 EECT [now 102 TFEU] was seen not as a means to check the size of business but as a vehicle for regulating the conduct of firms that had economic power, including publicly-owned companies dominating domestic markets.

For 40 years, application of the abuse of dominance article proceeded in a rather formalistic mode. Beginning in the late 1990s and proceeding especially in the early 2000s, the Commission's Directorate-General for Competition embarked on a programme to modernize European competition law, which entailed moving from formalistic rules to effects-based analysis and employing 'sound economics'. This resulted in the issuance of Guidance on the Commission's enforcement priorities in applying Article 82 ECT[5] to abusive exclusionary conduct by dominant undertakings ('Guidance Paper').[6] Skim it now and bookmark it for future reference. Keep also in mind that the issuance of the Guidance Paper in 2009 was preceded by the publication of a discussion paper at the end of 2005, which launched a consultation and an EU-wide debate on the underlying rationale and contours of Article 102 TFEU.[7]

The all-encompassing conversation that surrounded the adoption of the Guidance Paper, and is still unfolding today, brought back to the surface very

---

3 See E. Fox (1981), 'The modernisation of antitrust: A new equilibrium', *Cornell L. Rev.*, **66**, 1140.
4 A. Peacock and H. Willgerodt (eds) (1989), *German Neo-Liberals and the Social Market Economy*, London: Palgrave Macmillan.
5 Now Article 102 TFEU.
6 The Guidance Paper is available at: http://ec.europa.eu/competition/antitrust/art82/index.html.
7 See DG Competition discussion paper on the application of Article 82 [now Article 102 TFEU] of the Treaty to exclusionary abuses, available at: http://ec.europa.eu/competition/antitrust/art82/discpaper2005.pdf (accessed 15 June 2017).

fundamental questions, such as why does and should Europe have an abuse of dominance prohibition? Is it to protect small and powerless market actors from abuse, or only to protect consumers? Is it to assure a level playing field or only to enhance efficiencies? Is there a danger that the abuse of dominance prohibition would protect competitors from efficient and innovative competitors, or is there a danger that lax enforcement will protect dominant firms from the discipline of competition?

Should abuse of dominance law (equivalent to monopolization law in the US) be only reluctantly applied, on the theory that single-firm (non-cartel) action is usually aligned with consumers' interests, or should enforcers be vigilant to break the power of dominant firms and assure better access to markets for all market players? Which tilt in competition policy is likely to make firms better able to adjust and respond to the changing markets of the world, and to make Europe more competitive? Perspectives on these questions inform virtually every issue covered in this chapter, from whether dominance can be inferred from high market shares and high barriers, to whether dominant firms should have special responsibilities to firms without power, to whether specific dominant firm conduct amounts to a foreclosure of smaller firms that shifts the burden of justification to the dominant firm.

A. Dominance

Article 102 TFEU prohibits abuse of a 'dominant position'. The Court of Justice defined dominant position in *Hoffmann-La Roche v. Commission*,[8] and that definition has had lasting importance.

> 38 The dominant position ... referred to [in Article 102] relates to a position of economic strength enjoyed by an undertaking which enables it to prevent effective competition being maintained on the relevant market by affording it the power to behave to an appreciable extent independently of its competitors, its customers and ultimately of the consumers.
>
> 39 Such a position does not preclude some competition, which it does where there is a monopoly or a quasi-monopoly, but enables the undertaking which profits by it, if not to determine, at least to have an appreciable influence on the conditions under which that competition will develop, and in any case to act largely in disregard of it so long as such conduct does not operate to its detriment. * * *

---

8 Case 85/76, *Hoffmann-La Roche v. Commission* [1979] ECR 461, EU:C:1979:36.

> The existence of a dominant position may derive from several factors which, taken separately, are not necessarily determinative but among these factors a highly important one is the existence of very large market shares.
>
> 40 A substantial market share as evidence of the existence of a dominant position is not a constant factor and its importance varies from market to market according to the structure of these markets, especially as far as production, supply and demand are concerned. * * *
>
> 41 Furthermore, although the importance of the market shares may vary from one market to another the view may legitimately be taken that very large shares are in themselves, and save in exceptional circumstances, evidence of the existence of a dominant position.
>
> An undertaking which has a very large market share and holds it for some time, by means of the volume of production and the scale of the supply which it stands for—without those having much smaller market shares being able to meet rapidly the demand from those who would like to break away from the undertaking which has the largest market share—is by virtue of that share in a position of strength which makes it an unavoidable trading partner and which, already because of this secures for it, at the very least during relatively long periods, that freedom of action which is the special feature of a dominant position. * * *
>
> 48 On the other hand the relationship between the market shares of the undertaking concerned and of its competitors, especially those of the next largest, the technological lead of an undertaking over its competitors, the existence of a highly developed sales network and the absence of potential competition are relevant factors, the first because it enables the competitive strength of the undertaking in question to be assessed, the second and third because they represent in themselves technical and commercial advantages and the fourth because it is the consequence of the existence of obstacles preventing new competitors from having access to the market.

A dominant position connotes economic power in a defined market, power to impose market terms on consumers, or more generally power to hinder the maintenance of effective competition. Market definition—determination of both the product market and the geographic market—therefore precedes any determination of dominance (read again the note on market definition at p. 78 above).

There are no definite thresholds of dominance, though. Still, market shares are often relied upon as a first indicator of dominance. The Court of Justice in *AKZO* said, quoting from *Hoffmann-La Roche*: 'very large market shares are in themselves, and save in exceptional circumstances, evidence of the existence of a dominant position.' It then added: 'That is the situation where there is a market share of 50% such as that found to exist in this case.'[9] In *Hoffmann-La Roche*, a 47% share of one market (Vitamin A) was also held to be enough to confer dominance in view of the structure of the market (the next largest competitors had 27% and 18%), Roche's technological lead over its competitors, the absence of potential competition, and Roche's overcapacity. In contrast, the Court overturned a finding of dominance on another market (Vitamin B3) because a market share of 43% did not by itself 'constitute a factor sufficient to establish the existence of a dominant position' in the absence of sufficient corroborative support from other factors.

One fundamental question when assessing dominance is whether the firm in question does have the power to raise its prices significantly above its costs (and thus charge supracompetitive prices)? In its Guidance Paper, the Commission defines dominance and identifies factors necessary to assess it:[10]

> Dominance entails that the ... competitive constraints are not sufficiently effective and hence that the firm in question enjoys substantial market power over a period of time.[11]

An undertaking 'capable of profitably increasing prices above the competitive level for a significant period of time does not face sufficiently effective constraints and can thus generally be regarded as dominant.' Assessments of dominance will take account of the competitive structure of the market, including constraints by suppliers/competitors, by the credible threat of entry or expansion, and by buyer power.

Note on collective dominance

Article 102 prohibits abuse of a dominant position by 'one or more undertakings'. In theory, dominance can therefore exist on the part of one undertaking (single dominance) but also of two or more undertakings (collective dominance). What is collective dominance within the meaning of this clause?

In *Compagnie Maritime Belge*, members of a shipping conference in the liner market between northern Europe and western Africa collaborated as

---

9 Case 62/86, *AKZO Chemie BV v. Commission* [1991] ECR I-3359, EU:C:1991:286, para. 60.
10 See Guidance Paper, IIIA, paras. 9–18.
11 Guidance Paper, IIIA, para. 10.

'fighting ships' to destroy an independent competitor. The Court defined the critical question as whether 'from an economic point of view [the undertakings] present themselves or act together on a particular market as a collective entity.' '[A] liner conference . . . can be characterised as a collective entity which presents itself as such on the market vis-à-vis both users and competitors.'[12]

US law does not have an identical concept. But in *E.I du Pont de Nemours & Co. v FTC*,[13] the court stated in dictum that oligopolists' non-collusive adoption of the same oppressive, unjustified anticompetitive business practices could constitute an unfair method of competition within the prohibition of Section 5 of the Federal Trade Commission Act ('FTC Act').[14] Section 5 of the FTC Act, unlike the Sherman Act, requires neither joint action nor monopolistic power.

The Commission's practice in the area of collective dominance has historically been very limited and the few reportable cases have typically involved situations of strong structural links between the undertakings alleged to hold a collective dominant position. In addition to *Compagnie Maritime Belge*, see *Irish Sugar v. Commission*,[15] *Atlantic Container Line v. Commission*,[16] and *Piau v. Commission*.[17] Still, the notion of collective dominance raises interesting questions on the application of competition principles to oligopolistic conduct. Consider the notion of collective dominance together with the standard to find a concerted practice under Article 101 TFEU (see Chapter 2 above) and the notion of coordinated effects in merger analysis (see Chapter 6 below).

B. Abusive conduct

Article 102 TFEU lists four particular practices that may be abusive. The list includes some conduct that is directly associated with the existence of market power and is often referred to as exploitative in that it represents the use of power over price to extract more than 'fair' or 'competitive' prices from customers. Imposing unfair prices and limiting production fall within this

---

12 Joined Cases C-395/96 and C-396/96 P, *Compagnie Maritime Belge Transports SA v. Commission* [2000] ECR I-1365, EU:C:2000:132, paras. 42, 36, 48.
13 729 F.2d 128 (2d Cir.1984).
14 15 U.S.C. § 45.
15 Case T-228/97, *Irish Sugar v. Commission* [1999] ECR II-2969, EU:T:1999:246 (upheld in Case C-497/99 P, EU:C:2001:393).
16 Joined Cases T-191 and T-212 to T-214/98, *Atlantic Container Line v. Commission* [2003] ECR II-3275, EU:T:2003:245;
17 Case T-193/02, *Piau v. Commission* [2005] ECR II-209, EU:T:2005:22.

category. Other conduct on the list is coercive, such as requiring a contracting party to accept an obligation that has no relationship to the subject of the contract, forcing acceptance of a second product (a tie-in), or discriminating among customers and thereby placing the disfavoured customer at a competitive disadvantage.

This section deals with a variety of possible abuses of dominance, including excessive pricing, discriminatory pricing, refusals to deal, requirements and exclusive dealing contracts, tying, loyalty rebates, and price predation. It first discusses excessive and discriminatory prices. Excessive prices are by definition an exploitative abuse. Discriminatory pricing has two prongs—a higher price and a lower price—and typically lies at the intersection between exploitation and exclusion. It then turns to exclusionary practices, which are the subject of the Commission's Guidance Paper.

1. Excessive and discriminatory prices and unfair terms

Excessive pricing is usually a fraught subject because it is difficult for an authority or court to detect when prices are excessive, and then to do something about it without becoming a regulator. But occasionally a case arises that bypasses these issues.

CASE

British Leyland Plc v. Commission (Case 226/84)[18]

[The United Kingdom gave British Leyland the exclusive right to determine whether imported British Leyland cars conformed to UK national standards, and to issue certificates of conformity. British Leyland arbitrarily refused to grant certain certificates to applicants who had typically purchased their car outside of the UK, and it set much higher fees for left-hand-drive than for right-hand-drive cars.]

27   As the Court held in its judgement in *General Motors*, an undertaking abuses its dominant position where it has an administrative monopoly and charges for its services fees which are disproportionate to the economic value of the service provided.

28   It appears from the documents before the Court and the information provided by the parties that, in the case of both right-hand-drive and left-hand-drive vehicles, in order to issue

---

18   [1986] ECR 3263, EU:C:1986:421.

> **CASE** *(continued)*
>
> a certificate of conformity it is necessary to determine from the chassis number the date of manufacture of the vehicle. It is then possible to identify the number of the corresponding NTA certificate. It is, therefore, a simple administrative check which cannot entail significant costs. For left-hand-drive vehicles the certificate is in principle issued before conversion, if they are converted to right-hand-drive. The only difference in relation to the issue of a certificate for a right-hand-drive vehicle lies in the need to verify that the four alterations essential for a left-hand-drive vehicle have been made, namely the adjustment of headlights, full beam and dipped, the calibration of the speedometer in miles per hour, the adaptation of the rear fog lamp and the addition of a wing-mirror on the right front door. That verification does not require an inspection of the vehicle. It is effected on the basis of a certificate furnished by a garage and, on the basis of the cost incurred, cannot therefore justify the charging of different fees for the issue of certificates of conformity according to whether the vehicles are right-hand-drive or left-hand-drive. Initially the fee for left-hand-drive vehicles was six times greater than that for right-hand-drive vehicles.
>
> 29 Moreover, BL itself admitted at the hearing that the difference which existed at one time according to whether the certificate was requested by a dealer, who was charged UK £150, or by a private individual, who was charged only UK £100, was not based on the cost but on the consideration that the trader who was carrying out a transaction for gain could be required to pay a higher fee. The fact that the fee was first reduced to UK £100 and then UK £50, whilst for right-hand-drive vehicles it remained at UK £25, also suggests that it was fixed solely with a view to making the re-importation of left-hand-drive vehicles less attractive.
>
> 30 In those circumstances, the Commission was entitled to conclude that the fee was fixed at a level which was clearly disproportionate to the economic value of the service provided and that that practice constituted an abuse by BL of the monopoly it held by virtue of the British rules. * * *
>
> 33 Finally, BL's argument that the amount of the fee had no detrimental effect on the volume of the re-importations is, as the Court has already stated above, irrelevant.
>
> 34 In conclusion, it must be held that the complaints made by the Commission in the contested decision are established.

British Leyland was a toll-taker, enabled by government licence. Moreover, while the fact of excessiveness is usually extremely difficult to determine, in *British Leyland* it was obvious. Further, in this case, the exploitation was a means of market segmentation—a core offence.

Some years earlier, the Commission pressed a more ambiguous case of unfair pricing, and also a case of discriminatory pricing, against United Brands. *United Brands* is a flagship case for caution on finding 'excessiveness', while it also underscores the goal of market integration.

CASE

United Brands Co. v. Commission (Case 27/76) (pricing practices)[19]

[United Brands was the biggest banana producer in the world and in the EU. It was a vertically integrated company that grew bananas in South America, bought from other growers half of the bananas it sold, and accounted for some 40% of the sales of bananas in the Union, which was more than twice that of its nearest rival. It owned and promoted the Chiquita brand, the best known and the most heavily advertised brand in the world. Its system of distribution involved sales to ripeners/distributors, who would buy the green bananas, ripen them in special sheds and in specified gases, and resell them. The Commission alleged a series of abuses, including the cut-off of a Danish ripener/distributor, excessive pricing and discriminatory pricing.

United Brands sold all bananas to its distributors free on rail Rotterdam or Bremerhaven. There was a 100% difference between the prices charged to the distributor for Ireland, where Chiquita was an unknown brand and demand was low, and the prices charged to the distributor for Denmark, where the brand was well known and demand was strong. There were also disparities between the price charged to the Danish distributors and to the distributors for the other Member States. United Brands' prices were approximately 7% higher than the prices of its nearest rivals, and they were 30% to 40% higher than unbranded bananas. The Commission found discriminatory and excessive pricing violations and ordered United Brands to reduce its prices to distributors other than the distributors for Ireland by at least 15%.]

1. *Discriminatory prices* * * *

208   The Commission blames the applicant for charging each week for the sale of its branded bananas—without objective justification—a selling price which differs appreciably according to the Member State where its customers are established. * * *

212   The price customers in Belgium are asked to pay is on average 80% higher than that paid by customers in Ireland.

---

19 [1978] ECR 207, EU:C:1978:22.

CASE (continued)

213   The greatest difference in price is 138% between the delivered Rotterdam price charged by UBC to its customers in Ireland and the f.o.r. Bremerhaven price charged by UBC to its customers in Denmark, that is to say the price paid by Danish customers is 2.38 times the price paid by Irish customers. * * *

225   In fact the bananas sold by UBC are all freighted in the same ships, are unloaded at the same cost in Rotterdam or Bremerhaven and the price differences relate to substantially similar quantities of bananas of the same variety, which have been brought to the same degree of ripening, are of similar quality and sold under the same 'Chiquita' brand name under the same conditions of sale and payment for loading on to the purchaser's own means of transport and the latter have to pay customs duties, taxes and transport costs from these ports. * * *

232   These discriminatory prices, which varied according to the circumstances of the Member States, were just so many obstacles to the free movement of goods and their effect was intensified by the clause forbidding the resale of bananas while still green and by reducing the deliveries of the quantities ordered.

233   A rigid partitioning of national markets was thus created at price levels, which were artificially different, placing certain distributor/ripeners at a competitive disadvantage, since compared with what it should have been competition had thereby been distorted.

234   Consequently the policy of differing prices enabling UBC to apply dissimilar conditions to equivalent transactions with other trading parties, thereby placing them at a competitive disadvantage, was an abuse of a dominant position.

2.   *Unfair prices* * * *

252   The questions . . . to be determined are whether the difference between the costs actually incurred and the price actually charged is excessive, and, if the answer to this question is in the affirmative, whether a price has been imposed which is either unfair in itself or when compared to competing products. * * *

258   The Commission bases its view that prices are excessive on an analysis of the differences—in its view excessive—between the prices charged in the different Member States and on the policy of discriminatory prices which has been considered above.

259   The foundation of its argument has been the applicant's letter of 10 December 1974 which acknowledged that the margin allowed by the sale of bananas to Irish ripeners was much smaller than in some other Member States and it concluded from this that the amount by which the actual prices f.o.r. Bremerhaven and Rotterdam exceed the delivered Rotterdam

CASE (continued)

prices for bananas to be sold to Irish customers c.i.f. Dublin must represent a profit of the same order of magnitude.

260   Having found that the prices charged to ripeners of the other Member States were considerably higher, sometimes by as much as 100%, than the prices charged to customers in Ireland it concluded that UBC was making a very substantial profit.

261   Nevertheless the Commission has not taken into account in its reasoning . . . a confidential document . . . pointing out that the prices charged in Ireland had produced a loss.

262   The applicant also states that the prices charged on the relevant market did not allow it to make any profits during the last five years, except in 1975. * * *

264   However unreliable the particulars supplied by UBC may be (and in particular the document mentioned previously which works out the 'losses' on the Irish market in 1974 without any supporting evidence), the fact remains that it is for the Commission to prove that the applicant charged unfair prices.

265   UBC's retraction, which the Commission has not effectively refuted, establishes beyond doubt that the basis for the calculation adopted by the latter to prove that UBC's prices are excessive is open to criticism and on this particular point there is doubt which must benefit the applicant, especially as for nearly 20 years banana prices, in real terms, have not risen on the relevant market. * * *

267   In these circumstances it appears that the Commission has not adduced adequate legal proof of the facts and evaluations which formed the foundation of its finding that UBC had infringed Article [102] of the Treaty by directly and indirectly imposing unfair selling prices for bananas.

NOTES AND QUESTIONS

1. Excessive pricing is an exploitative violation. It signifies that a dominant firm uses its market power to overcharge consumers. Many antitrust regimes prohibit excessive pricing, which may be seen as the most direct economic evil of monopoly. But the challenges of detection, surveillance, and remedies are great and counsel caution in applying the law. For a recent policy statement on abusive exploitation, see EU Commissioner M. Vestager, 'Protecting consumers from exploitation' (Brussels, 21 November 2016): '. . . we need to act carefully when we deal with excessive prices. The best defence against exploitation remains the ability to walk away. So we can often protect consumers just by stopping powerful companies from driving their rivals out of the market. But we still have the option of acting directly against excessive prices. Because we have a responsibility to the public. And we should be willing to use every means we have

to fulfil that responsibility.' In that speech, Commissioner Vestager mentioned the *Gazprom* case,[20] prices of pharmaceuticals and standard-essential patents.[21]

The Commission thereafter opened an excessive pricing investigation against Aspen Pharma, after the Italian Antitrust Authority fined the company for increasing the price of anti-cancer drugs from 300% to 1500% after the patents expired. Apparently, the market was too small to induce generic competition. Similar huge price hikes in life-saving pharmaceuticals have induced several Member States to take action and to manoeuvre the difficult territory of not only determining dominance but also determining benchmarks for excessiveness and appropriate relief.

In that context, the Court of Justice issued an important judgement on 14 September 2017 providing guidance on the assessment of excessive prices under Article 102 TFEU in Case C-177/16, Latvijas Autoru, EU:C:2017:689.

2. What is the relationship between excessive and discriminatory pricing in *United Brands*? Is one offence more central than the other to EU objectives?
3. The Court called the differential prices for different Member States 'just so many obstacles to the free movement of goods' (para. 232). Is price discrimination a barrier to free movement? What was the real barrier to free movement? Why did the Court blame lack of mobility of the bananas on the price discrimination rather than on the green banana clause?
4. Price discrimination can be a way to get more money from those who are willing to pay more but alternatively it can be a way to compete—to lower prices and make more sales. United Brands was apparently charging high prices where consumers had a strong preference for bananas, and low prices to break into markets where Chiquita was not well known and other fruits were in strong demand. In areas in which demand for Chiquita bananas was strong, was the real question who would get the extra profits, United Brands or its distributor? Would prohibition of price discrimination mean all distributors would get the Irish price?
5. A recurrent question in relation to discrimination has been whether Article 102 TFEU forbids the mere charging of different prices for the same good or service within the same market, or whether it additionally requires evidence of harm to competition. In *British Airways v. Commission*,[22] one issue was whether BA's bonus schemes related to the achievement of sales targets caused discrimination between travel agents or produced exclusionary effects in relation to competing airlines. The Court of Justice found that the lack of equivalence between travel agents resulting from BA's linkage of the amount of rebates to specific sales targets amounted to a breach of Article 102 TFEU and that no 'actual quantifiable deterioration in the competitive position of [travel agents or competing airlines] taken individually' had to be adduced (para. 145). More recently, in *Post Danmark I*, the Court ruled to the contrary that 'charging different customers or different classes of customers different prices for goods or services whose costs are the same or, conversely, charging a single price to customers for whom supply costs differ, cannot of itself suggest that there exists an exclusionary abuse',[23] i.e., additional evidence of harm to competition is requisite or, put otherwise, the notion of 'competitive disadvantage' under Article 102(2)(c) cannot be merely inferred from the existence of differential treatment.[24]

---

20 AT/39.816 (upstream gas supplies in Central and Eastern Europe, pending).
21 For recent enforcement actions involving excessive prices in the pharmaceutical sector, see the UK Consumer and Market Authority ('CMA') decisions in cases CE/9742-13, Pfizer/Flynn Pharma (7 December 2016) and Actavis/Hydrocortisone (16 December 2016).
22 Case C-95/04 P, *British Airways v. Commission* [2007] ECR I-2331, EU:C:2007:166.
23 Case C-209/10, *Post Danmark I*, EU:C:2012:172, para. 30.
24 For a general discussion of the treatment of price discrimination under EU competition law, see D. Gerard (2005), 'Price discrimination under Article 82(2)(c) EC: Clearing up the ambiguities', GCLC Research Paper on the Modernisation of Article 82 EC [now Article 102 TFEU], 6 July 2005.

6. United States' antitrust law does not prohibit excessive pricing. It prohibits price discrimination only if the discriminatory pricing is likely to produce a monopoly (invoking the Sherman Act) or hurt disfavoured buyers in their competition with favoured ones (invoking the Robinson-Patman Act[25]). The US antitrust agencies seldom enforce the Robinson-Patman Act because they fear that most applications are anti-competitive. (Why?) As a result, most Robinson-Patman actions are private actions. Competitors of the price discriminator have been greatly restricted in their ability to sue, however, because they must prove antitrust injury and antitrust damages, and this requires proof that consumers are harmed. But consumers might benefit from the low prong of the price.[26]

As for excessive pricing, the Court of Appeals for the US Second Circuit said in *Berkey Photo, Inc. v. Eastman Kodak Co.*:[27]

> Excessive prices, maintained through exercise of a monopolist's control of the market, constituted one of the primary evils that the Sherman Act was intended to correct. . . .
>
> But unless the monopoly has bolstered its power by wrongful actions, it will not be required to pay damages merely because its prices may later be found excessive. Setting a high price may be a use of monopoly power, but it is not in itself anticompetitive. Indeed, although a monopolist may be expected to charge a somewhat higher price than would prevail in a competitive market, there is probably no better way to guarantee that its dominance will be challenged than by greedily extracting the highest price it can . . . . Judicial oversight of pricing policies would place the courts in a role akin to that of a public regulatory commission. . . . We would be wise to decline that function unless Congress clearly bestows it upon us.

Some 25 years later, the US Supreme Court went much further in a landmark case, *Trinko*, p. 177 below, stating that monopoly prices should be welcomed; high prices invite competition. Do the EU Treaty and *Trinko* reflect a major divide between US and EU competition law? What should happen when high prices do not attract entry?

2. Exclusionary conduct

The remainder of this chapter is devoted to the challenging subject of exclusionary or foreclosing violations. The subject is challenging because it highlights the tension between efficiency and equity; protecting consumers from higher prices and protecting competitors from foreclosure and the opportunity to contest a market segment. Sometimes these goals coincide and sometimes they diverge. A goal of protecting the competitive processes—which the EU includes—attenuates convergence; it may protect competition but it may sometimes result in protecting competitors at the expense of consumers. Should it be an important task of competition enforcement and adjudication to prevent that result? You will find different perspectives on these questions

---

25 15 U.S.C. § 13.
26 See, e.g., *Brooke Group Ltd v. Brown & Williamson Tobacco Corp.*, 509 U.S. 209, 113 S.Ct. 2578, 125 L.Ed.2d 168 (1993), p. 215 below.
27 603 F.2d 263, 294 (2d Cir.1979), cert. denied, 444 U.S. 1093 (1980).

in statements of the Commission and judgements of the courts; and even differences between different panels of the Court.

We start with the Commission's Guidance Paper, which applies contemporary economic learning, focusing on efficiency and consumers. The Commission begins its discussion of harm from foreclosure as follows:

> The aim of the Commission's enforcement activity in relation to exclusionary conduct is to ensure that dominant undertakings do not impair effective competition by foreclosing their rivals in an anticompetitive way and thus having an adverse impact on consumer welfare, whether in the form of higher price levels than would have otherwise prevailed or in some other form such as limiting quality or reducing consumer choice. In this document the term 'anticompetitive foreclosure' is used to describe a situation where effective access of actual or potential competitors to supplies or markets is hampered or eliminated as a result of the conduct of the dominant undertaking whereby the dominant undertaking is likely to be in a position to profitably increase prices to the detriment of consumers....[28]

Even where it finds anti-competitive foreclosure, the Commission will examine claims by the dominant undertaking that its conduct is justified by objective necessity or efficiency.

As you begin your study of refusal to deal, below, read the Commission Guidance on refusal to supply, paras. 74–89. A link to the Guidance Paper may be found at http://ec.europa.eu/competition/antitrust/art82/. The Commission's Guidance incorporates an economic approach, distancing itself from prior formalism. As you will see, the courts' judgements have not always followed suit. For all of the cases below, consider whether the Commission's analysis does or does not align with the Courts' analysis. If not, identify divergences.

a. *Refusal to deal*

(i) *Essential facility and duty to give access*

Ownership of or control over an essential facility presents a special case of duty to deal, duty not to exclude, and duty to treat competitors and customers fairly and non-discriminatorily.

---

28 Guidance Paper, para. 19.

The Commission first invoked the essential facility concept in the case of *Sealink*.[29] Sealink owned Holyhead Harbour, which was the only port in the UK serving Ireland for the transport of passengers and cars on the central corridor route. Sealink also operated a car ferry. B&I Line was a rival car ferry operator. Its berth was in the mouth of the narrow Holyhead Harbour. When a Sealink vessel passed a B&I vessel, it so agitated the water that B&I had to lift the ramp that connected the boat to the dock and stop loading or unloading. Sealink then scheduled more frequent sailings of its own vessels, making the disturbances intolerable to B&I. B&I sought interim measures, which the Commission granted. It said:

> 41   A dominant undertaking which both owns or controls and itself uses an essential facility, i.e., a facility or infrastructure without access to which competitors cannot provide services to their customers, and which refuses its competitors access to that facility or grants access to competitors only on terms less favourable than those which it gives its own services, thereby placing the competitors at a competitive disadvantage, infringes Article [102] if the other conditions of that Article are met. A company in a dominant position may not discriminate in favour of its own activities in a related market (Case C–260/89, Elliniki Radiophonia, para. 37–38). The owner of an essential facility which uses its power in one market in order to strengthen its position in another related market, in particular, by granting its competitor access to that related market on less favourable terms than those of its own services, infringes Article [102] when a competitive disadvantage is imposed upon its competitor without objective justification.
>
> This was accepted by Sealink through its subsidiary, SHL, when it stated that no agreement would be given to vary schedules if this compromised its ability to provide an acceptable level of service to all port users . . . . This is particularly so where the physical configuration of the port has obliged operators to accept differences in the services they are offered by the operator of the essential facility, in order to maximize its efficient utilization.
>
> 42   The owner of the essential facility, which uses the essential facility, may not impose a competitive disadvantage on its competitor, also a user of the essential facility, by altering its own schedule to the detriment of the competitor's service, where, as in this case, the construction or the features of the facility are such that it is not possible to alter one competitor's service in the way chosen without harming the other's. Specifically, where, as in this case, the competitor is already subject to a certain level of disruption from the dominant undertaking's activities, there is a duty on the dominant undertaking not to take any action which will result in further disruption. That

---

29   Commission Decision of 11 June 1992 in Case IV/34.174 – *Sealink/B&I – Holyhead* (interim measures).

is so even if the latter's actions make, or are primarily intended to make, its operations more efficient. Subject to any objective elements outside its control, such an undertaking is under a duty not to impose a competitive disadvantage upon its competitor in the use of the shared facility without objective justification . . .

Subsequent port cases, particularly where the State owned the port, confirmed the principle. See Chapter 7, below, section B.

Did Sealink have a legitimate reason to expand its schedule? Should this have been an objective justification? Should a firm that has made the investment in the essential infrastructure be allowed to prefer itself over its rivals in uses of the infrastructure?

For many years, US courts also applied an essential facility doctrine where the duty to grant access would not impair the defendant's own performance. Examples are the telecommunications cases before the break-up of AT&T, when AT&T held the nation's long distance telephone service monopoly, the local service monopolies, and the local loop bottleneck gateway to the local markets.[30] Sometime after the *AT&T* cases, US authorities and jurists began to fear that essential facility duties undermined incentives to invest, to innovate, and to compete. In *Verizon Communications Inc. v. Law Offices of Curtis V. Trinko*, below at p. 177, the US Supreme Court narrowed the law. Consider the effect of duties to deal on incentives to invest, innovate and compete as you read the following cases. Is the 'chilling-effect' concern well taken or not?

(ii)   Other duties to deal that may or may not involve an essential facility

CASE

Istituto Chemioterapico Italiano Spa v. Commission (Joined Cases 6 and 7/73) ('Commercial Solvents')[31]

[Commercial Solvents Corporation was a manufacturer of raw materials—nitropropane and aminobutanol—which were used to manufacture ethambutol, an antituberculosis drug.

---

30 See *MCI Communications Corp. v. American Telephone & Telegraph Co.*, 708 F.2d 1081 (7th Cir.1983); *United States v. American Telephone & Telegraph Co.*, 524 F.Supp. 1336, 1352 (D.D.C.1981).
31 [1974] ECR 223, EU:C:1974:18.

CASE *(continued)*

Aminobutanol was also used as an emulsifier for paint. Commercial Solvents Corporation acquired 51% of the shares of an Italian company, Istituto Chemioterapico Italiano ('Istituto'), which bought the raw materials from its parent, Commercial Solvents, and sold them to another Italian company, Zoja, which used them to manufacture ethambutol-based specialties.

Istituto sought to acquire Zoja, but the negotiations aborted. Istituto then increased the price at which it sold aminobutanol to Zoja. Zoja, however, discovered a cheaper source for aminobutanol—firms that bought the raw material from Commercial Solvents for use in paint. Zoja persuaded Istituto to cancel a large part of Zoja's order. Soon thereafter, Zoja's supply of cheaper aminobutanol dried up, largely because Commercial Solvents forbade its paint-making customers to resell aminobutanol for pharmaceutical use. Commercial Solvents then announced that it was withdrawing from the market for sales of the raw material, and it integrated vertically, using the raw material for its own production. When Zoja tried to reorder aminobutanol from Commercial Solvents, Commercial Solvents refused to accept the order.

The Commission held that Commercial Solvents had a dominant position in the market for the raw material and ordered Commercial Solvents to resume supplying Zoja and to pay a fine for the refusal to sell.]

23 The applicants state that they ought not to be held responsible for stopping supplies of aminobutanol to Zoja for this was due to the fact that in the spring of 1970 Zoja itself informed Istituto that it was cancelling the purchase of large quantities of aminobutanol which had been provided for in a contract then in force between Istituto and Zoja. When at the end of 1970 Zoja again contacted Istituto to obtain this product, the latter was obliged to reply, after consulting CSC, that in the meantime CSC had changed its commercial policy and that the product was no longer available. The change of policy by CSC was, they claim, inspired by a legitimate consideration of the advantage that would accrue to it of expanding its production to include the manufacture of finished products and not limiting itself to that of raw material or intermediate products. In pursuance of this policy it decided to improve its product and no longer to supply aminobutanol save in respect of commitments already entered into by its distributors. * * *

25 However, an undertaking being in a dominant position as regards the production of raw material and therefore able to control the supply to manufacturers of derivatives, cannot, just because it decides to start manufacturing these derivatives (in competition with its former customers) act in such a way as to eliminate their competition which in the case in question would amount to eliminating one of the principal manufacturers of ethambutol in the Common Market. Since such conduct is contrary to the objectives expressed in Article 3 [(1)

> **CASE** *(continued)*
>
> (g)] [now in a protocol] of the Treaty and set out in greater detail in Articles [101 and 102 TFEU], it follows that an undertaking which has a dominant position in the market in raw materials and which, with the object of reserving such raw material for manufacturing its own derivatives, refuses to supply a customer, which is itself a manufacturer of these derivatives, and therefore risks eliminating all competition on the part of this customer, is abusing its dominant position within the meaning of Article [102 TFEU]. In this context it does not matter that the undertaking ceased to supply in the spring of 1970 because of the cancellation of the purchases by Zoja, because it appears from the applicants' own statement that, when the supplies provided for in the contract had been completed, the sale of aminobutanol would have stopped in any case. * * *
>
> 28 ... [T]he applicants do not seriously dispute the statement in the Decision in question to the effect that 'in view of the production capacity of the CSC plant it can be confirmed that CSC can satisfy Zoja's needs, since Zoja represents a very small percentage (approximately 5–6%) of CSC's global production of nitropropane.' It must be concluded that the Commission was justified in considering that such statements could not be taken into account.

NOTES AND QUESTIONS

1. What main principle of law governs this case? Is this principle based on efficiency and consumer interests? Fairness and rights of competitors?
2. The Court gave recognition to a right to refuse to deal in *Oscar Bronner*,[32] where the complainant should have been able to fend for itself. The Court rejected the claim of Bronner, owner of a small daily newspaper, that the distribution system of Mediaprint, the near-monopolist publisher and owner of the only nationwide newspaper distribution system in Austria, was an essential facility to which he had a right of access. The Court said that Mediaprint's refusal to distribute Bronner's newspaper would not amount to an abuse of dominance unless it was 'likely to eliminate all competition in the daily newspaper market on the part of the person requesting the service and that such refusal be incapable of being objectively justified, [and] also that the service in itself be indispensable to carrying on that person's business, inasmuch as there is no actual or potential substitute in existence for that home-delivery scheme' (para. 41). Bronner had not made this case. Among other things, there were no technical or legal obstacles preventing Bronner, alone or in combination with other small papers, from setting up an alternative distribution system. How can *Oscar Bronner* be distinguished from *Commercial Solvents*?

* * *

---

[32] Case C-7/97, *Oscar Bronner GmbH & Co. KG v. Mediaprint Zeitungs-und Zeitschriftenverlag GmbH & Co.*, [1998] ECR I-7791, EU:C:1998:569.

US law applies a strong presumption of freedom of firms to choose to deal or not, as exemplified in the *Trinko* case below. *Trinko* embodies the philosophy and perspective of US antitrust—at least as the US Supreme Court sees it; and it is the prime referent for US law on abuse of dominance (monopolization). It paints the uniquely American perspective of trust in markets, and it has become the prime US authority cited as a contrast to much EU case law imposing special responsibilities on dominant firms.

CASE

Verizon Communications Inc. v. Law Offices of Curtis V. Trinko[33]

JUSTICE SCALIA:

[Verizon was the incumbent local exchange carrier ('ILEC') serving New York State. This meant that Verizon owned the elements of the local loop—facilities necessary to connect long distance lines with the local market. When competition in the local telephone service markets became technologically feasible, Congress passed the 1996 Telecommunications Act[34] to facilitate entry into the local markets. Among other things, the statute required the ILECs to give the new local exchange carriers (competitive LECs or CLECs) access to the elements of the local loop on reasonable non-discriminatory terms. Verizon, in order to keep its customers from defecting to new entrants and to limit entry, discriminated against the CLECs, disrupting their service and making it unreliable. Complaints to this effect were investigated and verified by the Federal Communications Commission, which fined Verizon and enjoined its discriminatory and exclusionary practices.

Plaintiffs were customers of the discriminated against CLECs. They sued for damages for their losses. (There was a serious question of plaintiffs' standing to sue, but this was not the basis of the decision.) Verizon moved to dismiss on the pleadings. Verizon maintained that it had no antitrust duty to the CLECs not to discriminate against them.

The Court first noted that the Telecommunications Act contained a savings clause preserving applicability of the antitrust laws; therefore the antitrust laws were not pre-empted by the Telecoms Act. The Court then turned to the question whether a telecom monopoly's denial of full interconnection services to rivals in order to limit their entry constituted a violation of Section 2 of the Sherman Act, which states: No person shall 'monopolize'.]

---

33 540 U.S. 398, 124 S.Ct. 872, 157 L.Ed.2d 823 (2004).
34 47 U.S.C.

> **CASE** (continued)
>
> III
>
> ... The mere possession of monopoly power, and the concomitant charging of monopoly prices, is not only not unlawful; it is an important element of the free-market system. The opportunity to charge monopoly prices—at least for a short period—is what attracts 'business acumen' in the first place; it induces risk taking that produces innovation and economic growth. To safeguard the incentive to innovate, the possession of monopoly power will not be found unlawful unless it is accompanied by an element of anticompetitive *conduct*.
>
> Firms may acquire monopoly power by establishing an infrastructure that renders them uniquely suited to serve their customers. Compelling such firms to share the source of their advantage is in some tension with the underlying purpose of antitrust law, since it may lessen the incentive for the monopolist, the rival, or both to invest in those economically beneficial facilities. Enforced sharing also requires antitrust courts to act as central planners, identifying the proper price, quantity, and other terms of dealing—a role for which they are ill-suited. Moreover, compelling negotiation between competitors may facilitate the supreme evil of antitrust: collusion. Thus, as a general matter, the Sherman Act 'does not restrict the long recognized right of [a] trader or manufacturer engaged in an entirely private business, freely to exercise his own independent discretion as to parties with whom he will deal.' *United States v. Colgate & Co.*, 250 U.S. 300, 307 (1919).
>
> However, '[t]he high value that we have placed on the right to refuse to deal with other firms does not mean that the right is unqualified.' *Aspen Skiing Co. v. Aspen Highlands Skiing Corp.*, 472 U.S. 585, 601 (1985). Under certain circumstances, a refusal to cooperate with rivals can constitute anticompetitive conduct and violate § 2. We have been very cautious in recognizing such exceptions, because of the uncertain virtue of forced sharing and the difficulty of identifying and remedying anticompetitive conduct by a single firm. The question before us today is whether the allegations of respondent's complaint fit within existing exceptions or provide a basis, under traditional antitrust principles, for recognizing a new one. * * *
>
> [The Court answered in the negative. Verizon did not engage in a voluntary course of dealing with its rivals; it supplied them because of statutory compulsion. Moreover, the unbundled elements to which rivals sought fair access did not even exist as a marketed product apart from the 1996 Act. Further, if there is an essential facilities doctrine, it was not available here.] The 1996 Act's extensive provision for access makes it unnecessary to impose a judicial doctrine of forced access. To the extent respondent's 'essential facilities' argument is distinct from its general § 2 argument, we reject it.

CASE (continued)

IV

Finally, we do not believe that traditional antitrust principles justify adding the present case to the few existing exceptions from the proposition that there is no duty to aid competitors. . . .* * *

. . . [Here, the regulatory] regime was an effective steward of the antitrust function.

Against the slight benefits of antitrust intervention here, we must weigh a realistic assessment of its costs. Under the best of circumstances, applying the requirements of § 2 'can be difficult' because 'the means of illicit exclusion, like the means of legitimate competition, are myriad.' *United States v. Microsoft Corp.*, 253 F.3d 34, 58 (CADC 2001) (en banc) (*per curiam*). Mistaken inferences and the resulting false condemnations 'are especially costly, because they chill the very conduct the antitrust laws are designed to protect.' *Matsushita Elec. Industrial Co. v. Zenith Radio Corp.*, 475 U.S. 574, 594 (1986). The cost of false positives counsels against an undue expansion of § 2 liability. . . .

Even if the problem of false positives did not exist, conduct consisting of anticompetitive violations of § 251 [Telecoms Act duty to give access] may be, as we have concluded with respect to above-cost predatory pricing schemes, 'beyond the practical ability of a judicial tribunal to control.' *Brooke Group Ltd v. Brown & Williamson Tobacco Corp.*, 509 U.S. 209, 223 (1993). Effective remediation of violations of regulatory sharing requirements will ordinarily require continuing supervision of a highly detailed decree. We think that Professor Areeda got it exactly right: 'No court should impose a duty to deal that it cannot explain or adequately and reasonably supervise. . . .' An antitrust court is unlikely to be an effective day-to-day enforcer of these detailed sharing obligations.[35]

The 1996 Act is in an important respect much more ambitious than the antitrust laws. It attempts '*to eliminate the monopolies* enjoyed by the inheritors of AT&T's local franchises.' . . . [535 U.S. at 476]. Section 2 of the Sherman Act, by contrast, seeks merely to prevent *unlawful monopolization*. It would be a serious mistake to conflate the two goals. The Sherman Act . . . does not give judges *carte blanche* to insist that a monopolist alter its way of doing business whenever some other approach might yield greater competition. We conclude that respondent's complaint fails to state a claim under the Sherman Act. * * *

---

[35] 'The Court of Appeals also thought that respondent's complaint might state a claim under a "monopoly leveraging" theory . . . . We disagree. To the extent the Court of Appeals dispensed with a requirement that there be a "dangerous probability of success" in monopolizing a second market, it erred. In any event, leveraging presupposes anticompetitive conduct, which in this case could only be the refusal-to-deal claim we have rejected.'

> **NOTES AND QUESTIONS**
>
> 1. *Trinko* is a regulated industries case but it also has modelled the law on refusals to deal and exclusionary strategies in non-regulatory contexts. Why is the Court so reluctant to allow an antitrust duty to deal?
> 2. How would the *Commercial Solvents* and *United Brands* cases be resolved under US law?

(iii) The special relevance of intellectual property

A firm may own intellectual property ('IP') rights, which typically grant the exclusive right to practice, use or license a patent, trademark, copyright or design. If the owner of IP has a dominant position and declines to license its IP, is the case for duty to deal stronger on grounds that the IP right reflects state-granted privileges that may be used to obstruct free movement of goods and to partition the internal market? Or is the right to refuse to deal stronger because IP is a protected form of property granted as a reward and incentive for innovation?

IP rights are a subject of Article 36 TFEU (ex Article 30 ECT), which provides that Articles 34 and 35, guaranteeing free movement of goods, shall not preclude 'restrictions on imports, exports or goods in transit justified on grounds of . . . the protection of industrial and commercial property' as long as such restrictions are not 'a means of arbitrary discrimination or a disguised restriction on trade between Member States.' The Court of Justice held, in *Deutsche Grammophon Gesellschaft GmbH v. Metro-SB-Grossmärkte GmbH*:[36]

> . . . Article [36] only admits derogations from [free movement principles] to the extent to which they are justified for the purpose of safeguarding rights which constitute the specific subject-matter of such property.

In 1988, the Court of Justice considered questions posed by national courts regarding exclusive design rights in automobile parts of Volvo and Renault. In the *Volvo* judgement the Court said:

> [T]he rights of the proprietor of a protected design to prevent third parties from manufacturing and selling or importing, without its consent, products incorporating the design constitutes the very subject-matter of his exclusive right. It follows . . . that a refusal to grant such a license cannot in itself constitute an abuse of a dominant position.

---

[36] Case 78/70, *Deutsche Grammophon Gesellschaft GmbH v. Metro-SB-Grossmärkte GmbH* [1971] ECR 487, EU:C:1971:59, para. 11.

[T]he exercise of an exclusive right by the proprietor of a registered design in respect of car body panels may be prohibited by Article [102 TFEU] if it involves, on the part of an undertaking holding a dominant position, certain abusive conduct such as the arbitrary refusal to supply spare parts to independent repairers, the fixing of prices for spare parts at an unfair level or a decision no longer to produce spare parts for a particular model even though many cars of that model are still in circulation, provided that such conduct is liable to affect trade between Member States.[37]

When is such a refusal to supply 'arbitrary', and when, on the other hand, does it go to the heart of the IP owner's right of exclusivity?

The principle of deference to IP holders' essential rights was tested in a case in which the copyright holders' right to refuse to license conflicted directly with the public's interest in competition. (But doesn't it always, if viewed in the short term?) The question arose whether each of the three significant TV broadcasters in Ireland was required to license its TV schedules to a third party who proposed to publish a consolidated TV guide.

CASE

Radio Telefís Eireann v. Commission (Joined Cases C-241 and C-242/91 P) (*'Magill'*)[38]

[Radio Telefís Eireann ('RTE'), BBC, and Independent Television Publications ('ITP') operated TV stations. Each published weekly listings of its programmes in Ireland and Northern Ireland, gave newspapers its schedule free on a daily basis, and claimed copyright protection over its programme listings. At that time, no composite TV guide existed. Magill conceived the idea of publishing a weekly magazine, the Magill TV Guide, listing all available TV programs in Ireland and Northern Ireland. It sought licenses from RTE, BBC and ITP, but the licenses were denied. Magill nonetheless proceeded with the publication. In a suit by the three copyright owners, the Irish High Court enjoined Magill from using the copyrighted listings of RTE, BBC and ITP. Magill complained to the Commission. The Commission found that each of the three broadcasters had and abused a dominant position. Two of the stations challenged the decision, claiming that they had done nothing more than exercise their rights under the Irish copyright law. The Irish copyright law protected a TV station's schedule of its programmes. Although this was a protection not extended by laws of other nations, the law itself was valid under Articles 34/36 TFEU, for it conferred IP rights

---

37 Case 238/87, *Volvo AB v. Erik Veng (UK) Ltd* [1988] ECR 6211, EU:C:1988:477, paras. 8–9.
38 [1995] ECR I-743, EU:C:1995:98.

CASE *(continued)*

and was not an arbitrary discrimination or disguised restriction on trade between Member States. [Re-read Articles 34, 36 and 345 TFEU.] The TV stations claimed that they had done nothing more than exercise their copyright right to refuse to license. Moreover, each station argued that it was not dominant; it supplied less than a third of the market. The General Court upheld the Commission, and the stations appealed.]

(a) Existence of a dominant position

46   So far as dominant position is concerned, it is to be remembered at the outset that mere ownership of an intellectual property right cannot confer such a position.

47   However, the basic information as to the channel, day, time and title of programmes is the necessary result of programming by television stations, which are thus the only source of such information for an undertaking, like Magill, which wishes to publish it together with commentaries or pictures. By force of circumstance, RTE and ITP, as the agent of ITV, enjoy, along with the BBC, a *de facto* monopoly over the information used to compile listings for the television programmes received in most households in Ireland and 30% to 40% of households in Northern Ireland. The appellants are thus in a position to prevent effective competition on the market in weekly television magazines. [They therefore] occupied a dominant position. . . .

(b) Existence of abuse

48   With regard to the issue of abuse, the arguments of the appellants and IPO wrongly presuppose that where the conduct of an undertaking in a dominant position consists of the exercise of a right classified by national law as 'copyright', such conduct can never be reviewed in relation to Article [102] of the Treaty.

49   Admittedly, in the absence of Community standardization or harmonization of laws, determination of the conditions and procedures for granting protection of an intellectual property right is a matter for national rules. Further, the exclusive right of reproduction forms part of the author's rights, so that refusal to grant a licence, even if it is the act of an undertaking holding a dominant position, cannot in itself constitute abuse of a dominant position.

50   However, it is also clear from that judgement . . . that the exercise of an exclusive right by the proprietor may, in exceptional circumstances, involve abusive conduct.

51   In the present case, the conduct objected to is the appellants' reliance on copyright conferred by national legislation so as to prevent Magill—or any other undertaking having the same intention—from publishing on a weekly basis information (channel, day, time and

> **CASE** *(continued)*
>
> title of programmes) together with commentaries and pictures obtained independently of the appellants.
>
> 52   Among the circumstances taken into account by the [General Court] in concluding that such conduct was abusive was, first, the fact that there was, according to the findings of the [General Court], no actual or potential substitute for a weekly television guide offering information on the programmes for the week ahead. On this point, the [General Court] confirmed the Commission's finding that the complete lists of programmes for a 24-hour period—and for a 48-hour period at weekends and before public holidays—published in certain daily and Sunday newspapers, and the television sections of certain magazines covering, in addition, 'highlights' of the week's programmes, were only to a limited extent substitutable for advance information to viewers on all the week's programmes. Only weekly television guides containing comprehensive listings for the week ahead would enable users to decide in advance which programmes they wished to follow and arrange their leisure activities for the week accordingly. The [General Court] also established that there was a specific, constant and regular potential demand on the part of consumers. . . .
>
> 53   Thus the appellants—who were, by force of circumstance, the only source of the basic information on programme scheduling which is the indispensable raw material for compiling a weekly television guide—gave viewers wishing to obtain information on the choice of programmes for the week ahead no choice but to buy the weekly guides for each station and draw from each of them the information they needed to make comparisons.
>
> 54   The appellants' refusal to provide basic information by relying on national copyright provisions thus prevented the appearance of a new product, a comprehensive weekly guide to television programmes, which the appellants did not offer and for which there was a potential consumer demand. Such refusal constitutes an abuse under heading (b) of the second paragraph of Article [102] of the Treaty.
>
> 55   Second, there was no justification for such refusal either in the activity of television broadcasting or in that of publishing television magazines. . . .
>
> 56   Third, and finally, as the [General Court] also held, the appellants, by their conduct, reserved to themselves the secondary market of weekly television guides by excluding all competition on that market since they denied access to the basic information which is the raw material indispensable for the compilation of such a guide.
>
> 57   In the light of all those circumstances, the [General Court] did not err in law in holding that the appellants' conduct was an abuse of a dominant position within the meaning of Article [102] of the Treaty. * * *

> **NOTES AND QUESTIONS**
>
> 1. From what facts did the Court find dominance? Was each of the three broadcasters dominant?
> 2. When does a dominant firm's refusal to license IP constitute an abuse? Does *Magill* erode the rule in *Volvo*? What is the significance of the fact that the TV stations 'prevented the appearance of a new product'? If the stations had formed a joint venture to produce a TV guide, could they have lawfully refused to grant a licence to Magill?
> 3. IP normally embodies the right to refuse to grant a licence. The right of exclusivity is the essence of IP rights, even if a holder of the right is dominant.[39] How and when does the right of exclusivity cease to become an essential ingredient of the IP right? Does it lose this character whenever competition and consumer interests would be better served by the grant of a licence? If so, does Article 102 TFEU eclipse Article 36 TFEU? How does the Court prevent this eclipse?
> 4. There is an unexplored question in *Magill*: Was the Irish copyright law excessive in protecting the mere listing of a TV schedule? Is copyright protection of a TV schedule even arguably necessary or important to preserve incentives to invent and to be creative? Few other jurisdictions protect a mere schedule. However, the Court could not have solved the *Magill* problem by declaring that Ireland stepped out of bounds by trying to give copyright protection to TV listings, for, under the Treaty, Ireland alone had the right to declare the scope of Irish property interests. (Article 345 TFEU). Could it have solved the problem by declaring that, on the particular facts, the Article 102 interests outweighed the Article 36 interests? Is part of the solution to consider the effect of antitrust enforcement on incentives to create? What impact was the antitrust enforcement in *Magill* likely to have on incentives to create or broadcast innovative programming?

CASE

IMS Health GmbH & Co. (Case C-418/01)[40]

[IMS Health Inc. was a market research company that provided services to the pharmaceutical industry. It devised a 'brick structure' in which it divided Germany into geographic areas that were used to measure and report sales of individual pharmaceutical products. Its efforts culminated in the development of the 1860 brick structure—a format for categorizing and reporting data that was the central feature of its regional and wholesaler data-information services. The format was protected by German copyright law.

National Data Corporation ('NDC') entered the German market to provide marketing data to the pharmaceutical industry, in competition with IMS. The pharmaceutical companies wanted the data only in the 1860 format. NDC asked IMS for a licence for the 1860 format, but IMS refused. It thereupon began selling marketing data to the pharmaceutical industry based on copies of the 1860 brick structure.

---

39 *Magill*, para. 49.
40 [2004] ECR I-5039, EU:C:2004:257.

> **CASE** *(continued)*
>
> IMS brought proceedings in a German court to prohibit NDC from using the IMS brick structure, on grounds that the brick structure was a database protected by copyright and IMS had the right to refuse to license it. The German court granted the injunction but then stayed the proceedings, observing that IMS could not refuse to license NDC if the refusal constituted an abuse of dominance under Article 102 TFEU. The national court referred to the Court of Justice questions concerning the circumstances under which such a refusal constitutes an abuse. The Court of Justice answered: Only in exceptional circumstances may the exercise of an exclusive (IP) right constitute an abuse of dominance. First, access to the product, service or IP must be indispensable to enable the undertaking to carry on business in a market.]
>
> 28 [To determine indispensability,] it must be determined whether there are products or services which constitute alternative solutions, even if they are less advantageous, and whether there are technical, legal or economic obstacles capable of making it impossible or at least unreasonably difficult for any undertaking seeking to operate in the market to create, possibly in cooperation with other operators, the alternative products or services . . . . [I]n order to accept the existence of economic obstacles, it must be established, at the very least, that the creation of those products or services is not economically viable for production on a scale comparable to that of the undertaking which controls the existing product or service. * * *
>
> 38 [Where access is indispensable,] it is sufficient that three cumulative conditions be satisfied, namely, that that refusal is preventing the emergence of a new product for which there is a potential consumers demand, that it is unjustified and such as to exclude any competition on a secondary market. * * *
>
> 44 . . . [I]t is sufficient that a potential market or even hypothetical market can be identified. Such is the case where the products or services are indispensable in order to carry on a particular business and where there is an actual demand for them on the part of undertakings which seek to carry on the business for which they are indispensable.
>
> 45 Accordingly, it is determinative that two different stages of production may be identified and that they are interconnected, the upstream product is indispensable in as much as for supply of the downstream product.
>
> 46 Transposed to the facts of the case in the main proceedings, that approach prompts consideration as to whether the 1860 brick structure constitutes, upstream, an indispensable factor in the downstream supply of German regional sales data for pharmaceutical products.
>
> 47 It is for the national court to establish whether that is in fact the position, and, if so be the case, to examine whether the refusal by IMS to grant a licence to use the structure at issue is capable of excluding all competition on the market for the supply of German regional sales data on pharmaceutical products. * * *

> **NOTES AND QUESTIONS**
>
> 1. If all four of the elements specified in *IMS* are proved (indispensability and the three 'sufficient' conditions), is IMS's copyrighted brick structure an essential facility?
> 2. Who won on the question whether there must be two interconnected markets?
> 3. How likely was NDC to prevail on each necessary element of its case? Which would be the hardest hurdle to overcome?

* * *

The next important refusal-to-deal case is *Microsoft*. The US Department of Justice had already brought a monopolization case against Microsoft and had won a large part of it. The European case involved practices later in time; and they were practices of a different sort. By the time the European Commission brought proceedings, Microsoft had eliminated the more blatantly predatory and coercive acts of the sort condemned in the US case.

(iv)   Interoperability

CASE

Microsoft Corp. v. Commission (Case T-201/04)[41]

[The European Commission brought proceedings against Microsoft, a 'super-dominant' firm with more than 90% of the PC operating systems market, for abusing its dominant position in violation of Article 102 TFEU. The Commission found two sets of Microsoft's practices to be illegal: (1) Bundling its media player with its operating system (Windows), which had become the standard in the market. RealNetworks had pioneered the media player and RealNetworks' player was popularly used with Windows. Thereafter Microsoft made its own media player and bundled it with Windows, foreclosing media player rivals from the most efficient channels to the market. (2) Refusal to deal, in the form of refusing to provide workgroup server software rivals with full interoperability information to connect with Windows and with Microsoft's workgroup server software. Workgroup servers are servers used by small enterprises to interconnect file, printing, document-sharing and management functions of all PCs within the enterprise. Novell and others had pioneered workgroup server software. Before Microsoft developed such software of its own, it gave full interoperability information to the workgroup server software providers. Then Microsoft made its own workgroup server software and withheld from its rivals the full information they needed for seamless interoperability. Microsoft noted that it provided a good deal of interoperability

---

[41] [2007] ECR II-3601, EU:T:2007:289.

CASE *(continued)*

information to the workgroup server software providers. Then Microsoft made its own workgroup server software and withheld from its rivals the full information they needed for seamless interoperability. Microsoft noted that it provided a good deal of interoperability information and claimed that it had no legal duty to help its rivals. Belatedly, it also claimed that its interface protocols containing the withheld interoperability information contained IP and that it had a right of absolute exclusivity of its IP.

For remedies, the Commission ordered Microsoft to supply the full interoperability protocols, offer an unbundled version of Windows without the media player, and pay a fine of €497 million for the two violations. Microsoft appealed to the General Court. At this point, we cover only the interoperability (duty to deal) issue.

Microsoft contended that disclosure of the interface protocols would entail disclosure of IP. The Commission disputed this claim but nonetheless argued that the circumstances satisfied the criteria of *Magill/IMS*: (1) access (here, to the complete interoperability information) must be indispensable, (2) the refusal must exclude any effective competition on a neighbouring market, and (3) the refusal must prevent the appearance of a new product for which there is a potential consumer demand. (4) If the criteria are satisfied, it then falls to the dominant firm to prove an objective justification.

The Court first held that the Commission did not err in finding that seamless interoperability was indispensable to efficient operation of rivals, and that the refusal gave rise to a risk of elimination of competition. The Court then summarized the evidence showing the sharp rise of Microsoft's share of workgroup server software, to more than 60%, and the decline of the competitors' shares, as soon as Microsoft stopped providing full interoperability information. It gave examples of how Microsoft killed off two of competitors' products, NDS for NT developed by Novell, and PC NetLink developed by Sun Microsystems, by withholding interoperability information. See facts at para. 654 below.] * * *

593   The above factors confirm that Microsoft's refusal has the consequence that its competitors' products are confined to marginal positions or even made unprofitable. The fact that there may be marginal competition between operators on the market cannot therefore invalidate the Commission's argument that all effective competition was at risk of being eliminated on that market. * * *

(3)   *The new product* * * *

647   The circumstance relating to the appearance of a new product, as envisaged in *Magill* and *IMS Health*, cannot be the only parameter which determines whether a refusal to license an intellectual property right is capable of causing prejudice to consumers within the

> **CASE** *(continued)*
>
> meaning of Article [102(b)]. As that provision states, such prejudice may arise where there is a limitation not only of production or markets, but also of technical development. * * *
>
> 650 ... [T]he Commission was correct to observe that '[owing] to the lack of interoperability that competing work group server operating system products can achieve with the Windows domain architecture, an increasing number of consumers are locked into a homogeneous Windows solution at the level of work group server operating systems'.
>
> 651 ... Microsoft's refusal prevented its competitors from developing work group server operating systems capable of attaining a sufficient degree of interoperability with the Windows domain architecture, with the consequence that consumers' purchasing decisions in respect of work group server operating systems were channelled towards Microsoft's products. The Court has also already observed that it was apparent from a number of documents in the file that the technologies of the Windows 2000 range, in particular Active Directory, were increasingly being taken up by organisations. As interoperability problems arise more acutely with work group server operating systems in that range of products than with those of the preceding generation, the increasing uptake of those systems merely reinforces the 'lock-in' effect referred to in the preceding paragraph.
>
> 652 The limitation thus placed on consumer choice is all the more damaging to consumers because, as already observed, they consider that non-Microsoft work group server operating systems are better than Windows work group server operating systems with respect to a series of features to which they attach great importance, such as 'reliability/availability of the ... system' and 'security included with the server operating system'.
>
> 653 In the second place, the Commission was correct to consider that the artificial advantage in terms of interoperability that Microsoft retained by its refusal discouraged its competitors from developing and marketing work group server operating systems with innovative features, to the prejudice, notably, of consumers. That refusal has the consequence that those competitors are placed at a disadvantage by comparison with Microsoft so far as the merits of their products are concerned, particularly with regard to parameters such as security, reliability, ease of use or operating performance speed.
>
> 654 The Commission's finding that '[i]f Microsoft's competitors had access to the interoperability information that Microsoft refuses to supply, they could use the disclosures to make the advanced features of their own products available in the framework of the web of interoperability relationships that underpin the Windows domain architecture' is corroborated by the conduct which those competitors had adopted in the past, when they had access to certain information concerning Microsoft's products. The two examples which the Commission gives . . ., 'PC NetLink' and 'NDS for NT', speak volumes in that regard.

CASE *(continued)*

PC NetLink is software developed by Sun on the basis of AS/U, which had been developed by AT&T using source code which Microsoft had licensed to it in the 1990s. A document submitted by Microsoft during the administrative procedure shows that the innovative features and added value that PC NetLink brought to Windows work group networks was used as a selling point for that product. Likewise, in its marketing material, Novell highlighted the new features which NDS for NT—software which it had developed using reverse engineering—brought to the Windows domain architecture (in this instance Windows NT).

655 The Commission was careful to emphasise, in that context, that there was 'ample scope for differentiation and innovation beyond the design of interface specifications'. In other words, the same specification can be implemented in numerous different and innovative ways by software designers. * * *

659 Last, Microsoft's argument that it will have less incentive to develop a given technology if it is required to make that technology available to its competitors is of no relevance to the examination of the circumstance relating to the new product, where the issue to be decided is the impact of the refusal to supply on the incentive for Microsoft's competitors to innovate and not on Microsoft's incentives to innovate. That is an issue which will be decided when the Court examines the circumstance relating to the absence of objective justification.

660 In the third place, the Commission is also correct to reject as unfounded Microsoft's assertion during the administrative procedure that it was not demonstrated that its refusal caused prejudice to consumers.

661 First of all, . . . the results of the third Mercer survey show that, contrary to Microsoft's contention, consumers consider non-Microsoft work group server operating systems to be better than Windows work group server operating systems on a number of features to which they attach great importance. * * *

664 Last, . . . it is settled case-law that Article [102] covers not only practices which may prejudice consumers directly but also those which indirectly prejudice them by impairing an effective competitive structure. In this case, Microsoft impaired the effective competitive structure on the work group server operating systems market by acquiring a significant market share on that market. * * *

(4) The absence of objective justification

666 In the first place, Microsoft claims that the refusal to supply the information was objectively justified by the intellectual property rights which it holds over the 'technology'

CASE *(continued)*

concerned. It has made significant investment in designing its communication protocols and the commercial success which its products have achieved represents the just reward. It is generally accepted, moreover, that an undertaking's refusal to communicate a specific technology to its competitors may be justified by the fact that it does not wish them to use that technology to compete with it.

667   In the reply, Microsoft relies on the fact that the technology which it is required to disclose to its competitors is secret, that it is of great value for licensees and that it contains significant innovation.

668   ... [T]he applicant adds that it had an objective justification for not licensing the technology 'given the prejudice to incentives to innovate that would have resulted if Sun (or others) had used that technology to build a "functional equivalent" that would compete against Microsoft's products on the same market'. * * *

697   The Court finds that, as the Commission correctly submits, Microsoft, which bore the initial burden of proof, did not sufficiently establish that if it were required to disclose the interoperability information that would have a significant negative impact on its incentives to innovate.

698   Microsoft merely put forward vague, general and theoretical arguments on that point.... Microsoft merely stated that '[d]isclosure would ... eliminate future incentives to invest in the creation of more intellectual property', without specifying the technologies or products to which it thus referred. * * *

701   It follows that it has not been demonstrated that the disclosure of the information to which that remedy relates will significantly reduce—still less eliminate—Microsoft's incentives to innovate.

702   In that context, the Court observes that it is normal practice for operators in the industry to disclose to third parties the information which will facilitate interoperability with their products and Microsoft itself had followed that practice until it was sufficiently established on the work group server operating systems market. Such disclosure allows the operators concerned to make their own products more attractive and therefore more valuable. In fact, none of the parties has claimed in the present case that such disclosure had had any negative impact on those operators' incentives to innovate. * * *

711   It follows from all of the foregoing considerations that Microsoft has not demonstrated the existence of any objective justification for its refusal to disclose the interoperability at issue. * * *

NOTES AND QUESTIONS

1. Were the *IMS/Magill* criteria faithfully applied to determine whether the refusal excluded 'any effective competition'? Were the *IMS/Magill* criteria faithfully applied to determine whether the refusal prevented the appearance of a new product for which there is a potential consumer demand? Should the *IMS/Magill* criteria be necessary conditions for determining whether Microsoft's withholding of interoperability information harmed competition and constituted abuse of dominance? If not, what would have been an appropriate framework for analysis?
2. How did the Court deal with the effect of the enforcement on incentives to innovate—Microsoft's incentives and the rivals' incentives? What role was played by burdens of proof in this regard? Do you agree with the Court's treatment?
3. How would the US *Trinko* Court have framed the question about incentives? Might it have asked: Did Microsoft have a duty to increase the incentives of rivals? Did it have a duty of forced sharing? What presumptions and burdens of proof flow from the way in which the question is asked?

    The closest US case to the EU *Microsoft* interoperability case is *Novell, Inc. v. Microsoft Corp.*[42] The court in *Novell* held that Microsoft did not run afoul of Section 2 of the Sherman Act (monopolization) by withdrawing from Novell, maker of WordPerfect software and the main competitor of Microsoft Word, access to interface shortcuts that had made WordPerfect viable. The court said that Microsoft had the right to refuse to deal; that it had no duty to share its IP; that Novell needed to show—but did not—that Microsoft's conduct was 'irrational but for its anticompetitive effect'. This is a tough standard to meet. Is it tougher than *Trinko* requires?
4. US cases have held that an IP owner has an absolute right to refuse to license its IP when the refusal is not part of an illegal scheme.[43] How would the US courts decide *Magill*, assuming the copyright protection was valid? How would they decide *IMS*? And the EU *Microsoft* case (interoperability)?
5. IP issues have become part of the regular fare of abuse of dominance cases. By one initiative, the European authorities are proceeding against patent holders of pharmaceuticals who are strategically blocking the competition of generic drugs—which usually sell for a fraction of the price of the brand. In *AstraZeneca*, the Court of Justice upheld the General Court and the Commission's findings that AstraZeneca, producer of the Losec ulcer drug, abused its dominant position by deliberately misleading patent offices in order to maintain supplementary protection certificates to delay entry of generic competitors, and that it applied for deregistration of marketing authorizations for Losec capsules to hinder parallel importers who could otherwise rely on those authorizations for regulatory approval. AstraZeneca's conduct offended the principles of freedom to compete on the merits and the responsibility of a dominant firm not to prejudice undistorted competition within the EU.[44]

    In a second initiative, the Commission has targeted patent holders who sue for injunctions against infringement in the following circumstances. The industry—such as mobile phones and tablets—has developed a standard and the members of the industry have agreed to license any patents essential to compliance with the standard on fair, reasonable and non-

---

42 731 F.3d 1064 (10th Cir. 2013).
43 See *Independent Service Organizations Antitrust Litigation (CSU v. Xerox)*, 203 F.3d 1322 (Fed. Cir. 2000), cert. denied, 531 U.S. 1143 (2001).
44 Case C-457/10 P, *AstraZeneca v. Commission*, EU:C:2012:770, para. 98.

discriminatory terms ('FRAND'). Before the FRAND terms are agreed, the holder of a standard essential patent ('SEP') sues a rival—for example, Samsung sues Apple—for infringement, and seeks an injunction against Apple's use of the essential patent; if the injunction is granted, Apple might have to take a generation of iPads off the market. In a case with a similar fact pattern, the Commission found an infringement of Article 102 TFEU by Motorola, and in another it agreed to commitments by Samsung.[45]

A similar case was subsequently referred to the Court of Justice for a preliminary ruling.[46] The case involved an alleged infringement by ZTE of a Huawei patent declared essential for a standard established by the European Telecommunications Standards Institute ('ETSI'). Huawei had undertaken to grant licences to third parties on FRAND terms but no licensing agreement could be finalized with ZTE at the end of the negotiations. Huawei subsequently sought an injunction against ZTE prohibiting the marketing of products operating on the basis of the standard embedding its patent, as well as the rendering of accounts, the recall of products and an award of damages. After distinguishing the case from precedents such as Volvo, Magill and IMS Health on account of the facts that 'the patent at issue is essential to a standard established by a standardisation body, rendering its use indispensable to all competitors' and that 'an undertaking to grant licenses on FRAND terms creates legitimate expectations on the part of third parties' (paras. 49 and 53), the Court took the following stance (para. 71):

> ... Article 102 TFEU must be interpreted as meaning that the proprietor of an SEP, which has given an irrevocable undertaking to a standardisation body to grant a licence to third parties on FRAND terms, does not abuse its dominant position, within the meaning of Article 102 TFEU, by bringing an action for infringement seeking an injunction prohibiting the infringement of its patent or seeking the recall of products for the manufacture of which that patent has been used, as long as:
>
> – prior to bringing that action, the proprietor has, first, alerted the alleged infringer of the infringement complained about by designating that patent and specifying the way in which it has been infringed, and, secondly, after the alleged infringer has expressed its willingness to conclude a licensing agreement on FRAND terms, presented to that infringer a specific, written offer for a licence on such terms, specifying, in particular, the royalty and the way in which it is to be calculated, and
> – where the alleged infringer continues to use the patent in question, the alleged infringer has not diligently responded to that offer, in accordance with recognised commercial practices in the field and in good faith, this being a matter which must be established on the basis of objective factors and which implies, in particular, that there are no delaying tactics.

Prior to reaching that conclusion, the Court of Justice underlined the need to find a fair balance between the interests protected by property rights, including that of effective

---

45 Commission Decisions of 29 April 2014 in Case AT.39985 – Motorola/Enforcement of GPRS Standard Essential Patents, and Case AT.39939 – Samsung/Enforcement of UMTS Standard Essential Patents.
46 Case C-170/13, *Huawei Technologies Co. Ltd v. ZTE Corp.*, EU:C:2015:477.

judicial protection and thus access to court, on the one hand, and those protected by competition principles in view of the risks of exclusionary conduct, on the other hand (paras. 52–55).

How do you assess the 'balance' struck by the Court? Is it fair, is it efficient? What do you make of the fact that the irrevocable commitment given by Huawei to ETSI, to the effect that it would license its patent on FRAND terms, triggered its exposure under Article 102 TFEU? What are the questions left unresolved by the Court and how significant are they?

b. *Exclusive dealing and loyalty rebates*

Refusals to deal are the tip of the iceberg of the abuse-of-dominance offence. From the early days in the application of abuse of dominance law, the Court of Justice cautioned dominant firms not to foreclose markets to the detriment of other market actors. Originally, the Court was particularly concerned with dominant firms' advantages over their smaller rivals. In later years, the Commission prioritized consumers' interests. As apparent from the cases discussed in this section, courts commonly assume that competitors' rights to access markets on their merits coincide with consumers' interests. However, these objectives might or might not coincide, depending on whether the dominant firm's conduct is an efficient way to reach consumers, and whether the conduct does or does not deprive the rivals of an efficient and important way for them to reach consumers.

Ask yourself as you read the cases: Who and what are the Commission and the Courts trying to protect? Competition? The competition process? Efficiency? Innovation? By what means are they trying to do so—protecting the process? Protecting competitors' access? Protecting the competitive structure of markets? Protecting freedom?[47] Many of the Court of Justice judgements, even contemporary ones, have not accepted the economic/consumer welfare approach of the Commission or (in some cases) of the General Court. In one modern case entailing a charge of selective price cuts, however, the Court of Justice did highlight consumers as the constituency to be protected.[48]

This section first presents excerpts from the three cases—*Hoffmann-LaRoche*, *Michelin II* and *British Airways*—that have formed the backbone of the EU law on special responsibility of the dominant firm and rights of all market players to contest markets on their merits.

---

47 For the Commission's Guidance, see Guidance Paper, paras. 31–45.
48 *Post Danmark I*, see below at p. 220.

CASE

Hoffmann-La Roche & Co. AG v. Commission (Case 85/76)[49]

[Hoffmann-La Roche ('Roche') had a dominant position in each of several vitamins. These included vitamin A, of which it held 47%, and vitamin B_6, of which it held more than 80%. Roche had contracted with 22 large purchasers, including Merck and Unilever, for the sale of vitamins to them.

Some purchasers agreed to buy several kinds of vitamins exclusively from Roche. Some contracts were requirements contracts, entered into at the request of purchasers who wanted assurance that their requirements would be filled.

In other cases, buyers agreed to buy most of their needs from Roche, and Roche agreed to give the buyer 'fidelity rebates'. These discounts became effective as to all past purchases when the buyer passed certain thresholds representing portions of the requirements of the buyer. The rebates applied cumulatively to the purchase of more than one kind of vitamin.

Many of the fidelity rebate contracts contained 'English clauses'. Under these clauses, if a customer received a better offer from a competitor and Roche refused to lower its price to meet the better offer, the customer was free to obtain supplies from the competitor without losing the benefit of the rebate. To meet the conditions of the escape clause, the better terms had to be offered by another competitor operating in Europe and on the same scale as Roche, and the offer had to be comparable.

Roche also entered into several contracts with large purchasers tailored to the parties' needs. For example, it had a contract with Merck for the sale of vitamin B_6. In the Merck contract, Roche recited that it planned to double its production capacity and would like to cover part of Merck's requirements. Merck agreed to buy from Roche its requirements above its own manufacturing capacity. Roche agreed to give Merck a 20% discount, Merck agreed not to resell the vitamins purchased at this discount, and Roche agreed to buy its requirements of phosphoric ester from Merck under the same conditions.

The Court of Justice held that the exclusive supply and requirements contracts were an abuse of a dominant position, even when entered into at the request of the purchaser. As for the Merck contract, the Court concluded that the purpose was to secure a stable market for

---

49 [1979] ECR 461, EU:C:1979:36.

CASE *(continued)*

Roche's increased production and to protect Roche from 'the risks of competition', and that it, too, offended Article 102.

The fidelity rebates were also singled out for condemnation. The rebates constituted price discrimination based on loyalty, not quantity discounts based on lower costs. Once a purchaser began to buy from Roche, the Court said, the customer had a 'powerful incentive' not to buy elsewhere.]

The Court

89   An undertaking which is in a dominant position on a market and ties purchasers—even if it does so at their request—by an obligation or promise on their part to obtain all or most of their requirements exclusively from the said undertaking abuses its dominant position within the meaning of Article [102] of the Treaty, whether the obligation in question is stipulated without further qualification or whether it is undertaken in consideration of the grant of a rebate.

The same applies if the said undertaking, without tying the purchasers by a formal obligation, applies, either under the terms of agreements concluded with these purchasers or unilaterally, a system of fidelity rebates, that is to say discounts conditional on the customer's obtaining all or most of its requirements—whether the quantity of its purchases be large or small—from the undertaking in a dominant position.

90   Obligations of this kind to obtain supplies exclusively from a particular undertaking, whether or not they are in consideration of rebates or of the granting of fidelity rebates intended to give the purchaser an incentive to obtain his supplies exclusively from the undertaking in a dominant position, are incompatible with the objective of undistorted competition within the Common Market, because—unless there are exceptional circumstances which may make an agreement between undertakings in the context of Article [101] and in particular of paragraph (3) of that article, permissible—they are not based on an economic transaction which justifies this burden or benefit but are designed to deprive the purchaser of or restrict his possible choices of sources of supply and to deny other producers access to the market.

The fidelity rebate, unlike quantity rebates exclusively linked with the volume of purchases from the producer concerned, is designed through the grant of a financial advantage to prevent customers from obtaining their supplies from competing producers. Furthermore the effect of fidelity rebates is to apply dissimilar conditions to equivalent transactions with other trading parties in that two purchasers pay a different price for the same quantity of the same product depending on whether they obtain their supplies exclusively from the undertaking in a dominant position or have several sources of supply.

> **CASE** *(continued)*
>
> Finally these practices by an undertaking in a dominant position and especially on an expanding market tend to consolidate this position by means of a form of competition which is not based on the transactions effected and is therefore distorted.
>
> 91 ... The concept of abuse is an objective concept relating to the behaviour of an undertaking in a dominant position which is such as to influence the structure of a market where, as a result of the very presence of the undertaking in question, the degree of competition is weakened and which, through recourse to methods different from those which condition normal competition in products or services on the basis of the transactions of commercial operators, has the effect of hindering the maintenance of the degree of competition still existing in the market or the growth of that competition. * * *

A few years later, the Court summarized the concept of abuse in another major exclusive dealing case, *Michelin I*:[50]

> 70 Article [102] covers practices which are likely to affect the structure of a market where, as a direct result of the presence of the undertaking in question, competition has already been weakened and which, through recourse to methods different from those governing normal competition in products or services based on traders' performance, have the effect of hindering the maintenance or development of the level of competition still existing on the market.

Michelin II came before the General Court 20 years later.[51] The Court reaffirmed that fidelity rebates harm competition. Thus:

> 97 ... [A]n undertaking in a dominant position has a special responsibility not to allow its conduct to impair genuine undistorted competition on the common market. Not all competition on price can be regarded as legitimate. An undertaking in a dominant position cannot have recourse to means other than those within the scope of competition on the merits.

What is the 'scope of competition on the merits'? Is a lower price to customers competition on the merits? If not, why and how to distinguish rebates from 'meritorious' price competition?

---

50 Case 322/81, *NV Nederlandsche Banden-Industrie Michelin v. Commission* [1983] ECR 3461, EU:C:1983:313 ('*Michelin I*').
51 Case T-203/01, *Manufacture Française Des Pneumatiques Michelin v. Commission* [2003] ECR II-4071, EU:T:2003:250 ('*Michelin II*').

By the time the next major fidelity rebate case came to the Court of Justice, the Court spoke in terms of harm to consumers as well as harm to excluded competitors and to competition.

Note on British Airways Plc v. Commission

British Airways ('BA') gave financial incentives to travel agents through discounts and bonuses variable in amount depending on the agent's performance in selling BA tickets. The Commission held that the loyalty and discounting plans abused BA's dominant position in the UK market for air travel agency services. The General Court and the Court of Justice dismissed the appeals.[52] The Court of Justice said:

> 75 ... [T]he Court took the view that the pressure exerted on resellers by an undertaking in a dominant position which granted bonuses with those characteristics is further strengthened where that undertaking holds a very much larger market share than its competitors.... It held that, in those circumstances, it is particularly difficult for competitors of that undertaking to outbid it in the face of discounts or bonuses based on overall sales volume. By reason of its significantly higher market share, the undertaking in a dominant position generally constitutes an unavoidable business partner in the market. Most often, discounts or bonuses granted by such an undertaking on the basis of overall turnover largely take precedence in absolute terms, even over more generous offers of its competitors. In order to attract the co-contractors of the undertaking in a dominant position, or to receive a sufficient volume of orders from them, those competitors would have to offer them significantly higher rates of discount or bonus.
>
> 76 In the present case,... BA's market share was significantly higher than that of its five main competitors in the United Kingdom.... [T]he rival airlines were not in a position to grant travel agents the same advantages as BA, since they were not capable of attaining in the United Kingdom a level of revenue capable of constituting a sufficiently broad financial base to allow them effectively to establish a reward scheme similar to BA's.
>
> 77 Therefore, the [General Court] was right to examine ... whether the bonus schemes at issue had a fidelity-building effect capable of producing an exclusionary effect. * * * [The General Court held that they did.]

---

52 Case C-95/04 P, *British Airways Plc v. Commission* [2007] ECR I-2331, ECLI:EU:C:2007:166.

[regarding objective economic justification:]

86   . . . It has to be determined whether the exclusionary effect arising from such a system, which is disadvantageous for competition, may be counterbalanced, or outweighed, by advantages in terms of efficiency which also benefit the consumer. If the exclusionary effect of that system bears no relation to advantages for the market and consumers, or if it goes beyond what is necessary in order to attain those advantages, that system must be regarded as an abuse.

87   [The General Court made no error in concluding] that those systems were not based on any objective economic justification. * * *

The second plea, alleging error in not examining the probable effects of the conduct or taking account of evidence that they had no material effect on competing airlines [also held to be unfounded] * * *

The third plea, alleging that the [General Court] erred in not examining whether BA's conduct involved a 'prejudice [to] consumers' within the meaning of [TFEU Article 102(b)]

106   Moreover, . . . Article [102] is aimed not only at practices which may cause prejudice to consumers directly, but also at those which are detrimental to them through their impact on an effective competition structure, such as is mentioned in Article 3(1)(g) EC [now moved to a protocol].

107   The [General Court] was therefore entitled, without committing any error of law, not to examine whether BA's conduct had caused prejudice to consumers within the meaning of subparagraph (b) of the second paragraph of Article [102], but to examine . . . whether the bonus schemes at issue had a restrictive effect on competition and to conclude that the existence of such an effect had been demonstrated by the Commission in the contested decision. * * *

NOTES AND QUESTIONS

1. Who were the victims of BA's conduct? What market effect was necessary to condemn BA's practice? What effect on consumers was necessary? Were consumers probably hurt? On what would consumer harm turn?

2. A case similar to the European *British Airways* case was brought by rival Virgin Atlantic Airways against BA in US courts. Virgin alleged that BA's incentive agreements with travel agencies and corporate customers, with incentive discounts based on target thresholds, shifted so much business away from Virgin that it frustrated Virgin's efforts to expand service from London Heathrow to five US markets. Virgin claimed that BA's agreements resulted in below-cost pricing, and that BA offset its loss by supra-competitive pricing on its monopoly routes. The court gave summary judgement to BA, stating that Virgin's evidence did not support its

below-cost claim or its recoupment claim, that the discounts were competition itself, and that Virgin failed to show how consumers were harmed.[53] What were the differences in concern, emphasis, and appreciation of consumer harm in the two cases against BA?

* * *

The Commission's Guidance Paper was adopted in 2009 and it was meant to add rigour to the assessment of exclusionary practices, focusing on harm to consumers. Did it succeed in adding economic rigour to the law? Consider the three contemporary cases below, *Tomra*, *Intel* and *Post Danmark II*. *Intel* is on appeal to the Court of Justice (see Case C-413/14 P) as the book goes to press; it is therefore discussed in an addendum.

CASE

Tomra Systems ASA v. Commission (Case C-549/10 P)[54]

[Tomra was the dominant operator of reverse vending machines—machines that accept empty bottles and return cash. It did business in Austria, Germany, the Netherlands, Norway and Sweden. It procured agreements from several supermarket chains that they would purchase from Tomra an agreed quantity of machines corresponding to all or a significant part of their requirements (exclusivity agreements), discount agreements keyed to Tomra's supplying their full or almost full demand (quantity commitments), and individualized retroactive rebates keyed to reaching a particular volume of purchases by the end of a period (loyalty rebates).

The Commission analysed the effects of the agreements, found that competition on the relevant markets was foreclosed, and held that Tomra violated Article 102 TFEU. The General Court affirmed the finding of infringement but held that it was not necessary for the Commission to do an effects analysis; following *Michelin II* and *British Airways*, the General Court said it was enough that the rebates conferred 'an advantage not based on any economic service justifying it' and the rebates tended to restrict the buyers choices, 'to bar competitors from access to the market, or to strengthen the dominant position by distorting competition.' [quoted from the General Court by the Court of Justice, para. 71]]

68   The General Court was correct to observe . . . that, for the purposes of proving an abuse of a dominant position within the meaning of Article 102 TFEU, it is sufficient to show that

---

53 *Virgin Atlantic Airways Ltd v. British Airways Plc*, 257 F.3d 256 (2d Cir. 2001).
54 EU:C:2012:221.

CASE *(continued)*

the abusive conduct of the undertaking in a dominant position tends to restrict competition or that the conduct is capable of having that effect. * * *

73   Contrary to what is claimed by the appellants, the invoicing of 'negative prices', in other words prices below cost prices, to customers is not a prerequisite of a finding that a retroactive rebates scheme operated by a dominant undertaking is abusive.

74   . . . The fact that the retroactive rebate schemes oblige competitors to ask negative prices from Tomra's customers benefiting from rebates cannot be regarded as one of the fundamental bases of the contested decision in showing that the retroactive rebate schemes are capable of having anti-competitive effects. Further, the General Court correctly stated . . . that a whole series of other considerations relating to the retroactive rebates operated by Tomra underpinned the contested decision as regards its conclusion that those types of practices were capable of excluding competitors in breach of Article 102 TFEU.

75   In that regard, the General Court observed, more particularly, that, according to the contested decision, in the first place, the incentive to obtain supplies exclusively or almost exclusively from Tomra was particularly strong when thresholds, such as those applied by Tomra, were combined with a system whereby the achievement of the bonus threshold or, as the case may be, a more advantageous threshold benefited all the purchases made by the customer during the reference period and not exclusively the purchasing volume exceeding the threshold concerned . . . . Secondly, the rebate schemes were individual to each customer and the thresholds were established on the basis of the customer's estimated requirements and/or past purchasing volumes and represented a strong incentive for buying all or almost all the equipment needed from Tomra and artificially raised the costs of switching to a different supplier, even for a small number of units. . . . Thirdly, the retroactive rebates often applied to some of the largest customers of the Tomra group with the aim of ensuring their loyalty. . . . Lastly, Tomra failed to show that their conduct was objectively justified or that it generated significant efficiency gains which outweighed the anti-competitive effects on consumers. . . .

[*Regarding proof of violation by means of loyalty rebates, the Court said:*]

79   The General Court was therefore justified in ruling, in essence . . . that the loyalty mechanism was inherent in the supplier's ability to drive out its competitors by means of the suction to itself of the contestable part of demand. When such a trading instrument exists, it is therefore unnecessary to undertake an analyse of the actual effects of the rebates on competition given that, for the purposes of establishing an infringement of Article 102 TFEU, it is sufficient to demonstrate that the conduct at issue is capable of having an effect on competition . . .

The Court eventually stated that the Commission's Guidance Paper, which was published in 2009 and requires an effects analysis, had no relevance to the legal assessment of the contested decision, which was adopted in 2006 (para. 81).

Note on Intel Corp. v. Commission (see also pp. xxix–xxxii)

Intel occupied approximately 70% of the European market for x86 CPU microprocessors, a key component to any computer's brain. Advanced Micro-Devices ('AMD') was its main competitor after other manufacturers exited the market in the first half of the 2000s. When AMD invented a superior chip, Intel developed a strategy to keep the AMD chip from gaining traction in the market for the crucial first months of the launch. According to the Commission, the strategy had two prongs. First, exclusivity rebates granted to computer manufacturers Dell, NEC, HP and Lenovo, as well as to Media-Saturn, a large European retailer. Second, direct payments to computer manufacturers HP, Acer and Lenovo to postpone or cancel the launch of AMD chips. The price of the chips was falling at all relevant times, and the strategy to exclude or marginalize AMD did not fully work; AMD remained a healthy company.

The Commission found a violation by object, and found that the conduct was not justified. As a result, it imposed a fine on Intel of €1.06 billion, which remains the highest fine ever imposed by the Commission on a single company for an infringement of the competition rules. The General Court affirmed. As discussed on pp. xxix–xxxii, the Court of Justice reversed. The appeal called into question, among other things, whether it was proper to treat Intel's conduct as an abuse 'by object'—thus provable without inquiry into effects; and whether it was proper to declare that, even in the case of an effects inquiry, there was no need for the Commission to prove that AMD was an equally efficient competitor.[55]

The General Court's judgement is 1650 paragraphs long; here is an excerpt from the General Court's press release (no. 82/14).

> *The General Court upholds the fine of €1.06 billion imposed on Intel for having abused its dominant position . . .*
>
> *Intel's action against the Commission's decision is dismissed in its entirety*

---

55 Case T-286/09, *Intel Corp. v. Commission*, EU:T:2014:547, appeal pending under Case C-413/14 P.

... In today's judgement, the General Court dismisses the action and thus upholds the Commission's decision.

The General Court finds, inter alia, that the rebates granted to Dell, HP, NEC and Lenovo are exclusivity rebates. Such rebates are, when applied by an undertaking in a dominant position, incompatible with the objective of undistorted competition within the common market. They are not based—save in exceptional circumstances—on an economic transaction which justifies such a financial advantage, but are designed to remove or restrict the purchaser's freedom to choose his sources of supply and to deny other producers access to the market. That type of rebate constitutes an abuse of a dominant position if there is no objective justification for granting it. Exclusivity rebates granted by an undertaking in a dominant position are, by their very nature, capable of restricting competition and foreclosing competitors from the market. It is thus not necessary to show that they are capable of restricting competition on a case by case basis in the light of the facts of the individual case.

In that regard, the General Court states that, in order to submit an attractive offer, it is not sufficient for a competitor to offer Intel's customer attractive conditions for the units that that competitor can itself supply to the customer; it must also offer that customer compensation for the potential loss of the exclusivity rebate for having switched supplier. In order to submit an attractive offer, the competitor must therefore apportion solely to the share which it is able to offer the customer the rebate granted by Intel in respect of all or almost all of the customer's requirements (including the requirements which Intel alone—as an unavoidable supplier—is able to satisfy).

Given that exclusivity rebates granted by an undertaking in a dominant position are, by their very nature, capable of restricting competition, the Commission was not required, contrary to what Intel claims, to make an assessment of the circumstances of the case in order to show that the rebates actually or potentially had the effect of foreclosing competitors from the market.

The General Court finds, in that context, that it is not necessary to examine, by means of the 'as efficient competitor test', whether the Commission correctly assessed the ability of the rebates to foreclose a competitor as efficient as Intel. More precisely, such a test establishes at what price a competitor as efficient as the undertaking in a dominant position would have had to offer its products in order to compensate a customer for the loss of the rebate granted by the undertaking in a dominant position. Since the exclusivity rebates granted by an undertaking in a dominant position are, by their very nature, capable of restricting competition, the Commission was not required to show, in its analysis of the circumstances of the case, that the rebates granted by Intel were capable of foreclosing AMD from the market. Moreover, even if the competitor were still able to cover its costs in spite of the rebates granted, that would not mean that the foreclosure effect did not exist. The mechanism of the exclusivity rebates is such as to make access to the market more difficult for competitors of the undertaking in a dominant position, even if that access is not economically impossible.

In so far as concerns the payments granted to Media-Saturn, the General Court finds that the same anti-competitive mechanism was in place as with the practices adopted vis-à-vis the computer manufacturers, but at a stage further down the supply chain. The Commission was thus not required to examine, in the light of the facts of the case, whether those payments were such as to restrict competition. It was required only to demonstrate that Intel had granted a financial incentive which was subject to an exclusivity condition.

Even supposing that the Commission was required to show, on a case by case basis, that the exclusivity rebates and payments granted to Dell, HP, NEC, Lenovo and Media-Saturn were capable of restricting competition, the General Court considers that the Commission demonstrated that capability to the requisite legal standard in its analysis of the facts of the case.

As regards the payments made to HP, Acer and Lenovo for them to postpone, cancel or restrict the marketing of certain products equipped with AMD CPUs, the General Court finds that those payments were capable of making access to the market more difficult for AMD. It also finds that Intel pursued an anti-competitive object, since the only interest that an undertaking in a dominant position may have in preventing in a targeted manner the marketing of products equipped with a product of a specific competitor is to harm that competitor. Such practices clearly fall outside the scope of competition on the merits. Those practices, which the Commission terms 'naked restrictions', amount to an abuse of a dominant position. * * *

On 20 October 2016, Advocate General Wahl issued his Opinion on the appeal lodged by Intel before the European Court of Justice ('ECJ') against the judgement of the General Court.[56] While not binding upon the ECJ, the Opinion was no less remarkable for it proposed to overturn the General Court on all grounds but for the amount of the fine. On substance, the Advocate General found that the General Court erred in law by assuming that so-called 'exclusivity rebates' are capable of having an anti-competitive effect without considering 'all the circumstances', i.e., the legal and economic context of the rebates including the conditions for the grant of the rebates, the market coverage

---

56 Opinion of Advocate General Wahl in Case C-413/14 P, *Intel Corp. v. Commission*, EU:C:2016:788.

thereof or the duration of the rebate arrangement. Thus, for Advocate General Wahl, the 'context is essential' because loyalty rebates (i.e., rebates that are not purely volume-based) are not always harmful and may instead enhance rivalry. As part of that contextual assessment, the outcome of the 'as efficient competitor's test' is relevant to ascertain the likelihood of anti-competitive effect beyond the mere theoretical possibility that such effect may occur, and so are the market performance of competitors or declining price trends. In contrast, the financial incentive derived by individual customers or even the existence of an overall foreclosure strategy are not conclusive as such when it comes to assessing the capability of a rebate to restrict competition.

NOTES AND QUESTIONS

1. In both cases, *Tomra* and *Intel*, the dominant firm offered customers a better price—but the better price was in exchange for loyalty. When is the better price that is linked to loyalty 'good' price competition, and when is it a 'bad' restraint?
2. Comment on the difference between the Commission's approach (must show negative effect on competition and consumers) and the General Court's approach (the strategies are abusive on their face; they create an irresistible draw of the buyer to the dominant firm). The *Tomra* court called this 'the suction effect'. Does one approach better protect a dynamic market? Induce lower prices (past the short term)? Induce innovation?
3. In *Intel*, comment on the difference between the exclusivity rebates, which the General Court said might in theory be justified, and the 'naked restrictions', i.e., the payments conditioned on the OEMs postponing or cancelling the launch of AMD CPU-based products, which may not be (because such practice 'clearly falls outside of the scope of competition on the merits', para. 205). Is the distinction well taken? Was Advocate General Wahl correct in proposing to uphold the relevance of Intel's argument that prices were falling and AMD was not excluded from the market; therefore competition could not have been harmed? Consult the Court of Justice judgement.
4. According to the Commission Guidance Paper (but not the General Court in *Intel*), exclusionary rebate strategies by dominant firms are not illegal unless they would exclude an 'as efficient' competitor. What is the reason for this condition? Is it a wise condition, to protect low prices? Or is it more likely to protect dominance? These questions were also at the center of the *Post Danmark II* case decided by the Court of Justice in 2015 on preliminary reference.

CASE

Post Danmark A/S v. Konkurrencerådet (Case C-23/14) ('*Post Danmark II*')[57]

[Post Danmark was the postal universal service operator in Denmark and held a statutory monopoly over the distribution of letters weighing up to 50 grams, including direct

---

57 EU:C:2015:651.

CASE *(continued)*

advertising mail. Post Danmark implemented a standardised rebate scheme for direct advertising mail consisting of a progressive scale of rates from 6 to 16% depending on the customer's aggregate purchases over a one-year reference period. Thus the price of mailings for each customer was adjusted at the end of the year, with retroactive effect from the beginning of that same year, on the basis of the quantity of items of mail actually sent.

Acting upon a complaint filed by Post Danmark's only serious competitor on the bulk mail market—which had withdrawn from that market in the meantime, the Danish competition authority (Konkurrencerådet) found the rebate scheme in question abusive for it had the effect of tying customers and foreclosing competition without benefiting consumers. On appeal, the Commercial Court came to the view that there was uncertainty as to the criteria to be applied in order to determine whether such a scheme was capable of having an exclusionary effect contrary to Article 102 TFEU, and therefore requested a preliminary ruling from the Court of Justice.]

[Regarding the abusive character of the rebate scheme]

32   As regards, in the first place, the criteria and rules governing the grant of the rebates, it must be recalled that the rebates at issue in the main proceedings were 'retroactive', in the sense that, if the threshold initially set at the beginning of the year in respect of the quantities of mail was exceeded, the rebate rate applied at the end of the year applied to all mailings presented over the reference period and not only to mailings exceeding the threshold initially estimated. * * *

34   In addition, it must be pointed out that the rebate scheme at issue in the main proceedings was based on a reference period of one year. However, any system under which discounts are granted according to the quantities sold during a relatively long reference period has the inherent effect, at the end of that period, of increasing the pressure on the buyer to reach the purchase figure needed to obtain the discount or to avoid suffering the expected loss for the entire period.

35   Consequently, . . ., such a rebate scheme is capable of making it easier for the dominant undertaking to tie its own customers to itself and attract the customers of its competitors, and thus to secure the suction to itself of the part of demand subject to competition on the relevant market. That suction effect is further enhanced by the fact that, in the case in the main proceedings, the rebates applied without distinction both to the contestable part of demand and to the non-contestable part of demand, that is to say, in the latter case, to addressed advertising mail weighing less than 50 grams covered by Post Danmark's statutory monopoly. * * *

CASE (continued)

42   In those circumstances [including the particularly high market share of Post Danmark], it must be held that a rebate scheme operated by an undertaking, . . . which, without tying customers to that undertaking by a formal obligation, nevertheless tends to make it more difficult for those customers to obtain supplies from competing undertakings, produces an anti-competitive exclusionary effect. * * *

48   [Still], a dominant undertaking may demonstrate that the exclusionary effect arising from its conduct may be counterbalanced, or outweighed, by advantages in terms of efficiency which also benefit the consumer.

[Regarding the relevance of the as-efficient-competitor test referred to in the Guidance Paper]

57   * * * [I]t is not possible to infer from Article 82 EC or the case-law of the Court that there is a legal obligation requiring a finding to the effect that a rebate scheme operated by a dominant undertaking is abusive to be based always on the as-efficient-competitor test.

58   Nevertheless, that conclusion ought not to have the effect of excluding, on principle, recourse to the as-efficient-competitor test in cases involving a rebate scheme for the purposes of examining its compatibility with Article [102 TFEU].

59   On the other hand, in a situation such as that in the main proceedings, characterised by the holding by the dominant undertaking of a very large market share and by structural advantages conferred, inter alia, by that undertaking's statutory monopoly, which applied to 70% of mail on the relevant market, applying the as-efficient-competitor test is of no relevance inasmuch as the structure of the market makes the emergence of an as-efficient competitor practically impossible.

60   Furthermore, in a market such as that at issue in the main proceedings, access to which is protected by high barriers, the presence of a less efficient competitor might contribute to intensifying the competitive pressure on that market and, therefore, to exerting a constraint on the conduct of the dominant undertaking.

[Regarding the standard of proof and appreciability]

65   * * * [T]he anti-competitive effect of a particular practice must not be purely hypothetical. * * *

69   Such an assessment [of whether a rebate scheme is capable of restricting competition] seeks to determine whether the conduct of the dominant undertaking produces an actual or likely exclusionary effect, to the detriment of competition and, thereby, of consumers' interests.

> **CASE** *(continued)*
>
> 73 It follows that fixing an appreciability (de minimis) threshold for the purposes of determining whether there is an abuse of a dominant position is not justified. That anti-competitive practice is, by its very nature, liable to give rise to not insignificant restrictions of competition, or even of eliminating competition on the market on which the undertaking concerned operates.

In addition, the Court of Justice observed that the Guidance Paper 'merely sets out the Commission's approach as to the choice of cases that it intends to pursue as a matter of priority; accordingly, the administrative practice followed by the Commission is not binding on national competition authorities and courts' (para. 52).

NOTES AND QUESTIONS

1. The Court of Justice emphasised that Post Danmark's rebate scheme was neither quantity-based (presumably lawful) nor tied to an exclusivity requirement (abusive 'by object'?) but was loyalty inducing, thereby requiring evidence of likely exclusionary effects. Likewise, it stressed that benefits for consumers could outweigh such exclusionary effects and thus defeat a *prima facie* finding of abuse. Does that mean that the Court introduced a condition akin to Article 101(3) in the assessment of abusive conduct under Article 102 TFEU? Is that appropriate and what are the consequences? How likely is it that dominant companies would succeed in invoking counteracting consumer benefits? Does Article 101(3) contain any leads in that regard?
2. The Court denied the need to resort to a price-cost test to assess the likelihood of exclusionary effects when the structure of the market allowed for a presumption of such effects, notably when dominance resulted from a statutory monopoly and translated in a very large market. Do you agree? In these circumstances, should Article 102 protect less efficient competitors, as the Court suggested? How do you reconcile this affirmation with the possibility for consumer benefits to outweigh exclusionary effects? What does it say about the relationship between competition and efficiency under EU competition law?
3. The Court of Justice dismissed the existence of some sort of appreciability threshold under Article 102 TFEU. Do you find the Court's justification persuasive? What does it say about the nature of the inquiry carried out under each of Article 101 and 102 TFEU, and about the nature of the anticompetitive conduct caught by each provision? Is market power a relevant factor, and to what extent? Is bigness a problem as such under EU competition law?

c. *Tying and bundling*

Tying, in the context of an abuse violation, involves a dominant firm's use of its power in one market to require buyers to purchase another product or service. Bundling is a similar practice; it involves offering several products together. Pure bundling implies that the firm offers the products only in a package and not separately. Mixed bundling involves offering the products both as a bundle and separately, with the bundled price being a discounted price. For a violation, must competition be harmed in one of the markets? Must the tie or bundling practice increase or maintain the dominant firm's market power or create market power in the second market? Or is it enough that the practice fences out competitors from significant opportunities otherwise open to them, and the dominant firm has no good defense, such as: the practice is pro-competitive or efficient and consumers get a fair share of the benefits?

A leading case on tying is *Tetra Pak International SA v Commission*.[58] Tetra Pak held 90% of EU sales of aseptic packaging machines and packaging (e.g. milk cartons). It required buyers of its non-aseptic machines to also use Tetra Pak cartons for the machines. The Court held the requirement illegal under Article 102 TFEU. For a general discussion of the treatment of tying under EU competition law, read the Commission's Guidance Paper, paras. 46–61.

For more than half a century, the United States has had a per se rule against forced tying by a firm with market power.[59] Justifications such as good will, safety and reputation have been rejected and also were seldom proved. However, the Supreme Court has retreated from per se concepts and has questioned the continued validity of the rule against tying.[60] Indeed, tying is a form of leveraging, and the Supreme Court said in *Trinko* that there is no leveraging violation in the absence of a dangerous probability of monopolizing a second market. See *Trinko*, above at p. 177.

In the US *Microsoft* case the court held Microsoft's tying illegal where it was combined with a clear predatory act. Microsoft tied its browser with its operating system and commingled code so that removal of Netscape's browser from Windows would disable other functions of Windows. But the court reversed the district court's holding that Microsoft's mere bundling of its browser with its operating system was illegal per se.[61]

The European *Microsoft* case was decided several years later. We have already summarized the facts and studied the interoperability portion of the

---

58 Case C333/94P, *Tetra Pak International SA v. Commission*, [1996] ECR I–5951, ECLI:EU:C:1996:436.
59 See e.g., *International Salt Co. v. United States*, 332 U.S. 392, 68 S.Ct. 12, 92 L.Ed. 20 (1947); *Eastman Kodak Co. v. Image Technical Services*, 504 U.S. 451, 112 S.Ct. 2072, 119 L.Ed.2d 265 (1992); *Jefferson Parish Hospital District No. 2 v. Hyde*, 466 U.S. 2, 32, 104 S.Ct. 1551, 80 L.Ed.2d 2 (1984).
60 *Illinois Tool Works Inc. v. Independent Ink, Inc.*, 547 U.S. 28, 126 S.Ct. 1281, 164 L.Ed.2d 26 (2006).
61 *United States v. Microsoft Corp.*, 253 F.3d 34 (D.C. Cir.), cert. denied, 534 U.S. 952 (2001).

judgement. Following are excerpts from the portion of the case on bundling the media player with the operating system.

> **CASE**
>
> ## *Microsoft Corp. v. Commission* (Case T-201/04)
>
> [See background facts at p. 186 above.]
>
> *The tying restricts competition on the media player market*
>
> *The foreclosure of competition*
>
> 1038   ... [I]n the first place, it is clear that owing to the bundling, Windows Media Player enjoyed an unparalleled presence on client PCs throughout the world, because it thereby automatically achieved a level of market penetration corresponding to that of the Windows client PC operating system and did so without having to compete on the merits with competing products. It must be borne in mind that it is common ground that Microsoft's market share on the client PC operating systems market is more than 90% and that the great majority of sales of Windows client PC operating systems (approximately 75%) are made through OEMs [original equipment manufacturers], who pre-install Windows on the client PCs which they assemble and distribute. Thus, the figures ... show that in 2002 Microsoft had a market share of 93.8% by units shipped on the client PC operating systems market and that Windows—and, as a result, Windows Media Player—was pre-installed on 196 million of the 207 million client PCs shipped in the world between October 2001 and March 2003. * * *
>
> 1088   It follows from the foregoing considerations that the final conclusion which the Commission sets out concerning the anti-competitive effects of the bundling is well founded. The Commission is correct to make the following findings:
>
> — Microsoft uses Windows as a distribution channel to ensure for itself a significant competitive advantage on the media players market;
> — because of the bundling, Microsoft's competitors are a priori at a disadvantage even if their products are inherently better than Windows Media Player;
> — Microsoft interferes with the normal competitive process which would benefit users by ensuring quicker cycles of innovation as a consequence of unfettered competition on the merits;
> — the bundling increases the content and applications barriers to entry, which protect Windows, and facilitates the erection of such barriers for Windows Media Player;
> — Microsoft shields itself from effective competition from vendors of potentially more efficient media players who could challenge its position, and thus reduces the talent and capital invested in innovation of media players;

> **CASE** *(continued)*
>
> — by means of the bundling, Microsoft may expand its position in adjacent media-related software markets and weaken effective competition, to the detriment of consumers;
> — by means of the bundling, Microsoft sends signals which deter innovation in any technologies in which it might conceivably take an interest and which it might tie with Windows in the future.
>
> 1089   The Commission therefore had ground to state that there was a reasonable likelihood that tying Windows and Windows Media Player would lead to a lessening of competition so that the maintenance of an effective competition structure would not be ensured in the foreseeable future. . . .* * *
>
> *Absence of objective justification*
>
> [Microsoft claimed that efficiency gains outweighed any anticompetitive effects; that consumers want one product, pre-installed; that the tying produces efficiencies and enhances technical performance; that adding components piecemeal can create conflicts and cause malfunction; and that removing components degrades the system. The Court held that the Commission appropriately rejected the factual assertions or found that the benefits could be attained in the less restrictive ways.] * * *
>
> 1159   Last, the Court notes that . . . Microsoft does not show that the integration of Windows Media Player in Windows creates technical efficiencies or, in other words, that it 'lead[s] to superior technical product performance'. * * *
>
> 1165   The Court further considers that Microsoft cannot contend that the removal of Windows Media Player from the system consisting of Windows Media Player and Windows will entail a degrading of the operating system. Thus, Windows XP Embedded can be configured in such a way as not to include Windows Media Player without having any effect on the integrity of the other functionality of the operating system. Furthermore, throughout the period between June 1998 and May 1999, when Microsoft first integrated WMP 6 in its Windows client PC operating system without allowing OEMs or users to remove it from that system, Microsoft offered its streaming media player as separate application software, without any effect on the functioning of the Windows operating system. . . .* * *

NOTES AND QUESTIONS

1. Microsoft owned a 'ubiquitous' network, which could and did carry its media player. If you were the BBC and had to decide how to distribute your content over the Internet, might you choose ubiquitous software over software with some better qualities? Does this mean that the owner of the ubiquitous network must share it with its competitors?

2. Would you predict that Microsoft's bundling would cause the total output of media player software to go down and the price to go up? That Microsoft would eventually get a monopoly in media players for PCs? Might the bundling have entrenched Microsoft in the PC operating system market? Explain.
3. How would the US *Microsoft* court have analysed the same problem?

d. Price predation and price discrimination (continued)

Antitrust proceedings are frequently triggered by complaints of rivals. Rivals often complain about prices that are too low. They complain that the dominant firm is pricing strategically low to drive the rivals out of the market, after which (they allege) the dominant firm will charge a yet higher monopoly price. For years, many jurisdictions, including the US, listened sympathetically to such complaints, and sometimes found violations and enjoined the 'predatory' pricing. (How might sympathy for the complaining firm be problematic for competition and consumers?)

In more recent times, jurisdictions have toughened their standards for a predatory pricing violation. Moreover, courts have reclassified some 'exclusionary' conduct as merely low price competition that should be encouraged and thus conduct that, if it is illegal at all, must fit demanding criteria.

This section starts with predatory pricing and discriminatory pricing (which we saw briefly in *United Brands*, above), and then turns to price squeezes imposed by vertically integrated dominant firms.

For Commission Guidance, see paras. 22–26 (cost benchmarks, and 'as-efficient-competitor concept'), paras. 62–73 (predation), and paras. 79–89 (margin squeeze) of the Guidance Paper, http://ec.europa. eu/competition/antitrust/art82. Note that the Commission values '[v]igorous price competition [as] generally beneficial to consumers .... [T]he Commission will normally only intervene where the conduct concerned has already been or is capable of hampering competition from competitors which are considered to be as efficient as the dominant undertaking.' However, 'in certain circumstances a less efficient competitor may also exert a constraint which should be taken into account. . . .' For example, an abusive practice excluding the competitor from network and learning effects may prevent the competitor from achieving efficiencies (paras. 22, 23).

CASE

AKZO Chemie BV v. Commission (Case C-62/86)[62]

[AKZO, a large Dutch multinational firm, and ECS (Engineering and Chemical Supplies Ltd), a small UK firm, both manufactured organic peroxides. AKZO had a market share of 50%. Benzoyl peroxide is the most important organic peroxide. Benzoyl peroxide is a bleaching agent for flour and is also used in plastics as an initiator of the polymer production process. ECS was engaged in the flour segment of the market. For a decade, ECS was content with its sales for the flour business, but in 1979 it developed excess capacity and started to sell to plastics makers, soliciting and selling to some of AKZO's customers. An AKZO official told ECS's manager Sullivan 'that AKZO would take aggressive commercial action on the milling products unless [Sullivan] refrained from supplying his products to the plastics industry.' The AKZO official told Sullivan AKZO would pry away ECS's flour customers at prices far below prevailing prices. When ECS ignored AKZO's threats, AKZO implemented selective, low prices, with the intent to damage the business of ECS.

From the end of 1980 for about four years, AKZO targeted ECS's customers in the flour segment, selling to them at prices that were below its average total cost and that were much lower than the previously prevailing rates. Meanwhile, AKZO charged its own loyal customers (whose business was not at risk) about 60% more than the targeted customers of ECS. As part of its strategy, AKZO sold these customers flour milling complements they needed at prices below AKZO's average variable cost, and it sold them some vitamin mixes (which it bought specifically for resale to these customers) below its own purchase price. ECS's business declined by about 70% in four years, and its profit margins fell.

The Commission initiated proceedings and obtained an interim order enjoining AKZO's conduct. In its decision on the merits, the Commission noted AKZO's 'clear predatory intent' as well as its scheme of price discrimination. However, the finding of predation had little effect on ECS. ECS's share in the flour additive sector went from 35% to 30%, and AKZO's share went from 52% to 55%.

Placing much weight on AKZO's intent to eliminate its competitor, the Commission found an infringement and levied a fine of 10 million ECUs (i.e., European Currency Units) on AKZO.]

---

62 [1991] ECR I-3359, EU:C:1991:286.

CASE (continued)

A. *Dominant position*

60   With regard to market shares the Court has held that very large shares are in themselves, and save in exceptional circumstances, evidence of the existence of a dominant position (judgement in Case 85/76 *Hoffmann-La Roche v. Commission* [1979] ECR 461, paragraph 41). That is the situation where there is a market share of 50% such as that found to exist in this case.

61   Moreover, the Commission rightly pointed out that other factors confirmed AKZO's predominance in the market. In addition to the fact that AKZO regards itself as the world leader in the peroxides market, it should be observed that, as AKZO itself admits, it has the most highly developed marketing organization, both commercially and technically, and wider knowledge than that of their competitors with regard to safety and toxicology...

62   The pleas put forward by AKZO in order to deny that it had a dominant position within the organic peroxides market as a whole must therefore be rejected.

B. *Abuse of a dominant position*

63   According to the contested decision (point 75) AKZO had abusively exploited its dominant position by endeavouring to eliminate ECS from the organic peroxides market mainly by massive and prolonged price cutting in the flour additives sector. * * *

69   It should be observed that... the concept of abuse is an objective concept relating to the behaviour of an undertaking in a dominant position which is such as to influence the structure of a market where, as a result of the very presence of the undertaking in question, the degree of competition is weakened and through recourse to methods which, different from those which condition normal competition in products or services on the basis of the transactions of commercial operators, has the effect of hindering the maintenance of the degree of competition still existing in the market or the growth of that competition.

70   It follows that Article [102] prohibits a dominant undertaking from eliminating a competitor and thereby strengthening its position by using methods other than those which come within the scope of competition on the basis of quality. From that point of view, however, not all competition by means of price can be regarded as legitimate.

71   Prices below average variable costs (that is to say, those which vary depending on the quantities produced) by means of which a dominant undertaking seeks to eliminate a competitor must be regarded as abusive. A dominant undertaking has no interest in applying such prices except that of eliminating competitors so as to enable it subsequently to raise

CASE *(continued)*

its prices by taking advantage of its monopolistic position, since each sale generates a loss, namely the total amount of the fixed costs (that is to say, those which remain constant regardless of the quantities produced) and, at least, part of the variable costs relating to the unit produced.

72   Moreover, prices below average total costs, that is to say, fixed costs plus variable costs, but above average variable costs, must be regarded as abusive if they are determined as part of a plan for eliminating a competitor. Such prices can drive from the market undertakings which are perhaps as efficient as the dominant undertaking but which, because of their smaller financial resources, are incapable of withstanding the competition waged against them.

73   These are the criteria that must be applied to the situation in the present case. * * *

114   The prices charged by AKZO to its own customers were above its average total costs, whereas those offered to customers of ECS were below its average total costs.

115   AKZO is thus able, at least partly, to set off losses resulting from the sales to customers of ECS against profits made on the sales to the 'large independents' which were among its customers. This behaviour shows that AKZO's intention was not to pursue a general policy of favourable prices, but to adopt a strategy that could damage ECS. The complaint is therefore substantiated. * * *

140   By maintaining prices below its average total costs over a prolonged period, without any objective justification, AKZO was thus able to damage ECS by dissuading it from making inroads into its customers. * * *

[The Court concluded that AKZO, at various times, offered customers of ECS prices lower than AKZO's total or average variable costs, and did so as part of its threat to obtain ECS's withdrawal from the plastics sector.]

162   . . . [I]t must be observed that the infringement committed by AKZO is particularly serious, since the behaviour complained of was intended to prevent a competitor from extending its activity into a market in which AKZO held a dominant position.

[The Court reduced the fine to 7.5 million ECUs—predecessor to the euro—on grounds that the controlling law had not previously been specified and the infraction did not have a significant effect on market shares.]

NOTES AND QUESTIONS

1. Why does the Court require below-cost pricing as a necessary element of the violation? Should it be sufficient that the dominant firm lowered its prices strategically to eliminate or wound its rivals? Explain.
2. Was AKZO's below-cost pricing a strategy to: (1) drive out the competitors and raise price? (2) compete? (3) divide markets? What is the significance of these different hypotheses?
3. In what respect does the Commission Guidance differ from the Court's analysis?
4. In the US, a pioneer in low-priced, no-frills, non-branded cigarettes sued a major tobacco company for embarking on a predatory pricing campaign to destroy or marginalize the new product. The resulting case, *Brooke Group*, was later cited to the EU Court of Justice by a low-pricing firm that was accused of predatory pricing by the Commission and tried to defend its conduct as pro-competitive. (See *Tetra Pak* at p. 218 below.) *Brooke Group* is the leading US case on price predation.

CASE

Brooke Group Ltd v. Brown & Williamson Tobacco Corp.[63]

JUSTICE KENNEDY:

[Cigarette manufacturing is a concentrated industry dominated by only six firms, including the two parties here. In 1980, petitioner (hereinafter Liggett) pioneered the economy segment of the market by developing a line of generic cigarettes offered at a list price roughly 30% lower than that of branded cigarettes. By 1984, generics had captured 4% of the market at the expense of branded cigarettes, and respondent Brown & Williamson entered the economy segment, beating Liggett's net price. Liggett responded in kind, precipitating a price war, which ended, according to Liggett, with Brown & Williamson selling its generics at a loss. Liggett filed this suit, alleging, inter alia, that volume rebates by Brown & Williamson to wholesalers amounted to price discrimination that had a reasonable possibility of injuring competition in violation of § 2(a) of the Clayton Act,[64] as amended by the Robinson-Patman Act. Liggett claimed that the rebates were integral to a predatory pricing scheme, in which Brown & Williamson set below-cost prices to pressure Liggett to raise list prices on its generics, thus restraining the economy segment's growth and preserving Brown & Williamson's supracompetitive profits on branded cigarettes. After a jury returned a verdict in favour of Liggett, the District Court held that Brown & Williamson was entitled to judgement as a matter of law. The Court of Appeals affirmed.] * * *

---

63 509 U.S. 209, 113 S.Ct. 2578, 125 L.Ed.2d 168 (1993).
64 15 U.S.C. § 13.

> **CASE** (continued)
>
> Liggett contends that Brown & Williamson's discriminatory volume rebates to wholesalers threatened substantial competitive injury by furthering a predatory pricing scheme designed to purge competition from the economy segment of the cigarette market . . . . [W]hether the claim alleges predatory pricing under § 2 of the Sherman Act or primary-line price discrimination under the Robinson-Patman Act, two prerequisites to recovery remain the same. First, a plaintiff seeking to establish competitive injury resulting from a rival's low price must prove that the prices complained of are below an appropriate measure of its rival's costs . . . . Although [we have] reserved as a formal matter the question 'whether recovery should ever be available . . . when the pricing in question is above some measure of incremental cost,' . . . the reasoning in [our] opinions suggests that only below-cost prices should suffice, and we have rejected elsewhere the notion that above-cost prices that are below general market levels or the costs of a firm's competitors inflict injury to competition cognizable under the antitrust laws . . . . As a general rule, the exclusionary effect of prices above a relevant measure of cost either reflects the lower cost structure of the alleged predator, and so represents competition on the merits, or is beyond the practical ability of a judicial tribunal to control without courting intolerable risks of chilling legitimate price-cutting. . . .
>
> Even in an oligopolistic market, when a firm drops its prices to a competitive level to demonstrate to a maverick the unprofitability of straying from the group, it would be illogical to condemn the price cut: The antitrust laws then would be an obstacle to the chain of events most conducive to a breakdown of oligopoly pricing and the onset of competition. Even if the ultimate effect of the cut is to induce or reestablish supracompetitive pricing, discouraging a price cut and forcing firms to maintain supracompetitive prices, thus depriving consumers of the benefits of lower prices in the interim, does not constitute sound antitrust policy. . . .
>
> The second prerequisite to holding a competitor liable under the antitrust laws for charging low prices is a demonstration that the competitor had a reasonable prospect, or, under § 2 of the Sherman Act, a dangerous probability, of recouping its investment in below-cost prices . . . . 'For the investment to be rational, the [predator] must have a reasonable expectation of recovering, in the form of later monopoly profits, more than the losses suffered.' . . . Recoupment is the ultimate object of an unlawful predatory pricing scheme; it is the means by which a predator profits from predation. Without it, predatory pricing produces lower aggregate prices in the market, and consumer welfare is enhanced. Although unsuccessful predatory pricing may encourage some inefficient substitution toward the product being sold at less than its cost, unsuccessful predation is in general a boon to consumers.
>
> That below-cost pricing may impose painful losses on its target is of no moment to the antitrust laws if competition is not injured: . . .

CASE *(continued)*

Even an act of pure malice by one business competitor against another does not, without more, state a claim under the federal antitrust laws; those laws do not create a federal law of unfair competition. . . .

For recoupment to occur, below-cost pricing must be capable, as a threshold matter, of producing the intended effects on the firm's rivals, whether driving them from the market, or, as was alleged to be the goal here, causing them to raise their prices to supracompetitive levels within a disciplined oligopoly. This requires an understanding of the extent and duration of the alleged predation, the relative financial strength of the predator and its intended victim, and their respective incentives and will . . . . The inquiry is whether, given the aggregate losses caused by the below-cost pricing, the intended target would likely succumb.

If circumstances indicate that below-cost pricing could likely produce its intended effect on the target, there is still the further question whether it would likely injure competition in the relevant market. The plaintiff must demonstrate that there is a likelihood that the predatory scheme alleged would cause a rise in prices above a competitive level that would be sufficient to compensate for the amounts expended on the predation, including the time value of the money invested in it. As we have observed on a prior occasion, '[i]n order to recoup their losses, [predators] must obtain enough market power to set higher than competitive prices, and then must sustain those prices long enough to earn in excess profits what they earlier gave up in below-cost prices.' Matsushita, 475 U.S., at 590–591.

Evidence of below-cost pricing is not alone sufficient to permit an inference of probable recoupment and injury to competition. Determining whether recoupment of predatory losses is likely requires an estimate of the cost of the alleged predation and a close analysis of both the scheme alleged by the plaintiff and the structure and conditions of the relevant market . . . . If market circumstances or deficiencies in proof would bar a reasonable jury from finding that the scheme alleged would likely result in sustained supracompetitive pricing, the plaintiff's case has failed. . . .

These prerequisites to recovery are not easy to establish, but they are not artificial obstacles to recovery; rather, they are essential components of real market injury. As we have said in the Sherman Act context, 'predatory pricing schemes are rarely tried, and even more rarely successful,' *Matsushita*, and the costs of an erroneous finding of liability are high . . . . * * *

. . . While a reasonable jury could conclude that Brown & Williamson's intent was anticompetitive and that the price of its generics was below its costs for 18 months, the evidence was inadequate to show a reasonable prospect of cost recoupment. * * *

Affirmed.

The *Brooke Group* assumptions and standards have been both defended and questioned in scholarly literature. The legal rule remains a strong one in the US.

Tetra Pak International SA v. Commission,[65] involved a predatory pricing claim as well as a tying claim. (See tying part of case above.) Tetra Pak noted that the sales below cost took place only on the non-dominated market (non-aseptic cartons) and argued that Tetra Pak had no realistic chance of recouping its losses since competition would prevent it from raising its prices; it urged the Court of Justice to adopt the rule in *Brooke Group*. The Court declined. It confirmed that recoupment is not a constituent element of a price predation case under European law. Thus:

> 41 In *AKZO* this court did indeed sanction the existence of two different methods of analysis for determining whether an undertaking has practised predatory pricing. First, prices below average variable costs must always be considered abusive. In such a case, there is no conceivable economic purpose other than the elimination of a competitor, since each item produced and sold entails a loss for the undertaking. Secondly, prices below average total costs but above average variable costs are only to be considered abusive if an intention to eliminate can be shown.

> 42 . . . For sales of non-aseptic cartons in Italy between 1976 and 1981, . . . prices were considerably lower than average variable costs. Proof of intention to eliminate competitors was therefore not necessary. In 1982, prices for those cartons lay between average variable costs and average total costs. For that reason . . . the [General Court] was at pains to establish—and the appellant has not criticised it in that regard—that Tetra Pak intended to eliminate a competitor. * * *

> 44 Furthermore, it would not be appropriate, in the circumstances of the present case, to require in addition proof that Tetra Pak had a realistic chance of recouping its losses. It must be possible to penalise predatory pricing whenever there is a risk that competitors will be eliminated. The [General Court] found . . . that there was such a riin this case. The aim pursued, which is to maintain undistorted competition, rules out waiting until such a strategy leads to the actual elimination of competitors.

Note on France Telecom SA v. Commission ('Wanadoo')

The Commission charged Wanadoo, later acquired by France Télécom, with charging residential customers a price below average variable cost for high speed Internet access, and later a price below average total cost, as part

---

[65] Case C-333/94 P, *Tetra Pak International SA v. Commission* [1996] ECR I-5951, EU:C:1996:436.

of a plan to pre-empt the market in high-speed Internet access during a key phase in its development. It found a violation of Article 102 TFEU. The General Court upheld the Commission's findings, and the Court of Justice affirmed.[66]

France Télécom made the following claims of error, all unsuccessfully.

1. The claim that Wanadoo's (WIN's) high market share did not prove its dominant position, because its share fell (from 72% to about 63%) and the market was fast-growing. The General Court said: WIN 'had a very high market share which, save in exceptional circumstances, proves that it had a dominant position within the meaning of the case-law. . . .' (para. 103). The General Court confirmed that WIN had a dominant position, noting that WIN itself forecast that it would hold at least 60% of the market. The Court stated that WIN's link-up with the network of France Télécom gave it competitive advantages that contributed to its dominance.
2. The claim that WIN had the right to align its prices to those of its competitors, even if those prices were below costs. The General Court said: 'Even a dominant firm must generally be allowed to take reasonable steps to protect its own interests, but this right is not absolute . . . . [S]uch behaviour cannot be countenanced if its actual purpose is to strengthen this dominant position and abuse it' (para. 185).
3. The claim that competition was robust, there was no possibility of ousting existing competitors, and barriers were low; there could be no anti-competitive effect. The General Court said, citing *AKZO*, where prices are below average variable costs, an anti-competitive effect is presumed, because the only interest the undertaking may have is eliminating competitors. Where prices are merely below average total costs, the Commission must prove predatory intent, and it did so—showing an express plan 'to pre-empt' the market. Moreover 'it is clear' that WIN's conduct 'had the effect of discouraging rival undertakings' (para. 214). Moreover, it was no defence that the low pricing would result in economies of scale and learning effects, promising profitability later (presumably at the same low price) (paras. 215–217).
4. The claim that the Commission should have been required to prove a realistic chance of recoupment of losses. Citing *Tetra Pak* (which rejected *Brooke Group*), the General Court reaffirmed that proof of recoupment is not necessary.

---

66 Case T-340/03, *France Telecom SA v. Commission* [2007] ECR I-107, EU:T:2007:22; Case C-202/07 P, *France Telecom SA v. Commission* [2009] ECR I-2369, EU:C:2009:214 (*'Wanadoo'*).

> **NOTES AND QUESTIONS**
>
> 1. Comment on each of the four rejected claims. Was the Court right to reject them?
> 2. In 2010, the Court of Justice had before it a preliminary reference regarding another challenge to low prices. This one was based on a targeted price cut to one customer, wrested away from a rival. The price was below Post Danmark's average total costs but higher than its average incremental costs. The Danish authority brought proceedings. It lost the predatory pricing part of the case because Post Danmark was not found to have eliminatory intent and prices were not below average variable costs. The preliminary reference concerned abuse of dominance merely by means of a targeted price cut (labelled by the referring court as price discrimination).

CASE

Post Danmark A/S v. Konkurrencerådet (Case C-209/10) ('*Post Danmark I*')[67]

[Post Danmark had a legal monopoly for the delivery of addressed letters and small parcels in Denmark. It had a universal service obligation to deliver this mail, for which it established a network that covered the whole national territory.

Post Danmark and Forbruger-Kontakt were the two largest firms in the sector of unaddressed mail, which includes phone directories, brochures, and local newspapers. Effective from 1 January 2004, Post Danmark concluded contracts with Forbruger-Kontakt's major customers, three supermarket chains. It lured one of the three, Coop group, by a price marginally lower than Forbruger Kontakt's, and the prices Post Danmark charged all three were lower than those Post Danmark charged to its own pre-existing customers. Forbruger-Kontakt complained.

The Danish competition authority found that eliminatory intent could not be established and, given also that it covered its average incremental costs, Post Danmark had not engaged in predatory pricing in the market for unaddressed mail. But the authority held that Post Danmark had abused dominance in unaddressed mail by 'practicing a targeted policy of reductions designed to ensure its customers' loyalty', by price-discriminations, by selectively low prices, by not putting its customers on an equal footing, and by favoring its new customers without cost-justification.

A Danish court affirmed. Post Danmark appealed the finding of illegal price discrimination, arguing that selectively low pricing cannot be an abuse in the absence of an intention to drive a competitor from the market. The Danish court made a preliminary reference to the Court of Justice. The Court of Justice said:]

---

67 EU:C:2012:172 (Grand Chamber).

CASE (continued)

19   ... [T]he court making the reference asks, in essence, what the circumstances are in which a policy, pursued by a dominant undertaking, of charging low prices to certain former customers of a competitor must be considered to amount to an exclusionary abuse, contrary to Article 82 EC [now Article 102 TFEU], and, in particular, whether the finding of such an abuse may be based on the mere fact that the price charged to a single customer by the dominant undertaking is lower than the average total costs attributed to the business activity concerned, but higher than the total incremental costs pertaining to the latter.

20   It is apparent from case-law that Article 82 EC covers not only those practices that directly cause harm to consumers but also practices that cause consumers harm through their impact on competition ... It is in the latter sense that the expression 'exclusionary abuse' appearing in the questions referred is to be understood. * * *

22   ... [N]ot every exclusionary effect is necessarily detrimental to competition ... Competition on the merits may, by definition, lead to the departure from the market or the marginalisation of competitors that are less efficient and so less attractive to consumers from the point of view of, among other things, price, choice, quality or innovation. * * *

25   Thus, Article 82 EC prohibits a dominant undertaking from, among other things, adopting pricing practices that have an exclusionary effect on competitors considered to be as efficient as it is itself and strengthening its dominant position by using methods other than those that are part of competition on the merits. Accordingly, in that light, not all competition by means of price may be regarded as legitimate .... * * *

31   In the present case, ... the Danish competition authorities had recourse, not to the concept of 'variable costs' mentioned in the case-law stemming from *AKZO* v. *Commission*, but to another concept, which those authorities termed 'incremental costs'. In this respect, ... those authorities defined 'incremental costs' as being 'those costs destined to disappear in the short or medium term (three to five years), if Post Danmark were to give up its business activity of distributing unaddressed mail'. In addition, that government stated that 'average total costs' were defined as being 'average incremental costs to which were added a portion, determined by estimation, of Post Danmark's common costs connected to activities other than those covered by the universal service obligation'.

32   However, as the Danish government stated in its written replies to those questions, a notable feature of the case in the main proceedings is that there are considerable costs related both to the activities within the ambit of Post Danmark's universal service obligation and to its activity of distributing unaddressed mail. These 'common' costs are due, in particular, to the fact that, at the material time, Post Danmark was using the same infrastructure and the same staff for both the activity of distributing unaddressed mail and the activity

> **CASE** *(continued)*
>
> reserved to it in connection with its universal obligation for certain addressed items of mail. That government states that, according to the Konkurrencerådet, because Post Danmark's unaddressed mail activity used the undertaking's 'common distribution network resources', the costs of its universal service obligation activities could be reduced over a period of three to five years if Post Danmark were to give up distributing unaddressed mail.
>
> 33   . . . [F]or the purpose of estimating what it described as 'average incremental costs', the Konkurrencerådet included, among other things, not only those fixed and variable costs attributable solely to the activity of distributing unaddressed mail, but also elements described as 'common variable costs', '75% of the attributable common costs of logistical capacity' and '25% of non-attributable common costs'.
>
> 34   In the specific circumstances of the case in the main proceedings, it must be considered that such a method of attribution would seem to seek to identify the great bulk of the costs attributable to the activity of distributing unaddressed mail.
>
> 35   When that estimation was completed, it was found, among other things, that the price offered to the Coop group did not enable Post Danmark to cover the average total costs attributed to the activity of unaddressed mail distribution taken as a whole, but did enable it to cover the average incremental costs pertaining to that activity, as estimated by the Danish competition authorities.
>
> 36   Moreover, it is common ground that, in the present case, the prices offered to the Spar and SuperBest groups were assessed as being at a higher level than those average total costs, as estimated by those authorities. In those circumstances, it cannot be considered that such prices have anti-competitive effects.
>
> 37   As regards the prices charged the Coop group, a pricing policy such as that in issue in the main proceedings cannot be considered to amount to an exclusionary abuse simply because the price charged to a single customer by a dominant undertaking is lower than the average total costs attributed to the activity concerned, but higher than the average incremental costs pertaining to the latter . . .
>
> 38   Indeed, to the extent that a dominant undertaking sets its prices at a level covering the great bulk of the costs attributable to the supply of the goods or services in question, it will, as a general rule, be possible for a competitor as efficient as that undertaking to compete with those prices without suffering losses that are unsustainable in the long term.
>
> 39   It is for the court making the reference to assess the relevant circumstances of the case in the main proceedings in the light of the finding made in the previous paragraph. In any

> **CASE** *(continued)*
>
> event, it is worth noting that it appears from the documents before the Court that Forbruger-Kontakt managed to maintain its distribution network despite losing the volume of mail related to the three customers involved and managed, in 2007, to win back the Coop group's custom and, since then, that of the Spar group.* * *

Post Danmark I stands out as a judgement decisively based on freedom of low pricing that benefits consumers. Should the consumer perspective of the Court in *Post Danmark I* apply to other price-related practices? How do you compare the Court's perspective in *Post Danmark I* and *Post Danmark II* (see above p. 204) Is the Court consistent in its reliance on the notion of 'as-efficient-competitor'? If not, what justifies the different perspectives developed by the Court? If so, how do you reconcile the two *Post Danmark* judgements?

The next important price-related case involved a price-squeeze (*TeliaSonera*) and while citing *Post Danmark*, the Court did not adopt a single-track consumer perspective. The presentation of *TeliaSonera* is preceded by the discussion of a price squeeze case in the US (*linkLine*), and then an EU Court of Justice case involving regulation (*Deutsche Telekom*).

e. *Margin squeeze*

A margin squeeze occurs when the difference between the cost of an upstream input product or service and the price of a downstream output product or service is either negative or insufficient to cover the specific costs incurred for the production or supply of the downstream output product or service. As a result, it may prevent a competitor as efficient as the supplier of the input product or service to compete effectively for the supply of the downstream product or service.

Note on *Pacific Bell Telephone Co. v. linkLine Communications, Inc.*

Pacific Bell was the incumbent telephone service provider in an area on the West Coast of the US. It provided a local telephone service and, as the historical incumbent (and former lawful monopolist before technology made competition feasible), owned the elements of the local loop in the area. It also supplied a digital subscriber line ('DSL') service—for fast computer access through phone lines—to Internet service providers ('ISPs') at wholesale, and sold DSL service to its own customers at retail. During some periods it charged its retail customers for DSL less than it charged the ISPs at wholesale. The price of wholesale service was regulated. That is, Pacific Bell proposed the rate; the Federal Communications Commission approved it, which it must do for all filed rates unless they are 'unjust and unreasonable'.

The ISPs sued for an unlawful price squeeze under Section 2 of the Sherman Act. Pacific Bell moved for judgement on the pleadings, arguing that, after *Trinko* (see p. 177 above), a monopolist in a regulated industry has no antitrust duty to deal and no duty to avoid a price squeeze; if there is a problem, it should be resolved by the regulatory agency. The lower courts declined to dismiss the price squeeze case, holding that price squeeze claims survive *Trinko*. The Supreme Court reversed the decision. Since there was no antitrust duty to supply the DSL transport service to the rivals, there was no antitrust duty to refrain from squeezing them out of business. Plaintiffs would have a cause of action only if they could meet the tough requirements for proving that defendant's low retail price was predatory.[68]

CASE

Deutsche Telekom AG v. Commission (Case C-280/08 P)[69]

[Deutsche Telekom ('DT') was the dominant provider of telecom services in Germany and had sole access to the local loop. DT was regulated by the German Regulatory Authority, which imposed price ceilings. DT charged new entrants into the local telecom service market higher fees for wholesale access to the local loop than it charged its customers for services including DSL for fast-speed Internet connection. The competing providers of DSL service complained to the European Commission. The Commission found a margin squeeze in violation of Article 102 TFEU. The General Court upheld the Commission's findings, and the Court of Justice affirmed. DT had a duty to provide competitors access to the local loop. It therefore had a duty not to create a margin squeeze. DT had sufficient scope to eliminate the margin squeeze on terms consistent with the regulation, and could go back to the German regulator if it needed an adjustment in price. The Court said:]

80   According to the case-law of the Court of Justice, it is only if anti-competitive conduct is required of undertakings by national legislation, or if the latter creates a legal framework which itself eliminates any possibility of competitive activity on their part, that Articles 81 EC and 82 EC [Articles 101 and 102 TFEU] do not apply. In such a situation, the restriction of competition is not attributable, as those provisions implicitly require, to the autonomous conduct of the undertakings. Articles 81 EC and 82 EC may apply, however, if it is found that

> **CASE** *(continued)*
>
> the national legislation leaves open the possibility of competition which may be prevented, restricted or distorted by the autonomous conduct of undertakings.
>
> 81 The possibility of excluding anti-competitive conduct from the scope of Articles 81 EC and 82 EC on the ground that it has been required of the undertakings in question by existing national legislation or that the legislation has precluded all scope for any competitive conduct on their part has thus been accepted only to a limited extent by the Court of Justice.
>
> 82 Thus, the Court has held that if a national law merely encourages or makes it easier for undertakings to engage in autonomous anti-competitive conduct, those undertakings remain subject to Articles 81 EC and 82 EC.
>
> 83 According to the case-law of the Court, dominant undertakings have a special responsibility not to allow their conduct to impair genuine undistorted competition on the common market.
>
> 84 It follows from this that the mere fact that the appellant was encouraged by the intervention of a national regulatory authority such as RegTP to maintain the pricing practices which led to the margin squeeze of competitors who are at least as efficient as the appellant cannot, as such, in any way absolve the appellant from responsibility under Article 82 EC.
>
> 85 Since, notwithstanding such interventions, the appellant had scope to adjust its retail prices for end-user access services, the General Court was entitled to find, on that ground alone, that the margin squeeze at issue was attributable to the appellant.
>
> 86 ... [A]ppellant does not challenge the General Court's findings ... that, in essence, the appellant was able to make applications to RegTP for authorisation to adjust its retail prices for end-user access services, specifically retail prices for narrowband access services for the period between 1 January 1998 and 31 December 2001, and retail prices for broadband access services for the period from 1 January 2002.
>
> ***
>
> 159 It is clear ... that, according to the General Court, it is not the level of the wholesale prices for local loop access services—which, as has already been stated ... cannot be challenged in the present appeal—or the level of retail prices for end-user access services which is contrary to Article 82 EC, but the spread between them. ***
>
> 172 As regards the abusive nature of the appellant's pricing practices, it must be noted that subparagraph (a) of the second paragraph of Article 82 EC expressly prohibits a dominant undertaking from directly or indirectly imposing unfair prices. ***

CASE *(continued)*

177   It follows from this [special responsibility] that Article 82 EC prohibits a dominant undertaking from, inter alia, adopting pricing practices which have an exclusionary effect on its equally efficient actual or potential competitors, that is to say practices which are capable of making market entry very difficult or impossible for such competitors, and of making it more difficult or impossible for its co-contractors to choose between various sources of supply or commercial partners, thereby strengthening its dominant position by using methods other than those which come within the scope of competition on the merits. From that point of view, therefore, not all competition by means of price can be regarded as legitimate.

178   In the present case, it must be noted that the appellant does not deny that, even on the assumption that it does not have the scope to adjust its wholesale prices for local loop access services, the spread between those prices and its retail prices for end-user access services is capable of having an exclusionary effect on its equally efficient actual or potential competitors, since their access to the relevant service markets is, at the very least, made more difficult as a result of the margin squeeze which such a spread can entail for them.

179   At the hearing the appellant submitted, however, that the test applied in the judgement under appeal for the purpose of establishing an abuse within the meaning of Article 82 EC required it, in the circumstances of the case, to increase its retail prices for end-user access services to the detriment of its own end-users, given the national regulatory authorities' regulation of its wholesale prices for local loop access services.

180   It is true . . . that Article 82 EC aims, in particular, to protect consumers by means of undistorted competition.

181   However, the mere fact that the appellant would have to increase its retail prices for end-user access services in order to avoid the margin squeeze of its competitors who are as efficient as the appellant cannot in any way, in itself, render irrelevant the test which the General Court applied in the present case for the purpose of establishing an abuse under Article 82 EC.

182   By further reducing the degree of competition existing on a market—the end-user access services market—already weakened precisely because of the presence of the appellant, thereby strengthening its dominant position on that market, the margin squeeze also has the effect that consumers suffer detriment as a result of the limitation of the choices available to them and, therefore, of the prospect of a longer-term reduction of retail prices as a result of competition exerted by competitors who are at least as efficient in that market.

183   In those circumstances, in so far as the appellant has scope to reduce or end such a margin squeeze . . . by increasing its retail prices for end-user access services, the General

CASE *(continued)*

Court correctly held . . . that that margin squeeze is capable, in itself, of constituting an abuse within the meaning of Article 82 EC in view of the exclusionary effect that it can create for competitors who are at least as efficient as the appellant. The General Court was not, therefore, obliged to establish, additionally, that the wholesale prices for local loop access services or retail prices for end-user access services were in themselves abusive on account of their excessive or predatory nature, as the case may be. * * *

(c) i) *The complaint concerning the misapplication of the as-efficient-competitor test* * * *

252   The General Court therefore held . . . without any error of law, that the anti-competitive effect which the Commission is required to demonstrate, as regards pricing practices of a dominant undertaking resulting in a margin squeeze of its equally efficient competitors, relates to the possible barriers which the appellant's pricing practices could have created for the growth of products on the retail market in end-user access services and, therefore, on the degree of competition in that market.

253   [A] pricing practice such as that at issue in the judgement under appeal that is adopted by a dominant undertaking such as the appellant constitutes an abuse within the meaning of Article 82 EC if it has an exclusionary effect on competitors who are at least as efficient as the dominant undertaking itself by squeezing their margins and is capable of making market entry more difficult or impossible for those competitors, and thus of strengthening its dominant position on that market to the detriment of consumers' interests.

254   Admittedly, where a dominant undertaking actually implements a pricing practice resulting in a margin squeeze of its equally efficient competitors, with the purpose of driving them from the relevant market, the fact that the desired result is not ultimately achieved does not alter its categorisation as abuse within the meaning of Article 82 EC. However, in the absence of any effect on the competitive situation of competitors, a pricing practice such as that at issue cannot be classified as exclusionary if it does not make their market penetration any more difficult. * * *

Then Competition Commissioner Kroes said, in a press release welcoming the judgement of the General Court: 'This [the margin squeeze] was clearly harmful to consumers, because competition between operators is the best means to bring overall prices down.'[70]

---

70   MEMO/08/232 of 10/04/2008.

Does it matter whether Deutsche Telekom lowers its wholesale price or raises its retail price? Does it matter whether the low retail price is not a predatory price?

How would the European Commission and courts decide the US *linkLine* case? What resolution is best for consumers? Note that the cases involve the relationship between a regulatory regime and antitrust rules. How is that relevant to the analysis?

CASE

Konkurrensverket v. TeliaSonera Sverige (Case C-52/09)[71]

[In Sweden, TeliaSonera was the dominant telecom supplier at retail. Historically it was the owner of exclusive rights and it still owned the local loop connecting the service provider to the subscriber's telephone. TeliaSonera also supplied ADSL—fast internet service—at wholesale and retail. It allegedly priced its wholesale service so high and retail service so low that ADSL retail competitors had no margin to supply service. Unlike the facts in *Deutsche Telekom*, TeliaSonera had no regulatory obligation to supply ADSL input services to telephone operators. The Swedish court asked the EU Court of Justice for a preliminary ruling on a number of questions. The Court first observed the function of the competition law, and then answered the questions.]

22   The function of [the Treaty's competition] rules is precisely to prevent competition from being distorted to the detriment of the public interest, individual undertakings and consumers, thereby ensuring the well-being of the European Union. * * *

30   ... [A]fter ascertaining whether the other conditions for the applicability of Article 102 TFEU are satisfied in the present case—including whether TeliaSonera holds a dominant position and whether trade between Member States was affected by its conduct—it is for the referring court to examine, in essence, whether the pricing practice introduced by TeliaSonera is unfair in so far as it squeezes the margins of its competitors on the retail market for broadband connection services to end users.

31   A margin squeeze, in view of the exclusionary effect which it may create for competitors who are at least as efficient as the dominant undertaking, in the absence of any objective

---

71   [2011] ECR I-527, EU:C:2011:83.

CASE *(continued)*

justification, is in itself capable of constituting an abuse within the meaning of Article 102 TFEU.

32   In the present case, there would be such a margin squeeze if, inter alia, the spread between the wholesale prices for ADSL input services and the retail prices for broadband connection services to end users were either negative or insufficient to cover the specific costs of the ADSL input services which TeliaSonera has to incur in order to supply its own retail services to end users, so that that spread does not allow a competitor which is as efficient as that undertaking to compete for the supply of those services to end users.

33   In such circumstances, although the competitors may be as efficient as the dominant undertaking, they may be able to operate on the retail market only at a loss or at artificially reduced levels of profitability.

34   It must moreover be made clear that since the unfairness, within the meaning of Article 102 TFEU, of such a pricing practice is linked to the very existence of the margin squeeze and not to its precise spread, it is in no way necessary to establish that the wholesale prices for ADSL input services to operators or the retail prices for broadband connection services to end users are in themselves abusive on account of their excessive or predatory nature, as the case may be. * * *

41   In order to assess the lawfulness of the pricing policy applied by a dominant undertaking, reference should be made, as a general rule, to pricing criteria based on the costs incurred by the dominant undertaking itself and on its strategy.

42   In particular, as regards a pricing practice which causes margin squeeze, the use of such analytical criteria can establish whether that undertaking would have been sufficiently efficient to offer its retail services to end users otherwise than at a loss if it had first been obliged to pay its own wholesale prices for the intermediary services.

43   If that undertaking would have been unable to offer its retail services otherwise than at a loss, that would mean that competitors who might be excluded by the application of the pricing practice in question could not be considered to be less efficient than the dominant undertaking and, consequently, that the risk of their exclusion was due to distorted competition. Such competition would not be based solely on the respective merits of the undertakings concerned.

44   Furthermore, the validity of such an approach is reinforced by the fact that it conforms to the general principle of legal certainty, since taking into account the costs and prices of the dominant undertaking enables that undertaking to assess the lawfulness of its own conduct,

CASE *(continued)*

which is consistent with its special responsibility under Article 102 TFEU . . . While a dominant undertaking knows its own costs and prices, it does not as a general rule know those of its competitors.

45   That said, it cannot be ruled out that the costs and prices of competitors may be relevant to the examination of the pricing practice at issue in the main proceedings. That might in particular be the case where the cost structure of the dominant undertaking is not precisely identifiable for objective reasons, or where the service supplied to competitors consists in the mere use of an infrastructure the production cost of which has already been written off, so that access to such an infrastructure no longer represents a cost for the dominant undertaking which is economically comparable to the cost which its competitors have to incur to have access to it, or again where the particular market conditions of competition dictate it, by reason, for example, of the fact that the level of the dominant undertaking's costs is specifically attributable to the competitively advantageous situation in which its dominant position places it.

46   It must therefore be concluded that, when assessing whether a pricing practice which causes a margin squeeze is abusive, account should as a general rule be taken primarily of the prices and costs of the undertaking concerned on the retail services market. Only where it is not possible, in particular circumstances, to refer to those prices and costs should those of its competitors on the same market be examined. * * *

59   It follows that the absence of any regulatory obligation to supply the ADSL input services on the wholesale market has no effect on the question of whether the pricing practice at issue in the main proceedings is abusive.

Whether an anti-competitive effect is required and whether the product offered by the undertaking must be indispensable

60   The referring court seeks to ascertain, thirdly, whether the abusive nature of the pricing practice in question depends on whether there actually is an anti-competitive effect and, if so, how that effect can be determined. Moreover, it seeks to ascertain whether the product offered by TeliaSonera on the wholesale market must be indispensable for entry onto the retail market. * * *

63   . . . [T]he practice in question, adopted by a dominant undertaking, constitutes an abuse within the meaning of Article 102 TFEU, where, given its effect of excluding competitors who are at least as efficient as itself by squeezing their margins, it is capable of making more difficult, or impossible, the entry of those competitors onto the market concerned.

CASE *(continued)*

64   It follows that, in order to establish whether such a practice is abusive, that practice must have an anti-competitive effect on the market, but the effect does not necessarily have to be concrete, and it is sufficient to demonstrate that there is an anti-competitive effect which may potentially exclude competitors who are at least as efficient as the dominant undertaking.

65   Where a dominant undertaking actually implements a pricing practice resulting in a margin squeeze on its equally efficient competitors, with the purpose of driving them from the relevant market, the fact that the desired result, namely the exclusion of those competitors, is not ultimately achieved does not alter its categorisation as abuse within the meaning of Article 102 TFEU.

66   However, in the absence of any effect on the competitive situation of competitors, a pricing practice such as that at issue in the main proceedings cannot be classified as an exclusionary practice where the penetration of those competitors in the market concerned is not made any more difficult by that practice. * * *

69   In particular, the first matter to be analysed must be the functional relationship of the wholesale products to the retail products. Accordingly, when assessing the effects of the margin squeeze, the question whether the wholesale product is indispensable may be relevant.

70   Where access to the supply of the wholesale product is indispensable for the sale of the retail product, competitors who are at least as efficient as the undertaking which dominates the wholesale market and who are unable to operate on the retail market other than at a loss or, in any event, with reduced profitability suffer a competitive disadvantage on that market which is such as to prevent or restrict their access to it or the growth of their activities on it.

71   In such circumstances, the at least potentially anti-competitive effect of a margin squeeze is probable. * * *

73   Secondly, it is necessary to determine the level of margin squeeze of competitors at least as efficient as the dominant undertaking. If the margin is negative, in other words if, in the present case, the wholesale price for the ADSL input services is higher than the retail price for services to end users, an effect which is at least potentially exclusionary is probable, taking into account the fact that, in such a situation, the competitors of the dominant undertaking, even if they are as efficient, or even more efficient, compared with it, would be compelled to sell at a loss.

74   If, on the other hand, such a margin remains positive, it must then be demonstrated that the application of that pricing practice was, by reason, for example, of reduced profitability,

> **CASE** *(continued)*
>
> likely to have the consequence that it would be at least more difficult for the operators concerned to trade on the market concerned. * * *
>
> 76   The assessment of the economic justification for a pricing practice established by an undertaking in a dominant position which is capable of producing an exclusionary effect is to be made on the basis of all the circumstances of the case. . . . In that regard, it has to be determined whether the exclusionary effect arising from such a practice, which is disadvantageous for competition, may be counterbalanced, or outweighed, by advantages in terms of efficiency which also benefit the consumer. If the exclusionary effect of that practice bears no relation to advantages for the market and consumers, or if it goes beyond what is necessary in order to attain those advantages, that practice must be regarded as an abuse. * * *

NOTES AND QUESTIONS

1. Note the *TeliaSonera* Court's expansive rendition of the goals of EU competition law in para. 22. Is this different from the perspective conveyed by the Court in *Post Danmark I*, para. 20? Is *Post Danmark* unique, in that its low (and above cost) price was merely price competition to lure a customer from a competitor? If the Court had declared such price competition to constitute an abuse of dominance, can you see the chilling effect on all price competition? The US analogue would be the now discredited case of Utah Pie (condemning price competition by means of a discriminatory price).[72]
2. Does the judgement in *TeliaSonera* have a chilling effect? Why does the US law (*Trinko*, *linkLine*) 'think' so?

f.   Abusive leveraging

In June 2017, the European Commission fined Google €2.42 billion for abusing its dominance as a search engine by pushing another Google product to highest prominence on search results and demoting the products of its rivals. Google offers Google Shopping, a comparative shopping site. After Google's initial forays in comparative shopping did not succeed well, the Commission found, Google began to place its own shopping comparison site number one. Thereafter, it received the highest share of clicks, and its demoted competitors suffered substantial losses of traffic on a lasting basis. The Commission's data showed that the top result of a search receives about 95% of all clicks and that results relegated to page 2 receive only about 1% of all clicks. More traffic generates more revenues. Google has appealed the decision (see Case T-612/17,

---

72   *Utah Pie Co. v. Continental Baking Co.*, 386 U.S. 685 (1967).

Google and Alphabet v. Commission), which was not yet publicly available at the time of printing. Excerpts from the Commission press-release can be found on pages xxxiii–xxxvi.

Reflect on the competitive effects of Google's strategy, assuming the Commission's fact-finding is accurate. What should be sufficient, and what should be necessary, to prove harm to competition? What duties should Google have to its rivals in comparative search? What is a good remedy for this offense?

* * *

Take stock, now, of the EU principles and rules that govern abuses of a dominant position. What is the overall perspective of the EU on how to identify whether practices of dominant firms that tend to exclude or make life hard for rivals constitute an abuse of dominance? What is the overall perspective of US law?

To what extent are the following observations true, and do they explain the differences?

- The US Supreme Court decisions presume that dominant firm conduct, unconstrained by antitrust, is generally good for consumers. They reflect a concern that antitrust authorities and courts will err, prohibiting pro-competitive and innovative conduct and chilling invention.
- EU competition law, influenced by its market integration tradition and by the fact that many of its markets do not operate optimally, privileges openness and access, is suspicious of dominant firm conduct that tends to fence out rivals, and reflects confidence that antitrust intervention can facilitate the functioning of the market.

6
Merger control

The competition articles of the 1957 Treaty of Rome establishing the European Economic Communities ('EEC') did not mention mergers. Facing trade barriers at every frontier, many business enterprises were too small to be efficient. As a result, mergers—especially mergers between firms from different Member States—held the promise of promoting market integration. However, the Member States were not prepared to yield to the Union over the structure of their economies, and EU competence over mergers was regarded by many as unreasonably intrusive. Article 85 EEC, now Article 101 TFEU, was designed to regulate agreements and ongoing collaborations. Article 86 EEC, now Article 102 TFEU, was designed to regulate the behaviour of dominant firms.

By contrast to the EEC Treaty, the European Coal and Steel Community ('ECSC') Treaty—which was adopted six years earlier and has now expired—specifically prohibited mergers that created power 'to determine prices, to control or restrict production or distribution or to hinder effective competition in a substantial part of the market . . .' (Article 66, para. 2) Thus, from the start, the Member States expressly conceded control over coal and steel mergers, underscoring the deliberateness of the omission of merger control in the EEC Treaty.

Finally, in 1989, the Council promulgated the Merger Regulation, officially providing a merger control system for the Union.

The adoption of European merger control coincided with important economic and political changes in the world. In November 1989, the Berlin Wall fell. Members of the former Soviet bloc and many others adopted merger control as part of the introduction of a domestic competition regime. More than 100 countries now have merger control/notification regimes. Since many of the possibly anti-competitive mergers are between firms that operate across national borders, problems of jurisdiction, conflict, and cooperation emerge. These challenges are considered in the present chapter, after a discussion of the concept and detail of the Merger Regulation.

A. The Merger Regulation

1. Coverage and procedures

After 16 years of debate, on 21 December 1989 the Council adopted the Merger Control Regulation, with an effective date of 21 September 1990.[1] It was amended in 2004. The Merger Regulation has three major purposes: (1) to provide specific authority for the Commission to challenge mergers and acquisitions that would harm competition, and thus to put an end to the debate whether the Treaty conferred such authority; (2) to provide a structure for merger control, giving the Commission necessary market information and the power to stop anti-competitive mergers before their consummation (standstill principle); and (3) to centralize merger enforcement in the hands of the Commission so that enterprises would not be subject to multiple and potentially inconsistent substantive standards, notice requirements and waiting periods ('one-stop-shop' principle).

Specifically, subject to exceptions, the parties to a concentration with a 'Community dimension' must file pre-merger notification forms and wait until final decision prior to closing their transaction. The Commission has exclusive power, vis-à-vis Member State authorities, to allow or disallow these transactions. The Member States have ceded authority to prevent or authorize such transactions, except when legitimate national interests such as security, plurality of media, and prudential concerns are at stake, and except in certain circumstances when a distinct State market is affected.

A concentration has a Community dimension when:

(a) the combined aggregate worldwide turnover of all the undertakings concerned is more than €5 billion; and
(b) the aggregate Community-wide turnover of each of at least two of the undertakings concerned is more than €250 million, unless each of the undertakings concerned achieves more than two-thirds of its aggregate Community-wide turnover within one and the same Member State.

---

1 Regulation 4064/89/EEC of 21 December 1989 on the control of concentrations between undertakings [1989] O.J. L 395/1 ('Merger Regulation'). The Merger Regulation was amended in 2004 and became Regulation 139/2004/EC, [2004] O.J. L 24/1. Various procedural issues are further governed by the Regulation 802/2004/EC [2004] O.J. L 133/1 (known as the 'Implementation Regulation'). The Merger Regulation and different sets of interpretative guidelines (e.g., jurisdictional notice, horizontal guidelines, non-horizontal guidelines, remedies notice, notice on ancillary restraints), may be found at: http://ec.europa.eu/competition/mergers/legislation/legislation.html (accessed 9 June 2017).

Concentrations also have a Community dimension and thus come within the Merger Regulation if:

1. the undertakings have combined aggregate worldwide turnover of at least €2.5 billion;
2. the undertakings have combined aggregate turnover of at least €100 million in at least three Member States;
3. at least two of the undertakings have at least €25 million turnover in the same three Member States; and
4. at least two undertakings have at least €100 million turnover in the Community,

unless each of the undertakings achieves more than two-thirds of its aggregate Community-wide turnover in the same Member State.[2]

Concentrations below the thresholds remain subject to the laws of the Member States. In some cases a concentration even with a Community dimension threatens competition in a distinct market within one Member State. Member State authority may ask the Commission to refer such a concentration to it, and the Commission *may* grant the reference; but if the affected territory is not a substantial part of the internal market, the Commission *must* grant the reference. The applicable clause—Article 9—was called the German clause, since it was proposed by Germany in response to its concerns that Germany would be stripped of its power to prohibit concentrations that uniquely harmed Germany. Another clause, Article 22, known as the Dutch clause, allows the Commission to investigate mergers not of Community dimension at the request of one or more Member States. Article 4(4) and (5) of the Merger Regulation also organize a pre-notification referral system at the initiative of the parties to the concentration, which allows for the allocation of the review thereof to the best-placed authority, e.g., the Commission in case a concentration is capable of being reviewed under the domestic merger regime of at least three Member States.

Joint ventures are 'concentrations' if they are created to 'perform on a lasting basis all the functions of an autonomous economic entity.'[3] These joint ventures are called 'full-function' joint ventures. Full-function joint ventures get the benefit of the one-stop-shop principle if they meet the thresholds. If the joint venture may give rise to coordination of the competitive behaviour of firms that remain independent, or if it entails ancillary agreements

---

2 Merger Regulation, Article 1(2).
3 Merger Regulation, Article 3(4).

that are not obviously directly related and necessary to the concentration, the Commission must appraise its potentially cooperative or exclusionary aspects under Article 101 or 102 TFEU.

Concentrative transactions with a Community dimension must be notified to the Commission and may not be put into effect before the Commission adopts a final decision. The Commission must evaluate the concentration to determine whether it is compatible with the internal market, i.e., whether or not it may result in a significant impediment to effective competition (so-called 'SIEC test', discussed in the next section). The vast majority of concentrations are cleared in Phase I, within 25 working days of the notification (or 35 days if the parties offer commitments). In case of serious doubts as to the compatibility of the concentration with the common market at the end of Phase I, the Commission then advances to the stage of initiating proceedings, i.e., an in-depth review called Phase 2, which may last for several months.

The Merger Regulation provides that the implementing legislation that empowers Commission enforcement of Articles 101 and 102 TFEU (especially Regulation 1/2003[4]) does not apply to concentrations, whether they fall above or below the thresholds. Moreover, the Commission has represented that it will not normally apply Articles 101 or 102 TFEU to concentrations. Therefore, the Merger Regulation has effectively become the only EU measure for controlling concentrations.

2. The substantive standard

Initially the Merger Regulation proscribed only such mergers that created or strengthened a *dominant position* that would significantly impede competition in the common market. This wording proved to be too narrow, because it seemed to ignore important oligopoly effects. The 2004 revision accordingly expanded the coverage.

The substantive standard is set forth in Article 2 of the revised Merger Regulation, which provides:

1. Concentrations within the scope of this Regulation shall be appraised in accordance with the following provisions with a view to establishing whether or not they are compatible with the common market.

---

[4] Regulation 1/2003/EC of 16 December 2002 on the implementation of the rules on competition laid down in Articles 81 and 82 of the Treaty [2002] O.J. L 1/1.

In making this appraisal, the Commission shall take into account:

(a) the need to maintain and develop effective competition within the common market in view of, among other things, the structure of all the markets concerned and the actual or potential competition from undertakings located either within or without the Community;

(b) the market positions of the undertakings concerned and their economic and financial power, the alternatives available to suppliers and users, their access to supplies or markets, any legal or other barriers to entry, supply and demand trends for relevant goods and services, the interests of the intermediate and ultimate consumers, and the development of technical and economic progress provided that it is to consumers' advantage and does not form an obstacle to competition.

2. A concentration which would not significantly impede effective competition in the common market or in a substantial part of it, in particular as a result of the creation or strengthening of a dominant position, shall be declared compatible with the common market.

3. *A concentration which would significantly impede effective competition, in the common market or in a substantial part of it, in particular as a result of the creation or strengthening of a dominant position, shall be declared incompatible with the common market.* [Italics added.]

This standard is called the SIEC test; the question is whether the merger would 'significantly impede effective competition'.

The body of the Merger Regulation is preceded by a number of recitals. Recital 23 states that the Community must place its competition appraisal within the framework of the fundamental objectives of the Union referred to in the Treaty. Recital 15 states:

(32) Concentrations which, by reason of the limited market share of the undertakings concerned, are not liable to impede effective competition may be presumed to be compatible with the common market. Without prejudice to Articles [101] and [102] of the Treaty, an indication to this effect exists, in particular, where the market share of the undertakings concerned does not exceed 25% either in the common market or in a substantial part of it.

NOTES AND QUESTIONS

1. Review the substantive standard for proscribing concentrations under the Merger Regulation. In considering whether the merger is compatible with the internal market, is the Commission limited to weighing pro-competitive and anti-competitive aspects of the concentration? If the acquisition impedes effective competition, is it relevant that the acquisition also saves jobs? That it produces productive efficiencies that help the firm compete in world markets? That it creates a European champion that by some measure might make Europe better off? If the acquisition is not likely to harm consumers, is it relevant that it will destroy small and middle-sized firms?

2. US law prohibits mergers 'the effect [of which] may be substantially to lessen competition.'[5] In Europe, this is sometimes called the 'SLC' test. (The UK also has an SLC test.) For the US, there is nothing magic in the words 'substantially to lessen competition'. The inquiry is whether the merger is anti-competitive.

US analysis of mergers of competitors is largely congruent with EU analysis, although US analysts have been more likely to use a robust-market assumption; namely, the assumption that actual or near competitive forces will constrain the merging parties from getting or using market power.

The US does not have one-stop shopping. The US federal merger law may be enforced by the Justice Department or the Federal Trade Commission, by the attorney general of any affected states, and by private parties threatened with antitrust injury.[6] In addition, the states that have anti-merger laws may seek to enforce them against mergers with local effects even though interstate commerce is also affected. Aware of the costs of multiple overlapping merger laws, the state attorneys general collaborate on the substantive standard for prohibition, and they invite merging parties to make joint filings with all interested states. Moreover, the state enforcers collaborate with the federal enforcers.

State enforcement has played an important role in the US, particularly in the 1980s when the federal government's market philosophy resulted in an unusually low level of merger challenges.

Should the US adopt the EU approach of centralized enforcement? Is there a need for multinational cooperation in merger control, as more and more mega-mergers have impacts around the world?

B. The economics of merger analysis

This section reviews some basic economics that may guide analysis of competitive harms, principally from a consumer or efficiency point of view. First, it analyses the effects of mergers on competition, assuming the relevant market. Second, it returns to the question of market definition, which is guided by the Commission's 1997 Notice on the definition of relevant market[7] and is often a controlling question in merger analysis.

1. Competition-lessening effects

Mergers may harm competition, causing output to fall and prices to rise or suppressing incentives to innovate, by creating or entrenching market power or facilitating its exercise. They can do this by one of two main routes: (i) creating or entrenching single firm power (dominance or other unilateral power, thereby causing unilateral or non-coordinated effects); or (ii) creating or entrenching a tight oligopoly wherein the few remaining firms in a market are likely to behave like collaborators rather than rivals (thereby causing coordinated effects). Other, less prominent, sources of concerns include vertical effects and conglomerate effects.

---

5 Clayton Act, § 7, 15 U.S.C. § 18.
6 See *California v. American Stores Co.*, 495 U.S. 271, 110 S.Ct. 1853, 109 L.Ed.2d 240 (1990).
7 [1997] O.J C 372/5.

The negative effects (principally higher price and lower output, and chilled incentives to invent)[8] cannot be expected if barriers to entry are low, strong potential competitors are waiting in the wings, smaller firms can easily and quickly expand without rising costs, or big buyers credibly threaten to integrate backwards if their suppliers do not perform competitively. In such cases the market may regulate itself. The economic forces put pressure on the existing market actors, causing them to be responsive to buyers' needs.

Of all mergers, mergers of competitors are most likely to harm competition. Also, mergers between a leading firm and a most important potential competitor can have the same unilateral or coordinated effects. Potential competitors can exert competitive pressure on prices. Incumbents may hold their prices down so as not to attract their entry. If a dominant firm acquires the most or only important potential competitor, the acquisition removes this competitive check. Also, if the potential entrant would have entered the market on its own and added a dynamic force to an oligopolistic or monopolistic market, the merger would prevent this force from materializing.

Mergers between buyers and suppliers ('vertical mergers') can also lessen competition, although in many cases they simply reshuffle buyer and supplier alliances. Vertical mergers may make it more likely that the firms will deal with each other to the exclusion of or in preference to dealing with others. Favouring one's own is especially likely in times of short supply or contracted demand.

Most often, a vertical merger is efficient and does not foreclose unintegrated rivals from access to needed supplies or outlets, raising their costs and pushing up price. The rivals may be able to buy from other suppliers or to supply other buyers, or to integrate vertically by contract or acquisition. But if leading firms in their respective fields merge, if barriers to entry are high, if concentration at the relevant market level is high, and if foreclosure of unintegrated rivals from necessary inputs or outlets threatens to squeeze rivals out of the market or incapacitate them, a vertical merger may increase dominance or facilitate oligopoly behaviour in the relevant market, raising consumer prices. EU competition law has been concerned also with competitors' access to markets, key assets and infrastructure (gateways), and with competitors' rights to compete on the merits free from blockage by a dominant firms' bundling and other strategies; but these factors must be linked with consumer harm.

---

8 Also, at high levels of concentration, loss of choice.

Mergers that are neither horizontal, potential-horizontal nor vertical are called conglomerate mergers. Conglomerate mergers are much less likely than horizontal, potential-horizontal or vertical mergers to lessen competition and harm consumers. In some cases, however, merging partners may be able to use leverage by engaging in tying or bundling strategies to create competition-lessening foreclosures (thereby causing 'conglomerate effects'). In the US today, the law treats anti-competitive effects of conglomerate mergers as negligible and speculative, and conglomerate mergers are substantially discounted as a source of competitive concern. In the EU, enforcers and policymakers are more likely to entertain arguments that the merger may cause conglomerate effects and/or that the merged firm will control the gateway to important inputs or outlets. If such claims are rarely decisive nowadays, they have played a significant role in some landmark cases discussed later in this chapter.

2. Positive effects

Mergers may produce efficiencies; they may increase competition; and mergers between firms from different Member States may increase market integration. A merger may create synergies, as vertical mergers are especially likely to do. Also, they may yield economies of scope as well as scale, as is often the case for mergers between firms that produce complementary products distributed through the same distribution channels. If the market is already competitive, market forces are likely to cause cost savings to be passed on to consumers. In contrast, if the market is monopolistic or oligopolistic, the merging partners are more likely to retain most of the savings and possibly raise prices as well.

3. Competitiveness

It is possible for a merger to yield efficiencies and increase the merged firm's competitiveness in world markets and at the same time to lessen competition in the domestic market. Despite world competition, domestic competition may be lessened if that local market is concentrated and the merged firm has (for example) locational or cultural advantages or the home market maintains barriers to foreign competition. To address the situation in which these two effects (efficiency in global competition and power at home) co-exist, the regulating nation must make a policy judgement as to which costs it wishes to avoid and which benefits it wishes to attain.

US law holds that a merger that lessens competition in the US is illegal regardless of the claim that the merger helps the firm compete in global markets.

The claim that a merger that increases market power in the US may enhance global competitiveness is regarded with scepticism and in fact is rarely substantiated. In contemplating this trade-off for the EU, policymakers typically do not consider the welfare of European consumers versus gains from greater economic strength abroad. However, as internal and European barriers have dismantled, imports from within and outside the EU have received increased attention for without barriers to entry, consumers are less likely to be subject to exploitation by local producers, in particular for traded and non-perishable goods (that is, those that move most freely).

4. Markets, concentration, barriers, and efficiencies

The above sections assumed well-defined markets, high concentration therein, and significant barriers to entry. All three of these concepts require detailed, fact-specific evaluation. Market definition is the crucial first step in merger analysis, particularly where the concern is that merging competitors will coordinate their behaviour and thus act like a cartel. Chapter 3 described the methodologies used to define markets, treating a market as an area in which, if there were a single seller, that firm would have market power; it would be able to raise the price of its product substantially and profitably for a significant period of time without fear that too many of its customers would shift to another product. All good substitutes are included in the market. Refer to the 1997 Notice on market definition.

Volvo wished to acquire control of Scania. Both firms were important Swedish truck makers. Neither made light trucks, and Scania had only a small position in medium trucks. Both were active in Europe and the world in sales of heavy trucks. In heavy trucks, they were particularly strong in Sweden, and also in Norway, Finland and Ireland. The merged firm would have held 31% of all heavy trucks in the European Economic Area ('EEA'). DaimlerChrysler was the number two firm with about 20%. The merged firm would have held 90% of Swedish sales and 50% of Irish sales. The two merging firms were the closest competitors to one another. Servicing contracts generally were valid only in the area within which the vehicle was sold.

Was there a product market of heavy trucks (more than 16 tons)? Was the geographic market national? European? Worldwide?

The Commission found a heavy truck market. Heavy trucks had a distinctive technical configuration. Engines and axles on heavy trucks were more sophisticated and more durable, which are qualities necessary for transporting heavy loads long distances. Heavy trucks are produced from different production lines than lighter trucks, and they appeal to different groups of customers. Therefore, competition from other (non-heavy) trucks was not a sufficiently good constraint to hold prices down and to incentivize responsive performance.

Moreover, the Commission found that the geographic markets were national. The Commission observed differences among nations in purchasing habits, technical requirements, price levels, and market shares. For example, prices were 10% to 20% higher in Sweden than in Denmark or Norway, and the price differentials did not lead to significant cross-border trade. Sales normally included a local service package that tended to attract local buyers to local sellers, and purchasing was normally done on a national basis.

Do you agree with the Commission's geographic market definition? Do you need more information? What would you like to know?[9]

A crucial product market definition question arose also in the case of the planned merger of the New York Stock Exchange Euronext and the Deutsche Börse. The parties would have had a near monopoly of exchange-traded European financial derivatives; but if the market included over-the-counter derivatives the firms' shares would be much smaller. The Commission rejected the parties' argument that over-the-counter derivatives were a good substitute and thus provided a check against exercise of market power, and it prohibited the merger.[10]

After defining the relevant market, the analyst normally counts sales or capacity of each firm in the market and assigns a market share to each. There are two accepted frameworks for counting what is in the market. One is the snapshot method—to count what is actually there; i.e., to record who sells/supplies how much of the relevant product/service. The other is the method employed both by the 1997 Commission Notice and by the 2010 US Federal Agency Merger Guidelines: to incorporate, as if already in the market, the goods that would quickly flow into the market if a hypothetical monopolist should try to raise price. The latter method incorporates the near potential competition. Whether or not near potential competition is incorporated directly into the market, it is a positive force that should be taken into account.

Next, one must measure concentration. There are two recognized ways of stating the measurement of concentration. One is the use of n-firm

---

9 See, the prohibition decision adopted by the Commission on 15 March 2000 in Case COMP/M.1672 – *Volvo/Scania*.
10 See the prohibition decision adopted by the Commission on 1 February 2012 in Case COMP/M.6166 – *Deutsche Börse/NYSE Euronext* (as upheld in Case T-175/12, *Deutsche Börse v. Commission*, EU:T:2015:148).

concentration ratios;[11] e.g., the top two firms account for *x*% of the market; the top four firms account for *y*% of the market. The second is the use of the Herfindahl-Hirschman Index ('HHI'). To calculate the HHI, one lists each firm in the market and its market share, squares each market share, and then adds the squares of the shares. The sum of the squares is the HHI index number and the delta between the pre- and post-merger HHI indexes captures the increased market concentration. Under each methodology, the key figures are those that represent the increase in concentration and the post-merger concentration. As a rule of thumb, a market is likely to be considered concentrated if the three leading firms have 75% or more of the market, or the market has an HHI of 2000 or more. The bare figures greatly overgeneralize facts, and the analysis should remain fact-specific.

Barriers and other hurdles to entry and expansion are then assessed. Even if a market is highly concentrated, the threat of entry may keep behaviour competitive if entry at an efficient scale can be easily achieved in a year or two.

Efficiencies may be relevant in two quite different ways. First, if the merger produces cost savings and the market is competitive (the firms behave rivalrously), the cost savings may be passed on to consumers and the cost-saving strategies may be mimicked by competitors. These effects are directly relevant to whether competition is helped or hurt by the merger. Second, in some cases even where a merger lessens competitive rivalry, cost savings may neutralize the price effect facing consumers, or in any event the producers' gain may be greater than the consumers' loss. This latter aspect is an efficiency *defence*. In practice, EU merger control law has not adopted an efficiency defence in this sense, where the merger lessens competition and raises prices to consumers. Neither has US law, despite a couple of outlier cases.[12]

C. Substantive law under the Merger Regulation

1. Mergers of competitors that create or increase dominance

In the first year of the Merger Regulation, the Commission cleared all notified mergers. Then, in the thirteenth month, the Commission examined the acquisition of de Havilland, the second largest commuter aircraft manufacturer in the world, by a joint venture owned by France and Italy ('ATR') that was the largest commuter aircraft manufacturer in the world. This is

---

11 'N' represents an unspecified number.
12 For a discussion, see D. Gerard (2003), 'Merger control policy: How to give meaningful consideration to efficiency claims?', *Common Market Law Review*, **40** (6), 1367.

an early case. Bear in mind that in cases prior to 2000 the Commission took short-cuts and perhaps sometimes too quickly presumed that merging firms' advantages that would make life tough for their rivals were also anticompetitive.

This section explores when advantages from mergers reflect efficiencies and are likely to benefit consumers, and when they are simply advantages of power likely to hurt consumers.

a. *Note on Aerospatiale-Alenia/De Havilland*

The US aircraft manufacturer, Boeing, agreed to sell its Canadian aircraft subsidiary de Havilland to a joint venture of two European firms, Aerospatiale of France and Alenia e Selenia of Italy. The joint venture, ATR, was the world's leading producer of turboprop or commuter aircraft; de Havilland was the number two producer. British Aerospace and Fokker were the only other significant European competitors. Japanese firms were not in the market and not likely to enter 'such a low-technology non-strategic market'. Other possible potential competitors, notably firms from Indonesia and Eastern Europe, were either in financial difficulties or not capable of producing a product of sufficient quality for the world market.

The acquisition would lead to an increase in market shares for ATR in the world market for commuters between 40 to 59 seats from 46% to 63%. The nearest competitor (Fokker) would have 22%. ATR would increase its share of the overall worldwide commuter market of 20 to 70 seats from 30% to 50%. Saab, the nearest competitor, would have 19%. The new entity would account for half the world market and more than two and a half times the share of its nearest competitor. The Commission was concerned that the merger would confer advantages on ATR/de Havilland that would seriously jeopardize the survival of the remaining small competitors and would thus lead to a monopoly and thus prohibited the merger.[13] This was the Commission's first merger prohibition.

The governments of France and Italy, owners of the would-be acquirer ATR, were highly critical of the Commission's decision. So, too, was Commissioner Bangemann, Commissioner for the Internal Market, who argued that the acquisition was good for Europe and that the Directorate-General for Competition had improperly failed to take account of the interests of

---

13 Commission Decision of 2 October 1991 in Case COMP/M.53 – *Aerospatiale/Alenia/de Havilland*.

Europe—as opposed to merely the interests of competition. They threatened to press for an amendment to the Merger Regulation to assure that the Commission could weigh industrial policy.

Look again at the Merger Regulation. (No relevant language has been changed since its adoption.) Can the Commission legally take industrial policy into account? On what basis, and if so, how and to what extent? Is it good or bad policy to allow an industrial policy counterweight to a dominance-creating merger?

Meanwhile, Canada, home to de Havilland, had cleared the merger. Canada had strongly supported the merger because de Havilland was in financial difficulties and constantly needed subsidies—which Canada paid—to protect Canadian jobs. The acquisition by ATR had seemed a promising route to turn around the fortunes of de Havilland. When the acquisition was declared illegal, Canada sought another suitor for de Havilland. It identified Bombardier, which acquired de Havilland but required a continuing and even greater subsidy.

After *de Havilland*, potential for international controversy increased. The EU, the US, and numerous other jurisdictions have pre-merger notification and reporting systems that are triggered by a significant but relatively modest level of sales in the jurisdiction. By the early 1990s, the EU, the US, and other jurisdictions freely applied their laws to mergers of firms located abroad that had effects within their territories. Conflict was sure to follow.

b. Note on Boeing/McDonnell Douglas

In the same year that *de Havilland* was decided, the EU and the US anticipated the need for greater cooperation, and entered into the Cooperation Agreement of 1991. In this agreement, each party agreed to notify the other upon becoming aware 'that their enforcement activities may affect important interests of the other party.' '[W]ithin the framework of its own laws and to the extent compatible with its important interests', each agreed 'to take into account the important interests of the other Party', and to seek 'an appropriate accommodation of the competing interests.' The agreement was invoked six years later, in connection with Boeing's plan to acquire McDonnell Douglas.

Boeing was the largest manufacturer of commercial jet aircraft in the world, accounting for about 64% of world market sales. Its only competitors were McDonnell Douglas, with about 5%, and Airbus Industrie, with about 30%.

Airbus was a consortium of manufacturers in Britain, France, Germany and Spain. Those countries had helped to finance Airbus.

Boeing and McDonnell Douglas were US companies and had no production assets in Europe, although they regularly made sales there. McDonnell Douglas also produced military jets, and its technology portfolio included patents from research and development undertaken with US government financing. In the commercial jet market, McDonnell Douglas had failed to invest in important new-generation developments and was facing financial and competitive difficulties. Its market share was withering. Boeing, meanwhile, had recently concluded 20-year exclusive supply agreements with the three big American airlines that were the most important launch customers for new generation aircraft—Delta, American, and Continental. The exclusive supply agreements represented about 11% of all world purchases of big commercial jets.

Commercial jet airplanes are very complex and expensive. An order from an airline is typically worth billions of dollars. In view of the fact that each sale to an airline is so significant, Airbus and Boeing were fierce competitors for sales around the world.

Boeing and McDonnell Douglas filed pre-merger notifications in the US and in the EU. European Competition Commissioner Karel Van Miert immediately expressed concerns about the merger and the exclusive agreements. On the US side, the Federal Trade Commission ('FTC') opened an investigation. The European Commission and the FTC made notifications to one another under the 1991 agreement, and the European and American officials shared their perspectives. They sharply disagreed on the analysis of anticompetitive effects.

Early on, politicians entered the fray, with Europeans declaring that the merger was blatantly anti-competitive and seriously harmful to competition and to Airbus, and Americans declaring that the merger was good for the American economy. Laura D'Andrea Tyson, former head of the Council of Economic Advisors, was quoted in the *Washington Post* as saying that this merger was good for America 'even if consumers of airplane seats are somewhat worse off.'[14] European Competition Commissioner Van Miert threatened that, if the merger should be consummated without European approval, the European Commission would impose prohibitive fines on Boeing and might seize Boeing planes flying into the EU.

---

14 *Washington Post*, 4 May 1997, p. H6.

On 1 July 1997, the US FTC issued a statement announcing the closing of its investigation.

Matter of Boeing Company/McDonnell Douglas Corporation
US Federal Trade Commission, Statement[15]

After an extensive and exhaustive investigation, the Federal Trade Commission has decided to close the investigation of The Boeing Company's proposed acquisition of McDonnell Douglas Corporation. For reasons discussed below, we have concluded that the acquisition would not substantially lessen competition or tend to create a monopoly in either defense or commercial aircraft markets.

[First, the FTC disclaims any attempt to support a national champion, which, it states, it has no power to do.]

On its face, the proposed merger appears to raise serious antitrust concerns. The transaction involves the acquisition by Boeing, a company that accounts for roughly 60% of the sales of large commercial aircraft, of a non-failing direct competitor in a market in which there is only one other significant rival, Airbus Industrie, and extremely high barriers to entry. The merger would also combine two firms in the U.S. defense industry that develop fighter aircraft and other defense products. Nevertheless, for reasons we will now discuss, we do not find that this merger will substantially lessen competition in any relevant market. * * *

The evidence collected during the staff investigation, including the virtually unanimous testimony of forty airlines that staff interviewed, revealed that McDonnell Douglas's commercial aircraft division, Douglas Aircraft Company, can no longer exert a competitive influence in the worldwide market for commercial aircraft. Over the past several decades, McDonnell Douglas has not invested at nearly the rate of its competitors in new product lines, production facilities, company infrastructure, or research and development. As a result, Douglas Aircraft's product line is not only very limited, but lacks the state of the art technology and performance characteristics that Boeing and Airbus have developed. Moreover, Douglas Aircraft's line of aircraft do not have common features such as cockpit design or engine type, and thus cannot generate valuable efficiencies in interchangeable spare parts and pilot training that an airline may obtain from a family of aircraft, such as Boeing's 737 family or Airbus's A–320 family.

In short, the staff investigation revealed that the failure to improve the technology and efficiency of its commercial aircraft products has lead to a deterioration of

---

15 (1 July 1997).

Douglas Aircraft's product line to the point that the vast majority of airlines will no longer consider purchasing Douglas aircraft and that the company is no longer in a position to influence significantly the competitive dynamics of the commercial aircraft market. * * *

* * *

Procedurally, the closing of the investigation was not a judicial finding that the merger was lawful under US law. Unlike a decision in Europe, an initial US decision not to challenge a merger does not preclude subsequent challenge. It remained theoretically possible for the merger to be tested in the US courts, e.g., in a private action by Airbus or in a suit by a state attorney general, if not by the Federal government. Nonetheless, immediately after the FTC closed its investigation, the US government (the Clinton administration) began to take an active political role in defending the merger to Europe. Key White House officials, including the President of the US, argued to key European officials, including the President of the European Commission, that the merger was not anti-competitive, that it was important to the defence interests of the United States (because the military assets of McDonnell Douglas would be best preserved in the hands of Boeing), and to employment in the US, and that the US was 'considering how to retaliate against Europe if it makes good on its threat to try and undermine the merger of [the] U.S. aerospace giants. . . .'[16] Reportedly, the administration officials were considering imposing tariffs on European planes, limiting flights between the US and France (the most adamant objector to the merger), and filing a protest with the World Trade Organization in view of European subsidies to Airbus.

Meanwhile, Boeing was negotiating with the European Commission, and at the eleventh hour it agreed to conditions acceptable to the Commission. The conditions were not acceptable to France, however, which maintained that only a prohibition would cure the essential problems. On 30 July 1997, the European Commission issued its decision in *Boeing/McDonnell Douglas*.[17]

The Commission concluded that Boeing held a dominant position and that the acquisition would strengthen its dominant position. It was expected to do so by, among other things, increasing Boeing's market share of large commercial aircraft from 64% to 70%, taking one of Boeing's only two remaining competitors off the market, further foreclosing the market,

---

16 *Washington Post*, 17 July 1997, p. C1.
17 Commission Decision of 30 July 1997 in Case COMP/M.877 – *Boeing/McDonnell Douglas*.

increasing Boeing's ability to entice airlines into exclusivity deals with it since it would be able to offer the advantages of a larger family of planes, and giving Boeing access to US government-funded research and development and intellectual property acquired from military and space functions of McDonnell Douglas. On the basis of significant commitments by Boeing, the Commission cleared the merger.

Boeing undertook, among other things: not to enforce its exclusivity rights under the agreements with American, Delta and Continental; not to enter into exclusive agreements until 2007; not to 'use its privileged access to the existing fleet in service of DAC [Douglas Aircraft Corporation] aircraft in order to leverage its opportunities for persuading current DAC operators to purchase Boeing aircraft'; to license to competitors upon request all US-funded patents usable in the manufacture or sale of commercial jet aircraft; and not to leverage its relationship with suppliers to refuse to deal with Boeing's competitors or to grant preferential treatment to Boeing.

c. *Contemporary mergers to monopoly*

The Commission blocked the merger of Deutsche Börse and the NYSE Euronext in 2012. The Commission found: in the market for exchange-traded European financial derivatives, the merger would have led to a near-monopoly and the elimination of the closest competitor; it would have diminished incentives to innovate, service offerings, and responsiveness to users. Moreover, each partner had its own clearing house, and the resulting single house would have raised the already high barriers to entry. Regarding efficiencies, the parties argued that the merger would produce greater liquidity and lower trading costs; but the Commission found that these benefits were overstated and in any event the proof of efficiencies did not hurdle the bar which is set quite high where the impediment to competition is so substantial.[18]

Likewise, and earlier, the Commission prohibited Ryanair's hostile takeover of Aer Lingus. The General Court affirmed. The merger would have produced overlaps on more than 30 routes from and to Ireland; it would have combined the two largest airlines at the Dublin airport, where the firms would have had 80% of European short-haul traffic; and the two airlines were the closest of competitors—both, no frills. Neither the threat of entry nor the claimed efficiencies were sufficient to offset the anticompetitive effects; and

---

18 Commission Decision of 1 February 2012 in Case COMP/M.6166 – *Deutsche Börse/NYSE Euronext*.

besides, the claimed efficiencies were not verifiable and had to be rejected for this reason too.[19]

NOTES AND QUESTIONS

1. In *Boeing*, how did the merger create or strengthen a dominant position if Airbus would remain a good competitive check on Boeing, which the Commission assumed?

    What is the significance of the fact that Boeing would gain a fuller line of jet planes, and that buyers (the airlines) saved money and time—including pilot training costs and replacement and maintenance costs—by dealing with one producer? What is the significance of the fact that Boeing would have access to technology that was funded by the US government?

    What is the significance of the facts that McDonnell Douglas was 'no longer a real force in the market for the sale of new aircraft on a stand-alone basis' (para. 58); no one but Boeing wanted to acquire McDonnell Douglas; and, if the merger was prohibited Boeing would probably absorb McDonnell Douglas' share anyway (all acknowledged in the decision)?

    Did the Commission confuse unfairness to Airbus (or a competitive advantage over Airbus) with harm to competition and consumers? Did it want to protect Airbus from efficient competition from Boeing?

2. If the merger did strengthen Boeing's dominance, was France correct that a prohibition was the best remedy?

3. Comment on the statement by the US Federal Trade Commission. Was the national aspect argument irrelevant? Should it be?

    Was *Boeing-McDonnell Douglas* purely a competition case? Who had the stronger side of the argument: the Europeans, most of whom seemed to believe that the US green light was industrial policy to promote Boeing as the US national champion? Or the Americans, most of whom seemed to believe that the EU opposition was industrial policy to protect Airbus as the European champion?[20]

4. Many mergers today are new economy mergers, involving high technology and fast-changing markets. In the face of fast-changing markets, where the market leader today may be eclipsed tomorrow, enforcers are more reluctant to intervene. Where, however, the merged firm may become the 'gatekeeper' to the market (control access), enforcement may occur.

    In 2000, the then Competition Commissioner Mario Monti described the Commission's approach to new economy mergers. He gave examples of two recent cases; one concerning a European market and the other a worldwide market:

    > First, the *Vodafone/Mannesmann* transaction raised competition concerns on the emerging market for pan-European seamless mobile telephony services. The merged company, with its extensive network, would be in a unique position vis-à-vis its competitors to roll out such services. In order to remedy these concerns, *Vodafone* accepted to give competitors non-discriminatory access to its integrated network. However, in order to ensure that competitors would not exclusively rely on the merged company, neglecting the development of their own infrastructure, the Commission limited the undertaking to three years. The Commission considered, inter alia, that in

---

19 Commission Decision of 27 June 2007 in Case COMP/M.4439 – *Ryanair/Aer Lingus*, upheld in Case T-342/07, *Ryanair Holdings v. Commission* [2010] ECR II-3457, EU:T:2010:280.

20 See E. Fox (1998), 'Antitrust regulation across national borders: The United States of Boeing versus the European Union of Airbus', *Brookings Review*, **16**, 30.

this period, UMTS licenses would be awarded in sufficient number to allow competitors to replicate the Vodafone network.

Second, in June this year [2000], the Commission prohibited the merger between the two US communications companies *MCI WorldCom* and *Sprint*. It found that the combination of the parties' extensive Internet networks and large customer bases would have allowed the merged entity to dictate terms and conditions for access to its Internet networks in a manner that could have had significant anti-competitive effects and hindered innovation. The Commission's investigation, which was carried out in close co-operation with the American antitrust authorities, showed that despite liberalisation, regional and local providers are still dependent on the largest top-level providers to gain full and effective access to the Internet.[21]

In the above examples, was the Commission wisely proactive or overly aggressive in intervening in new economy mergers?

5. Consider the parallel with Article 102 concerns when a single firm becomes a gatekeeper—but by internal growth and (perhaps) anti-competitive strategies? Look again at the *Microsoft* case in Chapter 5, the interoperability problem.

6. In recent years, the Commission has attracted criticisms for being too lenient with new economy mergers, including Facebook's acquisition of WhatsApp[22] and, particularly, Microsoft's acquisition of Skype.[23] In *Microsoft/Skype*, the Commission found that the parties' activities overlapped in the area of communication services but that consumer and enterprise services belonged to two separate markets. While the parties both offered consumer solutions, and held an estimated combined share of 80 to 90% for video calls, no competition concern arose because these services were deemed part of a nascent and growing market boasting numerous players, including Google and Facebook. Moreover, the Commission dismissed the value of market shares as an accurate indicator of market power given the rapid changes observable over a short period of time (para. 78); likewise, it considered that 'competition in the consumer communications services markets is driven by innovation' (para. 84), as exemplified by recent entries. In the dynamic area of enterprise communications, then, Skype had a limited presence, according to the Commission, and did not compete directly with Microsoft's Lync's service. The Commission also considered possible conglomerate effects, including the incentive and ability of Microsoft to: (i) degrade Skype's interoperability with competing services; and (ii) tie Skype to Windows, thereby limiting other players' ability to compete.

Cisco Systems, the leader and Microsoft's main competitor for enterprise communication solutions, appealed the decision to the General Court arguing, in essence, that the Commission had cleared a merger to monopoly in the consumer communications market (for video calls) and missed interoperability issues in relation to enterprise communication solutions. The General Court sided with the Commission on all counts pointing, in particular, to: (i) the instability of market shares and their inherent weakness as an indicator of market power in a 'fast-growing sector which is characterized by short innovation cycles' (paras. 68–69); (ii) the potential of consumers' multi-homing practices to defeat network effects (paras. 79–81); and (iii) the speculative character of alleged foreclosure effects arising from a possible integration

---

21 Mario Monti (2001), 'European competition policy for the 21st century', in B. Hawk (ed.), *International Antitrust Law & Policy, Fordham Corporate Law 2000*, New York: Juris, Ch. 15.
22 Commission Decision of 3 October 2014 in Case COMP/M.7217–*Facebook/ WhatsApp*.
23 Commission Decision of 7 October 2011 in Case COMP/M.6281–*Microsoft/Skype*.

of Skype and Lync, knowing that the existence, extent and nature of demand for such a product was uncertain (paras. 120–122).[24]

d.   *The failing firm defence*

CASE

France v. Commission (Joined Cases C-68/94 and C-30/95) ('Kali + Salz')[25]

[After the fall of the Berlin wall and in view of the plan and then the reality of German unification, Germany established the Treuhandanstalt ('Treuhand'), a public institution entrusted with the task of restructuring the firms of the former German Democratic Republic. The Treuhand had title to, among others, Mitteldeutsche Kali AG ('MdK'), which held all of the GDR's operations in potash and rock salt. The business had escalating losses and was likely to close down if not taken over by a private firm. The only available, willing purchaser was Kali und Salz AG ('K+S'), a subsidiary of BASF chemicals group. It was proposed that K+S buy 51% of the stock of MdK, leaving 49% with the Truehand. This would result in K+S's achieving 98% of the German market for potashsalt-based products for agricultural use.

With respect to the German market:]

11   . . . [A]pplying the theory of the 'failing company defence', [the Commission] reached the conclusion that the proposed concentration was not the cause of the strengthening of the dominant position of K+S on the German market . . . . [T]he conditions for the 'failing company defence' were met, namely that K+S's dominant position would be reinforced even in the absence of the merger, because MdK would withdraw from the market in the foreseeable future if it was not acquired by another undertaking and its market share would then accrue to K+S; it can be practically ruled out that an undertaking other than K+S would acquire all or a substantial part of MdK'. . . . The Commission further observed . . . that, given the severe structural weakness of the regions in East Germany which were affected by the proposed concentration, and the likelihood of serious consequences for them of the closure of MdK, the conclusion it had reached was also in line with the fundamental objective of strengthening the Community's economic and social cohesion, referred to in the 13th recital in the preamble to the Regulation.

---

24   Case T-79/12, *Cisco Systems v. Commission*, EU:T:2013:635.
25   [1998] ECR I-1375, EU:C:1998:148.

CASE (continued)

[France sought annulment of the Commission's decision to allow the acquisition with respect to the German market without imposing any conditions. The Court of Justice rejected this claim.] * * *

111 It appears from point 71 of the contested decision that, in the Commission's opinion, a concentration which would normally be considered as leading to the creation or reinforcement of a dominant position on the part of the acquiring undertaking may be regarded as not being the cause of it if, even in the event of the concentration being prohibited, that undertaking would inevitably achieve or reinforce a dominant position. Point 71 goes on to state that, as a general matter, a concentration is not the cause of the deterioration of the competitive structure if it is clear that:

— the acquired undertaking would in the near future be forced out of the market if not taken over by another undertaking,
— the acquiring undertaking would gain the market share of the acquired undertaking if it were forced out of the market,
— there is no less anticompetitive alternative purchase. * * *

[The Commission was entitled to conclude that there was an 'absence of a causal link between the concentration and the deterioration of the competitive structure of the German market. . . .' In this case 'it is not possible . . . to attach any condition whatever to [the] declaration of the concentration's compatibility.' (para. 124).]

NOTES AND QUESTIONS

1. The failing firm defence seldom justifies a merger, for the three criteria are seldom met. For example, in 2011, when the Greek airline Aegean sought to acquire the troubled Greek airline Olympic, and the merger would have produced a monopoly on six domestic routes, the Commission found the proof of imminent failure lacking and prohibited the transaction.[26] But by 2013, as Olympic's fortunes continued to plummet, Aegean tried again, and this time ultimately with success. It was highly unlikely that Olympic would become profitable in the foreseeable future, its benefactor was planning to discontinue support, no other purchaser was available, and, absent the merger, Olympic would exit the market. The merger was cleared.[27]
2. US caselaw also contains a failing firm defence.[28] It is similarly difficult to meet the necessary criteria.
3. Note the Commission's industrial policy argument, in para. 11 of *Kali + Salz*: saving MdK will save jobs in the former East Germany and strengthen economic and social cohesion. Is

---

26 Commission Decision of 28 January 2011 in Case COMP/M.5830 – *Olympic/Aegean Airlines*.
27 Commission Decision of 23 April 2013 in Case COMP/M.6796 – *Aegean/Olympic II*.
28 See *Citizen Publishing Co. v. United States*, 394 U.S. 131, 89 S.Ct. 927, 22 L.Ed.2d 148 (1969).

this argument admissible under the Merger Regulation? Would it have saved the merger if there were a causal link between the concentration and the entrenchment of monopoly power? Should it have? Look again at the statement referenced. Was it a part of the *ratio decidendi* of the judgement, or just an observation of a welcome by-product?

4. Why wasn't the causal link between the concentration and the harm to competition similarly lacking in *Boeing/McDonnell Douglas* (see above section b), given the Commission's concessions that: '[I]t has to be concluded that DAC is today no longer a real force in the market on a stand-alone basis.' (para. 59). '[D]ue to the deterioration of the situation of DAC ... only Boeing is prepared to take over MDC's commercial aircraft business.' (para. 60).

2. Mergers that create unilateral or non-coordinated effects

On revising the Merger Regulation in 2004, the Commission was aware of a class of anti-competitive mergers of competitors that would not fall into the language of single-firm dominance (or collective dominance). There was a gap. This was a major reason for the revision.

To understand the gap, consider two firms merging that are particularly close competitors to one another for each is the second choice of consumers who prefer the other; their combination may allow the merged firm to raise prices profitably even if other competitors on the market do not follow suit. This phenomenon is called 'unilateral effects' because the merged firm can get power acting on its own, even without reaching a threshold of dominance. The phenomenon is also referred to as 'non-coordinated effects' to emphasize that the effect may be not only unilateral, i.e., result from the loss of competition between the merging firms, but may also change the incentives of competitors and trigger a price adjustment upwards of the remaining firms on the market. Thus, Recital 25 of the Merger Regulation says:

> 25 In view of the consequences that concentrations in oligopolistic market structures may have, it is all the more necessary to maintain effective competition in such markets. Many oligopolistic markets exhibit a healthy degree of competition. However, under certain circumstances, concentrations involving the elimination of important competitive constraints that the merging parties had exerted upon each other, as well as a reduction of competitive pressure on the remaining competitors, may, even in the absence of a likelihood of coordination between the members of the oligopoly, result in a significant impediment to effective competition. The Community courts have, however, not to date expressly interpreted Regulation (EEC) No 4064/89 as requiring concentrations giving rise to such non-coordinated effects to be declared incompatible with the common market. Therefore, in the interests of legal certainty, it should be made clear that this Regulation permits effective control of all such concentrations by providing that any concentration which would significantly impede effective competition,

in the common market or in a substantial part of it, should be declared incompatible with the common market. The notion of 'significant impediment to effective competition' in Article 2(2) and (3) should be interpreted as extending, beyond the concept of dominance, only to the anti-competitive effects of a concentration resulting from the non-coordinated behaviour of undertakings which would not have a dominant position on the market concerned.

Since 2004, the notion of unilateral or non-coordinated effects is therefore aimed to capture the most direct way through which both concentrations giving rise to situations of dominance and those gap cases may significantly impede effective competition, 'by eliminating important competitive constraints on one or more firms, which consequently would have increased market power, without resorting to coordinated behaviour.' As the Commission puts it, the main concern is that '[t]he reduction in these competitive constraints could lead to significant price increases in the relevant market', either by creating or strengthening the dominant position of a single firm or by eliminating important competitive constraints that the merging parties previously exerted on each other and on their remaining competitors.[29]

* * *

Mobile telecoms consolidations provide good examples of gap cases giving rise to unilateral effects. In 2012, the Commission cleared the acquisition of Orange Austria by Hutchinson 3G Austria,[30] subject to significant commitments (including spectrum divestiture and wholesale access) in order to alleviate concerns of upward price pressure. Orange and Hutchinson were the third and fourth mobile telephony operators in Austria and their combined share of 27% was lower than that of the other two players T-Mobile (31%) and Mobilkom (41%). There was therefore no question of dominance. Still, the merging firms were the most significant competitors of each other. Hence, the Commission found that the market power of the merging parties would have been higher than what their market shares suggested. The analytical inquiry was whether one firm's price rise would divert so much sales to the other merger partner (rather than to the rest of the market) that a price rise would pay for the merging firms. It would not be necessary for all rivals to collectively follow suit to make the upward pricing worth it, though

---

29 Commission Guidelines on the assessment of horizontal mergers under the Council Regulation on the control of concentrations between undertakings [2004] O.J. C 31/5, paras. 22–25 ('Horizontal Merger Guidelines').
30 Commission Decision of 12 December 2012 in Comp/M.6497 – Hutchison 3G Austria/Orange Austria.

there was a risk that they would follow because of a reduction in overall competitive constraints.

A similar pattern of analysis was followed in subsequent mobile telecom cases leading either to clearance[31] or to prohibition/withdrawal.[32] Contrary to the Austrian case referred to before, the concentration between Hutchison and Telefonica mobile operations in the UK (respectively, 'Three' and 'O2') would have created a new market leader—though not a dominant player—and given the merged entity full overview of the network plans of their two remaining competitors, with which they had entered into network sharing arrangements. Hence, the Commission concluded that the concentration would remove an important competitor, thereby reducing significantly competition for mobile services, increasing the incentive and ability of the merging parties and other operators to raise prices and degrading quality of service over time. In the absence of acceptable commitments, the transaction was prohibited.

3. Mergers of competitors that facilitate coordinated behaviour (collective dominance)

As noted, the original text of the Merger Regulation prohibited the creation or strengthening of *dominance* that may impede effective competition. The Commission soon had to confront the limits of the word 'dominance'. Could the word be stretched to cover duopoly and oligopoly?

Part of the answer was given in the previous section when considering unilateral or non-coordinated effects. With respect to coordinated effects, the Court of Justice originally responded to the dilemma. In *Kali und Salz* the Court held that the 1989 Merger Regulation caught mergers that create or strengthen a 'collective dominant position' likely to have a significant effect on competition. It stated that collective dominance might be established if the firms remaining on the market have 'close commercial links' such as participation in export cartels to third countries, joint ventures, and buyer/supplier relationships.[33]

Gencor/Lonrho was decided in the wake of the case law language stating that 'links' may justify finding dominance in an oligopolistic market. The case is

---

31 Commission Decision of 28 May 2014 in COMP/M.6992 – *Hutchison 3G UK/Telefonica Ireland*; Commission Decision of 2 July 2014 in COMP/M.7018 – *Telefonica Deutschland/E-Plus*, under appeal in Cases T-307/15, *1&1 Telecom v. Commission* and T-305/15, *Airdata v. Commission*.
32 Commission Decision of 11 September 2015 in COMP/M.7419 – *TeliaSonera/Telenor*; Commission Decision of 11 May 2016 in COMP/M.7612 – *Hutchison 3G UK/Telefonica UK*.
33 [1998] ECR I-1375, EU:C:1998:148, paras. 165–178.

important not for the semantic challenge (which was cured by an amendment to the regulation) but for the substantive question: By what theory was this merger anti-competitive in view of the fact that other players remained on the market? After *Gencor/Lonrho*, the General Court's annulment of the Commission decision in *Airtours* ushered in modern analysis of how a merger of firms in an oligopoly may harm competition by cooperative effects.

CASE

Gencor Ltd v. Commission (Case T-102/96)[34]

[Two South African platinum and rhodium mining companies merged, combining Implats, a subsidiary of Gencor, having about 17% of world market sales, and LPD (a subsidiary of the UK firm, Lonrho), having about 15% of sales. The combined firm would have had 32% of sales. The leading firm, Anglo American ('Amplats'), had about 43% of sales. Together the two resulting South African firms would have held about 89% of world reserves. Russia, through its firm Almaz, had a 22% share of sales and 10% of reserves. North American producers accounted for 5% of sales and had 1% reserves; and recycling firms accounted for 6% of sales. Russia was expected to dispose of its stocks in two years.

The Commission found that the concentration would create a dominant duopoly and was therefore incompatible with the common market, and it prohibited the concentration. Gencor contested the decision. The General Court analyzed as follows the evidence regarding whether the merger did indeed create a market structure in which the resulting two leading firms would gain collective dominance.]

222   [G]iven the similarity in the market shares, shares of world reserves and cost structures of the undertakings at issue, the Commission was entitled to conclude that, following the concentration, the interests of Amplats and Implats/LPD with regard to the development of the market would have coincided to a higher degree and that this alignment of interests would have increased the likelihood of anticompetitive parallel behaviour, for example restrictions of output. * * *

Characteristics of the market

[The Commission was entitled to find high transparency of price, production, sales, reserves, and new investment; and that given slow growth in demand, new competitors would not be encouraged to enter the market and existing competitors would not be encouraged to adopt aggressive strategies to capture additional demand.]

---

34 [1999] ECR II-753, EU:T:1999:65.

CASE (continued)

248   The applicant points out in that regard that the South African government's letter of 19 April 1996 indicates that world reserves outside South Africa and Zimbabwe could theoretically satisfy world demand for 20 years. * * *

252   As regards the applicant's argument that the 37% of the market accounted for by the marginal sources of supply and other influences would have curbed price increases, the Commission points out that the South African producers alone accounted for 63% of the market in 1995, a figure that was to increase significantly (to a level approaching 80%) when, from 1997, Russia would no longer be selling from its stocks. Furthermore, a significant proportion of the marginal competition was hypothetical and could not in any event have exerted any pressure on the market for some years. * * *

254   The applicant's view has no factual basis . . . . * * *

264   The applicant claims that the Commission . . . has failed to demonstrate the existence of structural links or to prove that the merged entity and Amplats intended to behave as if they constituted a single dominant entity . . . . * * *

The Court

273   In its judgement in the *Flat Glass* case, the Court referred to links of a structural nature only by way of example and did not lay down that such links must exist in order for a finding of collective dominance to be made. * * *

276   Furthermore, there is no reason whatsoever in legal or economic terms to exclude from the notion of economic links the relationship of interdependence existing between the parties to a tight oligopoly within which, in a market with the appropriate characteristics, in particular in terms of market concentration, transparency and product homogeneity, those parties are in a position to anticipate one another's behaviour and are therefore strongly encouraged to align their conduct in the market, in particular in such a way as to maximise their joint profits by restricting production with a view to increasing prices. In such a context, each trader is aware that highly competitive action on its part designed to increase its market share (for example a price cut) would provoke identical action by the others, so that it would derive no benefit from its initiative. All the traders would thus be affected by the reduction in price levels.

277   That conclusion is all the more pertinent with regard to the control of concentrations, whose objective is to prevent anti-competitive market structures from arising or being strengthened. Those structures may result from the existence of economic links in the strict sense argued by the applicant or from market structures of an oligopolistic kind where each

> **CASE** *(continued)*
>
> undertaking may become aware of common interests and, in particular, cause prices to increase without having to enter into an agreement or resort to a concerted practice. * * *
>
> 279   The Commission was entitled to conclude, relying on the envisaged alteration in the structure of the market and on the similarity of the costs of Amplats and Implats/LPD, that the proposed transaction would create a collective dominant position and lead in actual fact to a duopoly constituted by those two undertakings. * * *

NOTES AND QUESTIONS

1. Gencor argued (and the South African authorities maintained) that the combination of Implats and LPD would create a more efficient number two firm that could and would better compete against the dominant firm, Amplats. Who was probably correct—Gencor and South Africa, or the European Commission? What are the most important points on each side?
2. Did the Commission have to prove that Amplats and the merged firm would collude, at least tacitly, and thereby behave like *one* dominant firm? Or was it enough for the Commission to prove that the firms would behave interdependently, taking into account the probable strategies of one another and estimating if and when they would be jointly served by higher prices?
3. What is the significance of the Russian stocks? Why wouldn't Implats/LPD raise prices immediately and expect Amplats and Almaz to follow or at least not increase their output?
4. South Africa argued that it was not necessary to stop the merger; that if the merger did create conditions that made collaborative behavior more likely, and if the merger did eventually produce such behaviour, it would (and authorities should) intervene at that point to stop the behaviour. Was this a plausible tack?

* * *

The theory of collective dominance was tested further in *Airtours/First Choice,* involving a merger from four to three firms in the short haul holiday (air and hotel) package market. The post-merger shares were 32% for Airtours/First Choice, 27% for Thomson, and 20% for Thomas Cook. The Commission found that the market was characterized by stagnant demand, a low level of innovation, low price sensitivity, and similar cost structures of the three market leaders, with commercial links, transparency, and interdependence among them. It found that the merger would have significantly reduced fringe firms' ability to provide charter airline seats, thereby reducing the competitive threat of mavericks. Stating that collective dominance is 'not just about tacit collusion', the Commission found that the resulting three leading firms would hold a collective dominant position after the merger, and it prohibited the merger.

CASE

Airtours v. Commission (Case T-342/99)[35]

[Airtours, a British firm operating in the UK, sold package holidays for short-haul destinations such as Spain, Greece and Turkey. Four significant firms occupied the UK market for short-haul foreign package holidays; namely: Thomson—27%, Thomas Cook—20%, Airtours—21%, and First Choice—11%. Thus, the four firms occupied 79% of the market. All four operated charter airlines and travel agencies as well as tour operations. Airtours sought to take over First Choice. The takeover would have made Airtours number one with 32% of the market.

Many small tour operators occupied the market. In general they did not own charter airlines or travel agencies. The three largest of these held between 1.7% and 2.9% of the market. Several hundred accounted for less than 1% each.

Agreeing with a 1997 UK Monopolies and Mergers Commission Report ('MMC Report'), the Commission observed that the market had been competitive. It determined, however, that increased concentration and vertical integration had occurred since the MMC Report; that Airtours' takeover of First Choice would further increase the transparency of the market and the interdependence of the big firms; and that the remaining three big players would mutually restrict capacity, knowing that, by doing so, they would all be better off and that if any one of the three decided not to go along there would be oversupply and serious financial consequences for all. The Commission determined further that the smaller operators, already marginalized, would be further marginalized, since they would lose First Choice as a supplier of airline seats and as a potential distribution channel; and in any event the small operators would not have the ability to offset capacity reductions by the big three. As a result, capacity would be tightened and prices would rise, thus creating a collective dominant position impeding competition in violation of the Merger Regulation.

Airtours brought suit in the General Court for annulment of the Commission's decision.]

59   It is apparent from the case law that 'in the case of an alleged collective dominant position, the Commission is . . . obliged to assess, using a prospective analysis of the reference market, whether the concentration which has been referred to it leads to a situation in which effective competition in the relevant market is significantly impeded by the undertakings involved in the concentration and one or more other undertakings which together, in the concentration and one or more other undertakings which together, in particular because of factors giving rise to a connection between them, are able to adopt a common policy

---

35 [2002] ECR II-2585, EU:T:2002:146.

> **CASE** *(continued)*
>
> on the market and act to a considerable extent independently of their competitors, their customers, and also of consumers.' [citing *Kali & Salz* and *Gencor*]. * * *
>
> 61 A collective dominant position significantly impeding effective competition in the common market or a substantial part of it may thus arise as the result of a concentration where, in view of the actual characteristics of the relevant market and of the alteration in its structure that the transaction would entail, the latter would make each member of the dominant oligopoly, as it becomes aware of common interests, consider it possible, economically rational, and hence preferable, to adopt on a lasting basis a common policy on the market with the aim of selling at above competitive prices, without having to enter into an agreement or resort to a concerted practice within the meaning of Article [101] and without any actual or potential competitors, let alone customers or consumers, being able to react effectively.
>
> 62 As the applicant has argued and as the Commission has accepted in its pleadings, three conditions are necessary for a finding of collective dominance as defined:
>
> — first, each member of the dominant oligopoly must have the ability to know how the other members are behaving in order to monitor whether or not they are adopting the common policy. As the Commission specifically acknowledges, it is not enough for each member of the dominant oligopoly to be aware that interdependent market conduct is profitable for all of them but each member must also have a means of knowing whether the other operators are adopting the same strategy and whether they are maintaining it. There must, therefore, be sufficient market transparency for all members of the dominant oligopoly to be aware, sufficiently precisely and quickly, of the way in which the other members' market conduct is evolving;
> — second, the situation of tacit coordination must be sustainable over time, that is to say, there must be an incentive not to depart from the common policy on the market. As the Commission observes, it is only if all the members of the dominant oligopoly maintain the parallel conduct that all can benefit. The notion of retaliation in respect of conduct deviating from the common policy is thus inherent in this condition. In this instance, the parties concur that, for a situation of collective dominance to be viable, there must be adequate deterrents to ensure that there is a long-term incentive in not departing from the common policy, which means that each member of the dominant oligopoly must be aware that highly competitive action on its part designed to increase its market share would provoke identical action by the others, so that it would derive no benefit from its initiative;
> — third, to prove the existence of a collective dominant position to the requisite legal standard, the Commission must also establish that the foreseeable reaction of current and future competitors, as well as of consumers, would not jeopardise the results expected from the common policy.

CASE (continued)

63 ... [W]here the Commission takes the view that a merger should be prohibited because it will create a situation of collective dominance, it is incumbent upon it to produce convincing evidence thereof. The evidence must concern, in particular, factors playing a significant role in the assessment of whether a situation of collective dominance exists, such as, for example, the lack of effective competition between the operators alleged to be members of the dominant oligopoly and the weakness of any competitive pressure that might be exerted by other operators.

64 Furthermore, the basic provisions of Regulation No 4064/89, in particular Article 2 thereof, confer on the Commission a certain discretion, especially with respect to assessments of an economic nature, and, consequently, when the exercise of that discretion, which is essential for defining the rules on concentrations, is under review, the Community judicature must take account of the discretionary margin implicit in the provisions of an economic nature which form part of the rules on concentrations. * * *

[Airtours claimed, successfully, that the Commission (1) had failed to prove that the market had become non-competitive, and (2) that it had failed to prove that the three remaining large tour operators would have an incentive to cease competing with each other. (3) In any event, cooperating industry members would have no means to discipline a cheating (competitive) member, and (4) in any event, smaller operators, new entrants, and consumers could and would react to any capacity restrictions by, in the case of suppliers, adding capacity, and in the case of consumers, shifting their business to the smaller operators. The Court annulled the decision.]

NOTES AND QUESTIONS

1. *Airtours* was framed as a case of collective dominance. Today (had the facts been stronger), the theory would be stated as: significant impediment to effective competition by producing coordinated effects, i.e., 'by changing the nature of competition in such a way that firms that previously were not coordinating their behaviour, are now significantly more likely to coordinate and raise prices or otherwise harm effective competition' or by making 'coordination easier, more stable or more effective for firms which were coordinating prior to the merger.' The 'Airtours criteria' have been integrated into the Horizontal Merger Guidelines and now form the established framework of analysis for the assessment of the incentives and ability of firms in a concentrated market to coordinate their conduct (on price, production, capacity, customers, etc.) as a result of a merger, even without entering into an agreement or concerted practice within the meaning of Article 101 TFEU.[36]
2. What level of scrutiny did the Court give to the Commission's findings of mixed basic and

---

36 Horizontal Merger Guidelines, paras. 22(b) and 39–57.

economic facts—such as whether the market was competitive, and whether the smaller firms would be marginalized? Why were the Commissions' findings not within the margin of appreciation to which the Commission is normally entitled?

3. In *Sony/BMG (Impala)*, the General Court annulled a Commission decision *authorizing* a joint venture between Sony and Bertlesmann that combined their recorded music activities. In its Statement of Objections, the Commission had concluded that the joint venture would probably produce collective dominance effects, in view of high concentration and the high degree of transparency in the market. On further investigation, the Commission concluded that the market was not transparent and that collective dominance effects were not likely to result.

Annulling the clearance, the General Court stated that the Commission had not sufficiently explained the reversal of its position since it issued the Statement of Objections. It thought that collective dominance effects were plausible. It disagreed that promotional discounting of music undermined the transparency necessary for coordinated effects, and it stated that retaliatory measures against cheaters appeared to be available. Thus, the General Court ruled, the Commission had committed manifest errors of assessment. On appeal, however, the Court of Justice set aside the judgement of the General Court.[37] The Court of Justice noted that nothing in the Merger Regulation 'imposes different standards of proof in relation to decisions approving a concentration, on the one hand, and decisions prohibiting a concentration, on the other' (para. 46), thus rejecting the Commission's argument that its burden was lighter in clearing than in prohibiting a merger. On the substance, the Court of Justice held that the General Court had misconstrued the principles for analysis concerning market transparency in the context of collective dominance.

The Court of Justice said:

> 122 A collective dominant position [today, 'coordinated effects'] significantly impeding effective competition in the common market or a substantial part of it may thus arise as the result of a concentration where, in view of the actual characteristics of the relevant market and of the alteration to those characteristics that the concentration would entail, the latter would make each member of the oligopoly in question, as it becomes aware of common interests, consider it possible, economically rational, and hence preferable, to adopt on a lasting basis a common policy on the market with the aim of selling at above competitive prices, without having to enter into an agreement or resort to a concerted practice within the meaning of Article 101 and without any actual or potential competitors, let alone customers or consumers, being able to react effectively.
>
> 123 Such tacit coordination is more likely to emerge if competitors can easily arrive at a common perception as to how the coordination should work, and, in particular, of the parameters that lend themselves to being a focal point of the proposed coordination. Unless they can form a shared tacit understanding of the terms of the coordination, competitors might resort to practices that are prohibited by Article [101] in order to be able to adopt a common policy on the market. Moreover, having regard to the temptation which may exist for each participant in a tacit coordination to depart from it in order to increase its short-term profit, it is necessary to determine whether such coordination is sustainable. In that regard, the coordinating undertakings must be able to monitor to a sufficient degree whether the terms of the coordination are being adhered to. There must therefore be sufficient market transparency for each undertaking concerned to be aware,

---

37 Case C-413/06 P, *Bertelsmann AG and Sony Corporation of America v. Independent Music Publishers and Labels Association (Impala)* [2008] ECR I-4951, EU:C:2008:392.

sufficiently precisely and quickly, of the way in which the market conduct of each of the other participants in the coordination is evolving. Furthermore, discipline requires that there be some form of credible deterrent mechanism that can come into play if deviation is detected. In addition, the reactions of outsiders, such as current or future competitors, and also the reactions of customers, should not be such as to jeopardise the results expected from the coordination. * * *

Interestingly, the Court also emphasized the need to 'avoid a mechanical approach involving the separate verification of each of [the Airtours] criteria taken in isolation', and thus the importance of taking into account 'the overall economic mechanism of a hypothetical tacit coordination' (para. 125). The assessment of the transparency of a particular market, the Court suggested, should be carried out 'using the mechanism of a hypothetical tacit coordination as a basis' so as to ascertain whether any elements of transparency that may exist on that market are, in fact, capable of facilitating the reaching of a common understanding on the terms of coordination and/or allowing competitors to monitor whether these terms are being adhered to (para. 126).

4. Mergers other than mergers of competitors: vertical and conglomerate effects

Mergers of firms that are not competitors (non-horizontal mergers) may be divided into two categories: vertical mergers and conglomerate mergers. Vertical mergers are mergers of firms in the buyer-supplier line. Conglomerate mergers are mergers other than horizontal or vertical. Vertical mergers may give rise to concerns whereby, because of the merger, unintegrated rivals will be foreclosed from an important source of supply or outlet, barriers to entry may rise, upping the stakes and thus likelihood of entry, and perhaps so insulating the market that the risk of oligopolistic coordination or of dominance is increased. Conglomerate mergers may entail similar foreclosure concerns when buyers of one partner's product also need the other partner's product, leading to a tying or bundling effect and steering business away from unintegrated rivals because of leverage, not innovative, cost or quality benefits.

In the early days of enforcement of the Merger Regulation, the Commission was worried about foreclosure; it was concerned that large firms, especially multi-product firms, would get unfair advantages over their rivals and distort the playing field. *Boeing/McDonnell Douglas* is an example. When consumers, not competitors, later became the focus of inquiry, the Commission— under prodding by the General Court, took seriously two important points: (1) a vertical or conglomerate merger may bring benefits to consumers; (2) it takes more than a loose foreclosure story (e.g., that life is more difficult for rivals) to harm competitors in a way that will harm market competition. Indeed, a merger that integrates complementary products or functions may benefit consumers in ways that rivals are incentivized to emulate, and the competitive pressure may cause rivals to find ways to outcompete the integrating firm, and (3) vertical and conglomerate mergers do not by their *nature* harm competition, as offending horizontal mergers do. They do not take a competitor off the market. They do not create a structure that may predictably produce a price rise even in the absence of an agreement. It takes *action* to foreclose rivals, such as forcing customers to accept a product they would not otherwise buy from that firm. If that conduct is itself illegal, is the law likely to deter the conduct, so that the whole merger need not be prohibited simply because the conduct might occur?

These aspects lurked in *Tetra Laval/Sidel*, and later in *GE/Honeywell*.

CASE

Tetra Laval BV v. Commission (Case C-12/03 P) (*'Tetra/Sidel'*)[38]

[Tetra Laval, a French firm and the world leader in the market for packaging milk, juice and other liquids in cartons, acquired the stock of its French rival Sidel, a leading producer of plastic containers for liquids by polyethylene terephthalate equipment ('PET'). The Commission declared the acquisition incompatible with the common market principally on grounds that Tetra Laval would use its dominance in the asceptic carton market to leverage itself into dominance in the PET packaging equipment market and that removing Sidel as a potential competitor to Tetra would strengthen Tetra's dominant position on the carton packaging markets.

The Commission ordered the parties to undo the merger. The parties sought an annulment. The General Court annulled the prohibition for lack of sufficient evidence and the Court of Justice upheld the General Court].

39   Whilst the Court recognises that the Commission has a margin of discretion with regard to economic matters, that does not mean that the Community Courts must refrain from reviewing the Commission's interpretation of information of an economic nature. Not only must the Community Courts, inter alia, establish whether the evidence relied on is factually accurate, reliable and consistent but also whether that evidence contains all the information which must be taken into account in order to assess a complex situation and whether it is capable of substantiating the conclusions drawn from it. Such a review is all the more necessary in the case of a prospective analysis required when examining a planned merger with conglomerate effect. * * *

---

38   [2005] ECR I-987, EU:C:2005:87.

CASE (continued)

44   The analysis of a 'conglomerate-type' concentration is a prospective analysis in which, first, the consideration of a lengthy period of time in the future and, secondly, the leveraging necessary to give rise to a significant impediment to effective competition mean that the chains of cause and effect are dimly discernible, uncertain and difficult to establish. That being so, the quality of the evidence produced by the Commission in order to establish that it is necessary to adopt a decision declaring the concentration incompatible with the common market is particularly important, since that evidence must support the Commission's conclusion that, if such a decision were not adopted, the economic development envisaged by it would be plausible.

45   It follows from those various factors that the [General Court] did not err in law when it set out the tests to be applied in the exercise of its power of judicial review or when it specified the quality of the evidence which the Commission is required to produce in order to demonstrate that the requirements of Article 2(3) of the Regulation are satisfied. * * *

75   However, it would run counter to the Regulation's purpose of prevention to require the Commission, as [the General Court held], to examine, for each proposed merger, the extent to which the incentives to adopt anticompetitive conduct would be reduced, or even eliminated, as a result of the unlawfulness of the conduct in question, the likelihood of its detection, the action taken by the competent authorities, both at Community and national level, and the financial penalties which could ensue. * * *

78   Consequently, the [General Court] erred in law in rejecting the Commission's conclusions as to the adoption by the merged entity of anti-competitive conduct capable of resulting in leveraging on the sole ground that the Commission had, when assessing the likelihood that such conduct might be adopted, failed to take account of the unlawfulness of that conduct and, consequently, of the likelihood of its detection, of action by the competent authorities, both at Community and national level, and of the financial penalties which might ensue. . . . * * *

NOTES AND QUESTIONS

1. Why are 'the chains of cause and effect' so 'dimly discernible, uncertain and difficult to establish' in conglomerate mergers as opposed to mergers of competitors? Consider the charge: Tetra, dominant in packaging liquids in aseptic cartons, a declining segment, will increase its dominance by acquiring Sidel, dominant in packaging liquids in stretch blown plastic bottles, a growing segment, and vice versa. How would the acquisition increase dominance? Would it happen naturally or would Tetra/Sidel have to *do* something to leverage power from one

market (assuming it is a market) to the other? What would it have to do? On what would the likelihood of its strategy and the success of its strategy depend? How is Article 102 TFEU relevant?

2. A few years before the Court judgement in *Tetra,* General Electric Company ('GE'), the world's largest producer of jet engines, announced that it planned to acquire Honeywell International, a leading firm in the production of navigating equipment and other jet aircraft components, as well as a producer of jet engines. Both firms were US companies, with assets also in Europe and elsewhere, doing business worldwide. GE first notified the planned merger to the US authorities. The Antitrust Division vetted the merger, found anti-competitive horizontal overlaps in engine production, and cleared the merger after requiring a spin-off of the offending assets. After the spin-off, it regarded the merger as almost entirely conglomerate. The US generally has no antitrust concerns with conglomerate mergers.

GE then sought clearance by the European Commission. The Commission identified a number of vertical and conglomerate (leveraging and foreclosure) concerns and a horizontal concern regarding jet engine overlap that was not worrisome to the US authority. It analysed the problems, found anti-competitive effects (e.g., that GE would prevail upon its engine customers to use Honeywell avionics in their aircraft, lowering prices for the bundle, marginalizing Honeywell's rivals, and later raising prices), and prohibited the merger. The prohibition evoked the ire of many Americans, including antitrust officials, the Secretary of the Treasury, and senators.

GE sought an annulment of the Commission decision. Its case came to the General Court after the judgement in *Tetra Laval,* which had set the standard of review and the standard of proof for vertical and conglomerate effects. The General Court upheld the Commission decision prohibiting the GE/Honeywell merger, but only on grounds of a horizontal overlap of engines. As for the conglomerate grounds, the General Court engaged in an extensive analysis of the facts and held that the Commission could not conclude from the facts that a merged GE/Honeywell was likely to engage in bundling. Its customers could not be pressured to accept a bundle they did not want.[39,40]

3. Regarding jet engine starters: GE was dominant in jet engines, Honeywell held more than 50% of the market for engine starters, and barriers to entry into engine starters were high. The Commission thought the merger would harm competition by giving GE incentives to manipulate the starter supply. The Court reversed this holding because the Commission had failed to consider the possible deterrent effect of Article 102 TFEU.

Should it have been enough, for proof of a violation, that the merged firm controlled an input essential to its rivals? Would you expect the merged firm to deny engine starters to its competitors? Would you expect the merged firm to manipulate the supply of this necessary ingredient in subtle and not always detectable ways?

4. Suppose the Commission had proved that the merged firm would probably have engaged in bundling. Would the Court have agreed that this was an anti-competitive practice? See Article 102 case law, above. Would US authorities and courts have so agreed? The US authorities that cleared the GE/Honeywell merger argued that if the merged firm bundled Honeywell's avionics products with GE's engines, it would save costs of double marginalization and the bundle would be efficient.

5. Energias de Portugal ('EDP') and Gas de Portugal ('GDP') proposed to merge. EDP was

---

39 Case T-210/01, *General Electric v. Commission* [2005] ECR II-5575, EU:T:2005:456 ('*GE/Honeywell*').
40 For the backstory of the star-crossed GE/Honeywell merger, see Eleanor Fox (2007), '*GE/Honeywell*: The U.S. merger that Europe stopped—A story of the politics of convergence', in Eleanor Fox and Daniel Crane (eds), *Antitrust Stories*, Foundation, Ch. 12.

dominant on all electricity markets in Portugal. GDP was dominant on most gas markets in Portugal, and was the monopoly supplier of gas to electricity producers, which used gas to power their new plants. GDP was the most likely important potential competitor in electricity. EDP was a major customer of GDP. Portugal owned significant shareholdings in both firms and 'appear[ed] to be the real architect' of the merger.

The Commission prohibited the merger.[41] It found anti-competitive horizontal effects in the electricity and gas markets through the elimination of GDP and EDP, respectively, as the most likely potential competitor to each other, in a context of nascent liberalization of the electricity and gas markets throughout the EU. Moreover, since gas was one of the most efficient way to produce electricity in Portugal, the concentration would have given rise to anti-competitive vertical effects on wholesale electricity markets in view of EDP's preferred access to the available gas resources in Portugal and the possible incentive and ability of the merged entity to increase the production costs of its competitors. Likewise, the concentration would have also led to foreclosure of a significant part of the gas demand (controlled by EDP), thus harming future competing gas producers.

Although the merging parties had offered commitments that held near-term benefits in the gas sector, the Commission determined that the advantages would not offer a better situation than GDP's potential entry into electricity markets and.The General Court upheld the prohibition.[42]

6. The Commission's experience with vertical and conglomerate mergers ultimately led to its guidelines on non-horizontal mergers.[43]

D. The international dimension

In 1988, the Court of Justice decided, in *Wood Pulp* (see Chapter 2 above), that European competition law reprehends offshore cartels 'implemented' in the Union. In 1997, the European Commission vetted Boeing's acquisition of McDonnell Douglas (two US firms with no assets in Europe but which did business in a world market). The Commission nearly enjoined the acquisition, which had been cleared by US authorities, but in the end allowed it subject to important conditions. See p. 246 above. (The US authorities, too, freely challenge offshore mergers that hurt their interests.)

In 1999, the European Commission enjoined the merger of Gencor and LPD (Lonrho), two South African firms, one of which had a presence in Europe. The General Court affirmed. See p. 258 above. This was the first merger prohibited and aborted on grounds of collective dominance (coordinated effects). In 2001, the Commission prohibited the GE/Honeywell merger, which had been approved by the US authorities. The General Court affirmed the prohibition. In 2012, the European Commission blocked a

---

41 Commission Decision of 9 December 2004 in COMP/M.3440 – *EDP/ENI/GDP*.
42 Case T-87/05, *EDP-Energias de Portugal SA v. Commission* [2005] ECR II-3745, EU:T:2005:333.
43 Available at: http://ec.europa.eu/competition/mergers/legislation/notices_on_substance.html (accessed 9 June 2017).

merger between Deutsche Börse and NYSE Euronext, which the US authorities had cleared; but the market effects were more serious in the EU than in the US.

All these situations illustrate the important jurisdictional questions lying at the heart of cross-border concentrations, which then translate in cooperation issues when it comes to their actual review and assessment. *Gencor/Lonrho* offers a good overview of these questions and their treatment in practice.

Note on *Gencor Ltd v. Commission*

See facts at p. 258 above.

After the South African platinum mining companies, Gencor and LPD, agreed to merge, the South African Competition Board vetted the merger and found no competition problem. The European Commission vetted the merger and was concerned that, when the Russian stocks were depleted in a couple of years, Gencor/LPD (Lonrho) and Anglo American, the world market leader, would jointly exercise dominant market power (collective dominance). Recall that LPD's parent, Lonrho, was a British firm, and Lonrho maintained its principal sales office in Belgium.

Examining the proposed merger, the Directorate-General for Competition of the European Commission invited comments from the South African authorities. The South African Deputy Minister of Foreign Affairs officially submitted his government's observations. He stated in a letter to the European Commission that the South African government favoured the consolidation. As to competitive effects, the Minister noted that the two remaining platinum firms in South Africa were now more equally matched, and he conveyed the South African view that the market would work better with two equally matched competitors than under market domination by Anglo American. The Minister did not contest the intervention of the Commission. However, he wrote: 'Having regard to the importance of mineral resources to the South African economy', South Africa favoured allowing the consolidation and attacking any collusion between Anglo American and Gencor/LPD if and when it arose (judgement, para. 3).

The Commission prohibited the merger. Gencor sought annulment in the General Court on both jurisdictional and substantive grounds. Gencor argued that the Union had no jurisdiction over this concentration since it involved economic activities conducted within the territory of a non-member country and had been approved by authorities of that country.

Gencor contended that the Merger Regulation applies only to concentrations carried out within the Union. It based its construction on the language of the Merger Regulation (especially recitals), the Treaty articles on which the regulation was based, and the international law principle of territoriality. Gencor distinguished the *Wood Pulp* case, wherein the Court of Justice had asserted jurisdiction over an offshore cartel designedly raising prices in Europe, on grounds that the cartel was implemented in Europe. Gencor said, of *Wood Pulp*, that while the high prices were agreed to offshore, the conspiracy to raise prices was implemented by selling at the conspiratorial prices into the Union. By contrast, the platinum merger was implemented in South Africa and 'is thus primarily relevant to the industrial and competition policy of that non-member country' (para. 56).

The General Court rejected Gencor's construction of the Regulation. The Court said:[44]

> According to *Wood Pulp*, the criterion as to the implementation of an agreement is satisfied by mere sale within the Community, irrespective of the location of the sources of supply and the production plant. It is not disputed that Gencor and Lonrho carried out sales in the Community before the concentration and would have continued to do so thereafter.

The Court proceeded to assess the legitimacy of jurisdiction under international law. Noting that the transaction entailed the merger of the firms' marketing operations throughout the world, including the Community, it said:

> Application of the Regulation is justified under public international law when it is foreseeable that a proposed concentration will have an immediate and substantial effect in the Community. [para. 90]

The Court concluded that the merger's effect in the Union (formerly, the 'Community') would be immediate, substantial and foreseeable. It construed 'immediate' to include 'medium term'—after Russian platinum stocks were exhausted and thus after a force that could be disruptive of Anglo and Gencor's duopoly behaviour would have been removed. It concluded that an *abuse* (a price rise resulting from collective behaviour) need not be immediate; it is enough that a transaction causes a lasting structural alteration, making abusive behaviour economically rational.

---

[44] Case T-102/96, *Gencor Ltd v. Commission* [1999] ECR II-753, EU:T:1999:65, para. 87.

As to substantiality of the effect, Gencor claimed that the merging parties' sales and market shares in Europe were too small to cause a substantial effect and that the merging parties' greater sales elsewhere—Japan and the United States—undermined 'substantiality.' The Court rejected this claim. It said:

> The fact that, in a world market, other parts of the world are affected by the concentration cannot prevent the Community from exercising its control over a concentration which substantially affects competition within the common market by creating a dominant position.

Likewise, the Court rejected the claim that the exercise of jurisdiction violated an international principle of non-interference, if there is such a principle, or the principle of proportionality. The Court said that there was no conflict between the laws of the two jurisdictions and therefore no interference because South Africa did not require the firms to do what the EU required them not to do. Nor was it shown how the completion of the merger would enhance South Africa's vital economic or commercial interests.

Moreover, as the Commission had argued, the merger was like an export cartel. Only a small amount of platinum was sold in South Africa. South Africa stood to gain more by exploiting the world than it stood to lose by exploiting its own consumers.

Thus, the Court held, it had jurisdiction.

South Africa did not further resist prohibition of *Gencor/Lonrho*. But when, two years later, the Commission signalled its serious problems with the GE/Honeywell merger, US senators, cabinet members, and the President declared the European 'intrusion' into the 'American' merger inappropriate. After the European prohibition, US Assistant Attorney General in charge of Antitrust, Charles James, issued a statement taking issue with the European analysis, not with the assertion of jurisdiction. 'Antitrust laws protect competition, not competitors', he said. The merger 'would have been procompetitive and beneficial to consumers . . . . [The European Commission] apparently concluded that a more diversified, and thus more competitive GE, could somehow disadvantage other market participants . . . . This matter points to the continuing need . . . to move toward a greater policy convergence.'[45]

---

45 81 Bureau of National Affairs (now Bloomberg BNA) Antitrust & Trade Reg. Rep. 15 (6 July 2001).

NOTES AND QUESTIONS

1. In *Gencor/Lonrho*, was the Court's concept of conflict the same as or different from that of the US Supreme Court in *Hartford* (see p. 59 above)? Was there really no conflict?
2. Does the European Commission have subject matter jurisdiction over offshore mergers? Does *Wood Pulp* help you answer the question? The US federal antitrust agencies' 1995 International Guidelines declare that the US agencies have jurisdiction to challenge an anti-competitive merger of foreign firms that hurts US consumers; and that they even may challenge an offshore merger that hurts US exporters as long as it also hurts foreign consumers (but query whether subsequent case law may have put such mergers beyond reach).[46]

    Is there anything to be said for a rule of law that would give only the US the right to enjoin a merger of US firms with substantial sales (and thus consumers) in the US, and only the EU the right to prohibit a merger of European firms with substantial sales in the EEA? What if the merger harms consumers beyond the borders of the home country (e.g., *Gencor/Lonrho*)? What if the merger harms only producer interests (e.g., rights of access to markets) and the foreign law protects these interests? (Compare *Boeing/McDonnell Douglas*.)
3. Do these cases—mergers in global markets having impacts around the world—suggest a need for international law or principles? Philip Condit, then Chairman of Boeing, told the *Washington Post*[47] at the conclusion of Boeing's negotiations with the EU to settle the merger challenge: 'In a global economy, a single set of rules is, in fact, preferable[.] Over time, we have to keep working in that direction.'

    Comment on Mr Condit's statement. Is it realistic? How is a single set of merger rules for the world achieved? How—and by whom—might the single set be applied, objectively and without nationalistic bias? Consider also the case of worldwide mergers creating monopolies in (third world) jurisdictions devoid of merger control regime or of the means to enforce merger rules.

    The competition-law nations of the world (more than 130) have achieved some convergence of procedure and process in pre-merger notification requirements. They are moving towards convergence of some substantive standards, albeit with a significant margin of difference on some points. The major forum for convergence is the International Competition Network—a virtual network of the antitrust authorities of the world.[48] A common approach, however, does not always mean common outcomes when several jurisdictions rule upon the same transnational merger. Market conditions sometimes differ from nation to nation, as in *Deutsche Börse/NYSE Euronext*. Moreover, as in *GE/Honeywell*, different analysts may apply different presumptions, often affecting market definition and assessment of competitive effects.

---

46 Antitrust Enforcement Guidelines for International Operations (April 1995), available at: hhttps://www.justice.gov/atr/antitrust-enforcement-guidelines-international-operations, Illustrative Example H (accessed 9 June 2017).
47 *Washington Post*, 24 July 1997, E1.
48 A description of their initiatives and the documents that comprise their growing work product are available at: www.internationalcompetitionnetwork.org (accessed 9 June 2017). (Select 'By Working Group'; select 'Mergers'.)

7

The State and competition

From the outset, State monopoly, State-granted benefits and privileges, and State power co-opted by private interests posed serious market interference issues. For some Member States, the State was *the* problem. In some States, business—especially in basic goods and services—was also run by State or State-privileged monopolies. These enterprises were dominant by reason of privilege, not by reason of skill, foresight or inventiveness. By the nature of their operations, these enterprises were a major obstacle to achieving a common market. They tended to procure goods only from their nationals (and procurement by State enterprises represented a sizeable percentage of GDP). In offering goods or services, they were often nationalistic and discriminatory. They often had leverage to exclude competitors, and their large presence and connections, themselves, chilled entry. It was predictable that several articles of the Treaty would be addressed to the problem of the State in the market and that from the outset the Commission would have a sharp eye on State monopolies of a commercial character and firms that held privileges bestowed by the State.

Ports, and discriminatory access to them, presented a good example of State monopoly abuses. The ports cases are also a good example of application, jointly, of two or more Treaty articles, such as Articles 102 and 106 TFEU—abuse of dominance, and limits on the conduct of public undertakings and those granted special or exclusive rights. Other combinations of Treaty articles that came into common use are the former Article 3(1)(g) stating that the EU must ensure that competition is not distorted (now in Protocol 27) and Article 4(3) TEU, whereby Member States have a duty to cooperate in carrying out the tasks of the EU, along with Articles 101 and 102 TFEU and the various articles facilitating free movement and prohibiting discrimination, such as Articles 18, 34, 35 and 56 TFEU.

State-granted aid and other subsidies to domestic businesses were likewise a major problem. Each of the Member States was subsidizing 'its' firms as and when it chose, often responding to powerful private interests or trying to puff-up domestic champions to give them a competitive edge over their neighbours, undermining competitive opportunities of out-of-state firms; thus, the importance of Articles 107–108 TFEU—prohibiting State aid unless authorized.

When the financial crisis hit Europe in 2008, the then Competition Commissioner, Neelie Kroes, gave a speech.[1] She decried State aids that would simply dump one nation's crisis onto the others. She said:

> Were it not for the State aid rules, there was a real risk that national governments would have been forced into a costly and damaging subsidy race, wasting billions upon billions of taxpayers' money competing with each other's largesse rather than focusing the money where it was most needed. Were it not for the State aid rules, we could have been faced with beggar thy neighbour policies that could have undermined the solutions that governments were putting in place . . . .* * *
>
> The European Single Market's role is all the more vital during periods of economic difficulties—together we stand, divided we fall. The Single Market will attenuate any economic downturn and accelerate recovery. Which is why, despite siren calls to the contrary, we need to ensure that the Single Market functions as well as possible at this crucial moment, which means enforcing the antitrust and State aid rules as diligently as ever.

Commissioner Kroes immediately gave guidance on circumstances in which State aid would be approved (in general, approval would be possible when the aid was focused on growth and the future), and when it would be disapproved. The intensifying financial crisis, however, put her principles under pressure.[2]

* * *

This chapter starts with ports cases as an example of abuse of power of State-owned or recently privatized firms, depriving rivals of access to infrastructure facilities. These cases are a fortiori examples of violation of Article 102 TFEU. It then reviews the compatibility of State monopoly and monopoly privileges with the Treaty. Subsequently, it deals with public restraints and asks when anti-competitive State measures violate the competition provisions in combination with other articles, such as Article 4(3) TEU and

---

[1] 'EU competition rules—part of the solution for Europe's economy', Speech/08/625, 18 November 2008.
[2] For an overview of the immediate response to the crisis, see D. Gerard (2009), 'EC competition law enforcement at grips with the financial crisis: Flexibility on the means, consistency in the principles', *Concurrences*, **1**, 46.

Article 101 TFEU, and when State measures shield anti-competitive private action that they facilitate. Finally, the chapter closes by discussing the Treaty provisions that control State distortions of competition by grants of subsidies, called State aids.

A. State ownership, and a note on liberalization

Ports and ports authorities were principally owned by States. They were literally and figuratively gateways to markets. Typically, States adopted measures to bolster ports' powers to exclude; and exclusion, discrimination and exploitation were common. The ports cases are, therefore, helpful illustrations of (1) factually, problems of State ownership and exclusive privilege, and (2) legally, the interrelationship of Treaty articles applied to address the problems of abuse, promote liberalization, and assure non-discriminatory access.

This section reviews specifically cases and measures revolving around two ports—the Port of Rødby, Denmark, and the Port of Genoa, Italy.

Port of Rødby
Commission Decision 94/119/EC[3]

[DSB was a Danish public undertaking which operated as a department of the transport ministry. It held the exclusive right to organize railroad traffic in Denmark, owned the Port of Rødby, and operated ferry services between Denmark and neighbouring countries. Stena was a Swedish shipping group which specialized in ferry services and wished to operate between Denmark and Germany (Puttgarden), which essentially links eastern Denmark with Germany and the rest of western Europe.

Stena requested permission from the Danish government to use the existing port facilities at Rødby or to build a port in the vicinity. The Danish government refused. Stena complained to the Commission.]

Abuse of dominant position

12   The refusal to allow 'Euro-Port A/S', a subsidiary of the Swedish group [Stena] to operate from Rødby has the effect of eliminating a potential competitor on the Rødby-Puttgarden route and hence of strengthening the joint dominant position of DSB and DB on that route.

---

3 Commission Decision 94/119/EC of 21 December 1993 [1994] O.J. L 55/52.

According to the case law of the Court, an abuse within the meaning of Article [102 TFEU] is committed in cases where, without any objective necessity, an undertaking holding a dominant position on a particular market reserves to itself an ancillary activity which might be carried out by another undertaking as part of its activities on a neighbouring but separate market, with the possibility of eliminating all competition from such undertaking.

Thus an undertaking that owns or manages and uses itself an essential facility, i.e. a facility or infrastructure without which its competitors are unable to offer their services to customers, and refuses to grant them access to such facility is abusing its dominant position.

Consequently, an undertaking that owns or manages an essential port facility from which it provides a maritime transport service may not, without objective justification, refuse to grant a shipowner wishing to operate on the same maritime route access to that facility without infringing Article [102 TFEU].

13 According to the case law of the Court, Article [106(1) TFEU] prohibits Member States from placing, by law, regulation or administrative provision, public undertakings and undertakings to which they grant exclusive rights in a position in which those undertakings could not place themselves by their own conduct without infringing Article [102 TFEU]. The Court added that, where the extension of the dominant position of a public undertaking or an undertaking to which the State has granted exclusive rights resulted from a State measure, such a measure constituted an infringement of Article [106], read in conjunction with Article [102] of the Treaty. . . .

Thus, for the reasons given above, any firm in the same position as DSB which refused to grant another shipping operator access to the port it controlled would be abusing a dominant position. Where, as in the present case, a Member State has refused such access and has strengthened the effects of the refusal by also refusing to authorize the construction of a new port, it constitutes a State measure in breach of Article [106 TFEU], read in conjunction with Article [102 TFEU].

14 The reasons given by the Danish Transport Ministry for rejecting both requests of 'Euro-Port A/S' . . . are the following:

— the plan of 'Euro-Port A/S' . . . (Stena), to build a new terminal is not acceptable as that undertaking has allegedly 'not established that there is an unsatisfied demand for a ferry service' and it is 'most unlikely that such a demand would arise' . . .

— Euro-Port A/S' (Stena) could not operate from the existing port facilities as this would have the effect of preventing the companies already operating in the port from expanding their activities. * * *

The Commission concludes . . . that:

— there was indeed an unsatisfied demand for ferry services in May 1990 since one year later DSB and DB had expanded their services,
— the increase in the activities of DB and DSB in 1991 confirms that the port of Rødby was not saturated.

15   The Commission also considers that there is no evidence that the existing facilities at Rødby would today be saturated or that, subject to alterations which Stena has informed the Commission it is prepared to finance, existing port capacity is unable to cope with an increase in trade. The Commission also notes that the Swedish group (Stena) has acquired land adjacent to the port facilities of Rødby which is perfectly suitable for development as a terminal by Stena.

It therefore concludes that there are no technical constraints preventing the Stena group from sailing between Rødby and Puttgarden.

16   In their letter of 22 February 1993 which constitutes the reply to the letter of formal notice sent by the Commission on 24 November 1992, the Danish authorities rejected the latter's request, stressing that their refusals were justified under Community law. They stated that it would be impossible to allow Stena access to the existing facilities, giving technical reasons and referring for the first time, without any further details, to obligations incumbent upon DB and DSB in the general interest.

This would appear to indicate that, in the view of the Danish authorities, the technical feasibility of access to the port is not a problem or is not the only problem and that they also have a duty to protect the public undertaking DSB from a competitor on the market for ferry services.

Nor can the Commission share the view of the Danish authorities that the alleged saturation of the existing port facilities would make pointless any attempt to introduce competition since this could not in any event lead to an increase in the number of sailings between Rødby and Puttgarden.

Even on a saturated market, an improvement in the quality of products or services offered or a reduction in prices as a result of competition is a definite advantage for consumers; this could also lead to an increase in demand which, in the present case, could be met by expanding the port. * * *

Article [106(2) TFEU]

18   The Commission considers that the application of the competition rules in the present case does not impede the particular task entrusted to the public undertaking DSB namely to organize rail services and manage the port facilities at Rødby. Therefore the exception provided for in Article [106](2) does not apply.

* * *

CONCLUSION

19   In view of the foregoing, the Commission considers that the measures referred to in paragraphs 1 and 2 constitute infringements of Article [106](1) of the Treaty, read in conjunction with Article [102].

* * *

The Commission subsequently refined the remedy. It 'became apparent that establishing competing facilities, especially in the case of nationwide networks, requires a great deal of investment and is usually inefficient. So the European Commission developed the concept of legally separating the provision of the network from the commercial services using the network.'[4] What are the merits of this structural remedy?

CASE

Merci Convenzionali Porto di Genova v. Siderurgica Gabrielli SpA (Case C-179/90)[5]

[The Italian Navigation Code established an exclusive right to organize dock work for third parties, and required retention of dock work companies that employed only registered workers of Italian nationality. Carriers coming to port were not permitted to use their crew to load and unload. The organizer of dock work was generally controlled by the port authority.

Merci enjoyed the exclusive right to organize dock work. Siderurgica Gabrielli SpA arrived in the Port of Genoa with goods, but Merci delayed in providing unloading services and Siderurgica Gabrielli suffered damages, for which it sought compensation. The Italian court asked the Court of Justice whether the Italian rules violated Article 4(3) TEU and Articles 34

---

4   See: http://ec.europa.eu/competition/liberalisation/overview_en.html (accessed 12 June 2016).
5   [1991] ECR I-5889, EU:C:1991:464.

> **CASE** *(continued)*
>
> (free movement of goods), 45 (free movement of workers), 102 and 106 TFEU, and whether Siderurgica Gabrielli had a remedy.
>
> Advocate General Van Gerven pinpointed the anticompetitive and discriminatory effects inherent in the Italian law:]
>
> 22 [W]e must now consider whether these abuses of a dominant position within the meaning of Article [102 TFEU]—in so far as the national court regards them as established—are imposed, or facilitated, or made inevitable by the relevant national legislation. I think there can be little doubt about this. In fact, the scale of charges and other, presumably unfair, contractual conditions applied by Merci and Compagnia are made possible, if not inevitable, by the national legislation applicable and are facilitated, if not made compulsory, by the port authorities under the powers conferred on them by national legislation. The other abuses too are made possible by that legislation. But for the monopoly for the performance of dock work conferred on it by the Italian legislation, Compagnia could certainly not have afforded to abstain from using modern technology, and it is clear also that the dissimilar treatment of trading parties was possible only as a result of the monopoly granted to Merci and the complexity and lack of transparency of the scale of charges devised by the authority.
>
> [The Court ruled:]
>
> 19 [I]t appears from the circumstances described by the national court and discussed before the Court of Justice that the undertakings enjoying exclusive rights in accordance with the procedures laid down by the national rules in question are, as a result, induced either to demand payment for services which have not been requested, to charge disproportionate prices, to refuse to have recourse to modern technology, which involves an increase in the cost of the operations and a prolongation of the time required for their performance, or to grant price reductions to certain consumers and at the same time to offset such reductions by an increase in the charges to other consumers.
>
> 20 In these circumstances it must be held that a Member State creates a situation contrary to Article [102] of the Treaty where it adopts rules of such a kind as those at issue before the national court, which are capable of affecting trade between Member States as in the case of the main proceedings, regard being had to the factors mentioned in . . . this judgement relating to the importance of traffic in the Port of Genoa.
>
> 21 As regards the interpretation of Article [34] of the Treaty requested by the national court, it is sufficient to recall that a national measure which has the effect of facilitating the abuse of a dominant position capable of affecting trade between Member States will generally be incompatible with that article, which prohibits quantitative restrictions on imports and

> **CASE** (continued)
>
> all measures having equivalent effect (see Case 13/77 *GB-INNO-BM v. ATAB* [1977] ECR 2115, paragraph 35) in so far as such a measure has the effect of making more difficult and hence of impeding imports of goods from other Member States.
>
> 22 In the main proceedings it may be seen from the national court's findings that the unloading of the goods could have been effected at a lesser cost by the ship's crew, so that compulsory recourse to the services of the two undertakings enjoying exclusive rights involved extra expense and was therefore capable, by reason of its effect on the prices of the goods, of affecting imports.
>
> 23 It should be emphasized in the third place that even within the framework of Article [106], the provisions of Articles [34], [45] and [102] of the Treaty have direct effect and give rise for interested parties to rights which the national courts must protect (see in particular, as regards Article [102] of the Treaty.
>
> 24 The answer to the first question, as reformulated, should therefore be that:
> Article [106(1)] of the . . . Treaty, in conjunction with Articles [34], [45] and [102] of the . . . Treaty, precludes rules of a Member State which confer on an undertaking established in that State the exclusive right to organize dock work and require it for that purpose to have recourse to a dock-work company formed exclusively of national workers; Articles [34], [45] and [102] of the Treaty, in conjunction with Article [106], give rise to rights for individuals which the national courts must protect.

Following the judgement, Italy revised its law to open up competition for port-handling. The Commission, however, was not satisfied. It found that local authorities systematically refused to grant operating licences to potential competitors of long-established dock services companies. Italy, in response, issued a license.[6] The Commission again found that the Italian reform was insufficient and indeed that it created new problems. It found additional infringements by Commission Decision 97/744.[7]

The port cases reflect principles and problems common to a range of infrastructure industries and regulated sectors, including transport, post,

---

6 European Community, XXVth Report on Competition Policy (1995), pp. 58–59.
7 Commission Decision 97/744/EC of 21 October 1997 pursuant to Article 90 (3) of the EC Treaty on the provisions of Italian ports legislation relating to employment [1997] O.J. L 301/17.

telecommunications and energy. The law that applies to restrictive State measures and to abusive action by undertakings is intertwined. In some sectors, notably energy and telecommunications, major liberalization projects, aided by framework directives, are under way. The objective is to improve conditions of competition, not just to prevent its restriction.[8]

B.   State monopolies of a commercial character: application of Articles 34 and 37 TFEU

While the ports cases clarify duties of State monopolies not to discriminate, exclude and thereby harm competition, a yet more conceptual, more basic question about the essence of the political economy of the EU was to arise: Did the Treaty adopt a rule of free enterprise? Did it tolerate State-owned monopoly? And even if so, were new nationalizations inconsistent with the Treaty?

In 1962, Italy nationalized its electricity industry, transferring all of the assets of the nationalized firms to ENEL. Mr Costa, a lawyer, refused to pay €3 of his electric bill and sued for a declaration that the nationalization act was void as inconsistent with the Treaty and that his debt was void. He came before an ideologically sympathetic magistrate in Milan, who agreed with him that nationalization violated EU law. He later came before a hostile Italian Supreme Court, and was derided by an indignant Italian government. He ultimately suffered dismissal of his case for lack of standing, without having received an answer from the Court of Justice whether nationalization was or was not permissible under the Treaty.[9]

Reflect on the unanswered question in *Costa:* Is the creation of a new State monopoly by nationalization consistent with the Treaty?

The principal relevant provision of the Treaty is Article 37 TFEU, which must be read together with Article 34 TFEU, which prohibits Member States from imposing quotas or tariffs or measures of equivalent effect; that is, from unduly restricting trade.

---

8   See N. Kroes (2008), 'Improving competition in European energy markets through effective unbundling', in B. Hawk (ed.), *International Antitrust Law & Policy, Fordham Competition Law 2007*, New York: Juris, Ch. 9, p. 247.
9   See Case 6/64, *Costa v. ENEL* [1964] ECR 585, EU:C:1964:66, ruling that Article 37 TFEU, prohibiting any new commercial monopoly giving rise to national discrimination in procuring or marketing goods, is directly effective.

Article 37 TFEU, ex 31 ECT

1. Member States shall adjust any State monopolies of a commercial character so as to ensure that no discrimination regarding the conditions under which goods are procured and marketed exists between nationals of Member States.

The provisions of this Article shall apply to any body through which a Member State, in law or in fact, either directly or indirectly supervises, determines or appreciably influences imports or exports between Member States. These provisions shall likewise apply to monopolies delegated by the State to others.

2. Member States shall refrain from introducing any new measure which is contrary to the principles laid down in paragraph 1 or which restricts the scope of the Articles dealing with the prohibition of customs duties and quantitative restrictions between Member States. * * *

To address a serious problem of alcohol abuse, Sweden brought the liquor business under State control. It formed a state-owned company, V&S, with exclusive rights to produce and export spirits and to import beer, wine and spirits. It formed another State-owned company, Systembolaget, and gave it the exclusive right to sell alcoholic beverages at wholesale to restaurants and the exclusive right to sell alcoholic beverages at retail.

To facilitate its accession to the EU, Sweden abolished the privileges of V&S and the wholesale privileges of Systembolaget and replaced them with a system of licences, while retaining for Systembolaget its retail monopoly. Licences for import, export, production, and wholesaling were to be issued at the discretion of the Alcohol Inspectorate upon the making of an application, which required documentation and the payment of a high, non-reimbursable fee. The fees, including annual renewal fees, were much higher per litre for low sales volume than for high sales volume, and thus the fee structure favoured the large incumbent supplier, V&S.

Advocate General Elmer, on a reference involving the criminal prosecution of an unauthorized wine importer, summarized the basis and workings of the Swedish system as follows:

> The fundamental aim of Swedish alcohol policy throughout the twentieth century has been to limit the effect of market forces, namely competition and private profits. The reason for this was the conviction that competition and private profits encourage active marketing and active selling, which lead to increased consumption. The greater the number of undertakings having an interest in increased

alcohol sales, the better alcoholic beverages will fare in the competition for consumers' money. In the case of a sector which society does not wish to see expand, market mechanisms such as competition and profit are not particularly suitable as means of control.

In the government's view, the principle of limiting private profits in the alcohol trade remains valid. . . . (*Franzen*; see additional excerpts from his opinion infra.)

CASE

Franzen (Case C-189/95) (*Swedish alcohol monopoly*)[10]

[Harry Franzen, without a licence, imported wine from Denmark and sold it in Sweden. Prosecuted for a criminal violation, he pleaded that the Swedish law was invalid for violating Articles 34 and 37 TFEU. The national court referred questions to the Court of Justice.

Advocate General Elmer agreed with Mr Franzen that the Swedish alcohol monopoly violated EU law. The advocate general said that Article 34 TFEU 'is intended to ensure access to the market of products from other Member States' (para. 59) and 'to prevent lacunae in the protection of free movement' (para. 65). As to Article 37 TFEU:]

[*Excerpts from the Opinion of Advocate General Elmer*]

68   . . . Article [37] of the Treaty refers to the traders who supply the market in products. That provision therefore differs from Article [34] of the Treaty, first by being limited to discrimination and secondly by not protecting the free movement of goods as such but by protecting the traders of the other Member States who participate in the free movement of goods.

69   That was confirmed in . . . *Commission v. Greece* [Case C-347/88,[1990] ECR I-4747, EU:C:1990:470], where the Court held that to maintain in force the State's rights with regard to the importation and marketing of petroleum products gave rise to discrimination within the meaning of Article [37(1) TFEU] against exporters established in other Member States. Presumably, the determining factor in that case was that the State's monopoly was of such a kind as to prevent certain traders, in particular those with whom the Greek State's monopoly did not have commercial relations, from exporting to the Greek market. There was therefore discrimination between nationals of the Member States, as mentioned in Article [37(1)].* * *

---

10   [1997] ECR I-05909, EU:C:1997:504.

CASE *(continued)*

72   Furthermore, in its decisions the Court has sometimes applied Articles [34] and [37 TFEU] concurrently to a national monopoly of a commercial character and sometimes applied only Article [34] to exclusive rights conferred on a national monopolistic undertaking. Thus in . . . *Commission v. Greece*, the Court held that the exclusive right to import and market finished petroleum products was contrary to both Article [34] and Article [37(1) TFEU]. In the telecommunications terminals judgement [Case C-202/88, *France v. Commission* [1991] ECR I-1223, EU:C:1991:120] the Court held that exclusive rights to import and market terminal equipment constituted a measure having equivalent effect to a quantitative restriction on imports within the meaning of Article [34] of the Treaty. * * *

[The Advocate General concluded that the Swedish monopoly and regulation necessarily hindered trade in violation of Article 34 TFEU; that it had the same effect as an import monopoly and therefore a discriminatory effect in violation of Article 37 TFEU; and that the system was not justified under Article 36 TFEU since health and life could be protected by less restrictive means. The Court did not entirely agree.]

The Court

The rules relating to the existence and operation of the monopoly

[*The Retail Monopoly*]

39   The purpose of Article [37] of the Treaty is to reconcile the possibility for Member States to maintain certain monopolies of a commercial character as instruments for the pursuit of public interest aims with the requirements of the establishment and functioning of the common market. It aims at the elimination of obstacles to the free movement of goods, save, however, for restrictions on trade which are inherent in the existence of the monopolies in question.

40   Thus, Article [37] requires that the organization and operation of the monopoly be arranged so as to exclude any discrimination between nationals of Member States as regards conditions of supply and outlets, so that trade in goods from other Member States is not put at a disadvantage, in law or in fact, in relation to that in domestic goods and that competition between the economies of the Member States is not distorted.

41   In the present case, it is not contested that, in aiming to protect public health against the harm caused by alcohol, a domestic monopoly on the retail of alcoholic beverages, such as that conferred on Systembolaget, pursues a public interest aim.

42   It is therefore necessary to determine whether a monopoly of this kind is arranged in a way which meets the conditions referred to in paragraphs 39 and 40 above. * * *

> **CASE** *(continued)*
>
> *The monopoly's sales network*
>
> 53   Mr Franzen contends that the sales network maintained by Systembolaget is restricted and does not offer the full range of beverages available, which restricts even more the possibilities of sale.
>
> 54   It is true that a monopoly such as Systembolaget has only a limited number of 'shops'. However, it does not appear from the information provided to the Court that the number of sales outlets are limited to the point of compromising consumers' procurement of supplies of domestic or imported alcoholic beverages.
>
> 55   First of all, under the agreement which it has made with the State, Systembolaget must establish or close sales outlets on the basis of management constraints, consumer demand and the necessities of alcohol policy and ensure that each commune which so wishes has a sales outlet and that all points of the territory are served at least by dispatch deliveries.
>
> 56   Second, according to the information provided to the Court, alcoholic beverages may be ordered and supplied in the monopoly's 384 'shops', through around 550 sales outlets as well as along 56 bus routes and on 45 rural post rounds. Furthermore, there is at least one 'shop' in 259 of the 288 Swedish communes and Systembolaget is planning for every commune to have at least one 'shop' in 1998.
>
> 57   Finally, even if the retail network of Systembolaget is still imperfect, this circumstance does not adversely affect the sale of alcoholic beverages from other Member States more than the sale of alcoholic beverages produced in Sweden.
>
> *The promotion of alcoholic beverages*
>
> 58   Mr Franzen also contends that the system for promoting alcoholic beverages favours the marketing of beverages produced in Sweden. He points out that the promotion of alcoholic beverages is confined to mere provision of information about the products, varying in form depending on whether the products are in the 'basic' assortment or in the 'by order' assortment, that the information is provided by the monopoly alone, without any control by suppliers and, furthermore, that suppliers may not canvas persons in charge of the monopoly's 'shops'.
>
> 59   As far as these points are concerned, it must be observed first of all that the restriction of the possibilities for promoting alcoholic beverages to the public is inherent in the situation where there is only one operator on the market for their retail.

CASE *(continued)*

60 Second, the monopoly rules do not prohibit producers or importers from promoting their products to the monopoly. . . .

61 It must also be pointed out that the promotion of alcoholic beverages to the public is subject, in the Member State in question, to a general restriction, the validity of which has not been called in question by the national court nor challenged by Mr Franzen. That restriction consists, in particular, of a ban on advertising on radio and television and in all newspapers or other periodicals, that is to say the means traditionally used by producers to promote their products to the public. However, alcoholic beverages selected by Systembolaget may be advertised in written material available at sales outlets. Furthermore, any alcoholic beverage may be mentioned in press articles. * * *

64 Finally, it must be noted that the method of promotion used by the monopoly applies independently of products' origin and is not in itself apt to put at a disadvantage, in fact or in law, beverages imported from other Member States in relation to those produced on national territory. * * *

66 So, having regard to the evidence before the Court, it appears that a retail monopoly such as that in question in the main proceedings meets the conditions for being compatible with Article [37] of the Treaty. . . .

Article 34 [The Production and Wholesaling Restrictions]

68 . . . Mr Franzen observes that the monopoly may obtain supplies only from holders of production licences or wholesale licences whose grant is subject to restrictive conditions and that such an obligation necessarily impedes imports of products from other Member States. * * *

70 In a national system such as that in question in the main proceedings, only holders of production licences or wholesale licences are allowed to import alcoholic beverages, that is to say traders who fulfil the restrictive conditions to which issue of those licences is subject. According to the information provided to the Court during the proceedings, the traders in question must provide sufficient personal and financial guarantees to carry on the activities in question, concerning in particular their professional knowledge, their financial capacity and possession of storage capacity sufficient to meet the needs of their activities. Furthermore, the submission of an application is subject to payment of a high fixed charge . . . which is not reimbursed if the application is rejected. Finally, in order to keep his licence, a trader must pay an annual supervision fee, which is also high. . . .

71 The licensing system constitutes an obstacle to the importation of alcoholic beverages from other Member States in that it imposes additional costs on such beverages, such as

CASE (continued)

intermediary costs, payment of charges and fees for the grant of a licence, and costs arising from the obligation to maintain storage capacity in Sweden.

72   According to the Swedish government's own evidence, the number of licences issued is low (223 in October 1996) and almost all of these licences have been issued to traders established in Sweden.

73   Domestic legislation such as that in question in the main proceedings is therefore contrary to Article [34] of the Treaty.

74   The Swedish government has, however, invoked Article [36] of the . . . Treaty. It maintains that its legislation was justified on grounds relating to the protection of human health.

75   It is indeed so that measures contrary to Article [34] may be justified on the basis of Article [36] of the Treaty. All the same, according to established case-law (Cassis de Dijon . . .), the domestic provisions in question must be proportionate to the aim pursued and not attainable by measures less restrictive of intra-Community trade.

76   Although the protection of human health against the harmful effects of alcohol, on which the Swedish government relies, is indisputably one of the grounds which may justify derogation from Article [34] of the Treaty, the Swedish government has not established that the licensing system set up by the Law on Alcohol, in particular as regards the conditions relating to storage capacity and the high fees and charges which licence-holders are required to pay, was proportionate to the public health aim pursued or that this aim could not have been attained by measures less restrictive of intra-Community trade.

77   It must therefore be held that Articles [34] and [36] of the Treaty preclude domestic provisions allowing only traders holding a production licence or a wholesale licence to import alcoholic beverages on conditions such as those laid down by Swedish legislation.

NOTES AND QUESTIONS

1. What is the practical effect of the judgement? Why can Sweden keep its retail monopoly? Must it abandon its import and wholesale monopoly?
2. The *New York Times* assessed the impact of the judgement on Sweden in an article, 'Europe making Sweden ease alcohol rules':[11]

---

11   *New York Times*, 28 March, 2001, Int'l edn, p. A1.

... [P]iece by piece, Sweden is being forced to take apart its anti-alcohol policies because most violate the European Union's rules of fair competition. Some liquor stores are open late and on Saturdays. A few have been remade into cheerfully decorated self-service stores. And wine lovers can delight in a wide selection. * * *

Experts say that what is happening in Sweden over alcohol policy is in many ways a prime example of the difficulties the European Union faces as it tries to extend its reach and harmonize policies. Stretching from freezing climates to desert regions and incorporating vastly different cultures, the union is seeing that what may be a market commodity in one country is a health issue in another.

'On this issue, we can't even really understand each other,' said Dr. Gunar Agren, the executive manager of Sweden's National Institute of Health. 'We just see things very differently and in fact we have different problems with alcohol.'

Is this criticism fair? Is the *Franzen* judgement a triumph of free movement and free competition over monopoly? Or a triumph of European regulation over national cultural choices?

3. How did the Swedish alcohol system harm competition? Who was hurt? Consider all of Mr Franzen's arguments. Were the harms Mr Franzen identified essentially costs the nation was willing to pay for a national social policy? Or were they harms also to the whole Union? When effects of national, market-restricting policies spill over to other nations, who should decide whether the costs are worth the benefits?

The Court of Justice has dealt with related problems in free movement cases; especially cases under Article 34 TFEU, which prohibits Member States from imposing 'quantitative restrictions on imports and all measures having equivalent effect.' The case law strongly disfavours restraints on free movement but admits an exception where the restriction (such as health and safety standards that may impede trade) is necessary to satisfy important public interest objectives that take precedence over free movement.[12] Moreover, if the allegedly offending measures are merely 'selling arrangements'—time, place and manner of sale, with no discriminatory effect in law or in fact—the State prerogative is recognized; the measure does not fall within Article 34 and no justification is necessary.[13] *Keck* overturned precedent that would have required France to justify the below-cost ban because of its effect on trade. Under the older precedent, France would have been required to show that the restraint was not only warranted by an important public interest but was proportional to it.

Is the Court's approach in *Franzen* consistent with its approach in *Keck*?

4. In view of *Franzen*, was Mr Costa right or wrong?
5. A decade later, Klas Rosengren and 10 other Swedes ordered Spanish wine through a Danish website, which offered wine at lower prices than Systembolaget, the Swedish retail alcohol monopoly. Systembolaget confiscated Rosengren's wine on the grounds that Swedish law prohibited its citizens from importing wine from other EU countries. Rosengren sued in a Swedish court. Systembolaget defended that its law was justified as a means of preventing alcohol abuse. The Swedish court referred the question of the legality of the Swedish ban to the Court of Justice, which ruled for Rosengren. The Court held that the ban restricted trade

---

12 Case 120/78, *Rewe-Zentral v. Bundesmonopolverwaltung Fur Branntwein (Cassis de Dijon)* [1979] ECR 649, EU:C:1979:42.
13 Joined Cases C-267 and C-268/91, *Keck and Mithouard* [1993] ECR I-6097, EU:C:1993:905 (holding not within Article 34 a French law prohibiting retail prices of less than acquisition cost, even though the law had the effect of keeping out of France low-priced, non-monopolistic cross-border trade).

in violation of Article 34 TFEU and was a disproportionate means to protect the health of Swedish citizens.[14]

C. Exclusive privileges: Article 106 TFEU

Article 106 TFEU prohibits public undertakings and undertakings to which Member States grant special or exclusive rights from violating the competition provisions insofar as application of those rules does not obstruct the performance of the tasks assigned. Specifically:

Article 106 TFEU, ex 86 ECT

1. In the case of public undertakings and undertakings to which Member States grant special or exclusive rights, Member States shall neither enact nor maintain in force any measure contrary to the rules contained in this Treaty, in particular to those rules provided for in Article 18 [non-discrimination] and Articles 101 to 109 [restrictive agreements, abuse of dominance, State aids].

2. Undertakings entrusted with the operation of services of general economic interest or having the character of a revenue-producing monopoly shall be subject to the rules contained in this Treaty, in particular to the rules on competition, insofar as the application of such rules does not obstruct the performance, in law or in fact, of the particular tasks assigned to them. The development of trade must not be affected to such an extent as would be contrary to the interests of the Community. * * *

The next two cases ask when enjoyment of a State-granted monopoly right, which is the right to keep out the competition, violates Article 106 TFEU.

CASE

Hofner v. Macrotron GmbH (Case C-41/90)[15]

[German law, intended to achieve a high level of employment and to improve the distribution of jobs, conferred on the Bundesanstalt für Arbeit (Federal Employment Office) the exclusive right of placement, i.e., exclusivity as employment agent. The law required the Office to provide the service free of charge. Placement activities by others were punishable by fine. Messrs Höfner and Elser contracted with Macrotron to present to Macrotron a suitable

---

14 Case 170/04, *Klas Rosengren and Others* [2007] ECR I-4071, EU:C:2007:313.
15 [1991] ECR I-1979, EU:C:1991:161.

CASE *(continued)*

candidate for the post of sales manager, for a fee. They presented such a candidate, but Macrotron decided not to employ him and refused to pay the fee stipulated, alleging, inter alia, that the contract was void by reason of the German law. Höfner and Elser rejoined that the German law was void because it unnecessarily restrained their competition in violation of Article 106 TFEU, and exclusion of their competition amounted to abuse of dominance under Article 102 TFEU. The national court referred questions to the Court of Justice.]

16   In its fourth question, the national court asks more specifically whether the monopoly of employment procurement in respect of business executives granted to a public employment agency constitutes an abuse of a dominant position within the meaning of Article [102 TFEU], having regard to Article [106(2) TFEU]. . . .

17   According to the appellants in the main proceedings, an agency such as the Bundesanstalt is both a public undertaking within the meaning of Article [106(1)] and an undertaking entrusted with the operation of services of general economic interest within the meaning of Article [106(2)] of the Treaty. The Bundesanstalt is therefore, they maintain, subject to the competition rules to the extent to which the application thereof does not obstruct the performance of the particular task assigned to it, and it does not in the present case. The appellants also claim that the action taken by the Bundesanstalt, which extended its statutory monopoly over employment procurement to activities for which the establishment of a monopoly is not in the public interest, constitutes an abuse within the meaning of Article [102] of the Treaty. They also consider that any Member State which makes such an abuse possible is in breach of Article [106(1) TFEU] and of the general principle whereby the Member States must refrain from taking any measure which could destroy the effectiveness of the Community competition rules.

18   The Commission takes a somewhat different view. The maintenance of a monopoly on executive recruitment constitutes, in its view, an infringement of Article [106(1)] read in conjunction with Article [102] of the Treaty where the grantee of the monopoly is not willing or able to carry out that task fully, according to the demand existing on the market, and provided that such conduct is liable to affect trade between Member States. * * *

21   It must be observed, in the context of competition law, first that the concept of an undertaking encompasses every entity engaged in an economic activity, regardless of the legal status of the entity and the way in which it is financed and, secondly, that employment procurement is an economic activity.

22   The fact that employment procurement activities are normally entrusted to public agencies cannot affect the economic nature of such activities. Employment procurement has not always been, and is not necessarily, carried out by public entities. That finding applies in particular to executive recruitment.

CASE *(continued)*

23   It follows that an entity such as a public employment agency engaged in the business of employment procurement may be classified as an undertaking for the purpose of applying the Community competition rules.

24   It must be pointed out that a public employment agency which is entrusted, under the legislation of a Member State, with the operation of services of general economic interest . . . remains subject to the competition rules pursuant to Article [106(2)] of the Treaty unless and to the extent to which it is shown that their application is incompatible with the discharge of its duties.

25   As regards the manner in which a public employment agency enjoying an exclusive right of employment procurement conducts itself in relation to executive recruitment undertaken by private recruitment consultancy companies, it must be stated that the application of Article [102] of the Treaty cannot obstruct the performance of the particular task assigned to that agency in so far as the latter is manifestly not in a position to satisfy demand in that area of the market and in fact allows its exclusive rights to be encroached on by those companies.

26   Whilst it is true that Article [102] concerns undertakings and may be applied within the limits laid down by Article [106(2)] to public undertakings or undertakings vested with exclusive rights or specific rights, the fact nevertheless remains that the Treaty requires the Member States not to take or maintain in force measures which could destroy the effectiveness of that provision . . . . ***

29   . . . [T]he simple fact of creating a dominant position of that kind by granting an exclusive right within the meaning of Article [106(1)] is not as such incompatible with Article [102] of the Treaty. A Member State is in breach of the prohibition contained in those two provisions only if the undertaking in question, merely by exercising the exclusive right granted to it, cannot avoid abusing its dominant position.

30   Pursuant to Article [102(b)], such an abuse may in particular consist in limiting the provision of a service, to the prejudice of those seeking to avail themselves of it.

31   A Member State creates a situation in which the provision of a service is limited when the undertaking to which it grants an exclusive right extending to executive recruitment activities is manifestly not in a position to satisfy the demand prevailing on the market for activities of that kind and when the effective pursuit of such activities by private companies is rendered impossible by the maintenance in force of a statutory provision under which such activities are prohibited and non-observance of that prohibition renders the contracts concerned void. ***

CASE *(continued)*

34   In view of the foregoing considerations, it must be stated in reply to the fourth question that a public employment agency engaged in employment procurement activities is subject to the prohibition contained in Article [102] of the Treaty, so long as the application of that provision does not obstruct the performance of the particular task assigned to it. A Member State which has conferred an exclusive right to carry on that activity upon the public employment agency is in breach of Article [106(1)] of the Treaty where it creates a situation in which that agency cannot avoid infringing Article [102] of the Treaty. That is the case, in particular, where the following conditions are satisfied:

— the exclusive right extends to executive recruitment activities
— the public employment agency is manifestly incapable of satisfying demand prevailing on the market for such activities
— the actual pursuit of those activities by private recruitment consultants is rendered impossible by the maintenance in force of a statutory provision under which such activities are prohibited and non-observance of that prohibition renders the contracts concerned void
— the activities in question may extend to the nationals or to the territory of other Member States.

CASE

Commission v. DEI (Case C-553/12 P) (*Greek lignite*)[16]

[Greece liberalized its electricity market as mandated by EU directives. It created a wholesale market in which electricity producers compete for the right to sell power for the next day. The cheapest source of electricity in Greece comes from lignite (brown coal).

Through various legislative tools, Greece had granted an exclusive licence to explore and exploit lignite to DEI, the former electricity monopoly still majority owned by the Greek government at the time of the decision.]

8   [In its decision] the Commission found, inter alia, that the grant and maintenance of those rights was contrary to Article [106(1) TFEU], read together with Article [102 TFEU],

---

16   EU:C:2014:2083.

> **CASE** *(continued)*
>
> since it created a situation of inequality of opportunity between economic operators as regards access to primary fuels for the purposes of generating electricity and allowed DEI to maintain or reinforce its dominant position on the Greek wholesale electricity market by excluding or hindering any new entrants. * * *
>
> 10   According to the Commission, DEI held a dominant position on both those markets [lignite and wholesale electricity], with a market share of more than 97% and 85% respectively. In addition, there was no prospect of new market entrants being capable of significantly reducing DEI's share of the wholesale electricity market, since imports, which represent 7% of total consumption, did not constitute a genuine competitive restraint on that market.
>
> 11   Concerning the State measures in question, the Commission notes that DEI had been granted, pursuant to Legislative Decree No 4029/1959 and Law No 134/1975, exploitation rights for 91% of public deposits of lignite for which rights were granted . . . . The Commission adds that power stations operating on lignite, which are the least costly in Greece, are the most used, since they produce 60% of the electricity permitting the supply of the interconnected network.
>
> 12   According to the Commission, by granting DEI and maintaining in its favour quasi-monopolistic lignite exploration rights which ensure that it has privileged access to the most attractive fuel in Greece for the purposes of generating electricity, the Hellenic Republic thereby created inequality of opportunity between economic operators on the wholesale electricity market and thus distorted competition, maintaining or reinforcing DEI's dominant position and excluding or hindering any new entrants, despite the liberalisation of the wholesale electricity market. * * *
>
> [DEI obtained the annulment of the Commission's decision before the General Court.] * * *
>
> 43   It is clear from the Court's case-law that a system of undistorted competition, such as that provided for by the Treaty, can be guaranteed only if equality of opportunity is secured as between the various economic operators.
>
> 44   It follows that if inequality of opportunity between economic operators, and thus distorted competition, is the result of a State measure, such a measure constitutes an infringement of Article [106(1) TFEU] read together with Article [102 TFEU].
>
> 45   The Court has moreover had occasion to state in that regard that, although the mere fact that a Member State has created a dominant position by the grant of exclusive rights is not as such incompatible with Article [102 TFEU], the [Treaty] nonetheless requires the Member

CASE *(continued)*

States not to adopt or maintain in force any measure which might deprive that provision of its effectiveness.

46   It follows . . . that . . . infringement of Article [106(1) TFEU] in conjunction with Article [102 TFEU] may be established irrespective of whether any abuse actually exists. All that is necessary is for the Commission to identify a potential or actual anti-competitive consequence liable to result from the State measure at issue. Such an infringement may thus be established where the State measures at issue affect the structure of the market by creating unequal conditions of competition between companies, by allowing the public undertaking or the undertaking which was granted special or exclusive rights to maintain (for example by hindering new entrants to the market), strengthen or extend its dominant position over another market, thereby restricting competition, without it being necessary to prove the existence of actual abuse. * * *

[The Court of Justice reversed the General Court's judgement and sent the case back for analysis of the other pleas raised by DEI.[17]]

NOTES AND QUESTIONS

1. Compare the standards for running afoul of Article 106 TFEU in *Höfner* and in *DEI*.
2. What type of abuse would DEI be led to commit due to its privileges? Would the abuses be exclusionary or exploitative? Could DEI avoid committing an abuse?
3. Does the Court in *Höfner* require an efficiency audit of the Federal Employment Office to determine whether it can satisfy demand? Isn't the Office's ability to satisfy demand a function of the resources the German government makes available to it? Why does the EU care whether Germany sufficiently funds its free employment service? Do all dominant firms abuse their dominance by simply not providing enough goods or services (at what price level?), or is it critical that the government-granted exclusive privilege prevents anyone else from serving the market?
4. Messrs Höfner and Elser also claimed a violation of Article 56 TFEU (Member States may not restrict freedom to provide services in respect of nationals of Member States) in conjunction with Article 18 TFEU (no discrimination on grounds of nationality); but since all parties, including the employment candidate, were German, the Court found Article 56 inapplicable. If the candidate or the private employment agency were Belgian, would Article 56 TFEU protect the private agency's right to its fee?
5. In *Régie des Postes v. Corbeau*,[18] a Belgian law—enacted before the development of courier service—gave exclusive mail delivery rights to the Belgian Post Office and prohibited private mail delivery. Mr Corbeau set up a private mail delivery service in Liège. Corbeau collected mail from his clients and guaranteed delivery before noon the following day to all addressees

---

17 Case T-169/08, ECLI:EU:T:2016:733.
18 Case C-320/91, *Régie des Postes v. Corbeau* [1993] ECR I-2533, EU:C:1993:198.

within town limits. He delivered in-town mail and dispatched the out-of-town mail by post. When prosecuted, Corbeau asserted a violation of Article 106 TFEU.

In an Article 267 reference, the Court of Justice advised the Belgian court that an undertaking charged with the provision of universal service may not restrict competition more than necessary to achieve its public mission in view of contemporary market conditions, leaving it to the national court to determine what was more than necessary.

Was Corbeau skimming the cream from the Belgian Post's business? At some point, would cream-skimming compromise the economic stability of the post office and disable it from fulfilling its obligation to provide universal service? How can the national court determine how much competition is too much competition for the Belgian Post to fulfill its public mission?

6. There is, however, a gap in the coverage of Articles 101, 102 and 106 TFEU. State bodies are subject to those Treaty obligations only if they carry out economic activities. Bodies that regulate the market but do not participate in it are not covered. In *FENIN v. Commission*,[19] the Court of Justice acknowledged that the public bodies that ran the Spanish national healthcare system and provided free services funded by social security contributions and other State funding were not 'undertakings', and it held that a State body that is not an undertaking does not become so in its role as purchaser of goods—here, medical goods and equipment. The purchasing activity is not 'dissociable from the service subsequently provided.' The holding of *FENIN* means that suppliers to State bodies carrying out public functions are not protected by Article 102 TFEU from the State body's exploitative and discriminatory purchasing conduct. Does this holding shield too much activity from the antitrust provisions? Is it sufficient protection that the State is subject to Article 18 TFEU, prohibiting discrimination based on nationality?

CASE

Albany International BV and Textile Industry Pension Funds (Case C-67/96)[20]
(see additional facts at p. 108 above, excerpt regarding Article 101—labour)

[Albany International, a textile firm that wished to provide pensions for its workers through an insurer of its choice, contended that the Dutch law granting to a specified fund an exclusive right to manage supplementary textile industry pensions violated Articles 102 and 106 TFEU. Citing *Höfner*, the Court repeated that mere creation of a dominant position (which the Netherlands conferred on the pension fund) is not incompatible with Article 102 TFEU. Rather, to run afoul of the law, the Member State must create a situation in which the undertaking cannot avoid abusing its dominance.]

98   It is therefore necessary to consider whether, as contended by the Fund, the Netherlands government and the Commission, the exclusive right of the sectoral pension fund to manage supplementary pensions in a given sector and the resultant restriction of competition may be

---

19   Case C-205/03 P, *FENIN v. Commission* [2006] ECR I-6295, EU:C:2006:453.
20   [1999] ECR I-5751, EU:C:1999:430.

CASE *(continued)*

justified under Article [106(2)] of the Treaty as a measure necessary for the performance of a particular social task of general interest with which that fund has been charged. * * *

102   It is important to bear in mind first of all that, under Article [106(2)] of the Treaty, undertakings entrusted with the operation of services of general economic interest are subject to the rules on competition in so far as the application of such rules does not obstruct the performance, in law or in fact, of the particular tasks assigned to them.

103   In allowing, in certain circumstances, derogations from the general rules of the Treaty, Article [106(2)] of the Treaty seeks to reconcile the Member States' interest in using certain undertakings, in particular in the public sector, as an instrument of economic or fiscal policy with the Community's interest in ensuring compliance with the rules on competition and preservation of the unity of the common market.

104   In view of the interest of the Member States thus defined they cannot be precluded, when determining what services of general economic interest they entrust to certain undertakings, from taking account of objectives pertaining to their national policy or from endeavouring to attain them by means of obligations and constraints which they impose on such undertakings.

105   The supplementary pension scheme at issue in the main proceedings fulfils an essential social function within the Netherlands pensions system by reason of the limited amount of the statutory pension, which is calculated on the basis of the minimum statutory wage. * * *

107   Next, it is not necessary, in order for the conditions for the application of Article [106(2)] of the Treaty to be fulfilled, that the financial balance or economic viability of the undertaking entrusted with the operation of a service of general economic interest should be threatened. It is sufficient that, in the absence of the rights at issue, it would not be possible for the undertaking to perform the particular tasks entrusted to it, defined by reference to the obligations and constraints to which it is subject or that maintenance of those rights is necessary to enable the holder of them to perform tasks of general economic interest which have been assigned to it under economically acceptable conditions.

108   If the exclusive right of the fund to manage the supplementary pension scheme for all workers in a given sector were removed, undertakings with young employees in good health engaged in non-dangerous activities would seek more advantageous insurance terms from private insurers. The progressive departure of 'good' risks would leave the sectoral pension fund with responsibility for an increasing share of 'bad' risks, thereby increasing the cost of pensions for workers, particularly those in small and medium-sized undertakings with older employees engaged in dangerous activities, to which the fund could no longer offer pensions at an acceptable cost.

CASE *(continued)*

109   Such a situation would arise particularly in a case where, as in the main proceedings, the supplementary pension scheme managed exclusively by the Fund displays a high level of solidarity resulting, in particular, from the fact that contributions do not reflect the risk, from the obligation to accept all workers without a prior medical examination, the continuing accrual of pension rights despite exemption from the payment of contributions in the event of incapacity for work, the discharge by the Fund of arrears of contributions due from an employer in the event of insolvency and the indexing of the amount of pensions in order to maintain their value.

110   Such constraints, which render the service provided by the Fund less competitive than a comparable service provided by insurance companies, go towards justifying the exclusive right of the Fund to manage the supplementary pension scheme.

111   It follows that the removal of the exclusive right conferred on the Fund might make it impossible for it to perform the tasks of general economic interest entrusted to it under economically acceptable conditions and threaten its financial equilibrium. * * *

[The Fund has the power to grant exemptions from its own exclusivity. It has the duty to grant such exemptions if specific criteria are met, thus providing a check against discriminatory or arbitrary denials.]

122   Finally, as regards Albany's argument that an adequate level of pension for workers could be assured by laying down minimum requirements to be met by pensions offered by insurance companies, it must be emphasised that, in view of the social function of supplementary pension schemes and the margin of appreciation enjoyed, according to settled case-law, by the Member States in organising their social security systems, it is incumbent on each Member State to consider whether, in view of the particular features of its national pension system, laying down minimum requirements would still enable it to ensure the level of pension which it seeks to guarantee in a sector by compulsory affiliation to a pension fund.

123   The answer to the third question must therefore be that Articles [102] and [106] of the Treaty do not preclude the public authorities from conferring on a pension fund the exclusive right to manage a supplementary pension scheme in a given sector.

NOTES AND QUESTIONS

1. Does the Court in *Albany* grant wide berth to the State to carry out its social purpose of solidarity, despite the fact that its chosen solution might block competition and not be efficient? Or

does the Court imply some level of serious scrutiny? If the Netherlands can assure an adequate level of pensions by laying down minimum requirements, must it abandon its system of granting an exclusive right to a chosen fund? See para. 122. Who determines whether adequate pensions can be assured by less restrictive means? Does para. 122 mean that a grant of exclusive rights can, in itself, violate the Treaty simply because it restricts competition and the restriction was unnecessary to achieve the public goal?

2. Since the late 1970s, the Commission and Courts have taken a number of actions to limit the power of State-owned monopolies and undertakings enjoying exclusive rights. In 1980, the Commission issued a directive under Article [106(3)] TFEU requiring Member States to reveal financial information about their State-owned enterprises.[21]

In a number of situations the case is a straightforward Article 102 case, and the fact of State ownership or State-granted privilege does not provide a shield. In *British Telecom*, the Court held that a State telecommunications monopoly abused its dominance by preventing private message-forwarding agencies from receiving and forwarding international telephone calls.[22] In *Telemarketing*, the Court stated that a broadcasting monopoly enterprise would abuse its dominant position by refusing to sell broadcasting time to a telemarketing firm that competed with the monopoly firm's subsidiary.[23]

3. EU competition law is in the vanguard in controlling State-granted privileges that harm competition.[24]

D. State measures that restrict competition or facilitate private restrictions

1. State responsibility

State legislation is a frequent source of distortion of competition. Distortions may result from national laws on price control, sector regulation (e.g., oil, tobacco, transport), taxation, and various social and national industrial policies.

To what extent does Article 4 TEU, the competition articles, and the freedoms of movement suggest a broad pre-emption by EU competition policy of anti-competitive State legislation? The Court bowed in the direction of a broad pre-emption in *INNO/ATAB*.[25] The Court said, regarding a Belgian

---

21 Commission Directive 80/723/EEC of 25 June 1980 on the transparency of financial relations between Member States and public undertakings [1980] O.J. L 195/35, amended by Commission Directive 85/413, [1985] O.J. L 229/20.
22 Case 41/83, *Italy v. Commission* [1985] ECR 873, EU:C:1985:120 ('*British Telecom*').
23 Case 311/84, *Centre Belge d'Études de Marché-Télémarketing SA v. Compagnie Luxembourgeoise de Télédiffusion SA* [1985] ECR 3261, EU:C:1985:394 ('*Telemarketing*').
24 See, for a study of various jurisdictions' competition-law coverage of State-related restraints, E. Fox and D. Healey (2014), 'When the state harms competition: The role for competition law', *Antitrust Law Journal*, 79, 769.
25 Case 13/77, *NV GB-INNO-BM v. Vereniging van de Kleinhandelaars in Tabak* [1977] ECR 2115, EU:C:1977:185 ('*INNO/ATAB*').

law requiring, for tax collection purposes, that tobacco products be sold at a price affixed to the label by the manufacturer or importer:

> [W]hile it is true that Article [102 TFEU] is directed at undertakings, nonetheless it is also true that the Treaty [now Article 4(3) TEU] imposes a duty on Member States not to adopt or maintain in force any measure which could deprive that provision of its effectiveness. [para. 31]

But in the years after *INNO/ATAB*, the Court backed away from a strong view of Member State duties not to restrain competition unnecessarily. Especially since the *Keck* 'revolution' in 1993 (see p. 289 above), the Court has been reluctant to condemn Member States' regulatory laws for undermining Articles 101 and 102 TFEU. Three competition cases decided at the time of *Keck* reflect the new deference in adopting measures that have anti-competitive effects; namely, *Ohra, Meng* and *Reiff*.

Ohra, a Dutch insurance firm that dealt directly with customers rather than through intermediaries, tried to become more competitive by giving credit cards to its customers. Ohra was prosecuted for violating a Dutch law that prohibited insurance companies and their agents from granting rebates or other things of value. Ohra responded that the law was anti-competitive and constituted a violation of Member States' obligations under Articles 3(1)(g) (now in a protocol) and Article 4(3) TEU, as linked with Articles 101 and 102 TFEU.[26]

In *Meng*, in the face of a similar German law, insurance agent Meng rebated his commissions to his clients. When prosecuted, he presented the same defence as Ohra: he was competing; the prohibition was illegal.[27]

Reiff involved a German law that delegated truck tariff-setting to tariff boards whose members were appointed by the Federal Minister upon the recommendation of the truckers themselves. In setting the tariffs, the board members were obliged to take account of the public interest criteria laid down by the public authority, and the Minister of Transport was entitled to participate in the meetings, to reject tariffs that were not in the public interest, and to set tariffs himself. A trucking company charged Reiff, a shipper, a price less than the mandated tariff. The federal office proceeded against

---

[26] Case C-245/91, *Ohra Schadeverzekeringen NV v. Netherlands* [1993] ECR I-5851, EU:C:1993:887 ('*Ohra*').
[27] Case C-2/91, *W. Meng v. Germany* [1993] ECR I-5751, EU:C:1993:885 ('*Meng*').

Reiff for the difference, and Reiff defended on grounds that the law was anti-competitive and void.[28]

The three cases came to the Court of Justice on Article 267 references. The Court held: A Member State would infringe Articles 3(1)(g) [now in a protocol] and 4(3) TEU if it 'requires or favours the adoption of agreements, decisions or concerted practices contrary to Article [101 TFEU], or reinforces such effects, or deprives its own legislation of its official character by delegating economic responsibility to private traders' (quoting from *INNO/ATAB*). It held that none of the three laws fit the prohibited category.

Do you agree? What are the anti-competitive effects in each case? In which of the cases can you make the best argument that the national measure would tend to reinforce a private cartel or that it delegated economic responsibility for an anticompetitive act to private traders?

The question remained: How broadly or narrowly would the Court construe its mandate that the State must not undermine the effectiveness of Articles 101 and 102 TFEU?

CASE

Consorzio Industrie Fiammiferi (Case C-198/01) ('Italian matches')[29]

[In *Consorzio Industrie Fiammiferi* (*Italian matches*), Italy organized a match cartel by relying on an 80-year-old Royal Decree. Italy required the Italian match producers to join a consortium. The minister was required to set the price for matches, and the consortium of competitors was required to allocate quotas. Government officials had the duty to oversee the quotas. A German match producer complained to the Italian Antitrust Authority that it was having difficulty entering the Italian market. Swedish producers later complained that they were denied a fair quota and could sell only to the Italian match consortium. The Italian Antitrust Authority opened proceedings. It found Treaty violations both by Italy and by the Italian producers. An Italian tribunal referred questions to the Court of Justice. Here is the response of the Court regarding Italy's responsibility.]

---

28 Case C-185/91, *Gebrüder Reiff GmbH & Co. KG v. Bundesanstalt für den Güterfernverkehr* [1993] ECR I-5801, EU:C:1993:886 ('*Reiff*').
29 [2003] ECR I-8055, EU:C:2003:430.

> **CASE** *(continued)*
>
> 45   ... [A]lthough Articles [101 and 102 TFEU] are, in themselves, concerned solely with the conduct of undertakings and not with laws or regulations emanating from Member States, those articles, read in conjunction with Article [4 TEU], which lays down a duty to cooperate, nonetheless require the Member States not to introduce or maintain in force measures, even of a legislative or regulatory nature, which may render ineffective the competition rules applicable to undertakings.
>
> 46   The Court has held in particular that Articles [4 TEU and 101 TFEU] are infringed where a Member State requires or favours the adoption of agreements, decisions or concerted practices contrary to Article [101 TFEU] or reinforces their effects, or where it divests its own rules of the character of legislation by delegating to private economic operators responsibility for taking decisions affecting the economic sphere.
>
> 47   Moreover, since the Treaty of Maastricht entered into force, the ... Treaty has expressly provided that in the context of their economic policy the activities of the Member States must observe the principle of an open market economy with free competition. ...
>
> 48   It is appropriate to bear in mind, second, that in accordance with settled case-law the primacy of Community law requires any provision of national law which contravenes a Community rule to be disapplied, regardless of whether it was adopted before or after that rule.
>
> 49   The duty to disapply national legislation which contravenes Community law applies not only to national courts but also to all organs of the State, including administrative authorities, which entails, if the circumstances so require, the obligation to take all appropriate measures to enable Community law to be fully applied.
>
> 50   Since a national competition authority such as the Authority is responsible for ensuring, *inter alia*, that Article [101 TFEU] is observed and that provision, in conjunction with Article [4 TEU], imposes a duty on Member States to refrain from introducing measures contrary to the Community competition rules, those rules would be rendered less effective if, in the course of an investigation under [101 TFEU] into the conduct of undertakings, the authority were not able to declare a national measure contrary to the combined provisions of Articles [4 TEU] and [101 TFEU] and if, consequently, it failed to disapply it.
>
> 51   In that regard, it is of little significance that, where undertakings are required by national legislation to engage in anti-competitive conduct, they cannot also be held accountable for infringement of Articles [101 and 102 TFEU]. Member States' obligations under Articles 3(1)(g) EC (now in a protocol), [4 TEU, 101 TFEU and 102 TFEU], which are distinct from those to which undertakings are subject under Articles [101 and 102 TFEU], nonetheless continue to exist and therefore the national competition authority remains duty-bound to disapply the national measure at issue.

> **CASE**
>
> ## Cipolla v. Fazari and Macrino v. Meloni (Joined Cases C-94 and C-202/04)[30]
>
> [Pursuant to a 73-year-old Italian law, Italy adopted maximum and minimum fee schedules for lawyers, from which there could be no derogation except in narrow circumstances. The schedules were based on a draft prepared by the National Lawyers' Council—a professional body of lawyers. In connection with three fee disputes, an Italian court referred to the Court of Justice questions regarding the validity of the Italian law.]
>
> 48 ... [T]he fact that a Member State requires a professional organisation composed of lawyers, such as the CNF, to produce a draft scale of fees does not, in the circumstances specific to the cases in the main proceedings, appear to establish that that State has divested the scale finally adopted of its character of legislation by delegating to lawyers responsibility for taking decisions concerning them.
>
> 49 Although the national legislation at issue in the main proceedings does not contain either procedural arrangements or substantive requirements capable of ensuring with reasonable probability that, when producing the draft scale, the CNF conducts itself like an arm of the State working in the public interest, it does not appear that the Italian State has waived its power to make decisions of last resort or to review implementation of that scale.
>
> 50 First, the CNF is responsible only for producing a draft scale which, as such, is not binding. Without the Minister of Justice's approval, the draft scale does not enter into force and the earlier approved scale remains applicable. Accordingly, that Minister has the power to have the draft amended by the CNF. Furthermore, the Minister is assisted by two public bodies, the Consiglio di Stato and the CIP, whose opinions he must obtain before the scale can be approved.
>
> 51 Secondly, Article 60 of the Royal Decree-Law provides that fees are to be settled by the courts on the basis of the criteria referred to in Article 57 of that decree-law, having regard to the seriousness and number of the issues dealt with. Moreover, in certain exceptional circumstances and by duly reasoned decision, the court may depart from the maximum and minimum limits fixed pursuant to Article 58 of the Royal Decree-Law.
>
> 52 In those circumstances, the view cannot be taken that the Italian State has waived its power by delegating to private economic operators responsibility for taking decisions

---

30 [2006] ECR I-11421, EU:C:2006:758.

CASE (continued)

affecting the economic sphere, which would have the effect of depriving the provisions at issue in the main proceedings of the character of legislation.

53   Nor . . . is the Italian State open to the criticism that it requires or encourages the adoption by the CNF of agreements, decisions or concerted practices contrary to Article [101 TFEU] or reinforces their effects, or requires or encourages abuses of a dominant position contrary to Article [102 TFEU] or reinforces the effects of such abuses. * * *

Free movement of services

58   The prohibition of derogation, by agreement, from the minimum fees set by a scale such as that laid down by the Italian legislation is liable to render access to the Italian legal services market more difficult for lawyers established in a Member State other than the Italian Republic and therefore is likely to restrict the exercise of their activities providing services in that Member State. That prohibition therefore amounts to a restriction within the meaning of Article [56 TFEU].

59   That prohibition deprives lawyers established in a Member State other than the Italian Republic of the possibility, by requesting fees lower than those set by the scale, of competing more effectively with lawyers established on a stable basis in the Member State concerned and who therefore have greater opportunities for winning clients than lawyers established abroad.

60   Likewise, the prohibition thus laid down limits the choice of service recipients in Italy, because they cannot resort to the services of lawyers established in other Member States who would offer their services in Italy at a lower rate than the minimum fees set by the scale.

61   However, such a prohibition may be justified where it serves overriding requirements relating to the public interest, is suitable for securing the attainment of the objective which it pursues and does not go beyond what is necessary in order to attain it.

62   In order to justify the restriction on freedom to provide services which stems from the prohibition at issue, the Italian government submits that excessive competition between lawyers might lead to price competition which would result in a deterioration in the quality of the services provided to the detriment of consumers, in particular as individuals in need of quality advice in court proceedings.

63   According to the Commission, no causal link has been established between the setting of minimum levels of fees and a high qualitative standard of professional services provided by lawyers. In actual fact, quasi-legislative measures such as, inter alia, rules on access to the legal

CASE *(continued)*

profession, disciplinary rules serving to ensure compliance with professional ethics and rules on civil liability have, by maintaining a high qualitative standard for the services provided by such professionals which those measures guarantee, a direct relationship of cause and effect with the protection of lawyers' clients and the proper working of the administration of justice.

64   In that respect, it must be pointed out that, first, the protection of consumers, in particular recipients of the legal services provided by persons concerned in the administration of justice and, secondly, the safeguarding of the proper administration of justice, are objectives to be included among those which may be regarded as overriding requirements relating to the public interest capable of justifying a restriction on freedom to provide services . . . on condition, first, that the national measure at issue in the main proceedings is suitable for securing the attainment of the objective pursued and, secondly, it does not go beyond what is necessary in order to attain that objective. * * *

70   Having regard to the foregoing, the answer to the fourth and fifth questions . . . must be that legislation containing an absolute prohibition of derogation, by agreement, from the minimum fees set by a scale of lawyer's fees such as that at issue in the main proceedings for services which are (a) court services and (b) reserved to lawyers, constitutes a restriction on freedom to provide services laid down in Article [56 TFEU]. It is for the national court to determine whether such legislation, in the light of the detailed rules for its application, actually serves the objectives of protection of consumers and the proper administration of justice which might justify it and whether the restrictions it imposes do not appear disproportionate in the light of those objectives. * * *

NOTES AND QUESTIONS

1. Do paras. 48 to 53 in *Cipolla* surprise you, after *Italian matches*?
2. What is the argument, contrariwise, that setting minimum lawyer fees harms free movement *and* consumers and is not justified on its face? What is the argument that the Italian law requires or facilitates an illegal agreement among lawyers? Note the Commission's argument that enforced price floors do not correlate with higher quality services. Note also that, in most jurisdictions, competitors have a right to combine to procure government action—a point relevant to 'Private responsibility', below.
3. How will the national court determine whether the law 'actually serves the objectives of the protection of consumers and the proper administration of justice' and whether the restrictions are 'disproportionate in light of those objectives'? Would a bright line (e.g., no minimum fees) have been superior? Italy, in fact, proceeded to abolish minimum lawyer fees.
4. Given their alleged public policy objectives, should public restraints be assessed exclusively under the free movement rules of the Treaty, instead of the competition rules? What would be

the possible benefits, or pitfalls, of such an approach? As a general rule, should State measures be subject to the same or another discipline than private conduct?[31]

5. See, for the Court's treatment of lawyers' agreements that restrict competition, *Wouters*, in Chapter 3. Is the Court especially deferential to agreements among professionals that may restrict competition, or has it struck the right balance?

In the US, professionals, when carrying on their commercial activities, are fully subject to the antitrust laws. But States may regulate lawyers and other professionals in the public interest. For example, the State may limit the number of lawyers in the State through State bar examinations.[32]

2. Private responsibility

Private actors may avoid responsibility on grounds that the anti-competitive act was not theirs; it was the act of the State and they had no room for autonomous conduct ('State compulsion' doctrine).

CASE

Commission and France v. Ladbroke Racing Ltd (Joined Cases C-359 and C-379/95 P)[33]

[French law created Pari Mutuel Urbain ('PMU') as a joint service of the authorized racing companies to manage their rights in off-track betting, and it granted PMU exclusive rights to run off-track betting on horse races held in France and horse race betting organized in France. French law prohibited anyone, other than PMU, to place or accept bets on horse races.

Ladbroke Racing Ltd, an operator of off-track betting, lodged with the Commission a complaint against France under Article 106 TFEU, and a complaint against the ten main racing companies in France and PMU under Articles 101 and 102 TFEU. Before taking a position on the Article 106 claim, which included allegations of illegal State aid, the Commission rejected the allegations of violation of Articles 101 and 102 on grounds that those articles did not apply.

The General Court annulled the Commission's decision to reject the complaint, on grounds that a definitive determination could not be made by the Commission before completing its investigation regarding the compatibility of the French law with the competition rules. The Commission and France appealed to the Court of Justice.]

---

31 For a discussion, see D. Gerard (2010), 'EU competition policy after Lisbon: Time for a review of the "state action doctrine"?', *Journal of European Competition Law & Practice*, **3**, 202.
32 See *Hoover v. Ronwin*, 466 U.S. 558, 104 S.Ct. 1989, 80 L.Ed.2d 590 (1984).
33 [1997] ECR I-6265, EU:C:1997:531.

> **CASE** (continued)
>
> 20   ... [T]he Commission submits that it is necessary to distinguish between State measures requiring undertakings to engage in conduct contrary to Articles [101] and [102 TFEU] and measures that do not require any conduct contrary to those rules but simply create a legal framework that itself restricts competition. In the first case, the Commission considers that Article [101] remains applicable to undertakings' conduct despite the existence of national statutory obligations and irrespective of the possible application of Articles 3(1)(g) [ECT, now in protocol 27], [4 TEU] and [101 TFEU] with regard to those State measures. In fact, the Commission argues that an undertaking can and, by virtue of the primacy of Community law and the direct effect of Articles [101(1)] and [102] of the Treaty, must refuse to comply with a State measure that requires conduct contrary to those provisions.
>
> 21   In the second case, by contrast, Article [101 TFEU] may in certain circumstances not apply. That is the case here, since the 1974 legislation does not require the conclusion of an agreement between the main racing companies but itself grants the PMU the exclusive right to organize off-course totalizator betting. The restriction of competition thus flowed directly from the national legislation, without any action on the part of undertakings being necessary.
> * * *
>
> 33   Articles [101] and [102] of the Treaty apply only to anti-competitive conduct engaged in by undertakings on their own initiative. If anticompetitive conduct is required of undertakings by national legislation or if the latter creates a legal framework which itself eliminates any possibility of competitive activity on their part, Articles [101] and [102 TFEU] do not apply. In such a situation, the restriction of competition is not attributable, as those provisions implicitly require, to the autonomous conduct of the undertakings.
>
> 34   Articles [101] and [102 TFEU] may apply, however, if it is found that the national legislation does not preclude undertakings from engaging in autonomous conduct which prevents, restricts or distorts competition.
>
> 35   When the Commission is considering the applicability of Articles [101] and [102] of the Treaty to the conduct of undertakings, a prior evaluation of national legislation affecting such conduct should therefore be directed solely to ascertaining whether that legislation prevents undertakings from engaging in autonomous conduct which prevents, restricts or distorts competition.
>
> [The Commission was therefore entitled to find Articles 101 and 102 TFEU inapplicable without completing its investigation into the compatibility of the French legislation with the competition law. The Court set aside the judgement of the General Court.]

> **NOTES AND QUESTIONS**
>
> 1. Describe the anti-competitive aspects of the French off-track betting system. Why might France desire such a system nonetheless?
> 2. The Commission held that there was no *private* anti-competitive action. Defend the result, including the distinction made by the Commission in paras. 20–21.
> 3. What do paras. 33 and 34 mean?
> 4. Were the State measures (apart from State aid) likely to be compatible with Article 106 TFEU? What if the PMU establishments shut their doors at 5:00 p.m. and gamblers claimed they were shut out of betting? (Consider *Höfner.*) Would the outcome of the case have been different if the PMU were an undertaking in the sole control of the ten racing companies?

CASE

Commission v. Italy (Case C-35/96) ('CNSD')[34]

[Customs agents are professionals who offer services to carry out customs formalities relating to the import, export and transit of goods, and related monetary, fiscal and commercial services. In Italy, the Departmental Councils of Customs Agents, whose members are elected by the customs agents, are constituted by Italian law to supervise the activity of the customs agents. Also constituted by Italian law, the Consiglio Nazionale degli Spedizionieri Doganali (National Council of Customs Agents, or 'CNSD') governs the Departmental Councils. It is legally responsible for setting the tariff for the services provided by customs agents on the basis of proposals from the Departmental Councils. Its members are customs agents elected by the Departmental Councils. Customs agents who deviate from the tariff are subject to discipline, which can include suspension or removal from the register of customs agents.

The Commission brought an action against Italy under Article 258 for a declaration that Italy failed to fulfill its obligations under Articles 4 TEU and 101 TFEU by requiring the CNSD to adopt a decision by an association of undertakings (a minimum compulsory tariff; i.e., to price fix) contrary to Article 101 TFEU.

In connection with Articles 4 TEU and 101 TFEU, Italy argued that the customs agents were professionals exercising a liberal profession; that their activity was intellectual, and that they and their association CNSD were not 'undertakings' subject to Article 101 TFEU.

The Court held first that CNSD engaged in economic activity on the market and therefore was an association of undertakings and second that its setting of maximum and minimum fees infringed Article 101(1) TFEU.] * * *

---

34 [1998] ECR I-3851, EU:C:1998:303.

> **CASE** *(continued)*
>
> 52 Thirdly, the question of the extent to which that infringement can be attributed to the Italian Republic must be considered.
>
> 53 Although Article [101] of the Treaty is, in itself, concerned solely with the conduct of undertakings and not with measures adopted by Member States by law or regulation, the fact nevertheless remains that Article [101] of the Treaty, in conjunction with Article [4 TEU], requires the Member States not to introduce or maintain in force measures, even of a legislative nature, which may render ineffective the competition rules applicable to undertakings (for Article [101] of the Treaty, see *Van Eycke, Reiff*).
>
> 54 Such would be the case if a Member State were to require or favour the adoption of agreements, decisions or concerted practices contrary to Article [101 TFEU] or to reinforce their effects, or to deprive its own rules of the character of legislation by delegating to private economic operators responsibility for taking decisions affecting the economic sphere (see *Van Eycke, Reiff*).
>
> 55 By adopting the national legislation in question, the Italian Republic clearly not only required the conclusion of an agreement contrary to Article [101] of the Treaty and declined to influence its terms, but also assists in ensuring compliance with that agreement.
>
> 56 First, Article 14(d) of Law No 1612/1960 requires the CNSD to compile a compulsory, uniform tariff for the services of customs agents.
>
> 57 Secondly, . . . the national legislation in question wholly relinquished to private economic operators the powers of the public authorities as regards the setting of tariffs.
>
> 58 Thirdly, the Italian legislation expressly prohibits registered customs agents from derogating from the tariff on pain of exclusion, suspension or removal from the register.
>
> 59 Fourthly, . . . the Decree of the Minister for Finance of 6 July 1988 bestowed upon [the tariff] the appearance of a public regulation. First, publication in the 'General Series' of the *Gazzetta Ufficiale della Repubblica Italiana* gave rise to a presumption of knowledge of the tariff on the part of third parties, to which the CNSD's decision could never have laid claim. Second, the official character thus conferred on the tariff facilitates the application by customs agents of the prices that it sets. Lastly, its nature is such as to deter customers who might wish to contest the prices demanded by customs agents.
>
> 60 In the light of the foregoing considerations, it must be held that, by adopting and maintaining in force a law which, in granting the relative decision-making power, requires the CNSD to adopt a decision by an association of undertakings contrary to Article [101], consisting of setting a compulsory tariff for all customs agents, the Italian Republic has failed to fulfil its obligations under Articles [4 TEU] and [101 TFEU]. ***

In *Consorzio Industrie Fiammiferi* (*Italian matches*), see facts at p. 301 above, the Italian Antitrust Authority also held that the Italian match producers violated the competition law to the extent that they took autonomous action in fixing quotas. Although the match producers were required by law to set quotas and government officials had the duty to oversee the quotas, the producers had the power to divvy up the quotas in the most anticompetitive way.

The Court of Justice substantially agreed with the Italian Authority. Not only did the national competition authority have the *duty* to disapply the national law, which required an agreement of competitors and legitimized and reinforced its anti-competitive effects. The private quota-setting could be sufficiently autonomous to merit antitrust condemnation even though the State fixed the price.[35]

NOTES AND QUESTIONS

1. In the aftermath of *CNSD*, can the Italian government take back its decision-making prerogative and set the tariff itself? If so, is the probable effect of the Court's judgement merely to cause the government to take on this tariff-setting task? Or is the government likely to rethink whether the public interest requires price-setting?
2. Is the judgement unfair to CNSD, which was held to have acted pursuant to the command of its government? Note the Court's choices. It could have regarded CNSD as protected from an Article 101 violation by State command. But if it had recognized CNSD's State action defence, could it have held Italy to be in violation of Article 4 TEU read together with TFEU Article 101? Re-read paras. 53–55.
3. Is *CNSD* consistent with *Ladbroke?* Where is the private autonomous action in *CNSD*?
4. In *Italian matches*, did the producers have sufficient autonomy to be held responsible? Is the problem only that the Italian producers were nationalistic quota-assigners? Will the ministry now set the quotas as well as the prices? Would it have any interest in doing so if it cannot divvy up the market among the Italians? Would a discriminatory allocation by the State violate Articles 18 and 34 TFEU?
5. What does *Cipolla* add to your assessment of the validity of the Italian law?
6. US law is nearly identical in result. A person or firm that merely follows an anti-competitive command of the state (e.g. not to advertise) is protected from antitrust liability by the state action defense; but a state of the US may not delegate to private parties the power (and duty) to fix prices and shield them from federal liability for price fixing.[36]
7. In other respects, also, US law is somewhat similar to EU law on state action and supremacy, but the EU institutions have far broader power than US courts to override anti-competitive state legislation by virtue of the free movement principles. When Congress passed the US antitrust laws, it could have chosen to pre-empt anti-competitive state law that adversely affected interstate commerce, but it did not. Accordingly, subject to the constraint of the commerce

---

35 See E. Fox (2004), 'State action in comparative context: What if *Parker v. Brown* were Italian', in B. Hawk (ed.) (2004), *International Antitrust Law & Policy, Fordham Corporate Law 2003*, New York: Juris, Ch. 19.
36 *California Retail Liquor Dealers Ass'n v. Midcal Aluminum, Inc.*, 445 U.S. 97, 100 S.Ct. 937, 63 L.Ed.2d 233 (1980); *Schwegmann Bros. v. Calvert Distillers Corp.*, 341 U.S. 384, 71 S.Ct. 745, 95 L.Ed. 1035 (1951).

clause in the US Constitution, states of the US may adopt and enforce regulatory statutes that have significant anti-competitive effects.[37] Moreover, antitrust laws of the US states—even law that is more prohibitory than federal antitrust law—is normally valid, and it functions in tandem with federal law.[38] Private parties acting under a lawful but anti-competitive state regime are protected from federal antitrust enforcement as long as the state has clearly articulated its policy that displaces competition with regulation and supervises the private action.[39]

A state may not impose an unreasonable burden on interstate commerce (e.g., discrimination against imports); but seldom is such a burden found when the law applies equally to residents and outsiders.[40] Even a law that gives preference to in-state facilities might be justified where, for example, it is part of an environmental program that internalizes costs.[41]

8. For a survey and analysis of antitrust laws of jurisdictions that reach and may prohibit anti-competitive measures of the nation/state and its subdivisions, see Eleanor Fox and Deborah Healey, When the State Harms Competition – The Role for Competition Law, 79 Antitrust L.J. 769 (2014). The European Union is the leader in this regard.

E. State aid

States are tempted to give money and other benefits to support local firms and to attract other business. Frequently they are asked to favour one competitor, sector or region over another, often to save a failing business and to save jobs. At mid-twentieth century, extensive State support of industry was the norm in Europe. If trade barriers had been removed but State aid flourished, Europe would never have become one common market. Thus, in order to contain State aid and provide transparency for permissible aid, the Treaty included Articles 107 to 109 TFEU. Over time, the control of State aid has evolved into a full-fledged discipline and a peculiar and discrete part of competition enforcement in Europe. Nowadays, it accounts for half of the enforcement activity of the Directorate-General for Competition. This section only offers a high-level presentation of the main principles governing State aid control; for an in-depth presentation, refer to specialized treatises.[42]

---

37 See, e.g., *Exxon Corp. v. Governor of Maryland*, 437 U.S. 117, 98 S.Ct. 2207, 57 L.Ed.2d 91 (1978) (prohibiting oil producers/refiners from operating retail service stations in the state for fear that they would favour their own stations), though, in recent years, the Supreme Court has taken a more aggressive view of pre-emption.
38 *California v. ARC America Corp.*, 490 U.S. 93, 109 S.Ct. 1661, 104 L.Ed.2d 86 (1989) (allowing California to authorize indirect purchaser lawsuits even though federal law disallows them).
39 *Southern Motor Carriers Rate Conference, Inc. v. United States*, 471 U.S. 48, 105 S.Ct. 1721, 85 L.Ed.2d 36 (1985).
40 Compare *Exxon Corp. v. Governor of Maryland*, above, with *West Lynn Creamery v. Healy*, 512 U.S. 186, 114 S.Ct. 2205, 129 L.Ed.2d 157 (1994).
41 *United Haulers v. Oneida-Herkimer Solid Waste Mgmt Authority*, 550 U.S. 330, 127 S.Ct. 1786, 167 L.Ed.2d 655 (2007).
42 Including C. Quigley, *European State Aid Law and Policy* (2015), 3rd edn, Oxford: Hart Publishing, 888 p.

1. Notion of State aid

State aid is 'any aid granted by a Member State or through State resources in any form whatsoever. . . .' Historically, direct subsidy has been the most common form of aid, but State aid also includes exemptions from fiscal or social charges, credit guarantees, credit at low interest, credit or equity investments that would not be available in the market, payment by the State of a higher price to domestic suppliers, sale by the State below the market price to domestic buyers, assumption by the State of part of an undertaking's risk, tax concessions (e.g., to encourage the takeover of an ailing firm), and virtually any other benefit conferred by the State on terms that would not be acceptable to a private investor.

a. State aid criteria and ex-ante review

Article 107(1) TFEU declares that any State aid that 'distorts or threatens to distort competition by favouring certain undertakings or the production of certain goods shall, insofar as it affects trade between Member States, be incompatible with the common market.' Hence, the notion of State aid requires: (i) an intervention by the State or through State resources; (ii) that is liable to affect trade between Member States; (iii) confers a selective advantage on the recipient(s); and (iv) distorts or threatens to distort competition.[43]

The Treaty, however, gives the Commission the power to approve State aid for the reasons listed in Article 107(2) and (3) TFEU. To obtain approval, Member States must notify to the Commission their plans to grant State aid, prior to implementation. The Commission may then authorize the aid without conditions, authorize the aid after agreed modifications, or open formal proceedings, after which it might prohibit the aid from being granted. The Commission must give notice to concerned parties to submit their comments.[44]

If the Commission finds that State aid is not compatible with the internal market or that aid is being misused, it must direct the State to abolish or alter the aid within a specified time period, or to recover aid unlawfully granted. If the Member State fails to comply, the Commission or an interested Member

---

[43] For a detailed discussion, see Commission Notice on the notion of State aid as referred to in Article 107(1) TFEU [2016] O.J. C 262/1.
[44] See Regulation 2015/1589/EU laying down detailed rules for the application of Article 108 TFEU [2015] O.J. L 248/9.

State may refer the matter to the Court of Justice. If aid is granted prior to its approval, in breach of the notification requirement and standstill principle, i.e., it is unlawful aid, its suspension and/or recovery can also be sought in front of national courts.

b. *Compatible aid*

The grounds to approve State aid are set out in paras. (2) and (3) of Article 107 TFEU.

Paragraph (2) lists forms of aid that 'shall be compatible' with the internal market. Aid that shall be compatible under paragraph (2) is:

(a) aid of a social character granted to individual consumers without discrimination as to origin of products,
(b) damage relief in natural disasters or exceptional occurrences, and
(c) aid to the economy of certain areas of the Federal Republic of Germany affected by the division of Germany insofar as it is required to compensate for economic disadvantages caused by that division.

Paragraph (3) specifies aid that the Commission *may* declare compatible with the common market. Frequently invoked by Member States, this section empowers the Commission to declare compatible aid in the following five categories:

(a) aid to promote the economic development of areas where the standard of living is abnormally low or where there is serious underemployment';
(b) aid to promote the execution of an important project of common European interest or to remedy a serious disturbance in the economy of a Member State';
(c) 'aid to promote cultural and heritage conservation where such aid does not affect trading conditions and competition in the Community to an extent that is contrary to the common interest'; and
(d) other categories added by decision of the Council.

To eliminate red tape and to concentrate on the cases that matter most, the Commission has enacted block exemption regulations that eliminate the need for notification if certain conditions are met. The General Block Exemption Regulation 651/2014[45] covers a wide array of State aid objectives, including

---

45 Commission Regulation 651/2014/EU of 17 June 2014 declaring certain categories of aid compatible with the internal market in application of Articles 107 and 108 of the Treaty [2014] O.J. L 187/1.

aid for environmental protection, risk capital, R&D and innovation, newly created small enterprises, and broadband rollout. The *de minimis* Regulation 1407/2013[46] also exempts Member States from the notification requirement for small amounts of aid. Various horizontal and sector-specific rules and guidelines clarify the Commission's policy to approve different forms of aid.

c. *The market economy operator test*

There is considerable case law on what is a State aid. Although Member States may not favour firms by using State aid, the Treaty does not prevent a State from participating in the economy as long as it acts as a 'market economy operator'. The State can therefore be a shareholder and participate in capital increases without breaching Article 107 TFEU if the transaction is at market rate.

In its progressive privatization of Electricité de France ('EDF'), the former electricity monopoly, France restructured EDF's accounts. It converted a debt it was owed by EDF into equity. The transaction had fiscal consequences; EDF avoided paying a tax by incorporating the debt into capital. France argued that this was neutral from a State aid perspective; it could have requested EDF to pay the tax and later make a capital injection to the amount of the tax. In other words, France argued, it acted as a market economy operator and provided no advantage to EDF.

The Commission disagreed. It found that it was not possible to apply the market economy operator test to a fiscal operation, since taxation is the exclusive province of the State and it is not possible to compare its fiscal policy with that of a hypothetical private investor.

The Court of Justice annulled the Commission decision in *EDF v. Commission*.[47] It recalled that Article 107(1) TFEU covers State aid 'in any form whatsoever.' The form of the measure does not matter, only its effects do. Therefore, the Commission must take a global view of the measures adopted and assess their overall effects. A Member State that wishes to rely on the market economy operator principle needs to demonstrate, using evidence prepared before or at the moment of its investment decision, that it was rational for it do so as an investor. Policy considerations such as social or

---

46 Commission Regulation 1407/2013/EU of 18 December 2013 on the application of Articles 107 and 108 of the Treaty on the Functioning of the European Union to de minimis aid [2013] O.J. L 352/1.
47 Case C-124/10 P, *EDF v. Commission*, EU:C:2012:318.

environmental objectives cannot be taken into account here (although they might be relevant in assessment of the compatibility of the aid).

d. *Public service compensation*

Does a privatized transport enterprise receive State aid when the State continues to cover the costs of public service obligations? Altmark Trans sought to organize public transport in a new East German länder. In *Altmark Trans GmbH*,[48] the Court of Justice held that public subsidies for transportation services are not State aids, and therefore do not require notification and justification, where they constitute proportionate compensation for the discharge of public service obligations (known as 'services of general economic interest' or 'SIEG'). Such subsidies fall outside of Article 107 TFEU if the following conditions are satisfied: (1) the recipient must be required to discharge clearly defined public service obligations, (2) the formula for calculating the compensation must be established beforehand in an objective and transparent matter, (3) the compensation must not exceed what is necessary to discharge the public service, and (4) either the undertaking must be chosen in a public procurement procedure or the level of compensation needed to fulfil the public service obligation must have been determined on the basis of the costs of a typical, well-run undertaking.

Given the importance of public services in the economy of most Member States and the ubiquity of compensations thereof, the Commission has elaborated detailed rules based on the *Altmark* principles in order to enable States to self-assess their practices and increase legal certainty. The SIEG package includes Commission communications, a decision and a Regulation setting forth specific de minimis thresholds for the compensation of public services.[49]

e. *State v. private resources*

Germany decided to promote windmill energy. German law obliged all regional public electricity suppliers to buy windmill power as a portion of their energy and to pay for the wind-generated electricity at a price higher than the price of other energy; and it obliged upstream electricity suppliers to pay to the regional suppliers a part of the extra costs. PreussenElektra, an

---

48 Case C-280/00, *Altmark Trans GmbH and Regierungspräsidium Magdeburg v. Nahverkehrsgesellschaft Altmark GmbH, and Oberbundesanwalt beim Bundesverwaltungsgericht* [2007] ECR I-7747, EU:C:2003:415 ('*Altmark Trans GmbH*').
49 Available at: http://ec.europa.eu/competition/state_aid/legislation/sgei.html (accessed 12 June 2017).

upstream supplier, tried to avoid paying part of the extra costs of windmill energy on the grounds that its supplementary payment to the regional supplier (Schleswag, which happened to be Preussen's own subsidiary) would constitute an illegal subsidy of wind energy. The Court rejected the argument. It ruled that PreussenElektra's supplementary payment, although commanded by the State, was merely a private payment and did not take the mantle of German aid.[50]

Why wasn't the supplementary payment in fact a subsidy? Did this interpretation bless an end run around Article 107 TFEU? Could Preussen and Schleswag sue Germany for maintaining a State measure that restrained trade by putting them at a competitive disadvantage vis-à-vis Electricité de France and others in violation of Article 34 or 35 TFEU?

Consider then the case of Pearle, a company trading optical equipment in the Netherlands that sought to obtain the refund of levies imposed by the Central Industry Board for Skilled Trade ('the Board'), a trade association governed by public law, to finance a collective advertising campaign for opticians. The Board exercised statutory delegated powers as the governing body of various trading professions, and its by-laws were approved by a State entity. Supported by the Commission, Pearle claimed that the advertising campaign financed by the levies amounted to unlawful State aid because it occurred through a body designated by the State and benefited selected businesses. On preliminary reference, the Court of Justice denied because the advertising campaign was not funded by resources made available by the State but rather by levies earmarked for the organization of the advertising campaign and paid by the beneficiaries thereof. 'Since the costs incurred by the public body for the purpose of that campaign were offset in full by the levies imposed on the undertakings benefiting therefrom', no advantage was granted that constituted 'an additional burden for the State or that body.'[51]

f. *Selectivity*

Many State aid cases revolve around the determination of whether the State measure in question is selective or not, and can thus result in a selective advantage. This is notably because the condition of distortion of competition in the context of State aid control is largely presumed whenever the State measure gives an advantage to its beneficiary/-ies in relation to their competitors. In other words, the notion of distortion of competition under

---

50 Case C-379/98, *PreussenElektra AG v. Schhleswag AG* [2001] ECR I-2099, EU:C:2001:160.
51 Case C-345/02, *Pearle BV* [2004] ECR I-7139, EU:C:2004:448, para. 36.

EU State aid law can be equated with that of harm to competitors, which is markedly different than the interpretation of that notion in the fields of antitrust or merger control.

In brief, the assessment of the notion of selectivity requires a determination whether a particular legal regime or national measure is such as to 'favour certain undertakings or the production of certain goods over other undertakings which, in the light of the objective pursued by that regime, are in a comparable factual and legal situation and who accordingly suffer different treatment that can, in essence, be classified as discriminatory.'[52] In turn, the Commission and the EU courts have construed the notion of selectivity broadly. Selectivity is deemed established when an aid is granted to one specific company or a category of companies depending on, e.g., its size (large undertakings v. SMEs[53]), its type of business (manufacturing v. services), its sector of activity (textile, transport, steel, etc.), its geographical location (particular region within a Member State), or its date of incorporation (such as newly created companies). Likewise, selectivity can derive from the scope of the measure itself (*de jure*), or from its practical effects (*de facto*).

The distinction between general and selective State measures is particularly arduous in relation to tax advantages. Generally, although not involving a direct transfer of State resources, national measures of a fiscal nature may procure a selective advantage if they place the addressees thereof in a more favourable position than other taxpayers. In order to classify a national tax measure as selective, the Court of Justice has held that the Commission must begin by identifying the ordinary or 'normal' tax system applicable in the Member State in question, and thereafter demonstrate that the tax measure is a derogation from that ordinary system and thereby differentiates between operators that are in a comparable factual and legal situation, 'in the light of the objective pursued by that ordinary tax system.'[54] How to then determine the ordinary tax system against which the existence of a derogation must be assessed?

In *World Duty Free Group*,[55] the Court of Justice considered the selectivity of a provision of Spanish corporate tax law whereby the goodwill resulting from the acquisition by an undertaking taxable in Spain of a shareholding of at least

---

52 See, e.g., Joined Cases C-106 and C-107/09 P, *Commission and Spain v. Government of Gibraltar and United Kingdom* [2011] ECR I-11113, EU:C:2011:732, paras. 75 and 101.
53 Small to medium-sized enterprises.
54 See, e.g., Joined Cases C-78 and C-80/08, *Paint Graphos and Others* [2011] ECR I-7611, EU:C:2011:550, para. 49.
55 Joined Cases C-20 and C-21/15 P, *World Duty Free Group and Others* EU:C:2016:981.

5% in a 'foreign company', thus to the exclusion of companies established in Spain, was deductible from the taxable base in the form of an amortization to the extent that the interest in question was retained for an uninterrupted period of at least one year. The General Court found no selectivity because the measure was not applicable to an identifiable group of undertakings with specific characteristics. The Court of Justice overturned:

> 68   It is apparent from the judgements under appeal that the Commission relied, in the contested decisions, in order to establish that the measure at issue was selective, on the fact that the consequence of that measure was that resident undertakings were not treated equally. Pursuant to that measure, only resident undertakings who acquired at least 5% shareholdings in foreign companies could, under certain conditions, qualify for the tax advantage at issue, whereas resident undertakings making the acquisition of such a shareholding in undertakings taxable in Spain could not obtain that advantage, notwithstanding the fact that, according to the Commission, they were in a comparable situation in the light of the objective pursued by the ordinary Spanish tax system.
>
> 69   However, the General Court considered that the measure at issue, on the grounds that it did not affect any particular category of undertakings or the production of any particular category of goods, that it was applicable regardless of the nature of an undertaking's activity and that it was accessible, a priori or potentially, to all undertakings that wanted to acquire shareholdings of at least 5% in foreign companies and that held those shareholdings without interruption for at least one year, had to be regarded not as a selective measure but as a general measure . . . In so doing, the General Court erred in law.
>
> 70   Thus, . . . the General Court held that, if the condition relating to the selectivity of a national measure relevant to the recognition of State aid, in respect of a measure that is a priori accessible to any undertaking, is to be satisfied, it is always necessary that a particular category of undertakings, who are exclusively favoured by the measure concerned and who can be distinguished by reason of specific properties, common to them and characteristic of them, be identified.
>
> 71   However, the imposition of such a supplementary requirement to identify a particular category of undertakings, additional to the analytical method applicable to selectivity in tax matters that may be deduced from the Court's settled case-law, which essentially involves ascertaining whether the exclusion of certain operators from the benefit of a tax advantage that arises from a measure derogating from an ordinary tax system constitutes discrimination with respect to those operators, cannot be inferred from the Court's case-law . . .

The Court of Justice further added that the selective nature of a measure is not affected by the fact that the number of undertakings able to claim entitlement under that measure is very large, that these undertakings belong to various economic sectors or that the measure apply to undertakings regardless of their activity; what matters is that the measure is discriminatory.

* * *

The implications of the Court of Justice's judgement in *World Duty Free Group* are potentially very significant. Why is it so? Consider the fact that the selective advantage in that case resulted from the mere fact of carrying out an investment, that is in a foreign *v.* a domestic company. Consider also the fact that Germany, Ireland and Spain intervened in support of the defendants and against the Commission.

According to the standard set by the Court of Justice in *World Duty Free Group*, which tax measure could still be deemed general, and not selective? Is the selectivity criterion still meaningful in your view to determine whether a tax measure qualifies as State aid? What are the practical consequences of this broad definition of selectivity for the system of State aid control?

Still, in view of the measure at issue, what kind of justification would you offer for the outcome of the Court of Justice's reasoning? How would such justification relate to the socio-historical context of EU competition policy and State aid policy in particular? Revisit this question after reviewing the next section.

2. State aid policy

As noted, State aid control is a major facet of EU competition policy and developed into a highly technical and somewhat distinct area of practice. It played a particularly important role in the wake of the financial crisis commencing in 2008, as nations were tempted to pour subsidies into 'their own' banks at the expense of cross-border competition. The following remarks of Competition Commissioners Joaquín Almunia and Margrethe Vestager highlight the place of State aid policy in the EU and in the world.

Competition, State Aid and Subsidies in the European Union
Joaquín Almunia, Vice President and Commissioner for Competition
9th Global Forum on Competition, Paris, 18 February 2010

Ladies and gentlemen,

I'm very pleased to be here today in only the second week as Competition Commissioner. . . .

My key priority for the next five years is the same as it was under my previous responsibility as Commissioner for Economic and Financial Affairs: to help overcome the current financial and economic crisis and ensure that Europe emerges better equipped for balanced and sustainable growth and more jobs. This is an ambition which we all share for our respective countries—and the reason why we are meeting here at the OECD, to work together to achieve this ambition.

This is also the aim of the proposals the new European Commission is preparing for what we call 'The EU 2020 Strategy': to lay the foundations for a more dynamic, knowledge-based, socially inclusive and greener economy that is both sustainable and fair.

I believe that competition policy has a vital role to play in this regard, by making markets work better, for the benefit of business and consumers. . . .

Competition policy is sometimes thought of as only addressing the behaviour of companies and businesses: cartels or abuses of market power, or mergers whose impact on competition needs to be assessed. But State subsidies to business ('State aid' in EU Treaty language) can also distort competition. A review of the impact of subsidies is, I believe, an important aspect of competition policy.

Subsidies are of course an essential tool for policy makers and governments. Government measures to support the financial system and other sectors of the economy over the past 18 months are a case in point. It is widely acknowledged that the money governments poured or committed in support of financial institutions prevented a catastrophic collapse of the global banking system.

On top of the immediate reactions needed to avoid a meltdown of the economy, in normal times subsidies can help remedy a market failure, promote investment in environmentally friendly technologies, or foster economic and social development in a particularly depressed region. These are important public policy objectives—and it is crucial to ensure that governments have the best-designed tools available to achieve these objectives.

Our aim in recent years, before the crisis emerged, has been to ensure that subsidies are targeted towards horizontal objectives such as these, and to prevent subsidies that merely keep inefficient firms on life-support. In the mid-1990s, around 50 per cent of government subsidies to industry and services in the EU were earmarked for horizontal objectives as opposed to individual bailouts. By 2008 this figure had risen to nearly 90 per cent.

Overall, government subsidies in the EU amounted to just over 0.5 per cent of EU GDP in the period 2004–2008, excluding measures to address the financial and economic crisis. Over the longer term subsidies are on a downward trend, since they are down from nearly 1 per cent of EU GDP in the 1990s.

The EU system for reviewing State subsidies

What we have in the EU is a system that requires the European Commission to review State subsidies to business and to assess their impact on competition. The fundamental principles were laid down in 1957, as a necessary condition to achieving a common market in goods and services in the EU, and remain unchanged today in the new Lisbon Treaty. A single market across the EU requires a level playing field between businesses in different Member States, so that our review of subsidies looks not only at the impact on competition between businesses in a given country, but also at the impact on cross-border competition.

What we do is essentially carry out a balancing exercise, weighing up the efficiency and equity benefits that are expected to result from a subsidy, against the negative effects the subsidy might have on competition in the EU and on trade between EU Member States.

Specifically we consider whether the government's objective in providing the subsidy does not run counter to the common interest of EU Member States— including growth, employment, regional development, the environment, or research and development.

One element we take into account is whether the subsidy addresses a market failure. For instance, we recognise that small businesses find it difficult to access risk capital because of high transaction costs to assess small projects compared to the expected gains from investment. So subsidies to facilitate access to risk capital may be acceptable. Similarly, we are happy to encourage subsidies for the extension of broadband to remote regions, which is not profitable under normal market circumstances. Likewise, we allow subsidies to cover part of the costs of a research project knowing that markets are not always ready to take on the full risk of research especially when the profitability horizon is very long.

We check that, in practice, the subsidy will help achieve that objective, that it creates the right incentives for companies to adjust their behaviour. We also check that the subsidy is proportionate, i.e. that the same adjustments to company behaviour could not be obtained with lower subsidy.

This balancing exercise, based on an economic assessment of the impact of the measure, is carried out before the subsidy is implemented. It can lead to the Commission imposing conditions to minimise the distortion of competition, for instance, a reduction in the amount of the subsidy. This helps ensure that subsidy measures do not have an unduly distortive effect on competition in the EU. It also gives Member States an insight into the effectiveness of a planned subsidy and whether it will give value for money to the taxpayer.

Of course, what we don't do—thankfully—is review every single subsidy measure adopted by EU Member States. Following recent reforms, far fewer measures require notification to the Commission. Some of them do not distort competition or trade between Member States, others benefit from a general exemption laid down by regulation, or a general scheme (for instance for aid to research and development, development of small businesses, training and the creation of new jobs, etc). The Commission only carries out an in-depth, individual, review of those large subsidies which have the potential to be really harmful to competition. And what I want to do is to make sure our procedures for notification and review are as simple and streamlined as possible, so as to keep the bureaucratic burden to a minimum.

However, where we find that a State subsidy is unlawful—that is, it violates our rules for its acceptance—it must be recovered in full. That is the only effective way of remedying the distortion of competition created by the subsidy.

Why it works

I've mentioned before the role of State subsidies in the global financial crisis. Let me come back to this issue.

Early action by the European Commission helped ensure a common approach by Member States to financial sector bail-outs. Member States may have adopted different measures—those which they felt were best suited to their respective market situation—whether guarantee schemes, recapitalisation measures, or impaired asset relief measures, or a mixture of these. But the European Commission required that all of these measures complied with certain fundamental principles—non-discriminatory access to national schemes, subsidies limited to what was necessary, mechanisms to prevent abuse of State support, restructuring measures for certain financial institutions that received large amounts of aid.

This helped keep to a minimum any distortions of competition between banks within and across national borders, and helped preserve the integrity of the EU internal market. It prevented costly and damaging subsidy races between Member States, with each trying to outdo the other in an attempt to prevent business moving away.

Going forward, EU policy on reviewing State subsidies—notably through the restructuring measures being agreed as a condition of approving bank subsidies—is helping rebuild viable financial institutions which are able to carry out the essential function of providing finance to the real economy.

Reviewing subsidies at national, supranational and international level?

Naturally, the EU perspective on the control of subsidies is closely associated with its powers and role as a supranational body, pursuing common EU objectives such as a level playing field for business and the internal market.

But the underlying principle—that subsidies should not unfairly distort competition between businesses so that companies can compete on merit to the benefit of consumers—is equally important at national level and on national markets for goods or services. Creating or supporting a national champion creates domestic casualties too—those companies that are not chosen for government support. Measures to support inward investment may result in obvious rewards—but it may be worth assessing for just how long those measures continue to produce net benefits, in particular if such support is open-ended.

National regimes for reviewing State subsidies do exist—for instance in Spain, my own country, the national competition authority has the power to issue opinions on subsidies granted by the regions or the central government. On the other hand, countries that are candidates to join the EU are required to set up systems for reviewing State subsidies. One of them, Croatia, has a system that mirrors the EU system—with the national competition authority entrusted with the relevant powers. Looking further afield, Russia also has a system of subsidy control and the Mexican competition authority has powers to deliver opinions on the impact of subsidies on inter-State trade.

I believe that there is scope for individual countries outside the EU to consider adopting a system of controlling State subsidies, for the benefit of business environment and quality of public policies.

What about the international level?

All of us here today recognise the benefits of open markets and the downsides of protectionism. Subsidies can be an instrument of protectionism, countering the benefits of trade liberalisation. The WTO rules on subsidies for goods can play a role in removing the most harmful subsidies—but no rule can be applied properly without transparency. So I fully endorse the OECD ministerial conclusions of last June which State that government measures to support industry must be transparent and WTO consistent. Transparency helps contain protectionist measures by opening them up to public scrutiny—and helps ensure a level playing field for business in markets across the world.

With this in mind, I welcome the initiative by WTO Director General Pascal Lamy to report quarterly on measures adopted by G20 countries to counter the crisis. This is particularly important since the G20 is leading the drive towards a coordinated route out of the crisis for the world economy. In a move which underlines the importance we attach to transparency, the EU has already introduced this principle and reports regularly on all Member State actions, regardless of their G20 status. The next report will be published in early March. I look forward for other countries to follow that lead.

Conclusion * * *

The EU rules on government subsidies are a key element of EU competition policy in that they help maintain a level playing field for business within Member States and across Europe. They have proved their worth in the context of the financial and economic crisis, helping avoid damaging subsidy races between EU Member States and minimising the distortions of competition resulting from large-scale government bail-outs for financial institutions.

But rules on government subsidies are not an exclusive EU issue. They have a place in all competition regimes—whether national, federal, supranational or international. They help maintain the level playing field between businesses implanted within a country, across regions, and across national borders. They help open up markets to international trade. Ultimately, they help governments assess the effectiveness of proposed subsidy measures, and help channel funds to where they are the most necessary and can deliver the most benefit to taxpayers.

The EU State Aid Rules: Working Together for Fair Competition
Margrethe Vestager, Commissioner for Competition
High Level Forum on State Aid Modernisation, Brussels, 3 June 2016

Businesses need State aid rules to protect them from unfair competition.

But they don't want our rules to slow down the delivery of support that doesn't hurt competition. . . . Less than one in ten State aid measures now come to us for a decision. The rest fall under the general block exemption regulation. . . .

But even with the best intentions, we can't always be sure whether State aid is doing good. I am often asked, does taxpayers' money actually deliver faster development in our poorest regions, or do companies just pocket the money, and go on doing exactly what they were doing before? . . .

State aid and corporate taxation

One of the biggest threats to fair competition is when multinationals don't pay their fair share of tax.

The Commission has made action against tax avoidance one of its top regulatory priorities . . . Because others have to pay more, when multinationals don't pay their share.

But tax avoidance also hurts competition. When a government lets a company avoid paying its share, that company gains just as if it received a handful of cash.

I know that's not news to you: State aid is about the benefit received, not the form it takes.

What is new about our work on State aid and tax is that, over the last three years, it has become clear that general rules and schemes are not the only way that governments hand out tax benefits. In fact, you often don't know what benefits a company has, until you look at the tax rulings it has received.

We've therefore looked at more than a thousand tax rulings, to see if they gave special treatment to the companies that received them.

Not because we think rulings are a bad thing. The vast majority of them don't give us any concern at all. We know tax codes can be complicated, and that many authorities simply use tax rulings to give companies clarity on what they can expect to be taxed. This is about giving legal certainty, in the interests of the companies and other taxpayers.

Applying the arm's length principle

But our investigations show that tax rulings are also sometimes used in other ways: to grant individual companies a benefit that's not available to others.

How do we know if that's the case? The principle is very simple.

Governments should treat multinationals in the same way as companies that operate individually.

Local companies have to pay the market price when they buy a service. They don't have the option to do anything else.

So when one company in a group buys from other group companies, it should report transfer prices that come as close as possible to the market price. This is where the arm's length principle comes in: it is the best way to be sure you're treating every company fairly.

I know it's not always easy to decide what the market price should be. It's often a good idea to just look at what prices are actually paid in the market. But even that can be misused to support tax avoidance. We've seen tax rulings that claim to use this method even though there's actually no market to compare against. . . .

The basic principle is simple. What really matters from a State aid angle is that the transfer pricing methodology used to calculate the profits of a group leads to a reliable approximation of a market-based price.

To see if that is the case for a particular ruling, you have to look at all the details. But our investigation shows that some methods are more often linked to aggressive tax planning than others.

For example, so-called 'one-sided' methods don't even try to split a company's profits between the countries that might have a claim to tax them. Instead, one country simply works out the taxable profit based on an indicator, such as operating expenses. But those figures can be a poor indicator of how successful a company is, so using them to set the taxable profit is only appropriate in a limited number of cases.

Of course, working out the right market price isn't straightforward. It's often a question of finding a reasonable approximation. And we don't object to that, as long as the approximation is as precise as it can be under the circumstances.

The Commission is not a tax authority. We are not there to reassess the work of national tax authorities. Tax rulings which reflect economic reality and actually make sense are not an issue for us.

But we have seen some examples of unrealistic transfer prices, without any sign that the authorities had a convincing reason to accept them. That's where State aid can be involved, and where the Commission does have to act.

Notice on the Notion of Aid: infrastructure

Of course, when a business doesn't have any rivals, you don't need the State aid rules to protect competition.

And our Notice on the Notion of Aid tries to make sure everyone knows when that's the case. That way, governments don't need to hold back on investment for fear of breaking the State aid rules.

Take infrastructure, for example.

Europe is full of entrepreneurs, with new ideas to make our lives better and create new jobs.

But they can't reach their potential without the right infrastructure. You can't provide the latest cloud computing services if there isn't a good broadband network. You can't ship your products across Europe without good rail, road and river networks. . . .

Some of those projects do affect competition. Many companies have built broadband networks with private money, for example. So when States invest in those networks, we have to make sure it doesn't discourage private companies from investing.

But that doesn't mean every infrastructure investment is State aid. If you look at roads, or railways, or water networks, you find that State investment is often the only type of investment. And it often doesn't make much sense to think of rail tracks or roads competing directly with each other.

So we don't need to worry too much that those investments will affect competition. We just need to get them done. As quickly and as efficiently as we can.

So our Notice makes clear when infrastructure investment isn't State aid.

And it makes clear that just because you run an infrastructure that was built with State aid, like an airport, doesn't necessarily mean you – the operator – get aid yourself. You just need to make sure you pay a market price for it. This is what we have the EU procurement rules for.

This should help to get investments going. I'd encourage the working group on State aid and Infrastructure to discuss that in more detail. . . .

Conclusion

For me, it's important to be clear when we think State support doesn't affect competition.

Because the State aid rules aren't supposed to be an obstacle. They're supposed to be an enabler, of fair competition and therefore of investment, growth and jobs.

Of course, we have to be open to the possibility that new situations might call for State aid. Take the area of energy for example.

Competition policy in energy markets has a very important role to play here. By making sure that dominant positions are not abused, that renewables compete in the market, and that electricity capacity mechanisms are introduced only if they are really needed, competiton policy helps keeping overall energy costs under control.

But even with strong enforcement of competition policy, total energy costs for energy intensive businesses might still be too high.

Today, governments pay for many parts of their energy policy through charges on companies' electricity bills. Those charges help pay, for example, for windmills and solar plants and combined heat and power stations that improve our energy efficiency by using heat that would otherwise be wasted.

To help make that support sustainable, our State aid rules allow energy-intensive industries like steelmaking to be exempted from charges that support renewable energy.

But as energy policy has become more ambitious, the other charges that companies have to pay have gone up. This means that we have to keep asking ourselves if the balance is right, or if energy intensive businesses should be exempted from paying some of the charges on their electricity bills that pay for energy policy.

Because that's what the State aid rules are for. To make sure business can get help when it's needed, without hurting competition.

NOTES AND QUESTIONS

1. Article 107(1) prohibits State aid that 'distorts or threatens to distort competition by favouring certain [firms or goods]. . . .' What does 'distort[ing] competition' mean? Does the phrase mean the same thing in Article 107(1) as in Article 101(1) TFEU?
2. Do you agree that State aid normally 'distorts competition'? In what sense? Does it harm competition from the viewpoint of consumers? From the viewpoint of competitors? From the

vantage of protecting the competition process and the right to compete on the merits? Can State aid intensify competition? How can or should the Commission and the Court deal with pro-competitive effects (lower prices, more business formation) of State aids?

3. The US, in contrast with the EU, has no national subsidy control, except as required by the General Agreement on Tariffs and Trade/World Trade Organization, and except for prohibition of discriminatory subsidies that impose a burden on interstate commerce.[56] US law reflects the belief that freedom of state and local governments to grant subsidies or other benefits, whether to compete for business establishment or to prop up business in financial difficulty, is a healthy form of state autonomy and competition.[57] Are there good reasons why Europe has State aid control and the US does not?

4. Firms in Europe frequently challenge a grant of State aid to their rivals, and typically they are accorded standing to do so. Thus, when Ford and Volkswagen set up a joint venture in Portugal to make multi-purpose vehicles—a new endeavour for both joint venture partners—Matra, the dominant maker of MPVs, complained that Portugal's grant of infrastructure aid to the new entrant violated Article 107 TFEU, and that the joint venture agreement itself violated Articles 101 and 102 TFEU in part because the aid distorted competition. (How would Matra argue this point?) Matra lost on the merits; both the aid and the joint venture were allowed.[58]

Why would a firm challenge a grant of aid to its rival? Why, in particular, would a dominant firm challenge a grant of aid to a new entrant? Is the complainant likely to be complaining about harm to competition, about unfair advantages, or about competition itself? Would buyers of the products produced by a subsidized firm ever have an interest in challenging a State aid? Would it be accurate to view rivals' complaints about grants of State aid as complaints about *unfair* competition?

5. Explain the relationship between the State aid body of law and the antitrust (Articles 101 and 102 TFEU) and merger control bodies of law. While there are many differences, Europe took advantage of the synergies of its laws in the financial crisis of 2008, using its combined powers of subsidy control, merger control and restructuring, and doing so on an emergency basis.[59]

Note on tax rulings and Apple

Since 2013, the Commission has been investigating allegations of favourable tax treatment given to certain companies by means of so-called 'tax rulings', i.e., the advanced clarification of tax arrangements applicable to the companies in question. By mid-2016, that investigation had led to the opening of formal proceedings against the Netherlands for aid granted to Starbucks, Ireland for aid granted to Apple, Luxembourg for aids granted to Fiat, McDonald's and Amazon, as well as against Belgium for operating an excess

---

56 See *West Lynn Creamery v. Healy*, 512 U.S. 186, 114 S.Ct. 2205, 129 L.Ed.2d 157 (1994).
57 See *Camps Newfound/Owatonna, Inc. v. Town of Harrison*, 520 U.S. 564, 589, 117 S.Ct. 1590, 137 L.Ed.2d 852 (1997); and see Justice Scalia, dissenting, at 605–608.
58 See Case T-17/93, *Matra Hachette SA v. Commission* [1994] ECR II-595, EU:T:1994:89.
59 See N. Kroes, 'Competition law in an economic crisis', Opening address at the 13th Annual Competition Conference of the International Bar Association, Fiesole, 11 September 2009 (SPEECH/09/385). For a discussion, see also D. Gerard (2009), 'EC competition law enforcement at grips with the financial crisis: Flexibility on the means, consistency in the principles', *Concurrences*, **1**, 46.

profit exemption scheme. As expressed by Commissioner Vestager in the speech excerpted above, the overall concern is that Member States artificially reduce certain companies' tax base and overall burden by means of rulings relying on transfer prices and/or allocation of profits not reflecting economic reality, with the effect of underestimating taxable profits.

The Commission is not shy to present its investigation into Member States' tax ruling practices as part of an overall plan for 'fair and effective taxation' aimed at tackling tax avoidance (and, conversely, fiscal dumping). But it has also attracted criticisms for its extensive interpretation of core State aid concepts, such as that of 'advantage' and 'selectivity'. How does the Commission establish selectivity in relation to the application of domestic corporate taxes by means of tax rulings? What is the system of reference that would allow the identification of selected beneficiaries? Is it relevant that transfer pricing issues arise only for multinational companies? Is the 'arm's length principle' mentioned by Commission Vestager useful and legally sound? Is the Commission right to compare Member States' practices against a certain 'realistic' counterfactual? Isn't the Commission confusing the notions of advantage and selectivity?

In the most contentious case, the Commission ordered Apple to reimburse €13 billion (plus interest) to Ireland due to the alleged 'artificial allocation' of Apple's EU profits.[60] The Commission took issue with two tax rulings issued by Ireland to Apple in 1991 and 2007 allowing it to allocate almost all of its sales profits to a 'head office' that existed only on paper instead of to its subsidiaries established in Ireland, namely Apple Sales International (ASI) and Apple Operations Europe (AOE), thus avoiding paying taxes on a very large share of its earnings. The allocation of profits to that 'head office', with virtually no employees or physical existence, had allowed Apple's effective corporate tax rate to be set as law as 1% in 2003 and 0.005% in 2014, compared to the 12.5% tax rate provided for in Ireland's corporate tax legislation. Relevant excerpts of the Commission decision follow.

> 220 .... It is ... well-established that, for a measure to be categorised as State aid, there must, first, be an intervention by the State or through State resources; second, the intervention must be liable to affect trade between Member States; third, it must confer a selective advantage on an undertaking and, fourth, it must distort or threaten to distort competition.

---

60 See Commission Decision of 30 August 2016, State Aid SA.38373 (2014/C) (ex 2014/NN) (ex 2014/CP) – Ireland, Alleged aid to Apple; appeal pending in Case T-778/16, *Ireland v. Commission* and Case T-101/17, *Apple Sales International and Apple Operations Europe v. Commission*.

221. As regards the first condition for a finding of aid, the contested tax rulings were issued by Irish Revenue, which is the tax administration of the Irish State. . . . The contested tax rulings are therefore imputable to Ireland. As regards the financing of the measures through State resources, the Court of Justice has consistently held that a measure by which the public authorities grant certain undertakings a tax exemption which, although not involving a positive transfer of State resources, places the persons to whom it applies in a more favourable financial situation than other taxpayers constitutes State aid. . . . the Commission will demonstrate that the contested tax rulings result in a lowering of ASI's and AOE's tax liability in Ireland by deviating from the tax that those undertakings would otherwise have been obliged to pay under the ordinary rules of taxation of corporate profit in Ireland. By renouncing tax revenue that Ireland would otherwise have been entitled to collect from ASI and AOE under those rules, the contested tax rulings gives rise to a loss of State resources.

222. As regards the second condition for a finding of aid, ASI and AOE are part of the Apple group, a globally active multinational group operating in all Member States, so that any aid in their favour is liable to affect intra-Union trade. Similarly, a measure granted by the State is considered to distort or threaten to distort competition when it is liable to improve the competitive position of its recipient as compared to other undertakings with which it competes. . . . To the extent the contested tax rulings relieve ASI and AOE of a tax liability they would otherwise have been obliged to pay under the ordinary rules of taxation of corporate profit in Ireland, the aid granted under those rulings constitutes operating aid, in that it relieves those undertakings from a charge that they would normally have had to bear in their day-to-day management or normal activities. The Court of Justice has consistently held that operating aid in principle distorts competition, so that any aid granted to ASI and AOE should be considered to distort or threaten to distort competition by strengthening the financial position of ASI, AOE and the Apple group on the markets on which they operate. In particular, by relieving those undertakings of a tax liability they would otherwise have had to bear and which competing undertakings have to carry, the contested tax rulings free up resources for those undertakings to invest in their business operations, thereby distorting competition on the market, so that the fourth condition for a finding of aid is also fulfilled in this case.

223. As regards the third condition for a finding of aid, an advantage for the purposes of Article 107(1) of the Treaty is any economic benefit that an undertaking would not have obtained under normal market conditions, that is to say, in the absence of the State intervention. Thus, whenever the financial situation of an undertaking is improved as a result of a State intervention, an advantage is present. Such an improvement is shown by comparing the financial situation of

the undertaking as a result of the contested measure with the financial situation of that undertaking had the measure not been granted. . . . As regards fiscal measures, an advantage may be granted through different types of reduction in an undertaking's tax burden and, in particular, through a reduction in the taxable base or in the amount of tax due. . . ., the contested tax rulings result in a lowering of ASI's and AOE's corporation tax liability in Ireland by reducing those undertakings' annual taxable profits, and thus their taxable bases, for the purposes of levying corporation tax on those profits under the ordinary rules of taxation of corporate profit in Ireland. The contested tax rulings therefore confer an economic advantage on those companies through a reduction in their taxable base.

224. As regards the selective nature of that advantage, the Court of Justice has previously held that in the case of an individual aid measure, as opposed to a scheme, the identification of the economic advantage is, in principle, sufficient to support the presumption that it is selective, without it being necessary to analyse the selectivity of the measure according to the three-step analysis devised by the Court of Justice for fiscal State aid schemes. Since the contested tax rulings are individual aid measures granted only to ASI and AOE, a finding that those measures grant an advantage to ASI and AOE already suffices to conclude that that advantage is selective in nature. [The Commission subsequently went on to examine those measures according to the three-step analysis devised by the Court of Justice for fiscal aid schemes to demonstrate that they are also selective under that analysis.]

In reflecting on the above reasoning, consider critically the statement released by Tim Cook, the CEO of Apple: 'The European Commission has launched an effort to rewrite Apple's history in Europe, ignore Ireland's tax laws and upend the international tax system in the process. The opinion issued on August 30th alleges that Ireland gave Apple a special deal on our taxes. This claim has no basis in fact or in law. We never asked for, nor did we receive, any special deals. We now find ourselves in the unusual position of being ordered to retroactively pay additional taxes to a government that says we don't owe them any more than we've already paid . . . . The Commission's move is unprecedented and it has serious, wide-reaching implications. It is effectively proposing to replace Irish tax laws with a view of what the Commission thinks the law should have been. This would strike a devastating blow to the sovereignty of EU Member States over their own tax matters, and to the principle of certainty of law in Europe.'[61]

---

61 To follow recent developments and consult the Commission's working paper on State aid and tax rulings (3 June 2016), see: http://ec.europa.eu/competition/state_aid/tax_rulings/index_en.html (accessed 12 June 2016). See also Case T-755/15, *Luxembourg v. Commission*, pending; Case T-759/15, *Fiat Chrysler Finance Europe*

The US government is reported to have applied for leave to intervene in support of Apple's appeal before the General Court against the Commission decision, allegedly to contest the retroactive application of State aid rules to Apple.

* * *

This chapter examined State interventions, considered how State actions may harm trade and competition, and observed how the Treaty limits anti-competitive State actions. It is often said that, for harms to competition, the State is the biggest culprit because it can erect impenetrable barriers and privilege itself, its businesses and its friends as no private actor can do without the help of the State. But of course the State is also a guardian of the public good. Through Article 4 TEU and Articles 34, 35, 37, 56 and 106 in tandem with 101 and 102, and 107–109 TFEU, the EU attempts to do the job of limiting the anti-competitive, trade-restraining excesses of the Member States, particularly when they undermine the coherence of the internal market. Thus, in matters of constraining excessive and unjustified State action, competition and internal-market policy converge.

---

v. Commission, pending; Case T-131/16, *Belgium v. Commission*; and Case T-778/16, *Ireland v. Commission*; and Case T-892/16, *Apple Sales International and Apple Operations Europe v. Commission*, pending.

Afterword

The competition policy of the EU has been an ambitious, evolving, and largely successful enterprise, despite some false starts entailing overregulation and rigid rules. The genius of the enterprise is hard to dispute. Europe has proved that undue public anti-competitive restraints and undue private anti-competitive restrains are often integral, and that a common market cannot be created without coherent, community-wide, competition law. Even while US antitrust looks inward in the sense of dissociating antitrust from political economy and from links with adjacent disciplines such as trade, European competition policy acknowledges the links and seeks a coherent conception that takes account of neighbouring values and objectives. The EU model, as it has evolved to incorporate more economics and less formalism, appears to have become the model or referent of choice for the newer antitrust jurisdictions of the world. Thus, this study of the competition law of the EU has relevance and application well beyond Europe.

Index

Abuse of dominance
  generally, xxix–xxxvi, 159–233
    consumer interests *vs.* competitor rights, 193
    definitions, 159, 161–3, 213–14
    dominance thresholds, 162–3
    as efficient competitor test, xxv, 202–3, 227–32
    FRAND terms, role of, 191–3
    Guidance Paper 2005, 160, 163, 172
    historical development, 159–60
    intellectual property rights, 182
    legal basis, 159
    market share, 162–3, 213
    proof and appreciability, standard of, 206–7
    scope of competition on the merits, 196–7, 204
    treaty provisions, 159
    US law, 159–60, 164, 233
  abusive conduct
    generally, 164–5
    British Leyland v. Commission, 165–7
    discriminatory prices, 167–71
    excessive prices, 165–71
    market segmentation, 165–7
    policy investigations, 169–70
    unfair prices, 168–9
    unfair terms, 165–71
    United Brands v. Commission, 167–9
    US law, 171
  Article 102 TFEU
    generally, xxix–xxxii, 159–233
    applicability, 19–20
    background policy, 10–16
    individual rights of action, 15
    introduction to, 16–17
    text, 18, 159
  definitions
    abuse, 159, 213
    collective dominance, 163–4, 262
    dominance, 161–3, 213–14, 257
  exclusionary conduct
    generally, 171–2
    duties to deal, 174–80
    duty to give access, 172–4
    as efficient competitor test, xxv, 202–4, 206
    eliminatory intent, 220–23
    essential facility, 172–4, 277–8
    Guidance Paper 2005, 172
    IMS Health case, 184–6
    indispensability, 184–6
    intellectual property rights, and, 180–86
    interoperability, and, 186–93
    Istituto Chemioterapico Italiano v. Commission, 174–6
    market foreclosure, 193
    Microsoft v. Commission, 186–93
    objective justification, 189–90
    Radio Telefis Eireann v. Commission, 181–4
    refusal to deal, 172–93
    Sealink case, 173–4
    tying and bundling, 186–93
    US law, 177–80, 191
    Verizon Communications v. Trinko, 177–80
  exclusive dealing
    British Airways v. Commission, 197–9
    'by object' abuses, 201–4
    consumer benefits, relevance of, 204–7
    discount agreements, 197–201
    as efficient competitor test, xxv, 202–4, 206
    Guidance 2009, 199, 201, 204, 207
    Hoffmann-La Roche v. Commission, 194–6
    Intel Corp v. Commission, xxiv, 201–4
    loyalty rebates, xxiv, 194–201
    Michelin I and *Michelin II*, 196–7
    negative pricing, xxiv, 199–201
    Post Danmark II, 204–7
    proof and appreciability, standard of, 206–7
    retroactive rebate schemes, 204–7
    scope of competition on the merits, 196–7, 204
    Tomra Systems v. Commission, 199–200
  leveraging, 232–3
    Google case, xxxiii, 232
  margin squeeze
    anti-competitive effect requirement, 230–32

Deutsche Telekom v. Commission, 224–8
  duty to avoid, 224–8
  as efficient competitor test, 227–32
  Konkurrensverket v. TeliaSonera Sverige, 228–32
  legal certainty, 229–30
  national law conflicts, 224–6
  Pacific Bell Telephone v. linkLine Communications, 223–4
  US law, 223–4, 232
parallel imports, 134–5
  Sot.Lelos KAI SIA EE v. GlaxoSmithKline, 134–5
price predation and discrimination
  generally, 211
  AKZO Chemie v. Commission, 212–15, 218, 221
  Brooke Group v. Brown & Williamson Tobacco, 215–18
  exclusionary intent, 220–23
  France Telecom v. Commission (Wanadoo), 218–20
  interpretation conflicts, and, 211, 216–17, 220–23
  Post Danmark I, 220–23
  recoupment requirement, 216–20
  Tetra Pak v. Commission, 215, 218
  US law, 215–18
refusal to deal, 172–93
  duties to deal, 174–80
  duty to give access, 172–4
  essential facility, 172–4
  IMS Health case, 184–6
  intellectual property rights, 180–86
  interoperability, 186–93
  justification, 189–90
  Microsoft v. Commission, 186–93
  Radio Telefis Eireann v. Commission, 181–4
  Sealink case, 173–4
  tying and bundling, 186–93
  US law, 177–80
  Verizon Communications v. Trinko, 177–80
state ownership
  essential facility, 277–8
  national court interpretation, 280–81
  port control cases, 274, 276–82
tying and bundling
  generally, 207–8
  foreclosure of competition, 209–11
  loyalty rebates, 194–6, 204–7
  Microsoft v. Commission, 186–93, 208–11
  objective justification, 210
  Tetra Pak v. Commission, 208
  US law, 208

Anti-competitive practices, *See also* Article 101 TFEU; Cartels
  economic activities, interpretation, 18–20, 307–8
  justification, 118
  purpose, 36–8
  US law, and, 118
Appreciable competitive effect
  horizontal restraints, 83–5, 88–90, 109–10
  vertical restraints, 88–90, 147–51
Article 34 TFEU
  generally, 180
  free movement cases, 289
  state monopoly violations, 180, 282–4
Article 36 TFEU
  intellectual property rights, free movement, 180
Article 37 TFEU
  generally, 282–3
  Franzen case, 283–90
  purpose, 285
  text, 283
Article 56 TFEU
  state measure violations, 303–6
  violations of, 295
Article 101 TFEU
  generally, 33–158
  applicability, 18–20
  background policy, 10–16
  individual rights of action, 15
  internal activities, 19–20
  introduction to, 16–17
  limitations and exclusions, 19–20
  restrictive agreements, justification, 18
  text, 17
Article 101(1) TFEU
  cartels, 33
  principle, 16, 69
Article 101(2) TFEU
  principle, 16–17, 69
Article 101(3) TFEU
  principle, 17, 69
Article 102 TFEU
  applicability, 19–20
  background policy, 10–16
  individual rights of action, 15
  introduction to, 16–17
  state ownership violations, 274–5
  text, 18, 159
Article 106 TFEU
  exclusive privileges conflicts, 290–99

non-economic activities, 296
state monopoly violations, 274, 279
text, 290
Article 107 TFEU
generally, 275
compatible aid, 313–14
de minimis aid, 314
prohibition, principle of, 312–13
subsidies and public service compensation, 315
Article 108 TFEU
generally, 275

Block exemptions
criticism of, 156–7
development, 9–10, 70–71, 156–8
eligibility criteria, 153–4
horizontal restraints
generally, 70–71
R&D, 120–21
specialization, 121–2
US law, 121
individual exemptions, 70
limitations, 10
market share thresholds, 81, 89
motor vehicles, 28–30, 157–8
price controls, and, 122
resale price maintenance, 136
safe harbours, 81
State aid, 313–14, 325
technology transfer, 157–8
vertical restraints
history and reform, 29–31, 124–5
internet distribution restrictions, 152–5
Bundling agreements, *See* Tying and bundling
'By effect' restrictions, 77–88
appreciable competitive effect, 83–5, 88–90
competitive harm, interpretation, 77–8
counterfactual hypothesis, 84–8
de minimis agreements, 88–91
Guidelines 2011, 77, 87
market definition, interpretation, 78–82
market power, definition, 78
Mastercard v. Commission, 82–8
'By object' restrictions, 72–7, 90
Cartes Bancaires v. Commission, 73–7
competitive benefits *vs.* competitive harms, 76
de minimis agreements, 89–90
Guidelines 2011, 72, 77
Intel Corp v. Commission, xxiv, 201–4

national law prohibitions, 76
'pay for delay' settlements, 75–6
rule of reason, and, 76
US analysis differences, 76–7

Cartels
generally, 20–21, 33–4, 69
cooperation
concerted practices, 47–53
international agreements, 61–2
coordinated effects, 40
crisis, justification, 62–8
economics of, 36–40
effects doctrine, 54–60
development, 54
EU interpretation, 60
judicial acceptance, 56
UK interpretation, 60
enforcement, 33
cooperation agreements, 61–2
criminal prosecutions, 34–5
detection challenges, 35
fines, 34–5
leniency programmes, 35
forms, 33–4, 38–40
concerted practices, 47–53
domestic market protection, 42–3
market allocation, 39
mutual deference, 39–40
parallel conduct, 45–6
price-fixing, 38–9, 44–5
price-leadership, 45–6
quotas, 39
horizontal restraints, as, 69
jurisdiction
globalization, and, 54–5
international law conflicts, 55–8
non-interference principle, and, 57
State obligations, 57–8
US law, 58–60
Wood pulp case, 55–60, 269, 271
justification for, 40
Beef Industry Development Society (BIDS) case, 62–6
crisis cartels, 62–8
prohibition, 33, 40
purpose, 36
US provisions, 48–9
proof of, 48–9

ACF Chemiefarma v. Commission, 41–5
  concerted practices, 47–53
  Dyestuffs case, 45–6
  interdependence, 45–6
  justification, 40
  law and fact questions, 40
  parallel conduct, 45–6
  Quinine case, 41–5, 48
  Sugar cartel case, 47–8
  Wood pulp case, 49–53
  static effects, 39
  x-inefficiency effect, 39
Cellophane fallacy, 80, 83
Collective dominance
  close commercial links, and, 257–8
  definitions, 163–4, 257–8, 262
  justification for, 257–8
  mergers that facilitate, 257–65
    Airtours v. Commission, 261–4
    Gencor v. Commission, 258–60
Competition, *See also* Mergers; State actions; State aid; State ownership
  enforcement
    appeals and annulments, 9
    Court of Justice role, 9, 14
    damages, actions for, 15–16
    dawn raids, 9
    economic approach, 10–13
    effects-based approach, 12–15
    Framework Directive 2014, 16
    national proceedings, 9
    preliminary decisions, 8–9
    private mechanisms, 15–16
    procedures, 8–9
    resolutions, 9
    responsibilities, 8
    Statement of Objections, 8
  purpose, 1, 36–8
  Regulation (implementing)
    development, 9–10
    effects-based approach, 12–15
    reform, 10
    theory of harm, 82
Concerted practices, 47–53
Cooperative agreements
  interpretation
    generally, 69–70
    appreciable competitive effect, 83–5, 88–90, 109–10

Article 101(1), applicability of, 70–72
'by effect' restrictions, 77–90
'by object' restrictions, 72–7, 89–90
cartels, 69
Cartes Bancaires v. Commission, 73–7
counterfactual hypothesis, 84–8
de minimis agreements, 88–91
exception rule, 91–2
Guidelines 2011, 72, 77, 87, 101
justification, burden of, 91–2
market definition, interpretation, 78–82
Mastercard v. Commission, 82–8
policy development, 71–2
US analysis, differences, 76–7

De minimis agreements, 88–91
  market share thresholds, 81, 89–90
  Notice 2014, 88–90
De minimis aid exception, 314
Dead weight loss, 38–9
Demand substitution, 79
Directorate-General for Competition (DG COMP), 8–9
Dominant position, *See* Abuse of dominance

Economic activities
  definition and interpretation, 18–20, 307–8
  exclusive privilege, abuse of, 296
  internal activities, 19–20
  undertakings, definition, 307–8
Effects-based approach, 12–15
Environmental measures
  recycling initiatives, 118–20
Essential facility, 172–4, 277–8
European Competition Network (ECN), 9–10, 14
Exclusionary conduct
  generally, 171–2
  duties to deal, 174–80
  duty to give access, 172–4
  as efficient competitor test, xxv, 202–4, 206
  essential facility, 172–4, 277–8
  exclusionary intent, 220–23
  Guidance Paper, 172
  IMS Health case, 184–6
  indispensability, 184–6
  intellectual property rights, and, 180–86
  interoperability, and, 186–93
  Istituto Chemioterapico Italiano v. Commission, 174–6
  market foreclosure, 193

Microsoft v. Commission, 186–93
   objective justification, 189–90
   Radio Telefis Eireann v. Commission, 181–4
   refusal to deal, 172–93
   Sealink case, 173–4
   tying and bundling, 186–93
   US law, 177–80, 191
   Verizon Communications v. Trinko, 177–80
Exclusive dealing
   British Airways v. Commission, 197–9
   consumer benefits, relevance of, 204–7
   discount agreements, and, 197–201
   as efficient competitor test, xxv, 202–4, 206
   Guidance Paper, 199, 201, 204, 207
   Hoffmann-La Roche v. Commission, 194–6
   Intel Corp v. Commission, xxix, 201–4
   loyalty rebates, and, 194–201
   Michelin I and *Michelin II*, 196–7
   negative pricing, 199–201
   Post Danmark II, 204–7
   proof and appreciability, standard of, 206–7
   retroactive rebate schemes, 204–7
   scope of competition on the merits, 196–7, 204
   Tomra Systems v. Commission, 199–200
Exclusive selling agreements, 124

FRAND terms, 100–101, 191–3
Free riding
   vertical restraints, 123, 138, 141–2, 151

Horizontal restraints
   block exemptions
      generally, 70–71
      individual exemptions, 70
      price controls, 122
      R&D, 120–21
      specialization, 121–2
      US policy, 121
   'by effect' restrictions, 77–88
      appreciable competitive effect, 83–5, 88–90
      competitive harm, interpretation, 77–8
      counterfactual hypothesis, 84–8
      de minimis agreements, 88–91
      Guidelines 2011, 77, 87
      market definition, interpretation, 78–82
      market power, definition, 78
      Mastercard v. Commission, 82–8
   'by object' restrictions, 72–7, 90
      Cartes Bancaires v. Commission, 73–7

      competitive benefits *vs.* competitive harms, 76
      de minimis agreements, 89–90
      Guidelines 2011, 72, 77
      national law prohibitions, 76
      'pay for delay' settlements, 75–6
      rule of reason, 76
      US analysis differences, 76–7
   competitive effects of agreement
      generally, 74, 91–2
      Article 101(3), applicability of, 91–3, 99–100
      Atlas/Global One case, 106–7
      AUSBANC case, 97–100
      burden of proof, 92, 96
      consumer benefits, and, 99–100
      cross-border services, 109–10
      defences, 92, 108
      European economic activities, harmony in, 110–11
      European Night Services v. Commission, 101–6, 101–6
      exemption, duration of, 104–5
      fair competition agreements, 92
      Guidelines 2004, 91–3
      information exchange agreements, 72–3, 75, 93–100
      innovation, 106–8
      Iridium case, 107–8
      John Deere v. Commission, 94–5
      joint ventures, 101–6
      loose agreements, 93–101
      market characteristics, influences of, 97–9
      market transparency, 96–7
      non-competition justifications, 92, 108
      potential competitive effects, 94–6, 99, 102–4
      principles, 91–3
      standard setting, 100–101
      tighter agreements, 101–6
      Wirtschaftsvereinigung Stahl case, 96–7
   cooperative agreements, interpretation
      generally, 69–70
      appreciable competitive effect, 83–5, 88–90, 109–10
      Article 101(1), applicability of, 70–72
      'by effect' restrictions, 77–90
      'by object' restrictions, 72–7, 89–90
      cartels, 69
      Cartes Bancaires v. Commission, 73–7
      counterfactual hypothesis, 84–8
      de minimis agreements, 88–91

exception rule, 91–2
Guidelines 2011, 72, 77, 87, 101
justification, burden of, 91–2
market definition, interpretation, 78–82
Mastercard v. Commission, 82–8
policy development, 71–2
US analysis differences, 76–7
justification
burden of, 91–2, 96
non-competition, 92, 108–12
US policy, 118
policy development, 71–2
Guidelines 2010, 72
public policy/non-competition exceptions
generally, 92, 108, 115
Albany v. Textile Industry Pension Funds, 108–12
collective bargaining, 108–12
consumer harm, and, 113–15
domestic appliance recycling agreements, 118–20
energy consumption agreements, 116–17
environmental measures, 116–20
European policy harmonisation, 110–11, 116–20
labour agreements, 108–12
legal profession agreements, 112–15
multi-disciplinary partnerships, 114–15
self-regulatory restraints, 112–15
US policy, 112, 115, 118
waste management agreements, 117–20
Wouters et Cie case, 113–15
relevant markets, definition, 78–9, 83

Imports, *See* Block exemptions; Parallel imports
Information exchange agreements
horizontal restraints, 72–3, 75, 93–100
John Deere v. Commission, 94–5
Intellectual property rights
abuse of dominance, and, 182
exclusionary conduct, 180–86
IMS Health case, 184–6
indispensability, 184–6
national protection rules, 182–3
pharmaceutical licences, 191–2
Radio Telefis Eireann v. Commission, 181–4
refusal to deal, 180–86
standard essential patents, infringement, 192–3
patents ambushes, 100–101
International Competition Network (ICN), 61–2, 81
Internet
place of establishment, 153–4

selective distribution restrictions, 152–7
Adidas, 155–6
Pierre Fabre Dermo-Cosmetique v. President, 152–5

Joint ventures
concentrations, as, 236–7
full function joint ventures, 236–7
horizontal restraints, 101–6
R&D, and rule of reason, 121

Labour agreements
horizontal restraints, 108–12
Legal profession
horizontal restraints, 112–15
multi-disciplinary partnerships, 114–15
self-regulation, 112
Wouters et Cie case, 113–15
Licensing agreements
exclusionary conduct, 180–86
refusal to deal, 181–4
tying and bundling, 186–93

Margin squeeze
Deutsche Telekom v. Commission, 224–8
Konkurrensverket v. TeliaSonera Sverige, 228–32
Pacific Bell Telephone v. linkLine Communications, 223–4
Market allocation, 39
Market concentration
analysis methods, 243–4
Herfindah-Hirschman Index (HHI), 244
n-firm concentration ratios, 243–4
Market definition
analysis, 80–82
cellophane fallacy, 80, 83
competitive constraints, sources of, 79, 81
demand substitution, 79
geographical markets, 78–9, 83, 242–3
interpretation, 78–82, 242–3
market concentration, 243–4
market power, 81
market share thresholds, 81
Notice 1997, 78–80, 242–3
potential competition, interpretation, 79, 82
purpose, 78
relevant markets, 78–9, 83, 242–3
snapshot method, 243
supply substitution, 79
Market division agreements, 38

Market economics
  generally, 36–7
Market efficiency
  competition policy, and, 13, 26–7, and throughout
Market integration, 36, *See also* Cartels; Parallel imports
  generally, 20–21
  economics of competition, and, 36–8
  market partitioning, rule against, 27–31
Market partitioning
  parallel imports, 133
  rule against, 27–31
Market power
  analysis, 81
  incentives of, 36
Market segmentation, 165–7
Market share
  dominant position, 162–3
  thresholds, 81, 89–90, 213
Merger Control
  generally, 234–73
  analysis of
    barriers to entry, 244
    competition-lessening effects, 239–41
    conglomerate mergers, 241, 265–9
    global competitiveness, 241–2
    horizontal mergers, 244–65
    market concentration, 243–4
    market definition, and, 242–3
    market power increases, 241–2
    positive effects, 241
    vertical mergers, 239–40, 265–6, 268–9
  Community dimension
    definition, 235–6
    investigations, Commission powers, 236
    notification requirement, 237
  competition-lessening effects, 239–41
    conglomerate effects, 241
    methods, 239–40
    vertical mergers, 239–40
  concentrations
    definition, 235–6
    joint ventures, 236–7
    thresholds, 236
  jurisdictional conflicts
    generally, 269–70
    Gencor v. Commission, 270–73
  US law
    Boeing/McDonnell Douglas, 246–51, 255, 273
    conglomerate mergers, 268

  enforcement, 239
  failing firm defence, 254
  general prohibition, 239, 241–2, 269
  jurisdiction conflicts, 270–73
  mergers that create or increase dominance, 246–51, 254–5
  substantial lessening of competition (SLC test), 239
Merger Regulation
  generally, 8
  adoption, 235
  background, 234
  Community dimension, 235–7
  coverage, 237–8
  development and reform, 237–8, 255
  horizontal merger guidelines 2004, 256, 263
  Implementation Regulation, 235
  internal market compatibility, and, 238–9
  Member State role, 236
  purpose, 235
  unilateral/non-coordinated effects, 255–7
  US law, compared, 239, 241–2
mergers other than of competitors
  generally, 265–6
  conglomerate mergers, 265–9
  Tetra Laval v. Commission, 266–8
  vertical mergers, 265–6, 268–9
mergers that create or increase dominance, 244–55
  Aerospatiale-Alenia/De Haviland, 245–6
  Boeing/McDonnell Douglas, 246–51, 255
  failing firm defence, 253–5
  France v. Commission, 253–5, 257
  monopoly/gatekeeper outcome, 250–53
  new technology mergers, 251–4
  US law, under, 246–51, 254–5
mergers that create unilateral or non-coordinated effects, 255–7
  telecoms cases, 256–7
mergers that facilitate coordination/collective dominance
  generally, 257–8
  Airtours v. Commission, 261–4
  Gencor v. Commission, 258–60
  justifications for, 257–8
  Sony/Impala case, 264–5
procedures
  Dutch/German clauses, 236
  investigation, Commission powers, 236
  pre-merger notification, 235–6

significant impediment to effective competition test (SIEC test), 237–8
Modernisation
    effects-based approach, 12–15
    history, 10–15, 71, 90
    Regulation 1/2003, 10–15
    State aid, 324
    vertical restraints, 124–5
Motor vehicles
    block exemption, 28–30, 157–8

N-firm concentration ratios, 243–4

Parallel imports
    abuse of dominant position, 134–5
    balancing exercises, 130–32
    Consten and Grundig v. Commission, 21–7, 125–6, 128
    GlaxoSmithKline Services v. Commission, 30, 128–32
    market integration, 21–7, 125–6, 128
    market partitioning, 27–31, 133
    Pioneer case, 27–8
    Sot.Lelos KAI SIA EE v. GlaxoSmithKline, 30–31, 132–5
    vertical restraints
        Distillers Company v. Commission, 127–8
        dual pricing, 28–30, 127–8
        Volkswagen AG v. Commission, 28–30
Patents ambushes, 100–101
Price
    generally, 21
    abuse of dominance
        British Leyland v Commission, 165–6
        discriminatory prices, 167–8
        excessive or unfair prices, 165–71
        loyalty rebates, 194–201
        negative pricing, 199–201
        unfair prices, 168–9
        United Brands v. Commission, 167–9
        US law, 171
    block exemptions, 122
    margin squeeze
        Deutsche Telekom v. Commission, 224–8
        Konkurrensverket v. TeliaSonera Sverige, 228–32
        Pacific Bell Telephone v. linkLine Communications, 223–4
    parallel imports
        GlaxoSmithKline v. Commission, 128–32

        Sot.Lelos KAI SIA EE v. GlaxoSmithKline, 30–31, 132–5
    price ceilings, 128–32
    price-fixing cartels, 38–9, 44–5
    price-leadership, 45–6
    price predation and discrimination
        generally, 211
        AKZO Chemie v Commission, 212–15, 218, 221
        Brooke Group v. Brown & Williamson Tobacco, 215–18
        exclusionary intent, 220–23
        France Telecom v. Commission (Wanadoo), 218–20
        interpretation conflicts, 211, 216–17, 220–23
        Post Danmark I, 220–23
        recoupment requirement, 216–20
        Tetra Pak v. Commission, 215, 218
        US law, 215–18
    resale price maintenance
        generally, 135–6, 143
        cartels, and, 138–9
        justification for, 137–8
        Leegin Creative Leather v. PSKS, 125, 136–43
        per se rules, 137, 139–40
        rule of reason, 140–41, 143
        US development, 135–43
    SSNIP test, 79–80
    vertical restraints, 127–32
        Distillers Company v. Commission, 127–8
        dual pricing, 28–30, 127–8

Quotas, 39

Refusal to deal, 172–93
    duties to deal, 174–80
    duty to give access, 172–4
    essential facility, 172–4
    IMS Health, 184–6
    intellectual property rights, and, 180–86
    interoperability, and, 186–93
    justification, 189–90
    Microsoft v. Commission, 186–93
    Radio Telefis Eireann v. Commission, 181–4
    Sealink case, 173–4
    tying and bundling, 186–93
    US law, 177–80
    Verizon Communications v. Trinko, 177–80
Regulation 1/2003, 10–16
Regulation 17/62, 9–10, 12

Regulation 67/67, 156
Regulation 139/2004, 8, 235
Regulation 316/2014, 158
Regulation 773/2004, 12
Regulation 802/2004, 235
Regulation 1218/2010, 121–2
Regulation 2015/1589, 312
Regulation 2790/1999, 153–4
Regulation 4064/89, 235
Resale price maintenance
  generally, 135–6, 143
  bright line rule, 142–3
  cartels, 138–9
  justification for, 137–8
  Leegin Creative Leather v. PSKS, 125, 136–43
  per se rules, 137, 139–40
  rule of reason, 140–41, 143
  US law, 135–43
Research and development
  block exemptions, 120–21
  joint ventures, 121
  US policy, 121
Restraints of trade, *See* Cartels; Horizontal restraints; Vertical restraints
Rule of reason
  generally, 14
  resale price maintenance, 140–41, 143
  research joint ventures, 121

Safe harbours, 81, 89–90
SIEC test, 237–8
SSNIP test, 79–80
Standard setting
  benefits, 100
  patents ambushes, 100–101
State actions
  generally
    anti-competitive effects, 300–301
    duty not to contravene Community provisions, 300–302, 306–8
    effects, interpretation, 307
    freedoms, conflicts with, 299–300, 303–6
    interstate commerce, unreasonable burden on, 311
    public policy and consumer protection goals, 305–6
  restricting competition or facilitating private restrictions
    generally, 299–301, 306

Cipolla v. Fazari/Macrino v. Meloni, 303–6
Commission and France v. Ladbroke Racing, 306–8, 310
Commission v. Italy, 308–11
Consorzio Industrie Fiammiferi case, 301–2, 310
private responsibility, 306–11
state compulsion doctrine, 306–11
state responsibility, 299–306, 310
undertakings, interpretation, 307–8
US law, 310–11
State aid
  generally, 311
  Apple case, 330–33
  definition, 312, 314
  enforcement trends, 311
  exceptions, 275
  financial crisis, and, 275
  regime development, 311–12
  state ownership, and, 314–15
  tax rulings, 329–33
  policy
    arm's length principle, 325–6, 330
    corporate taxation, 325–6, 329–33
    General Block Exemption, 325
    Global Forum 2010 review, 319–24
    infrastructure investment, 327
    priorities, 320
    State Aid Rules, 324–8
    subsidies, review of, 321–4
    subsidies, role of, 320–21, 324
    US law, compared, 329
  regime
    abolition/removal, 312–13
    advantage *vs.* selectivity, 316–19, 330
    approval, 312
    Commission powers, 312–13
    compatible aid, 313–14
    de minimis aid exception, 314
    ex ante review, 312–13
    General Block Exemptions, 313–14, 325
    general prohibition, 275
    market economy operator test, 314–15
    selective *vs.* general measures, 316–19
    state *vs.* private resources, 315–16
    subsidies and public service compensation, 315
State ownership, *See also* State actions
  generally
    competition challenges, 274–5

limits on conduct of public undertakings, 274–5
State aid restrictions, and, 314–15
treaty obligations, 274–5
abuse of dominance
essential facility, 277–8
Franzen case, 283–90
Merci Convenzionali Porto di Genova v. Siderugica Gabrielli, 279–82
national court interpretation, 280–81
port control cases, 274, 276–82
state monopolies of commercial character, 282–90
Article 106
Albany International and Textile Industry Pension Funds, 296–9
Commission v. DEI, 293–6
exclusive privileges, 290–99
Hofner v. Macrotron, 290–93, 295–6
non-economic activities, and, 296
state monopoly violations, 274, 279
state monopolies of commercial character
Article 34 and 37 TFEU, application of, 282–90
Franzen case, 283–90
Statement of Objections, 8

Tax avoidance
Apple tax ruling, 330–33
arm's length principle, 325–6, 330
Technology licensing agreements, 124
Technology transfer block exemption, 157–8
Tying and bundling
abuse of dominance
generally, 207–8
foreclosure of competition, 209–11
loyalty rebates, 194–6, 204–7
Microsoft v. Commission, 186–93, 208–11
objective justification, and, 210
Tetra Pak v. Commission, 208
US law, 208
vertical restraints
generally, 144
appreciable competitive effect, 147–51
individual exemptions, criteria for, 148
market access restrictions, 144–51
Schöller Lebensmittel v. Commission, 147–51
Stergios Delimitis v. Henninger, 144–7

Undertakings
association of, 19–20
definition and interpretation, 18–20

US law
abuse of dominance
generally, 159–60, 164, 233
Brooke Group v. Brown & Williamson Tobacco, 215–18
excessive pricing, 171
exclusionary conduct, 177–80, 191
margin squeeze, 223–4, 232
Pacific Bell Telephone v. linkLine Communications, 223–4
price predation, 215–18
prohibition, 159–60, 164
refusal to deal, 177–80
state action restricting competition or facilitating private restrictions, 310–11
Trinko, 177–80, 199, 208, 224
tying and bundling, 208
anti-competitive practices
cartels
judicial challenges, 34
jurisdiction, 58–60
prohibition, 48–9
horizontal restraints
'by object' restrictions, 76–7
cooperative agreements, interpretation, 76–7
justification, 118
public policy/non-competition exceptions, 112, 115, 118
mergers
Boeing / McDonnell Douglas, 246–51, 255, 273
conglomerate mergers, 268
enforcement, 239
failing firm defence, 254
general prohibition, 239, 241–2, 269
jurisdiction conflicts, 270–73
mergers that create or increase dominance, 246–51, 254–5
substantial lessening of competition (SLC test), 239
resale price maintenance, 135–43
state aid regime, 329
vertical restraints, 135–43

Vertical restraints
generally, 123–58
agreements, analysis of
Adalat case, 126
applicability of Article 101(1), 125–6
appreciable competitive effect, 88–90, 147–51

block exemptions
  eligibility criteria, 153–4
  history and reform, 29–31, 124–5
  market integration, and, 124–5
distribution agreements, 123–4
effects of
  generally, 123–4
  modernization, 124–5
exclusive purchasing/tying agreements
  generally, 144
  Adidas, 155–6
  appreciable competitive effect, 147–51
  individual exemptions, criteria for, 148
  market access restrictions, 144–51
  Schöller Lebensmittel v. Commission, 147–51
  Stergios Delimitis v. Henninger, 144–7
exclusive selling, 124
forms of, 123–4
free riding, 123, 138, 141–2, 151
Guidelines 2010, 151
inter-/intrabrand restraints, 123–4
internet freedoms policies, 151
  Pierre Fabre Dermo-Cosmetique v. President, 152–5
  selective distribution, 152–5
notification process, 124
parallel imports
  abuse of dominant position, and, 134–5
  Consten and Grundig v. Commission, 21–7, 125–6, 128
  Distillers Company v. Commission, 127–8

dual pricing, 28–30, 127–8
  GlaxoSmithKline Services v. Commission, 30
  Pioneer case, 27–8, 126
  R&D investment, and, 133–4
  Sot.Lelos KAI SIA EE v. GlaxoSmithKline, 30–31, 132–5
  Volkswagen AG v. Commission, 28–30, 126
policy developments, 30, 151
  block exemptions, 29–31, 124–5
  modernization, 124–5
resale price maintenance
  generally, 135–6, 143
  justification for, 137–8
  Leegin Creative Leather v. PSKS, 125, 136–43
  per se rules, 137, 139–40
  rule of reason, 140–41, 143
  US development, 135–43
selective distribution
  freedom of movement, and, 152–3
  internet marketing restrictions, 152–5
  Pierre Fabre Dermo-Cosmetique v. President, 152–5
technology licensing agreements, 124
US policies, 135–43, 151

Welfare loss, 38–9
World Trade Organization
  competition agreements, 61
  R&D block exemptions, compatibility, 121

X-inefficiency, 39